THE WOMEN WHO CHANGED ARCHITECTURE

This book is made possible through the generous support of Robert and Arlene Kogod

Published by
Princeton Architectural Press
70 West 36th Street
New York, New York 10018
www.papress.com

ISBN 978-1-61689-871-7

Editor: Kristen Hewitt
Designer: Natalie Snodgrass

Library of Congress Control Number: 2021943860

Front Cover, Clockwise from top left:
© Mary Otis Stevens and Thomas McNulty Collection, MIT Museum
(p. 115); © Kate Joyce Studios. Courtesy Ross Barney Architects (p. 103);
Courtesy Interboro Partners (p. 285); Photo James Ewing (p. 298);
© Manuel Bougot (p. 41); Photo Bill Timmerman (p. 127)
Center: © Kate Joyce Studios. Courtesy Ross Barney Architects (p. 159)

Back Cover, Clockwise from top left:
Florence Knoll Bassett Papers (p. 83); © Hufton+Crow (p. 169);
Photo Iwan Baan (p. 181); Courtesy Höweler + Yoon Architecture (p. 251);
Photo Kawasami Kobayashi (p. 249)

THE WOMEN WHO CHANGED ARCHITECTURE

Edited by Jan Cigliano Hartman

Foreword by Beverly Willis
Introduction by Amale Andraos

Sarah Allaback, Julie Sinclair Eakin,
Katherine Flynn, Laurel Frances Rogers

With Lori Brown, Doris Cole,
Julia Gamolina, Mary McLeod,
Victoria Rosner, Margaret Birney Vickery

Beverly Willis Architecture Foundation · New York
Princeton Architectural Press · New York

V. RAISING THE ROOF

VI. INNOVATING FOR A BETTER WORLD

FOREWORD
Beverly Willis

The reluctant acceptance of women in architecture, historically, mirrored the larger societal acceptance of women in all areas of work life. At the turn of the twentieth century, architecture schools were reluctant to admit women, forcing Julia Morgan, one of the first practicing women architects, to travel to Paris to attend the École des Beaux-Arts. Long after the end of her career and fifty-seven years after her death, in 2014, she was awarded the American Institute of Architects' (AIA) highest honor, its Gold Medal. With this, the AIA finally took a huge step forward to recognize and accept women in the profession.

Architecture, as we know it today, was first organized as a profession in the United States around 1857. The first professional female architect in the world was possibly Signe Ida Katarina Hornborg, a Finnish architect. She attended the Helsinki Polytechnic Institute between the spring of 1888 and 1890, graduating as an architect "by special permission." Louise Blanchard Bethune was the first American woman known to have worked as a professional architect and the first woman elected to membership in the AIA. American Marion Mahony Griffin was the first US-licensed woman architect. In 1895, Mahony Griffin was the first employee hired by Frank Lloyd Wright and was his head designer for fourteen years.

The Harvard Annex, a private program for the instruction of women by Harvard faculty, was founded in 1879, after prolonged efforts by women to gain access to Harvard College. In 1916, Harvard professors collaborated to establish the Cambridge School of Architectural and Landscape Design for Women because the college did not admit women at the time. Word about the informal program spread, and by the 1916–17 academic year, the college was already advertising the experimental program and its curriculum.

Educational assistance for women came from an unexpected source, Frank Lloyd Wright. His family of Unitarians strongly supported a women's right to vote. In 1920, women won the right to vote, establishing them as more equal members of society. Wright opened a school, the Taliesin Fellowship, in 1932, where a remarkable 20 to 25 percent of the students were women. Wright liked to joke that "a Girl is a Fellow Here," the title of a movie that premiered at the Solomon R. Guggenheim Museum in June 2009, subtitled

Beijing Daxing International
Airport, Langfang, China,
Zaha Hadid Architects, 2019.
© Hufton+Crow

"100 Women Architects in the Studio of Frank Lloyd Wright." Men and women were treated equally; the men were just as likely to cook and clean as the women were to pour concrete and pitch hay.

Change doesn't come easily—or quickly. It would take two World Wars to convince men that women were capable of participating in the profession sphere. Between 1940 and 1945, women were trained to build ammunition plants, tanks, airplanes, and ships, to manage manufacturing plants, medical facilities, and farms, and to be engineers and architects. There was little they could not or did not do.

And yet, most women designers are woefully underrepresented in architectural history books. Books largely tell the stories of men. Architectural history students are led to believe that an exceptionally few women actually practiced architecture. Most students cannot recall the names of even two or three women. Female role models do not exist in the text-books, even if they do in schools

This book is a big step toward correcting the misimpression that celebrated women architects do not exist. In reality, there is an amazing number of them. This book illustrates the work of both past and present designers. It resolutely demonstrates that, today, some of the most outstanding and influential designs are and have been executed by women.

PREFACE
Jan Cigliano Hartman

As a woman studying the history of architecture since the 1970s, I have long been alert to the imbalance in printed knowledge about women and men designers. My growing discovery that women in architecture were underrepresented in publications—and therefore also online—ultimately led to my developing a collective biography of the women who changed architecture through the ages. I knew they existed. I knew of the influential work they had done. I also knew that many of their stories were buried under the weight of their dominant and more prominent male peers.

This book will change the history of architecture, bringing female architects into the central narrative. Until as recently as last year, the teaching of architectural history was about the men who designed remarkable buildings or introduced some innovative technique or style. Students didn't hear about Lilly Reich's pivotal role in the design of Ludwig Mies van der Rohe's world-renowned chairs or Barcelona Pavilion or about Anne Tyng's hand in the interior design (at least) of Louis Kahn's Yale University Art Gallery and Design Center, his first significant commission and widely considered his breakthrough masterpiece. And what about the many female associates of Frank Lloyd Wright's studio? They are the unsung heroes.

Documented in a couple dozen laudable historic and contemporary monographs are the significant architectural works of Mary Colter, Julia Morgan, Eileen Gray, Charlotte Perriand, Florence Knoll Bassett, Phyllis Lambert, Denise Scott Brown, Judith Chafee, Billie Tsien, Zaha Hadid, Patricia Patkau, Elizabeth Plater-Zyberk, Toshiko Mori, Elizabeth Diller, Maya Lin, Yvonne Farrell and Shelley McNamara of Grafton Architects, and Jeanne Gang—eighteen of the 122 architects featured in *The Women Who Changed Architecture*.

Many architects remain undocumented and virtually unknown. Ethel Bailey Furman of Richmond, Virginia, for one, an African American architect who designed over two hundred buildings in her native city, is largely unknown and underrepresented in local, regional, state, and national archives. Most of her residential buildings are gone, the victim of urban renewal that demolished hundreds of Black neighborhoods across the country.

Icefjord Center, Ilulissat, Greenland, Dorte Mandrup, 2021. Image by MIR

In addition to the United States, the architects in *The Women Who Changed Architecture* hail from Israel, France, Italy, the United Kingdom, Spain, Lebanon, Sri Lanka, Latvia, Iraq, Denmark, Finland, Sweden, the Netherlands, the Czech Republic, Germany, Poland, Austria, Pakistan, India, Australia, South Africa, Mexico, Peru, Jamaica, Argentina, Japan, and South Korea. Five African American architects and six Pritzker Prize recipients are featured. Worldwide, these women indelibly influenced the evolution of architecture across several decades.

Selecting these architects followed a strict criteria: design excellence and distinction, cultural and social progressiveness, and leadership in architectural practice—superior work, research, teaching, publications, and organizational engagement. Each of the six generations of "groundbreakers" practiced in distinctive social and cultural circumstances, and each approached architectural practice in ways that both responded to their environment and also introduced exceptional innovations that validated their practice and advanced the foundation for a future generation of women architects to gain recognition.

Throughout much of the twentieth century, the professional practice of architecture was regarded as generally exclusive rather than inclusive of women practitioners and designers—as were most professions. Yet, emerging even as early as the late nineteenth century, talented and daring women entered architectural practice, making solid strides toward acknowledgment and esteem. It is our hope that *The Women Who Changed Architecture* will alter architectural history, becoming more inclusive of women, people of color, and individuals representing our world heritage.

Earlier milestones advancing women in architecture include Susanna Torres's 1977 exhibition at the Architectural League in New York City, *Women in American Architecture: A Historic and Contemporary Perspective*, appearing in tandem with the book by the same name. Additionally, in 1998, the British *Architects' Journal* established, with the Royal Institute of British Architects, the Jane Drew Prize, created to recognize innovation and creativity by female architects and named after English architect Dame Jane Drew, the first female full professor at Harvard University and Massachusetts Institute of Technology (MIT). And in 2002, Beverly Willis (who wrote the Foreword) founded the Beverly Willis Architecture Foundation, Princeton Architectural Press's copublication partner, celebrating through education and research the very fact that women had changed design construction.

The Women Who Changed Architecture establishes a comprehensive and encyclopedic record of pioneering women in architecture, from 1881 to 2021. Although presenting an unprecedented record of these remarkable individuals, together with their revolutionary educations, innovations, awards, and influential design, the book, no doubt, has inadvertently overlooked worthy individuals. The record will continue to grow and develop.

INTRODUCTION
Amale Andraos

We live in a time when it is cool to be a "woman architect." A simple Google search today
surfaces countless lists and compendia on women architects who have been assembled
in the last few years, a proliferation of events and public conversations around women in
design and architecture, and a relatively significant number of profiles on women architects
and, more broadly, on gender equity in the field in mainstream general interest magazines.[1]
Few architects have received the celebrity status and attention that Zaha Hadid once
commanded—and her sudden death at the age of sixty-five spurred a rare outpouring of
reflections by the media around the world about her extensive and groundbreaking body
of work, her legacy and the architecture it embodied, and her identity as an Iraqi-born
British woman.

Trailing the professional world, academia is finally catching up. There are now numerous female deans, chairs, and directors at the helm of leading institutions in the United
States and in Europe, as well as at schools in the Middle East and Asia.[2] Beyond the growing
visibility that accompanies this new leadership, there is also a renewed and spirited activism demanding more recognition and more respect.[3] The slow but certain transformation of
the field is loud: it speaks to the blunt realization that there are many more ceilings to break
(and many more marginalized perspectives to include), and it can be heard advocating for
a kind of a new reality. There are enough women now in positions of power to make uncom-
fortably clamorous noise against the status quo.[4]

While the effort to inscribe feminist positions in architecture has been the subject of
much scholarly work—and recognizing current women architects and revealing forgotten
ones constitutes an important and ongoing task as this book represents—it is nevertheless
important to note some of the shifting frames of this struggle. Whereas earlier generations
aspired to move beyond the constructed opposition between being a woman and being
an architect—as demonstrated by Walter Gropius's Bauhaus—today, we are striving to
move beyond the far-too-recently-held notion that being an architect and being a woman
architect are different things. Well aware of the limitations and trappings of identity, many

Giant's Causeway Visitor
Centre, County Antrim,
Northern Ireland, Heneghan
Peng Architects, 2012.
© Hufton+Crow

contemporary female professionals are also well versed in what it means to ignore the limits set as a result of identity. While both asking how architecture produces gender (or forms feminine and masculine identities) and engaging in the kind of critical theory between body and space of the 1990s is still very much relevant, it is also time to let facts and figures speak for themselves—because they too will reveal the way in which the field of architecture has been designed to bias certain people over others.[5] As such, today, the urgent question is not how different architecture would be if it were designed by women but, rather, how deadly architecture would become if it didn't take seriously the multitude of identities, perspectives, imaginations, cultures, and contexts that constitute it and contribute to its continuous reinvention.

It is within this contemporary frame that this book registers the sheer number of architects who have shaped the discipline and practice of architecture across the decades. Yet, as with any endeavor with such encyclopedic aspirations, *The Women Who Changed Architecture* cannot escape the kind of critical questioning that its ambition provokes: Why these architects and not others? Why so many American architects? Why so many practicing architects at a time when practice is being so thoroughly redefined? And why so few collaborating architects at a time when so many architects work in pairs, in couples, in partnerships?

Countering these immediate questions is what I believe to be the most interesting aspect of this book: that it should not be read as a chronology of women architects but as a framework for understanding generations and the possibility of (inter)generational shifts. Indeed, the structure of *The Women Who Changed Architecture* constructs a fascinating archaeology of knowledge, turning every era's sediment into a stronger foundation for the next. By shifting away from chronology toward a narrative about transformation throughout generations, a new project emerges. The individual names, practices, and biographies recede to reveal more nuanced and complex stories, connections, and relationships, which taken together point to more fundamental questions: What, if any, common traits can be traced within and across generations? What, in contrast, are the events and bodies of work that resist the possibility of framing "women architects" as a category or significant object of study in itself?

Ohio State University South Campus Chiller Plant, Columbus, OH, Ross Barney Architects, 2013. Photo Brad Feinknopf

In the introductory essay to the book's first section, "Groundbreakers," Sarah Allaback reveals fascinating contrasts: while women were battling their way into the academic world to become architects, many were also carving their way outside of the academy through a multitude of other paths, such as by apprenticing as drafters or simply starting to design and build buildings across scales, typologies, and programs, often imbued with strong cultural, political, and social concerns. This was the generation of the Woman's Building at the 1893 World's Columbian Exposition, a fascinating affirmation of women's creative practices displayed on the world stage, an event one would not dream about today. In the introduction to "Paving New Paths" in the second section, Victoria Rosner and Mary McLeod register a generation's greater access to formal training and to the formal precepts of modernism while also noting how modernism's deployment as a "universal" architectural style led to anything but universality—especially in terms of the canon it produced.

With Doris Cole's introduction to the third section, "Advancing the Agenda," we find the ebullient and transformative activism of the time make its way into architecture as questions of feminist space and form, and of feminist education and organization, permeated architectural practice, which in turn redefined the field through the lens of feminism and the diversity of approaches and possibilities it opens up. Margaret Birney Vickery's opening to the fourth section, "Rocking the World," traces second-wave feminism in architecture as a new set of rising stars embraced critical theory and confronted the patriarchal modernist hegemony. Giving themselves the freedom to sample, explore, and hybridize from an open archive of art and architecture, this generation engaged new technologies to produce bold form and fresh approaches out of existing traditions and histories of architecture. Yet, despite some strident successes, this generation wrestled with the ongoing struggle for equal recognition that women still face today.

Julia Gamolina foregrounds social history in the introduction to the fifth section, "Raising the Roof," an account of architectural practice at a moment when architecture's disciplinary boundaries were increasingly blurred and when women architects pioneered new forms of hybrid practice at the intersection of architecture and art, architecture and

landscape, architecture and the city, and architecture and advocacy—all with a sharp awareness of architecture's civic values and responsibilities. Finally, with Lori Brown's introduction to the sixth section, "Innovating for a Better World," on the concluding generation,
we glimpse the way in which women architects moved from expanding architecture as a
discipline to expanding it as practice, weaving together new forms of working and engaging
across scales and medias. Set in contrast to the manifestos of previous generations, this
generation is at once pragmatic and idealistic, modeling new forms of practice committed
to renewing architecture's commitment to the public good.

Beyond these generational themes, which capture a sense of progress but also a continued struggle, one can trace exciting commonalities, which cut across generations and/or
jump from one generation to another. With a conceptual squint, a number of strong patterns
emerge. The first pattern is the significant number of working collaborations and partnerships between architects (and their husbands, partners, and peers) and between disciplines.
The women architects in this book seem to always be redefining architecture by challenging
its limits and boundaries, intersecting its expertise with that of fields beyond it, hybridizing
its focus to advance new forms of practice and knowledge, and engaging with the social,
political, environmental, or cultural issues of their respective times.

The second pattern to emerge is a shared concern and deep love of history and a certain
intellectual curiosity and generosity to inspire and produce original architectural expression
at all scales. And finally, there is always the relentless fight for recognition. Indeed, not
being "at the center" means a constant struggle to pierce whatever center of power exists,
but it also means a position of power from which to critique and displace those centers. And
with increasingly greater freedoms and advantages of adjacency, the women architects in
this book defined and redefined their own orbit of influence and interest.

This book is invaluable for the way it renders tangible the great specificity of every
architect and her work and the multigenerational interests that clearly emerge when
engaging architecture at its most fundamental: as the art and science of building. While
some architects explored their love of structures and others invested in the explorations of
materials and new technologies, they all materialized their ideas—whether on preservation,
on the environment, or on form—for the field and the world to see, feel, and inhabit. Taken
together, the collection of architectural practices in this book constructs shared narratives
while also letting the specificity and diversity of each body of work and their individual
trajectories stand on its own—simultaneously preserving the framings of "woman" or
"generational" without becoming reductive.

To be both a woman architect and an architect without ever having to choose, to create
a dialogue about the destabilizing lens of identity while also rejecting the limits cast in the
name of identity, and to enable myriad approaches that pull freely from within the archive
that is architecture: these are the goals we should aspire to for all architects, as a means
to critique, reinvent, and weave together knowledge once held separate. *The Women Who
Changed Architecture* helps create new ways of seeing, of representing, of communicating,
and, maybe, of understanding ourselves and each other better, through architecture.
These new ways of seeing are tied to the long historical and ever-changing evolution of
architecture. More importantly, this book enables us to build a new lens through which to
understand the struggles and successes of women architects not in a vacuum, but taken
together, across time and place, as they decenter and recenter the field around their ideas
and practices.

7 World Trade Center, New York,
NY, Nicole Dosso for SOM,
2006. © Dave Sundberg, Esto.
Courtesy SOM

I. GROUND-BREAKERS
Introduction by Sarah Allaback

When Louise Blanchard Bethune announced the opening of her firm in 1881, she delivered a powerful message to women interested in practicing architecture: the profession had no need for them.[1] Bethune challenged her peers to enter the profession as architects, ready to do the same work as their male colleagues. By not echoing the conventional sentiment that women architects had nothing to add to the field—that they were not particularly suited to designing homes or kitchens—she instead offered them limitless opportunities. The women profiled here held a range of opinions regarding women's inherent talents, but they all made the commitment to succeed by meeting the established professional criteria of their day. The first step, in every case, began with acquiring the necessary education.

In 1848, Sarah Worthington Peter opened the Philadelphia School of Design for Women, the first opportunity for American women to learn design skills in an institutional setting. When the popular Swedish writer Fredrika Bremer visited the school, she congratulated the women of the United States on "the new-found California for women... better than silver and gold."[2] As the design-school movement gained momentum, women interested in design careers could find instruction in Boston, Pittsburgh, Cincinnati, and New York. The Franklin Institute Drawing School in Philadelphia, an early sponsor of the Philadelphia School, began accepting women into its drafting classes in 1870, and Minera Parker Nichols, the city's first professional woman architect, was one of many trained there.

By the late 1870s, women aspiring to become architects found additional ways of pursuing their ambition: they might apprentice to an architect, as Bethune did; learn from a private tutor, like Theodate Pope Riddle and Ethel Bailey Furman; or enroll in an architectural program at one of the land-grant colleges, the coeducational colleges established on federal land grants under the 1862 Morrill Act. Mary L. Page, the first to graduate from such a program, earned a degree from the University of Illinois in 1879, and Margaret Hicks graduated from Cornell a year later. Although MIT's school of architecture remained closed to women until 1885, more than a dozen women had earned MIT architectural degrees by the end of the century, Lois Lilley Howe among them.

The 1893 World's Columbian Exposition brought female architects into the national spotlight for the first time. As the head of the fair's Board of Lady Managers, Bertha Palmer planned a competition for a woman's building to showcase women's achievements and charitable work.[3] Bethune, now an AIA fellow, declined to participate in the competition, which she viewed as establishing the unfortunate precedent of paying women much less than their male peers and forcing them to compete for the privilege.[4] The plan drafted by Sophia Hayden, a recent MIT graduate, was selected from thirteen submissions. Although the architect suffered a nervous breakdown, in part because of the board's excessive demands, this high-profile event introduced the concept of the woman architect to a broad public.

At the turn of the century, more than two hundred women were practicing architects. Julia Morgan made international news by becoming the first woman to graduate from the prestigious École des Beaux-Arts, an exceptional achievement regardless of gender.[5] In regions near universities with coeducational architecture schools, women architects and architecture students were beginning to mentor one another and to form supportive organizations. In 1910, Lilian Rice was one of the first woman to graduate from the new architecture school at the University of California, Berkeley, Morgan's alma mater, and, eight years later, Lutah Maria Riggs enrolled in a class with three other women. MIT graduates, including Lois Howe and Eleanor Manning, established their own firms and hired the second generation of young alumnae. In 1915, Mae Steinmesch founded a sorority at Washington University in St. Louis that would become the Association for Women in Architecture, and Bertha Yerex Whitman established the T-Square Society at the University of Michigan. The opening of the Cambridge School for Domestic Architecture and Landscape Architecture in 1916 brought more women design students into the stimulating environment surrounding Harvard, MIT, and the city of Boston. In the early 1920s, the architect Eleanor Raymond launched a home office with fellow Cambridge School graduates, a supportive network for her flourishing practice. Her career as a designer of innovative energy-efficient modernist homes with solar heating anticipated today's sustainable building practices.[6]

Aspiring European women architects of the early nineteenth century had fewer educational resources and female mentors than their American counterparts. The Finnish architect Signi Ida Katarina Hornborg received special dispensation to graduate from the Helsinki Polytechnic Institute in architecture, but the other architects profiled here received early training in the arts and discovered architecture later in their careers. The Irish architect Eileen Gray and the German architect Lilly Reich were educated in design schools and earned the respect of male teachers and architects. The Finnish architect Aino Alto graduated from the Institute of Technology before becoming the personal and professional partner of fellow architect Alvar Aalto. After earning a degree from the University of Applied Arts Vienna, Margarita Schutte-Lihotzky worked on social housing projects with the architects Adolf Loos and Josef Frank. The careers of all but Hornborg were inspired, in part, by the growing popularity of the modern design movement.

As the following profiles illustrate, the careers of many groundbreaking women architects flourished in the 1920s, a time of national prosperity and of growing respect for women, who had not only gained the vote but also demonstrated expertise in engineering and architectural design. Their achievements included designing nearly every type of building—from hotels in national parks to university buildings on college campuses, not to mention churches, hospitals, factories, and residences. Although some women-run firms survived the Depression and continued after World War II, these decades were difficult, discouraging times. The social pressure for American women to stay at home—to give up jobs and nurture families—impeded their progress in the profession. As "Paving New Paths" in section two will illustrate, however, women were making significant strides as architects and designers across the globe.

LOUISE BLANCHARD BETHUNE

BORN
Waterloo, NY, 1856

DIED
Buffalo, NY, 1913

EDUCATION
Richard A. Waite,
apprenticeship, 1876–81

PRACTICE
R. A. and L. Bethune,
Architects, 1881–83; Bethune,
Bethune & Fuchs, 1883–ca.
1900

NOTABLE HONORS
AIA, 1887; Fellow, AIA, 1888

In the mid-1870s, before any woman had entered a university architecture program, much less opened an architectural practice, Louise Blanchard Bethune decided to become an architect. Over the course of a career lasting nearly two decades, she not only owned her own firm but also gained membership into her discipline's highest professional organization. The first woman to achieve such status, she was also the first to address a wide audience on the topic of "women and architecture" and to suggest that women practitioners should receive equal pay for equal work. A leading business woman opposed to professional agitators, she chose to become an example of equal rights in the workplace rather than a promoter of them. When she died at age fifty-seven, she and her firm had completed more than 150 projects.[7]

Bethune's early life offers no explanation for her unprecedented later success as a professional architect. She was homeschooled by her parents, both of whom were educators, until age eleven. The family moved to Buffalo in 1866, and a year later she enrolled at Buffalo High School. As a student, she became interested in architecture, and, according to one account, a negative remark about women as architects led her to take on the challenge of becoming one.[8] After graduating in 1874, she taught, traveled, and studied on her own—all with the intent of preparing herself to enter Cornell's architecture program—but when presented with the opportunity of working as a draftsperson for Buffalo architect Richard A. Waite, she embarked on this more typical route into the profession. After five years of full-time employment at Waite's office, Bethune was not only proficient at drafting but also had gained experience at construction sites.

In October 1881, the twenty-five-year-old architect announced her decision to launch her own business. That December, she married Robert A. Bethune, a former coworker, and they became partners, opening R. A. and L. Bethune, Architects. Two years later, when their only child, Charles William, was born, they promoted draftsman William L. Fuchs to become the third partner. Bethune was the owner of the firm for several years before she started receiving payment for her work and sharing the financial rewards of the business with her partners.[9]

Bethune, Bethune & Fuchs came to be widely known for its design of local schools—eighteen commissions in all—but was also equally sought to design houses and the small factories, churches, and other buildings demanded by the growing city of Buffalo, newly linked to the world of commerce by the Erie Canal. Among her firm's projects unique to the growing city were the Cataract Power and Conduit Company, Hall and Sons brick factory, and the Buffalo Weaving Company mill. The partners designed buildings in other areas of New York and in Pennsylvania, Connecticut, and Canada. Just seven years after establishing her firm, Bethune became a member of the AIA and a year later, in 1888, a fellow of the organization. In 1898, Bethune took on her best-known commission, the Hotel Lafayette, a 225-room Renaissance revival building designed to accommodate guests attending the 1901 Pan-American Exposition. The celebrated hotel remains a landmark in downtown Buffalo, a city profoundly influenced by the country's first professional woman architect. —*SA*

Hotel Lafayette, Buffalo, NY,
rendering, Bethune, Bethune
& Fuchs, 1904. Courtesy Kelly
Hayes McAloni

SIGNE IDA KATARINA HORNBORG

BORN
Turku, Finland, 1862

DIED
Helsinki, Finland, 1916

EDUCATION
Helsinki Polytechnic College, 1890

PRACTICE
Kiseleff & Heikel, 1890; Lars Sonck, 1891–ca. 1900

NOTABLE HONORS
First trained female architect in Finland

Signe Hornborg was the first professionally trained female architect in Finland and possibly in the whole of Europe. Though information about her life and work remains scarce, she is widely celebrated as a trailblazer in the notoriously exclusionary field of architecture and for her important contributions to the National Romantic style in Finland.

Hornborg came of age during a period of nascent social transformation in Finland, when the women's movement succeeded in securing a measure of access to higher education for women. The establishment of the Finnish Women's Association in 1884 is largely regarded as a milestone in the women's movement, one of the central objectives of which was the improvement of women's educational opportunities.[10] Hornborg was among the first wave of women to benefit from this new legislation. She enrolled at the Helsinki Polytechnic College (now Aalto University) in 1887 and completed her studies in 1890, thereby becoming the first woman to receive a degree in architecture.[11] Like other women in academia at the end of the nineteenth century, Hornborg was granted status as a supernumerary student and could only complete her degree by special permission.

After graduating, Hornborg first worked in the Helsinki office of Kiseleff & Heikel and then later for Lars Sonck. (Sonck had played a leading role in the development of National Romanticism, a Nordic style similar to *Jugendstil*, which attempted to establish a new national spatial identity independent from Russian influence.[12]) Although landmark educational and professional gains had been made for many upper-class women in architecture, they were largely excluded from leadership roles. While it remains uncertain how many buildings Hornborg worked on over the course of her architectural career, she is recognized for having made significant contributions to the Newander House apartment building (1892) in Pori and the Sepänkatu Apartment Building (1897) in Helsinki, for which Hornborg planned the elevation. She is also known to have designed a children's workshop in Helsinki and a voluntary fire brigade house (1890) in Porvoo, which today is the oldest surviving building designed by a female architect in Europe.

The Newander House, also known as Signelinna (Signe Castle), is an eclectic, historicist work located in the center of Pori, which survives to this day. The Sepänkatu Apartment Building was demolished in the 1960s. Remarkably, Hornborg is credited with having supervised the building process in addition to designing the exterior facade, roles that were typically reserved for men.[13]
—*LFR*

The Newander House (Signe
Castle), Pori, Finland, 1892.
Photo Hanna Tyvelä

LOIS LILLEY HOWE

BORN
Cambridge, MA, 1864

DIED
Cambridge, MA, 1964

EDUCATION
School of Museum of Fine Arts, Boston; MIT, 1890

PRACTICE
Lois Lilley Howe, 1894–1913; Howe and Manning, 1913–26; Howe, Manning & Almy, 1926–37

TEACHING
Copley Society of Boston, director, 1895–1919; Society of Arts and Crafts, Boston, director, 1916–19; MIT Women's Association, president, 1922–24

NOTABLE HONORS
Second Prize, Women's Building, 1893 World's Fair

In a career spanning nearly five decades, Lois Lilley Howe led a firm responsible for more than 425 projects, ranging from home and office building remodels to housing developments. First on her own and later with partners Eleanor Manning and Mary Almy, she set a standard of quality that would gain her patronage from the established families of Boston and the surrounding region.

An 1890 graduate of MIT, Howe was exceptionally prepared for her venture into the field of architecture, having also worked in the institute's school of architecture as a drafter, artist, and librarian. She spent two years as a draftsperson at the Boston office of Allen and Kenway and maintained a private moonlighting practice before establishing her own firm on Tremont Street in 1894. Just a year later, the architect Robert Peabody sponsored her successful election into the AIA, an achievement that may have resulted because voting members had mistakenly thought she was a man, assuming Lois was a version of Louis. Over time, Howe proved herself more than worthy of the honor, as she became known for original residential designs, for fine renovations of older homes, and for striving to achieve historical accuracy by salvaging doors, windows, and other items from structures undergoing demolition. Her work, and that of her firm, soon appeared in *Architecture*, *Architectural Record*, *Architectural Forum*, and other professional journals of the day.[14]

In 1913, after publishing *Details of Old New England Houses*, with Constance Fuller, Howe hired the architect Manning as a partner. A former MIT graduate, Manning brought a new dimension to the practice appropriate to the Progressive Era—interest in the development of public housing and urban renewal projects. While Howe focused on restoration work, including the first seventeenth-century revival house restored in Cambridge, Manning led the partnership's foray into garden-city housing, garnering the firm a role in the design of city planner John Nolen's Mariemont, Ohio. One of twenty-five firms involved in the development, Howe and Manning were the architects of Denny Place, seven single-family and two two-family English cottages near the center of the development.[15]

The longevity of Howe's firm was due, in part, to her staggered hiring of MIT graduates, each of whom brought a new generation's energy and fresh perspective to the drawing board. In 1926, she welcomed Almy, a 1917 MIT graduate recently elected to the AIA.[16] Almy, who walked with crutches due to childhood polio, appears to have handled the business aspects of the firm during a rapidly modernizing era while also contributing design and drafting skills. Howe kept her firm afloat during most of the Depression, but finally closed the highly successful business upon her retirement in 1937. Six years earlier, she had been elected a fellow of the AIA on her own merits and under her own highly esteemed name, only the third woman to receive that honor. As the founder of the first firm of women architects in the twentieth century, Howe elevated the level of historic restoration in New England—preserving countless houses along the way—and proved that women architects could compete on the national stage in cutting-edge, garden-city planning projects. —*SA*

Above
Mrs. A. M. Griswold House
interior alterations, watercolor
sketch, Cambridge, MA, 1901.
Courtesy MIT Libraries

Left
Anne M. Paul House,
Newburyport, MA, 1911.
Courtesy MIT Libraries

THEODATE POPE RIDDLE

BORN
Salem, OH, 1867

DIED
Farmington, CT, 1946

EDUCATION
Private tutor

PRACTICE
Theodate Pope, 1907–ca. 1927

NOTABLE HONORS
AIA, 1918

When Effie Pope was nineteen, she changed her name to Theodate, an early indication of her decision to shape her own life as an art collector, preservationist, and influential architect. The only child of a prominent Cleveland, Ohio, industrialist and his wife, Pope was educated in Midwestern private schools before spending a year being "finished" at Miss Porter's School in Farmington, Connecticut. In the Farmington Valley, she discovered a legacy of American colonial architecture, working farms, and the natural beauty of the Farmington River landscape. When she returned to Cleveland, she yearned for that place, and rather than "coming out" for the season, she convinced her parents to allow her to move East.

At a time when most women of her social status busied themselves as hostesses and philanthropists, Pope pursued an interest in architectural design. In the mid-1890s, she received informal instruction in art history at Princeton University but was otherwise self-taught.[17] She studied current architecture publications to inform her first project, the remodeling of an old farmhouse, and used the lessons learned about its design and construction to design her parent's home, Hill-Stead, near her beloved school. The house, commissioned by her father, was at heart a "Pope House," not a "McKim, Mead and White House," though that renowned architecture firm was called in to draw up Pope's plan and make the drawings. Inspired by the Colonial Revival trend then sweeping the nation, her design suggested the classic traditions of early American building.[18]

Although she maintained an office at Hill-Stead, Pope opened a New York office in 1907. Over the next two decades, she designed three private schools in Connecticut: Westover School (1909) in Middlebury, Hop Brook School (1915) in Naugatuck, and Avon Old Farms (1927), a boys' school in Avon. Her fascination with historical architecture and its accurate reproduction particularly informed her design for Avon Old Farms, which not only replicated the cottages of the Cotswolds but also actually led her to visit that region for inspiration and to hire British craftsmen to work on the buildings.

In 1918, after eleven years of practice, Pope became the fifth female member of the AIA and the first from Connecticut. Her reputation for "faultless taste" and her ability to design in a style *Architectural Record* praised as "just fine old-fashioned American" led to a nationally significant commission in 1920.[19] The Women's Roosevelt Memorial Association hired her to reconstruct Theodore Roosevelt's birthplace, a Gothic Revival brownstone demolished four years earlier, as a memorial to the recently deceased president. Basing her design on the extant adjacent "twin" residence, Pope reconstructed the house in a way that is both commemorative and modern to her contemporaries.[20] Her meticulous restoration of the 1865 residence was significant within the historic-preservation movement. The Theodore Roosevelt Birthplace is now a national historic site run by the National Park Service.

Before her death in 1946, Pope envisioned her own house museum, bequeathing the landscape, house, and collection of art and decorative arts. Today, Hill-Stead is a National Historic Landmark. —*SA*

Above
Hill-Stead, Farmington, CT,
1901. Photo James F. O'Gorman.
Courtesy Hill-Stead Museum

Right
Westover School, Middlebury,
CT, 1909. Photo James F.
O'Gorman. Courtesy Hill-Stead
Museum

MARY COLTER

BORN
Pittsburgh, PA, 1869

DIED
Santa Fe, NM, 1958

EDUCATION
California School of Design, 1890

PRACTICE
Fred Harvey Company, 1910–47

TEACHING
Stout Manual Training School, Menomonie, WI, 1891–92; Mechanic Arts High School, St. Paul, MN, 1892–1907

NOTABLE HONORS
Pioneer of Pueblo Revival architecture; four National Historic Landmarks in Grand Canyon National Park: Hermit's Rest, Lookout Studio, Hopi House, Desert View Watchtower; eleven buildings on the National Register of Historic Places

Born into a family of Irish immigrants, Mary Colter lived in Pennsylvania, Colorado, and Texas before permanently settling in the newly prosperous and progressive city of St. Paul, Minnesota, in 1880. Shortly after the death of her father in 1886, Colter moved to Oakland, California, with her mother and sister, to attend the California School of Design in San Francisco.[21] While studying drawing and painting, Colter was likely influenced by her mentor, Arthur Frank Mathews, a leading figure of the California Decorative Style, which was an offshoot of the Arts and Crafts Movement.

Upon graduating, Colter returned in 1891 with her family to St. Paul, where she soon took up a position teaching freehand and mechanical drawing at the Mechanic Arts High School. During this time, Colter became very active in the local arts scene and pursued a self-directed study of history, archaeology, architecture, and design.[22] Her renown in St. Paul as a talented artisan with substantial knowledge of Native American art and culture eventually caught the attention of Fred Harvey, the proprietor of a chain of hotels, dining establishments, and shops along the Atchison, Topeka and Santa Fe Railway lines.[23] After two successful commissions in 1902 and 1905, the ambitious Midwesterner was eventually hired as master architect and decorator for the Fred Harvey Company in 1910.

Though Colter was based in Kansas City, where the Harvey Company was headquartered, she spent the vast majority of her time in the Four Corners region of the Southwest on various job sites or traveling on horseback to study Indigenous ruins and artifacts. The Hopi House (1905)—Colter's architectural debut and the first of eight projects she directed at the Grand Canyon—serves as a nascent demonstration of her unorthodox approach based on extensive historical and field research. Adjacent to the El Tovar hotel on the canyon's South Rim, the multistory complex was modeled after ten-thousand-year-old pueblo dwellings in the nearby village of Oraibi, Arizona, that Colter had visited.[24]

Colter's commitment to the preservation of Native American culture was further exemplified in the iconic Desert View Watchtower (1932), which drew direct inspiration from the Round Tower of Cliff Palace in Mesa Verde.[25] Decorating the tower's interior walls and ceilings are murals by the celebrated Hopi artist Fred Kabotie, depicting the origins of Hopi life, and pictographs and petroglyphs by Harvey Company artist Fred Geary, copied from various prehistoric sites in the region (many of which have since been destroyed).[26]

Hermit's Rest (1914) and Lookout Studio (1914) demonstrate the great lengths that Colter went to ensure that her structures were carefully integrated into their natural surroundings, often incorporating materials and geographical features found on site. Her buildings were inspiring, frequently enhancing tourists' experiences of the canyon's geologic and ethnographic wonders.

In addition to her work at the Grand Canyon, Colter designed a handful of hotels along the Atchison, Topeka and Santa Fe Railway, including El Navajo (1918) in Gallup, New Mexico, an expansion of La Fonda Hotel (1929) in Santa Fe, and La Posada (1930) in Winslow, Arizona. After a long, distinguished career, Colter retired at the age of seventy-eight to Santa

Fe, where she died in 1958. Her pioneering projects at the Grand Canyon—four of which were designated as National Historic Landmarks in 1987—had a lasting effect on the rustic style of architecture that was implemented in the National Park System throughout the mid-twentieth century.[27]

Moreover, the legacy of Colter's craftsmanship and ingenuity extended beyond the canyon's rim, playing an instrumental role in developing the renowned Spanish-Pueblo revival style of the Southwest. —*LFR*

Desert View Watchtower, Grand Canyon National Park, AZ, 1932. Courtesy Grand Canyon National Park

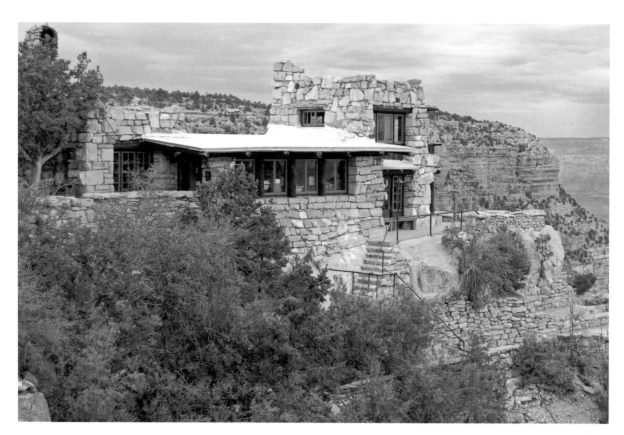

Above
Lookout Studio, Grand Canyon
National Park, AZ, 1914. Photo
Michael Quinn. Courtesy Grand
Canyon National Park

Right
Hopi House, Grand Canyon
National Park, AZ, 1905.
Courtesy William L. Bird
Postcard Collection

Bright Angel Lodge, Grand
Canyon National Park, AZ, 1935.
Photo Carol M. Highsmith,
Library of Congress

MARION MAHONY GRIFFIN

BORN
Chicago, IL, 1871

DIED
Chicago, IL, 1961

EDUCATION
MIT, 1894

PRACTICE
Dwight Perkins, 1894–95; Frank Lloyd Wright, 1895–1911; Walter Burley Griffin and Marion Mahony Griffin, 1911–14; Griffin and Mahony, 1914–37

NOTABLE HONORS
First licensed woman architect, AIA, 1894; winning design (with Walter Burley Griffin), Australian Federal Capital, Canberra, 1912

Marion Mahony Griffin spent the majority of her career in the daunting shadow of Frank Lloyd Wright, the most famous American architect of her generation. Historians continue to speculate about the extent to which her skills facilitated his tremendous success. Because of this association, and her acknowledged success as a member of the Prairie School, she is one of the best-known female architects.

When Mahony was only eleven, her father died, and she was left to help care for her three younger siblings while her mother earned a teaching degree, becoming a school principal. The family was further tried when their house burned down. Relatives and other women pitched in to help. In fact, Mahony's own aspirations were supported by these women, including civic leader Mary Wilmarth, who helped pay for her education.[28]

Mahony followed her cousin, architect Dwight Perkins, to MIT in 1890 and graduated from the architectural program four years later. After working for more than a year as a drafter at Perkins's office, she was hired by Wright as the only employee when he launched his first private practice. An avid practitioner in the Prairie School, Mahony worked in Wright's office for fifteen years.

During her association with Wright, she also worked for other architects and took on commissions of her own.[29] Mahony's first attributed independent project was All Soul's Church (1903) in Evanston, Illinois. The client evidently asked for a more conventional plan, and she altered her original design accordingly.[30] When Wright left for Europe in 1909, Mahony turned down his request to supervise the office. Architect Hermann V. von Holst stepped in, but only after the assurance that Mahony would serve as lead designer. During Wright's absence, Mahony designed the Adolph Mueller House at 4 Millikin Place, Decatur, Illinois (1910), and the David M. Amberg House in Grand Rapids, Michigan (1911). She also executed drawings for the famous Wasmuth Portfolio, a collection of Wright's designs published in Germany that led to his international recognition as a master architect. As much as half of the portfolio drawings have been attributed to Mahony.[31] Indisputably one of the most accomplished delineators of her day, she developed the iconic artistic style recognized as Wrightian.

Mahony left Wright's office in 1911 and married architect Walter Burley Griffin. A year later, the couple won a competition to design and plan the capital of Australia, in Canberra, most likely due to her compelling drawings. They collaborated on many significant Australian buildings, and Mahony Griffin is credited with important designs of the Creswick residence (1921), located in the Castlecrag neighborhood on the banks of the Sydney harbor, and the Capitol Theater in Melbourne (1923). In 1935, Walter Griffin decided to move his practice to India, where the couple had several projects. He died in 1937, and Mahony Griffin completed their joint work while overseeing the design of more than a hundred houses, designed in the Prairie School style. Mahony Griffin returned to the United States in the late 1930s. At age ninety, she died in poverty, but not obscurity. She is memorialized at Chicago's Graceland Cemetery (known as the cemetery of architects) in the company of such renowned peers as Louis Sullivan, Daniel Burnham, and William Le Baron Jenney. **—SA**

Above
Robert Mueller House,
Decatur, IL, 1909. Photo
© Mati Maldre, 1991

Right
Pioneer Press Office, Lucknow,
India, architectural drawing,
Walter Burley Griffin and
Marion Mahony Griffin, 1936.
Avery Architectural & Fine Arts
Library, Columbia University

JULIA MORGAN

BORN
San Francisco, CA, 1872

DIED
San Francisco, CA, 1957

EDUCATION
University of California,
Berkeley, 1894; École des
Beaux-Arts, 1901

PRACTICE
Bernard Maybeck, 1894–98;
John Galen Howard, 1902–4;
Julia Morgan, 1905–6; Morgan
and Hoover, 1907–10; Julia
Morgan, Architect, 1910–51

NOTABLE HONORS
First woman graduate, École
des Beaux-Arts, 1901; Honorary
Doctor of Laws, University of
California, Berkeley, 1929; Gold
Medal, AIA, 2014

In the early twentieth century, Julia Morgan was the first woman to earn an education and build a practice that rivaled those of her most accomplished male peers. Throughout her nearly six-decade career, she refused to enter competitions, write articles, or lecture about her work, leaving such distracting tasks to "talking architects."[32] Despite this lack of internal promotion, her firm flourished through the two World Wars and the Depression. The quality of Morgan's work, both in its engineering and craftsmanship, as well as her ability to please her clients, served as its own publicity.

The second child of an upper-middle-class family, Morgan exhibited an early talent for mathematics. Her parents encouraged her to pursue her career of choice at a time when such ambition rarely figured into the future of her female peers. In 1890, she entered the engineering program at the University of California, Berkeley, years before the founding of its first school of architecture. There, she became a student of the architect Bernard Maybeck, a charismatic alumnus of the École des Beaux-Arts, and developed a passion for architecture. Morgan worked briefly as a draftsperson in Maybeck's office after graduation. When Maybeck heard that the École might soon open its doors to women, he encouraged Morgan to apply. Morgan traveled to Paris in 1896, and, two years later, became the first woman allowed to take the school's entrance exam.[33] Her graduation from the École in 1901 made international news.[34]

Having secured her qualifications from the world's most prestigious architectural school, Morgan returned to the US in the fall of 1902. Her early years of practice benefited from the patronage of wealthy female clients, including Phoebe Apperson Hearst and Susan Mills. Beginning in 1902, Morgan began work in the architectural office of John Galen Howard, UC Berkeley's campus architect, working as a draftsperson on the Hearst Mining building and the Greek Theater. El Campanil was the bell tower she designed for Mills College in 1903.

After passing the California state architectural exam in 1904, Morgan left Howard to open her first office, only to see it destroyed during the 1906 San Francisco earthquake. She joined with junior partner Ira Hoover ca. 1907 as Morgan and Hoover, continuing the work on the Mills College Oakland Campus with the Margaret Carnegie Library (1905); a gymnasium (1909); an infirmary (1910); a recreation center (1922); and a residence (1926). The college's El Campanil bell tower was one of the few lofty structures to survive the earthquake, and Morgan soon became known for her skill as an engineer. Her postdisaster commissions, which employed reinforced concrete, included renovation of the severely damaged Fairmont Hotel and the Viavi Building on Nob Hill.[35] She remodeled the interior lobby of the Merchant's Exchange building, a fifteen-story skyscraper designed by Daniel H. Burnham and Willis Polk, and relocated her office to its thirteenth floor. Morgan and Hoover disbanded their practice in 1910, when her firm was renamed Julia Morgan, Architect. By 1927, her staff of fourteen included six women.

During World War I, the National War Council of the YWCA commissioned Morgan to design accommodations for female relatives and friends of troops stationed at army camps along the Pacific

Saint John's Presbyterian
interior, Berkeley, CA, 1910.
Julia Morgan Collection,
Environmental Design
Archives, UC Berkeley

Coast. Two other women architects—Katherine Cotheal Budd and Fay Kellogg—were responsible for the Southern, Midwest, and Eastern regions.[36] From 1913 to the 1930s, Morgan designed dozens of Hostess Houses and YWCA sites, including the thirty-acre campus of Asilomar, a conference center in Pacific Grove, California.[37]

After the death of Phoebe Hearst, her son, William Randolph, began planning a home on a property he called the Ranch. To develop its design, he hired his mother's architect of choice. La Questa Encantada, or Hearst Castle, as it has come to be known, was a collection of art and antiquities and an architectural tour de force. Morgan's skill at accommodating her client's vast acquisitions—from early Renaissance tapestries and illuminated books to Italian choir stalls and Roman relics—would prove crucial to the success of the massive design project that unfolded over the next few decades. Just months before the stock market crashed, the *New York Times* featured a story comparing "the business system by which the building and collecting is done" to that of the "Medici, d'Este, and Visconti." As architect, Morgan was "allowed a virtually free hand."[38] When completed, the 250,000-acre San Simeon ranch featured a more than 150-room main house, several guest houses, and eight acres of landscaped gardens.

In the 1920s, Morgan collaborated with Maybeck on two buildings at Berkeley, the Phoebe Apperson Hearst Memorial Auditorium and Art Museum and a women's gymnasium. Beginning in 1924, she worked on Wyntoon, the Hearst family retreat in Siskiyou County, near Mount Shasta. After the Gothic castle Maybeck had designed there in 1902 was lost to a fire, Morgan created a "Bavarian village," a complex of three guesthouses (each three stories), quarters for servants and superintendents, and grand accommodations for a theater and for recreation.[39] Her work at Wyntoon, a long-standing commission lasting through the early 1940s, approached the magnitude of San Simeon in terms of her time and personal devotion. Although Morgan's most lucrative commissions came from Hearst, she also accepted projects from clients of modest income.

In recent decades, Morgan has been increasingly recognized as a major figure in the Arts and Crafts Movement. Although her buildings often incorporated historic sources and were compellingly intricate, her focus on function, structure, and space anticipated early modernist design. One of her employees, Dorothy Wormser Coblentz, recalled that "she didn't build in a style. She built functionally; the plan came first."[40] Morgan retired in 1951, at the age of seventy-nine, with more than seven hundred commissions to her credit.

In 2014, fifty-seven years after her death, she posthumously became the first woman to receive the AIA Gold Medal, the highest honor, presented for a lifetime of professional achievement.[41] —*SA*

Left
Hearst Castle, San Simeon, CA, 1947. © Hearst Castle/CA State Parks

Below
The Hacienda, Milpitas Ranch House, Jolon, CA, 1930. Photo Frank C. Aston

MARY ROCKWELL HOOK

BORN
Junction City, KS, 1877

DIED
Siesta Key, FL, 1978

EDUCATION
Wellesley College, BA, 1900;
Art Institute of Chicago, 1904

PRACTICE
Howe, Hoit and Cutler, 1913–21;
Hook and Remington, 1923–32;
Mary Rockwell Hook, 1932–50

NOTABLE HONORS
Architectural Achievement,
AIA, 1977

During a career spanning nearly four decades, Mary Rockwell Hook designed houses for Kansas City's fashionable neighborhoods, rustic buildings in mountain settings, and vacation homes on the Florida coast. Her work changed with the times, reflecting the influence of the City Beautiful movement, the craftsman style, and, by the 1930s, the new materials and ideals of the modern movement. All the while, Hook's work retained a timeless originality and popular appeal. An international traveler, she infused her designs with foreign influences, as well as her own innovations with found objects and recycled building materials.

The third of five daughters born to Bertrand Rockwell, a successful grain merchant, and Julia Marshall Snyder, Hook benefitted from her parents' wealth and commitment to women's education. She attended the Dana Hall School and Wellesley College, graduating in 1900. Three years later, she enrolled at the Art Institute of Chicago and, after a year of study, moved to France and joined the atelier of Jean-Marcel Auburtin to prepare to enter the École des Beaux-Arts. Although she became the second woman to take and pass the École's entrance exam, she decided not to continue her study. Returning to the United States, Hook apprenticed for Howe, Hoit and Cutler.

Rockwell supported his daughter's career by purchasing the building lots for many of her projects. This freedom to design without restrictions inspired her to experiment with materials, such as concrete and earthen insulation, and to design the first attached garage and swimming pool in the region.[42]

In 1913, Hook planned the campus of the Pine Mountain Settlement School in Harlan County, Kentucky—a fifty-mile hike or horseback ride into the southern Appalachian Mountains. Here she created the Open House, a guest cabin praised as having "grown of its own vitality from the walks and woods," and other rustic buildings crafted from native boulders and wood milled on the site.[43] The school, considered an early example of the urban-settlement house reinterpreted for a rural landscape, was designated a National Historic Landmark in 1991 by the US Department of the Interior.[44]

Mary Rockwell married attorney Inghram D. Hook in 1921. Two years later, she launched Hook and Remington with architect Eric Douglas Macwilliam Remington. Much of the firm's residential work incorporated elements Hook discovered during her frequent visits to Italy, including timber, frescoes, and tile. Long before it became fashionable, she integrated recycled paving blocks, wood from an old railroad bridge, and other materials culled from razed buildings into her built works. The exceptional nature of her residential design in Kansas City has been acknowledged by a National Register district bearing her name.[45]

In 1935, Hook purchased and developed Whispering Sands, a fifty-five-acre property on Siesta Key, an island off Sarasota, Florida. The resort featured the Whispering Sands Inn, which heated its water using an early type of solar panel. Ten years later, she sold the inn and retained half of the land for Sandy Hook, where she designed two houses and commissioned a third from architect Paul Rudolph.[46] She completed her final Sarasota work, the Florence R. DeWalt House, in 1950.[47] Hook died at her Siesta Key home on her 101st birthday. **—SA**

Top
Julia M. Rockwell House, 5011
Sunset Drive, Kansas City, MO,
1932. Photo Frank Lauder.
Missouri Valley Special
Collections. Courtesy Kansas
City Public Library

Bottom
Whispering Sands Inn (now a
condominium), Sarasota, FL, 1935.
© Allan F. Blackman, 1974, Hook
Papers. Courtesy State Historical
Society of Missouri

EILEEN GRAY

BORN
Enniscorthy, Ireland, 1878

DIED
Paris, France, 1976

EDUCATION
Slade School of Fine Art, 1902;
Académie Colarossi, 1902;
Académie Julian, 1905

PRACTICE
Seizo Sugawara-Eileen Gray,
1910; Jean Désert gallery,
1922–30; Roquebrune-Cap-
Martin, 1926–49

NOTABLE HONORS
Royal Designer for Industry,
Royal Society for Arts,
Manufactures and Commerce,
1972; Honorary Fellow, Royal
Institute of the Architects of
Ireland, 1973

Eileen Gray was a leading figure in the French decorative arts of the 1910s and 1920s, a visionary architect whose conscientious and imaginative designs challenged the dehumanizing aspects of Heroic Modernism.

Gray was born near Enniscorthy, Ireland, into a family of Irish aristocrats. Her father, James Maclaren Smith, was a Scottish landscape painter who encouraged young Gray to develop her artistic skills.[48] She studied drawing at the Bohemian Slade School of Fine Art in London before moving to Paris, where she completed her education at the Académie Julian in 1905. While at Slade, Gray solicited lessons in traditional Asian lacquer techniques from the Soho-based furniture restorer Dean Charles. She later continued her training with the Japanese lacquer master Seizo Sugawara in Paris, with whom she opened a workshop in 1910. By 1913, Gray was exhibiting her pieces in the Salon des Artistes Decorateurs and soon established herself as one of the leading designers of lacquered furniture.[49]

The nascent success of Gray's designs was halted by the outbreak of World War I. Gray volunteered as an ambulance driver for the French army before retreating to London with Sugawara to wait out the remainder of the war.[50] After the armistice was declared in 1918, Gray returned to Paris and was soon commissioned to redesign the Rue de Lota apartment of the successful dressmaker Juliette Lévy, featured in *Harper's Bazaar* in 1920.[51] In 1922, Gray opened the Jean Désert gallery in Paris as a means to exhibit and sell her designs.

Over the course of the 1920s, Gray reoriented her practice toward architecture, encouraged by her relationship with Romanian architect Jean Badovici, who introduced her to the work of avant-garde European designers, such as Le Corbusier, Adolf Loos, and de Stijl. She began a self-directed study of architecture, pouring through books, taking drafting lessons, and visiting building sites with Polish architect Adrienne Górska. By the mid-1920s, Gray was immersed in the world of architecture, now favoring the restrained elegance of industrial modernism.

Gray's first major architectural accomplishment was E.1027 (1929), the vacation house she designed for herself and Badovici on the coast of Roquebrune-Cap-Martin, France. Though the seaside villa borrowed freely from Le Corbusier's "Five Points of the New Architecture" (1926) in its use of cement pilotis and open-plan layout, the design was highly original in its treatment of interior space. In an interview between Gray and Badovici about their collaboration on the Maison en Bord de Mer, she described the project as a critique of the modernist movement, declaring that "the poverty of modern architecture stems from the atrophy of sensuality."[52] Rather than a machine for living, Gray conceived of E.1027 as a living organism, filled with dynamic and evolving spaces imbued with intimate and kinesthetic qualities. In her attempts to achieve a self-conscious unity between architecture and the decorative arts, Gray devoted considerable energy toward constructing a domestic environment that was as functional and comfortable as it was playful and tactile.

By the time the effects of the Great Depression set in, Gray had abandoned

Villa E.1027, Roquebrune-
Cap-Martin, France, 1929.
© Manuel Bougot, 2014

her craft as a luxury furniture maker and closed Jean Désert. In 1931, Gray began drafting plans for a new house in Castellar, France. Built solely for herself, Tempe à Pailla (1934) was more modest than E.1027, a mixture of modern and vernacular. Constructed on top of an old stone foundation, the reinforced concrete house with flat roof opened onto a large terrace with breathtaking views of the surrounding mountains and sea. Despite the fact that the narrow property was wedged between a public road and a pathway to a neighboring house, Gray managed to create a secluded haven elevated amid the tree canopy.[53] Similar to E.1027, every square inch of Tempe was envisaged with imagination, featuring a variety of surprising built-in features, clever space-saving solutions, and transformable furniture.[54] Blurring the distinctions between architecture, furniture, and art, Gray's houses can be regarded as "total works."

In the mid-1930s, Gray's architectural undertakings broadened to address the pressing social and political issues of the day. With the emergence of paid vacation enacted by the French Popular Front in 1936, there arose a great deal of interest in the creation of leisure centers for working-class citizens.[55] Gray immediately got to work developing a scheme for a seaside resort with recreational and cultural facilities that sought to overcome the challenge of social integration. A long-time admirer of Gray's work, Le Corbusier enthusiastically included a model of her Vacation Centre (1937) in his Pavillon des Temps Nouveaux at the 1937 International Exhibition in Paris.[56]

When World War II overtook Europe, Gray was interned as a foreign national and forced to leave France. Her houses were looted and her projects were largely destroyed.[57] After the war, Gray returned to her house in Castellar and began work on what would prove to be her last major project, an ambitious Cultural and Social Center (1947), a communal gathering place for this remote, provincial town.

With her eyesight failing, Gray retired to her apartment in Paris and slowly faded from public view. Even though Gray designed more than forty-five architectural projects in her lifetime, only nine were realized. Four of her buildings, including E.1027, were incorrectly attributed to her collaborator, Badovici—an error that architectural historians eventually amended in 2000. Beyond the brief success she enjoyed during the 1920s, Gray had a surprisingly limited impact on the field until architectural historian Joseph Rykwert initiated a reappraisal of Gray's work in a series of articles published in *Domus* in 1968 and *Architectural Review* in 1972.

At the age of ninety-five, the reclusive designer, who had fallen into relative obscurity, incurred the sort of critical acclaim that would have served her well earlier in life. In 1972, the Royal Society for Arts appointed her a Royal Designer for Industry, and the following year, the Royal Institute of the Architects of Ireland elected her an Honorary Fellow in "recognition of her outstanding contribution to the development of modern architecture and design."[58] E.1027 was declared a historic monument in 1999 and is now widely regarded as a modern masterpiece. —*LFR*

LILLY REICH

BORN
Berlin, Germany, 1885

DIED
Berlin, Germany, 1947

EDUCATION
Wellesley College, BA, 1900;
Art Institute of Chicago, 1903

TEACHING
Bauhaus, Dessau, 1932–33;
Berlin University of the Arts,
1945–46

NOTABLE HONORS
German Werkbund, 1912, first
woman on board; second
female Bauhaus Master, 1931

Lilly Reich was a pioneering German designer and architect of modern exhibitions in the 1920s and 1930s. Through her integral role in the German Werkbund's exhibitions, she revolutionized the art of the display and introduced the general public to avant-garde concepts commonly associated with the Bauhaus.

Formally trained as an industrial embroiderer, Reich began her career designing textiles and women's clothing.[59] Her early ties to the textile industry influenced her later displays and interiors, demonstrating a mastery of material, texture, and color. In 1908, the Vienna Workshop invited Reich to join; here, she studied under Josef Hoffman and Else Oppler-Legband.[60] Through her connection with Oppler-Legband, Reich designed clothing displays for the highly fashionable Wertheim department store in Berlin in 1911.[61]

A critical development for Reich came in 1912, when she was elected a member of the Werkbund, an association of artists, architects, designers, and industrialists who aimed to bolster Germany's performance in the global market through mass production and standardization. To meet these ends, the Werkbund deployed various strategies toward shaping consumer taste, placing particular emphasis on exhibitions and window displays as optimal public interfaces—domains that Reich specialized in.[62]

In 1914, the Werkbund staged an exhibition in Cologne in an effort to elevate German design to an international audience. Working alongside Oppler-Legband and Anna Muthesius, Reich worked as general coordinator for the Haus der Frau (House of Women), which boldly asserted the centrality of women's roles in the design-reform movement. In the shockingly stark pavilion designed by Margarete Knüppelholz-Roeser, exhibits of objects and interiors promulgated the Werkbund principles of *Sachlichkeit* (objectivity) and functionalism.[63] In the heart of the exhibition were passages of shop windows designed by Reich.[64]

The defining moment of Reich's career occurred in 1926 with the exhibition *From Fiber to Textile* at the Frankfurt International Fair. In the cavernous arena of the Festhalle, Reich developed an archetype for a new method of display that emphasized the materials and processes involved in manufacturing rather than the finished product.[65] Lauded for their straightforward, nearly scientific presentation, Reich's minimalist installations caught the attention of fellow board member Ludwig Mies van der Rohe, who subsequently recommended her appointment as coordinator and designer of a major exposition on modern architecture in Stuttgart the following year.[66]

An influential Werkbund exhibition known as *The Dwelling* showcased an array of modern appliances and housewares, along with construction materials and methods, at the forefront of a new, rational architecture modeled nearby at the landmark Weissenhof Housing Estate. Reich was responsible for eight of the nine exhibition halls, two of which she designed in collaboration with Mies van der Rohe. In the main hall, freestanding white walls delineated and framed the exhibits of each manufacturer—a technique that has since become standard exhibition practice.[67]

Following the tremendous success of their work in Stuttgart, Reich and Mies

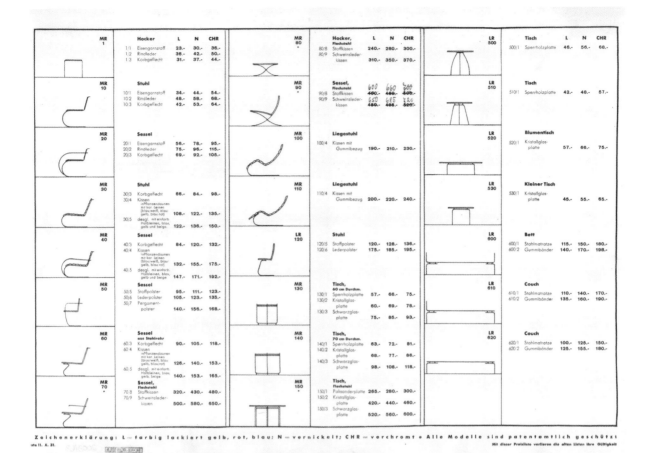

Above

Bamberg metal workshop, furniture designs, Ludwig Mies van der Rohe and Lilly Reich, 1931. Courtesy Bauhaus Archive Berlin. © 2020 Artists Rights Society (ARS), New York / VG Bild-Kunst, Bonn

Right

Werkbund exhibition, Stuttgart, Germany, 1927. © The Museum of Modern Art. Licensed by SCALA/Art Resource, NY

van der Rohe returned to Berlin and struck up a close professional relationship that would last until the late 1930s. Though they frequently worked together, Reich and Mies van der Rohe maintained separate studio practices. Their next project ensued the following year for the Women's Fashion exhibition in Berlin. Within a massive open-plan hall, their Velvet and Silk Café utilized hanging panels of yellow, red, and black fabric suspended by curved metal rods to create a continuous space populated by the tubular steel tables and chairs designed by Mies van der Rohe.[68] This innovative use of curtains as a temporary, flexible partition was famously featured in Reich's interior designs for Mies van der Rohe's Villa Tugendhat (1930) as well as the iconic Barcelona Pavilion (1929)—two pioneering prototypes of modern architecture.[69]

At the 1929 Barcelona International Exposition, Reich acted as the artistic director for twenty-five exhibits for the German Pavilion, most notably the textile exhibit, the chemistry exhibit, and the Hackerbräu beer exhibit.[70] Reich's functionalist installations attempted to neutralize the function of the display and elevated the consumer good to the status of a museum object. Despite unsuccessful attempts to have no label narration, desiring to let the object speak for itself, her displays took on a mannerism of their own. This was perhaps best demonstrated in her textile exhibit, in which large swaths of fabric draped over chrome bars were framed against free-standing panels of colored glass, portraying the textiles as graphic objects.

Reich's next large-scale project with the Werkbund was *The Dwelling of Our Time*, a prominent representation of architecture at the German Building Exhibition in Berlin in 1931. This time, Reich participated as both artistic director and architect. In addition to an exhibit of building materials on the hall's mezzanine and an exhibit of furnishings for Wertheim department store, Reich designed two apartments—one for a married couple and one for a single person—and a single-story house, all furnished with her own designs.

From 1932 to 1933, Reich taught as the head of the weaving studio and the workshop for interior design at the Bauhaus in Dessau.[71] After Gunta Stölz, Reich was the second woman to head a department at the Bauhaus. In 1933, the school was pressured to close by the newly empowered Nazi regime. That same year, the Third Reich assumed control of the Werkbund, henceforth suspending the exhibitions program. Despite this dire shift in leadership and policy, Reich maintained her allegiance to the Werkbund and continued her exhibition work for the government. Before the outbreak of World War II, she worked on several exhibitions that functioned as state propaganda, most notably *German People— German Work* (1934) and the German textile industry exhibit at the famously tense 1937 Paris World Exposition.[72]

The war played a definitive role in Reich's career, which floundered under the Nazi regime. She was conscripted into the military engineering group Organization Todt (OT) and later worked in the office of architect Ernst Neufert, who had been commissioned by Albert Speer to work out standards for residential buildings.[73] Her most important undertaking during the postwar years was her participation in the revival of the German Werkbund. Reich devoted the last year of her life to transmitting Werkbund principles and restructuring the programs in trade and applied-arts schools.[74] She died in 1947, before the Werkbund's official reestablishment in 1950. —*LFR*

Boarding House, *The Dwelling of Our Time*, German Building Exhibition, Berlin, 1931.
© The Museum of Modern Art. Licensed by SCALA/Art Resource, NY

ELEANOR RAYMOND

BORN
Cambridge, MA, 1887

DIED
Boston, MA, 1989

EDUCATION
Wellesley College, 1909;
Cambridge School of
Architecture and Landscape
Architecture for Women, 1919

PRACTICE
Frost & Raymond, 1919–28;
Eleanor Raymond, 1928–73

NOTABLE HONORS
AIA, 1924; Fellow, AIA, 1961

A Cambridge native, architect Eleanor Raymond created some of the most original houses of her generation, introducing modern design and technologies to tradition-bound neighborhoods in Boston and nearby New England towns. After graduating from Wellesley College in 1909, she took a course taught by landscape architect Fletcher Steele and subsequently worked for his office without pay. Inspired by the experience and her mentor's fresh perspective on contemporary design, Raymond enrolled in the Cambridge School of Architecture and Landscape Architecture for Women in 1917. While still a student, she formed a partnership with Henry Atherton Frost, one of her professors and a cofounder of the school.[75] Her first independent commission, the Cleaves House (1919) in Winchester, Massachusetts, was widely praised in contemporary architecture journals.[76] The art historian Henry Russell Hitchcock Jr. admired the house for its modernist details, which equaled those by European masters.[77]

In 1923, Raymond embarked on a project of personal importance, the transformation of a derelict property on Beacon Hill into a townhouse, which she shared with friends and relatives for the next thirty years. Fellow residents included her partner, Ethel Power, editor of *House Beautiful*, and the landscape architect Mary Cunningham, both of whom also attended the Cambridge School. Raymond profited from the support of her former classmates and also enjoyed the collaboration with other Cambridge School graduates who were eager for office experience, such as Laura Cox, her drafter for three decades.[78]

Despite the region's preference for traditional residential design, Raymond continued to pursue her interest in modern architecture and opened her own office in 1928. She and Power traveled to Europe to see the work of European modernists, particularly the International Style buildings by Gropius and Le Corbusier. In 1931, Raymond designed a house for her sister, Rachel Raymond, in Belmont, Massachusetts, drawing on aspects of the Bauhaus design school. One of the first International Style houses in New England, the house paid homage to traditional American design in the wood construction and stylistic aspects Raymond had gleaned through comprehensive study of vernacular architecture. The year of its design, Raymond published her only book, *Early Domestic Architecture of Pennsylvania*.

Throughout her career, Raymond experimented with new technologies to further her goal of designing simple buildings that suited the landscape, referred to the past, and fulfilled the hopes of their residents. She designed thirteen structures for the Boston sculptor and conservationist Amelia Peabody, including an experimental plywood house and an all-Masonite house. In the late 1940s, Raymond worked with Dr. Maria Telkes of the MIT solar laboratory to design the Dover Sun House (1949), one of the country's first solar buildings. Even though her most innovative modern designs displayed an unusual sensibility toward the American vernacular, they also expressed an ardent desire to bring the convenience and momentum of modern architecture to New England.

She was in her mid-eighties when she completed her final project in 1973. The Institute of Contemporary Art, Boston, launched a retrospective exhibition of her work in 1981, eight years before her death at the age of one hundred two.[79] —*SA*

Dover Sun House, Dover,
MA, 1949

LILIAN RICE

BORN
National City, CA, 1889

DIED
Rancho Santa Fe, CA, 1938

EDUCATION
University of California,
Berkeley, 1910

PRACTICE
Santa Fe Land Improvement
Company, 1921–29; Lilian Rice
Architect, 1929–38

NOTABLE HONORS
AIA, 1931; AIA honor awards
for La Valenciana Apartments
(1928), Arnberg House (1928),
and ZIAC Rowing Club (1932)

During her seventeen-year career, the architect Lilian Rice designed buildings that evoked California's history, as well as its promising future, significantly contributing to the development of a regional architectural style. Rice grew up in National City, where her father was a prominent local educator, and benefitted from the cultural diversity of a town located just a dozen miles from the Mexican border. As a teenager, she enrolled in the new school of architecture at the University of California, Berkeley, and studied under the architect John Galen Howard. After graduating in 1910, she supported herself by teaching at San Diego High School and San Diego State University teacher's college, where she became a mentor to Sam Hamill, FAIA. She also worked as an apprentice draftsperson in the office of architect Hazel Wood Waterman, a protégé of the pioneering modern architect Irving Gill. When Rice joined her firm, Waterman was completing a restoration of the Estudillo House in San Diego, one of the oldest examples of Spanish architecture in the state.[80] Rice's future work, particularly her 1920s restoration of the Osuna adobe on the former Rancho San Dieguito, was informed by this project.

In 1921, the local firm of Richard S. Requa and Herbert L. Jackson hired Rice to be a draftsperson and designer for Rancho San Dieguito, a development about thirty miles north of San Diego, launched by the Santa Fe Land Improvement Company. After just two years, she became the supervisory architect of the project, now called Rancho Santa Fe, and took on the full responsibility for laying out one of the state's first planned communities.

Her design centered around a civic center, including an inn, school, library, and commercial buildings, designed in the Spanish Mission style. While employed by Requa and Jackson, Rice supervised the work of fellow Berkeley graduate Olive Chadeayne (1904–2001), who was later elected to the AIA.

In 1929, after almost a decade of designing adobe and stucco buildings evoking Old California, Rice opened her own office in Rancho Santa Fe. She continued to take on new architectural projects for the community, such as the La Valenciana Apartments (1928)—the recipient of an AIA honor award—but also began to experiment with her own version of regional modernist style.[81] Her designs for the Arnberg House in La Jolla (1928) and a boathouse and clubhouse for the ZIAC Rowing Club in San Diego (1932) also received honor awards. In the mid-1930s, she designed San Dieguito Union High School in Encinitas and an elementary school in Chula Vista that now bears her name.

Rice was in the prime of her career when she succumbed to cancer in 1938, but little notice was taken of her death. Eighty years later, the *New York Times* published an obituary retrospectively crediting her for popularizing the Spanish Colonial Revival style in designs that also addressed the surrounding native landscape. Today, Rice homes have sold for more than $10 million, a testament to the quality and enduring aesthetic value of her vision.[82] **—SA**

Garage quadrangle,
Rancho Santa Fe, CA, 1923.
Courtesy Diane Y. Welch
Private Collection

ETHEL BAILEY FURMAN

BORN
Richmond, VA, 1893

DIED
Richmond, VA, 1976

EDUCATION
Private tutor; Chicago
Technical College, 1946

PRACTICE
Ethel Bailey Furman, 1918–76

NOTABLE HONORS
First woman architect in
Virginia; first Black woman
architect in the United States

Although never licensed to practice architecture, Ethel Bailey Furman is acknowledged as both the first female architect in Virginia and the first Black woman architect in the United States.[83] The daughter of a contractor, Furman grew up in Richmond, Virginia, surrounded by the tools of the building trade. Her parents, Madison J. Bailey and Margaret Jones Bailey, encouraged her interests, and she likely accompanied her father to building sites and assisted him in drafting and other tasks.

During her high school years, the family moved to Philadelphia, where she graduated from Germantown High School in 1910. Two years later, she married, and by 1916 had two children, born in New York State. According to family history, her father arranged for her to receive architectural tutoring in New York City about this time. In 1918, she divorced and married a Pullman porter, whose work with the New York railroad involved extensive travel. Furman moved her family, which now included a third child, back to Richmond. There, she set up her own office in the home her father had designed in 1890 at 3024 Q Street.[84] Furman continually strove to improve her professional skills and connections; in 1928, she was the only female participant in the Negro Contractors' Conference at the Hampton Institute in Hampton, Virginia.

In a career lasting more than five decades, Furman designed more than two hundred buildings in Richmond and the surrounding region. She was known for making her houses affordable by reducing unnecessary architectural details, without ever compromising quality. Her first house in Richmond, designed for Robert J. Wilder at 99 North Twenty-Eighth Street, became the childhood home of the state's first elected Black governor, Lawrence Douglas Wilder.[85] Identifying Furman's built work is complicated by the fact that she did not leave a portfolio of presentation drawings in an archive; instead, her working drawings were simply approved by local administrators or her male contractors.

The earliest mention of Furman's status as the first Black architect in Virginia appeared in the January 23, 1937, *Pittsburgh Courier*, at least a decade after she began her practice. Although she appears to have been accepted as a qualified professional, she sought out additional architectural training at the Chicago Technical College from 1944 to 1946.[86] Her experience in Chicago allowed her to keep up with stylistic changes in the field and resulted in additional commissions. In 1962, she designed a modern educational wing, "influenced by the popular International Style, for Richmond's Fourth Baptist Church."[87] An active member of civic and religious groups, Furman designed more than a dozen churches and donated two of her designs to the Lott Carey Missionary League, which constructed the designs in Liberia, Africa.[88] In 1976, the year of her death, she completed designs for Springfield Baptist Church in Hanover County, Virginia, and Rising Mount Zion Baptist Church in Sandston, Virginia. In 1985, the city of Richmond named a Church Hill park in her honor. —*LFR*

Above
Fourth Baptist Church,
educational wing, Richmond,
VA, 1961. Photo John Murden

Left
Negro Contractors'
Conference, Hampton
Institute, VA, 1928. Photo
Cheyne's Studio. Courtesy
Mr. and Mrs. J. Livingston
Furman

AINO MARSIO-AALTO

BORN
Helsinki, Finland, 1894

DIED
Helsinki, Finland, 1949

EDUCATION
Helsinki University of
Technology, 1920

PRACTICE
Oiva Kallio, 1920–23; Gunnar
Achilles Wahlroos, 1923; Alvar
Aalto Architects, 1924–35;
Artek, cofounder and head
designer, 1935–49, managing
director, 1941–49

NOTABLE HONORS
Alfred Kordelin Foundation
Grant, 1934; Bölgeblick
Glassware, Gold Medal,
Milan Triennale, 1936; Artek
installation, Gran Prix, Milan
Triennale, 1936; winning entry,
Finland Pavilion, Paris World's
Fair, 1937; winning entry,
Finnish Pavilion, New York
World's Fair, 1939

Aino Marsio-Aalto was a pioneering figure of modern Scandinavian design in the 1930s and 1940s and a founding figure of the Finnish furniture company Artek. Born to a large, working-class family, Marsio-Aalto enrolled at the Helsinki University of Technology in 1913, where she studied architecture and interior design. After graduating in 1920, she worked for Oiva Kallio in Helsinki and Gunnar Achilles Wahlroos in Jyväskylä before joining the studio of Alvar Aalto, whom she had met at the university. Six months later, Aino and Alvar married.[89]

Although many of Marsio-Aalto's specific contributions on projects produced under the name of Alvar Aalto's office remain uncertain, her particular area of expertise included interior and exhibition design and she is believed to have prepared the majority of the plans and sketches. Marsio-Aalto was essential to the firm's management, particularly with deadlines and finances.[90]

In the late 1920s, the Aaltos began two major projects that launched the firm into the international spotlight, the Viipuri Library (1935) and Paimio Tuberculosis Sanatorium (1932), among the earliest works of Finnish architecture to adopt the modern functionalist style. Largely regarded as one of the Aaltos' most important works, the Paimio sanatorium expanded on the notion of rational design by prioritizing the psychological and affective needs of the clinic's tuberculosis patients. In addition to overseeing the interiors of the clinic's staff housing, Marsio-Aalto assisted in the designs of the customized furniture and fixtures throughout the complex.[91]

In the early 1930s, Marsio-Aalto achieved professional notoriety independent of her work with Aalto. She is best known for the Bölgeblick series of molded glassware (1932), an elegant approach to utilitarian design characterized by concentric rings resembling ripples of water. The Bölgeblick series won the gold medal in the pressed-glass category in the Karhula-Iittala at the Milan Triennale, 1936. The Aaltos received the gold medal for the Finland Pavilion at the 1937 Paris World's Fair.[92]

The most significant development in Marsio-Aalto's career came in 1935 with the founding of Artek alongside Aalto, Maire Gullichsen, and art historian Nils-Gustav Hahl. Artek—a portmanteau of *art* and *technology*—was conceived as a multiplatform venture with the goal of importing industrial production and standardization into the domestic sphere while simultaneously bringing architecture and design into the realm of fine art.[93] Artek emerged as a highly influential force in the dissemination of modernist design.[94] As head designer and later managing director, Marsio-Aalto laid the foundation for the aesthetics and standards of Artek, prioritizing affordability, simplicity, comfort, and quality.

Through Artek, Marsio-Aalto ran a thriving interior design practice. Among her notable commissions were the lobby, boardroom, and managing director's office of the Sunila Pulp Mill (1937), a single-family house in the Pirkkola section of Helsinki (which was also part of the 1939 Helsinki Housing Fair), and the modern masterpiece Villa Mairea in Noormarkku (1939).

Despite her untimely death in 1949, Aino's legacy lives on with Artek, through which many of her designs remain in production to this day. —*LFR*

Top
Glassware, Bölgeblick
collection, Aino Marsio-
Aalto, 1932. Photo Maija
Holma. Courtesy Alvar Aalto
Foundation, 2001

Bottom
Villa Mairea, Noormarkku,
Finland, Aino Marsio-Aalto
and Alvar Aalto, 1938–39.
Photo Maija Holma. Courtesy
Alvar Aalto Foundation, 2001

AMAZA LEE MEREDITH

BORN
Lynchburg, VA, 1895

DIED
Ettrick, VA, 1984

EDUCATION
Virginia State Normal and
Industrial Institute, 1922;
Teachers College, Columbia
University, BA, 1930, MS, 1935

PRACTICE
Amaza Lee Meredith, 1935–

TEACHING
Virginia State University,
instructor, 1930–35, Fine Arts
Department, director, 1935–58,
Azurest South (Alumni House)

NOTABLE HONORS
Azurest South, Virginia
Landmarks Register, 1993, and
National Register of Historic
Places, 1993

Amaza Lee Meredith was a regionally celebrated artist and educator who was one of the first Black women to practice architecture in the United States. Despite having no formal training or license to practice, she designed a handful of buildings for herself and friends, bringing a strong African American aesthetic to modern architecture.

Meredith was born in Lynchburg, Virginia, in 1895, to a Black mother and a white father, Samuel Peter Meredith, a master stair builder. His expertise undoubtedly influenced Meredith's interest in architecture later in life.[95] Meredith graduated at the top of her class from Jackson Street High School in 1915—the same year that her father committed suicide.[96] Despite the painful events surrounding her father's death, Meredith persevered.

She taught in a one-room schoolhouse in Indian Rock, Virginia, and later at an elementary school in Lynchburg, before receiving her teaching certificate from Virginia Normal and Industrial Institute (later Virginia State University), graduating as the valedictorian of her class.[97] Meredith continued her teaching career at Dunbar High School in Lynchburg until 1928, when she moved to Brooklyn, New York, and enrolled in the Teachers College at Columbia University to study art. Meredith's long career at Virginia State University (VSU) began in 1930, with only a short leave of absence during the 1934–35 school year to obtain a master's degree in arts education from Columbia.[98] Upon her return in 1935, she founded and directed VSU's art department, a position she held until her retirement in 1958.

In addition to her active role as an educator, Meredith was a successful painter, with works exhibited at the Virginia Museum of Fine Arts and in galleries in New York and North Carolina.[99] In the mid-1930s, her training in the fine arts matured into a self-taught pursuit of interior design and architecture. Meredith's first and best-known building, Azurest South (1938), was designed as a home for herself and her partner, Dr. Edna Meade Colson, the dean of the VSU School of Education. Located on the eastern edge of the university campus in Ettrick, the dwelling's International Style stood in stark contrast to the Colonial Revival architecture that was popular in Virginia at the time. The bold, geometric form of the white stucco exterior is accented by glass block windows and bright turquoise roof coping. The relatively restrained exterior yields an experimental interior characterized by bold uses of color, geometric patterns, material finishes, and inventive lighting fixtures.[100] Significantly, Azurest South is a rare example of a modern architecture infused with a strong African American aesthetic, and in recent years, it has taken on additional significance as a nascent prototype for a queer, Black approach to design and material culture. In 1993, Azurest South was listed in the Virginia Landmarks Register and in the National Register of Historic Places.[101]

In 1947, Meredith and her sister, Maude Terry, began collaborating on Azurest North, an African American leisure community in Sag Harbor, Long Island. They worked with several others to establish the Azurest Syndicate, which brokered sales and financed mortgages for African Americans who were otherwise barred from obtaining loans due to widespread discriminatory practices, such as redlining.[102]

Meredith is believed to have designed four houses at Azurest North, including one for herself and one for her sister. Azurest North has thrived as a resort area for middle- and upper-class African American families since the 1950s.

In 1949, Meredith completed plans for an alumni house on the VSU campus, which were never realized. She retired from teaching in 1958 but continued to paint and design buildings, including the Gillfield Baptist Church education wing in Petersburg and several homes for family and friends in Virginia and Texas. Two years after her death in 1984, the Virginia State University Alumni Association designated Azurest South the Alumni House. —*LFR*

Top
Azurest South, Ettrick, VA, 1938. Virginia Department of Historic Resources

Bottom
Azurest South, picture window, Ettrick, VA. Photo Michael Borowski, 2018

LUTAH MARIA RIGGS

BORN
Toledo, OH, 1896

DIED
Montecito, CA, 1984

EDUCATION
University of California,
Berkeley, 1919

PRACTICE
Ralph D. Taylor, 1920; George
Washington Smith, 1921–30;
Horning & Riggs, 1930–31;
Lutah Maria Riggs, 1931–42;
MGM and Warner Brothers
studios, 1943–45; Riggs and
Shaw Architects, 1946–50;
Lutah Maria Riggs, 1951–80

NOTABLE HONORS
Licensed, AIA, 1928;
Commissioner, California
State Board of Architectural
Examiners; President, Santa
Barbara AIA, 1941, 1953; Fellow,
AIA, 1960; Los Angeles Times
Woman of the Year, 1967

A self-made woman, Lutah Maria Riggs worked her way through school, discovering her exceptional design talent on her own and becoming one of the most influential Southern California architects of her generation. Her father died when she was a child, and after her mother remarried, the family moved to Indianapolis. Upon completion of high school, Riggs and her mother joined her stepfather in Santa Barbara, where he had found employment. She enrolled in the Santa Barbara State Normal School, probably intending to become a teacher, and subsequently received a scholarship to the University of California, Berkeley, by winning the local newspaper's subscription-selling contest. At the university, she studied under the architect John Galen Howard, who became a mentor and friend. When she graduated in 1919, Riggs received the Alumni Prize, which helped finance additional graduate coursework, as did the various drafting assignments she took on for local firms.[103]

In 1921, the Pennsylvania-born architect George Washington Smith hired Riggs. After three years with the firm, Smith invited Riggs to accompany him on a trip to Mexico—explicitly to sketch the local architecture for a potential book—an experience that influenced Riggs's future work.[104] In 1925, Santa Barbara was hit by a devastating earthquake, and in its wake, the city took on the challenge of remaking itself, specifically in the Spanish Colonial Revival style. During this busy time, Riggs played a significant role in establishing the firm's national reputation. She became a licensed architect in 1928, and after Smith's death two years later, launched a practice of her own.[105]

Throughout the Depression, Riggs worked on Rolling Hills, a gated community in Palos Verdes, as well as taking on remodels and additions for former Smith clients and designing one of her most significant estates, the von Romberg villa in Montecito. In 1941 she became president of the Santa Barbara chapter of the AIA and attended the association's annual meeting at Yosemite.[106] She found work in Hollywood movie studios throughout the war years, designing MGM stage sets for *The White Cliffs of Dover* and *The Picture of Dorian Gray*. Her practice expanded significantly in 1946, when she engaged in a four-year partnership with the architect Alvin Benjamin Shaw III.[107]

An original, independent designer, Riggs drew on the region's cultural heritage while incorporating aspects of modernist architecture and new technologies. In the 1950s, she designed the Vedanta Temple in Los Angeles, inspired by Japanese and Chinese models, as well as a remodel of El Paseo, one of downtown Santa Barbara's landmark shopping destinations. As the city grew in popularity and population, Riggs contributed to the resort's charm by designing dozens of Spanish Colonial Revival houses, with modernist lines and details as requested by her clients. She completed her final commissions in 1980, four years before her death. In recent years, Riggs has been increasingly recognized for her extensive and invaluable role in preserving the essence of Santa Barbara's cultural legacy and for diffusing its beauty throughout Southern California. —*SA*

Above
Kiler House, Montecito, CA,
1956. Architecture and Design
Collection, Art, Design &
Architecture Museum, University
of California, Santa Barbara

Right
Vedanta Temple, Los Angeles,
CA, 1955. Architecture and
Design Collection, Art, Design &
Architecture Museum, University
of California, Santa Barbara

MARGARETE SCHÜTTE-LIHOTZKY

BORN
Vienna, Austria, 1897

DIED
Vienna, Austria, 2000

EDUCATION
University of Applied Arts
Vienna, 1919

PRACTICE
City of Vienna, housing
program, 1921–26; New
Frankfurt Team, 1926–30;
Soviet Union Department of
Children's Services, 1930–34

NOTABLE HONORS
Max Mauthner Prize, 1917;
Lobmeyr Prize, 1919; first
female architect in Austria,
1919; Architecture Award,
City of Vienna, 1980; Austrian
Decoration for Science and
Art, 1992; Grand Decoration
of Honor for Services to the
Republic of Austria, 1997

Born and raised in Vienna with a middle-class, liberal upbringing, Margarete (Grete) Schütte-Lihotzky enrolled, in 1915, as the first female student at what is now the University of Applied Arts Vienna.[108] Studying under Oskar Strnad, a pioneer of social housing, Schütte-Lihotzky was exposed firsthand to the appalling living conditions of the working class, a formative experience in her architectural and political career. After graduating, Schütte-Lihotzky earned a position with the City of Vienna's public housing program, assisting in the design of settlement blocks, model-unit types, and modular kitchens for war veterans alongside Adolf Loos and Otto Neurath.[109]

Impressed by Schütte-Lihotzky's designs on the rationalization of housework in these settlements, city planner and architect Ernst May invited her to join his New Frankfurt initiative dedicated to solving the city's desperate housing shortage resulting from World War I.[110] In 1926, Schütte-Lihotzky relocated to Frankfurt and began drafting plans for a lost-cost, compact kitchen with fully built-in features. Schütte-Lihotzky's innovative Frankfurt Kitchen was conceived as a "housewife's laboratory," a model of culinary efficiency with the objective of improving the social position of women. Beginning in 1927, ten thousand of these prefabricated kitchens were installed in new working-class apartments throughout the city. In addition to her kitchen, Schütte-Lihotzky made many other significant contributions to the social housing effort in Frankfurt, including schemes for single-women's lodgings, modern automatic laundries, and a kindergarten pavilion predicated on the ideas of

Maria Montessori, an Italian physician and educator whose philosophy of education inspired schools worldwide.

In 1930, Schütte-Lihotzky and her husband, Wilhelm Schütte, relocated to Moscow to join the so-called May Brigade, which was commissioned by the Soviet Union's Communist Party to build housing developments for the influx of industrial workers in the brand new socialist cities, or *Sotsgorods*. In these cities, the integration of women into the workforce resulted in the collectivization of tasks such as cooking and childcare. Schütte-Lihotzky addressed this reorganization of the social fabric through her role as director of the department of children's services, which was responsible for designing schools, kindergarten pavilions, daycare centers, and children's furniture.[111] Her most notable work during this time was a large daycare facility in Bryansk, Russia, which was unfortunately destroyed during World War II.

With the outbreak of war, Schütte-Lihotzky put her architectural practice on hold to join the Communist resistance against the Nazi regime. After the war, she traveled to Sofia, Bulgaria, where she helped to establish a department dedicated to the development of children's equipment and facilities and supervised the construction of four kindergartens. Schütte-Lihotzky's architectural activities were limited during the Cold War era, largely due to her leadership position with the Federation of Democratic Women, which possessed close ties to the Communist Party. Finding herself excluded from municipal work, Schütte-Lihotzky worked as a consultant for Communist Bloc countries and their allies, receiving commissions

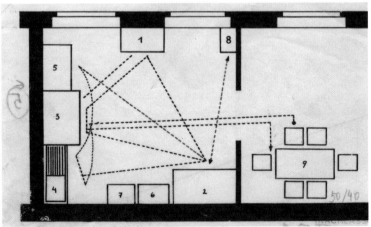

from the Academy of Architecture of the German Democratic Republic in 1954 and 1966 and from the Cuban Ministry of Education in 1963.

Through her designs for standard-ized kitchens and for housing, schools, kindergartens, and daycare facilities, Schütte-Lihotzky effectively mobilized the built environment as a tool of political and women's advocacy.[112] Her innumerable contributions to the field of architecture were officially recognized in 1980, when she received the Architecture Award of the City of Vienna. In 1988, she was offered the Austrian Decoration for Science and Art, which she declined due to the fact that it would be presented by Austrian president Kurt Waldheim, a former officer in the Nazi army. Years later, she would accept the award. —*LFR*

Top

Frankfurt Kitchen, forerunner of the efficient modern kitchen, 1927. Photo Hermann Collischonn. © University of Applied Arts Vienna, Collection and Archive. Courtesy of Luzie Lahtinen-Stransky

Bottom

Frankfurt Kitchen, efficiency diagram, 1927. © University of Applied Arts Vienna, Collection and Archive. Courtesy of Luzie Lahtinen-Stransky

II. PAVING NEW PATHS

Introduction by Mary McLeod and Victoria Rosner

Speaking to a group of women students at Cambridge in 1928, Virginia Woolf emphasized the opportunities newly available to their sex: "May I…remind you that most of the professions have been open to you for close on ten years now?"[1] It seemed potentially a watershed moment: in the United States, at the time of Woolf's speech, a full fifty years had passed since the first woman graduated from a professional architecture school; and in 1888, the AIA had named its first woman associate member. Still, the welcoming of women was uneven: in England, women were not admitted to the Architectural Association (AA) School of Architecture in London until 1917, while in other countries, architectural education remained closed to women as late as the 1940s. The situation was more difficult in practice. As Woolf conceded, "Even when the path is nominally open…there are many phantoms and obstacles, as I believe, looming in her way."[2]

The women profiled in this chapter did pave new paths, but they also contended with explicit bias, limited opportunities, and unequal compensation. The scale of their achievements is a testament to their perseverance and talent. While women architects of the previous generation were often restricted to domestic and design practice, the women in the "Paving New Paths" generation found opportunities to work at a variety of scales, creating universities and school buildings, hospitals and medical centers, housing developments, government buildings, and even skyscrapers. To obtain and execute these projects, women architects battled biased beliefs that women could not master large-scale engineering and were more suited to designing individual homes, long considered to be the sphere of women. Contrary to this belief, women architects of this time took a special interest in the design of large-scale urban projects: in the 1950s, Anne Griswold Tyng worked extensively on the City Tower project initially intended as part of Louis Kahn's Civic Center plan for Philadelphia; in the 1960s, Halina Skibniewska designed the much praised Bialowi district in Warsaw; and in 1967, Zofia Garlińska-Hansen was a coauthor of the Linear Continuous System, a visionary project that attempted to dissolve the boundaries between city and country, urban center and periphery.

Another thread that draws these women together is their strong social commitment and belief in the potential of the built environment to improve people's lives. Minnette de Silva advocated for the involvement of residents in the design of a large public housing project in Kandy, Sri Lanka, a rare and early example of participatory planning in the 1950s, and Jane Drew was dedicated to improving health care through her design of hospitals in both Ghana and Britain. A broad concern with social justice informs the work of Lina Bo Bardi and Charlotte Perriand, both active leftists, committed in both their designs and political activities to improving the conditions of the poor and the working class.

Both saw the incorporation of vernacular features into design as an important way to honor local traditions and craft—a practice they embraced while still advocating standardization and industrial techniques when appropriate.

In surveying these women, it is noteworthy how many of them also had professional lives beyond architecture. Most striking is the number who taught architecture as well as practicing it. This was truly the first generation during which an academic career in architecture was possible for women. Previous generations of women were not permitted to pursue formal professional training themselves, and so they could not offer it to others. Teaching provided many of these architects with a source of regular income and status, stabilizing earnings when architectural commissions might not be consistently available. Perhaps there was pleasure, too, in the new authority women could command in the professional classroom. Additionally, teaching was not the only side career to be found among this group. A number engaged in activities allied to architecture but distinct from traditional professional practice: photography (Esther Baum Born), furniture design (Perriand, Greta Magnusson Grossman, Florence Knoll Bassett), and writing (de Silva and Tyng).

It must be said that some of the women profiled here might bristle at the label "woman architect" and prefer to be known simply as "architect." Most began and established their careers during a relative lull in feminism that followed the general success of women's suffrage movements and that preceded the second-wave Women's Liberation Movement of the late 1960s and 1970s. For a number of women at this time, activism for social justice took the form of socialism rather than feminism, while the Polish architects in this group—Garlińska-Hansen, Jadwiga Grabowska-Hawrylak, and Skibniewska—worked in a socialist society that officially proclaimed women as equals, employing them in large numbers in state agencies. A surprising number of these architects worked actively to promote the standing of women in their profession, both incrementally and through imaginative initiatives. Sarah Pillsbury Harkness was a founding member of The Architects Collaborative (TAC), an American firm organized around a new collaborative model of practice, one that dispensed with hierarchy and gender roles and was also more amenable to women's lives, permitting, for example, flexible schedules. Drew went even further, attempting in the 1940s to create an all-women architectural firm, though it did not take hold. Natalie Griffin de Blois and Gertrude Kerbis, both of whom began their careers in corporate firms, embraced second-wave feminism and, in 1973, helped found Chicago Women in Architecture, an organization that continues to support and advocate for women architects today.

The focus here on women architects is not meant to suggest that women practice architecture in a particular way, but rather to contribute to the history of the field, from which women have been largely excluded. Today, women architects are beginning to receive public recognition for their achievements. In the winter of 2019–2020, the Louis Vuitton Foundation mounted a large retrospective of Perriand's career; and in 2019, Norma Merrick Sklarek, the first African American woman to become a member of the AIA, received the AIA Los Angeles Gold Medal.

ESTHER BAUM BORN

BORN
Palo Alto, CA, 1902

DIED
San Diego, CA, 1987

EDUCATION
University of California,
Berkeley, BArch, 1924,
MArch, 1926

PRACTICE
Wallace K. Harrison, 1929–33;
Ernest Born Architect, 1936–71

The best way to know Esther Baum Born, other than through the buildings she designed in partnership with her husband at their San Francisco firm, is through the photographs she took. By way of a friendship with Frida Kahlo and Diego Rivera, neighbors during a stint in New York during the 1930s, she became interested in Mexico, traveling there between 1935 and 1936 to photograph the country's modernist architecture. *The New Architecture in Mexico*, first published by William Morrow in 1937, depicted sweeping modern buildings in black and white, monuments to a new, emerging era. Born spent ten months there, photographing and drawing the regional architecture with a careful eye for details and ultimately garnering international attention for the movement.

Born in 1902 in Palo Alto, California, Esther was the oldest of three, the daughter of an electrical engineer and inventor and a homemaker. She graduated from Oakland Technical High School in 1920, after which she pursued architectural studies at the University of California, Berkeley. She studied under John Galen Howard, completing her undergraduate degree in 1924. She worked briefly for architect Henry H. Gutterson, then traveled for a year in Europe, studying languages and the history of art. She completed her graduate studies at the University of California, Berkeley, in 1926, and married architect Ernest Born the same year.

Ernest Born, originally from San Francisco, worked for some of the city's most prominent architects between 1923 and 1928, including Howard, John W. Reid Jr., and George Kelham. After a sabbatical in France and Italy, Esther and Ernest moved to Greenwich Village, where Esther took a job with Wallace K. Harrison, the architect overseeing the creation of Rockefeller Center. From 1929 to 1936, both Ernest and Esther worked in architectural offices across the city, eventually establishing their own studio with associate Carl Bertil Lund, who became their partner for over forty years.

One of the Borns' first projects was the New York offices and tasting room for the wine importers Bates & Schoonmaker (1935). Ernest was credited as the architect and Esther the photographer for pieces published in *Architectural Forum* and *Architectural Review*. The year 1933 found Esther taking an intensive course in architectural photography with photographer Ben Rabinovitch, showcasing her work in a group exhibition and solo shows at the Rabinovitch Gallery.

Returning to San Francisco in their native northern California, the Borns established an architecture and design studio. Their projects included a plan for Fisherman's Wharf, signage for the Bay Area Rapid Transit (BART) System, and the design of the Balboa Park Station. Esther continued to work on photography projects in the Bay Area, taking pictures of Frank Lloyd Wright's Northern California Usonian houses and the Golden Gate International Exposition.

Esther and Ernest had a fruitful partnership, despite the firm's singular name, Ernest Born Architect—which may have been because she wasn't licensed. The firm closed in 1971, when a decline in Esther's health prevented her from working. In 1984, to be closer to their daughter, the couple moved to San Diego, where Esther died in 1987 and Ernest in 1992. —*KF*

Above
Balboa Park Station, BART, San
Francisco, CA, Ernest Born
and Esther Baum Born, 1973.
Photo Roger Sturtevant. Ernest
and Esther Born Collection,
Environmental Design Archives,
UC Berkeley

Right
Monument to General Alvaro
Obregon, Parque de la Bombilla,
Mexico City, Mexico. Photo
Esther Baum Born, 1935.
© Esther Born Estate. Courtesy
Center for Creative Photography,
University of Arizona

CHARLOTTE PERRIAND

BORN
Paris, France, 1903

DIED
Paris, France, 1999

EDUCATION
École de L'Union Centrale des
Arts Décoratifs, 1925

PRACTICE
Le Corbusier Atelier, 1927–37;
independent practice, 1937–ca.
1982; Japanese Ministry for
Trade and Industry, advisor,
1940–42

NOTABLE HONORS
Lifetime Achievement Award,
Brooklyn Museum of Art
Modernism Design, 1997

"The extension of the art of dwelling is the art of living," said Charlotte Perriand in her essay "L'Art de Vivre" (1981).[3] These words testify to her belief in the modernist precept that architecture and furniture are the one and the same, underscoring the belief that functional, efficient design should be purposed for everyday life and society as a whole.

Born in Paris and raised by her father and mother, a tailor and seamstress, respectively, Perriand's early talent for drawing and craftsmanship led her to enroll in 1920, on a scholarship, at the École de L'Union Centrale des Arts Décoratifs, where she studied furniture design. After school, Perriand attended lectures and workshops by the Art Deco designer Maurice Dufrêne, who encouraged her to exhibit work at the 1926 Exposition Internationale des Arts Décoratifs et Industriels Modernes.

The following year, Perriand's designs underwent a radical transformation. At the 1927 Salon d'Automne, the twenty-four-year-old Perriand exhibited her provocative *Bar sous le Toit*, an attic bar inspired by Le Corbusier's machine-age aesthetics, equipped with a nickel-plated counter and tubular steel furniture. Virtually overnight, Perriand was thrust into the public eye. Le Corbusier invited her to join his team as a furniture designer—a title Perriand would come to renounce in favor of "interior architect."[4]

For the next decade, Perriand worked with Le Corbusier and Pierre Jeanneret, playing a central role in developing the signatory style of the studio's influential *Equipment d'Habitation* series. In 1928, the trio collaborated on the designs for a series of chairs that defined three standard seating positions: the LC2 Grand Confort armchair, the B301 reclining chair, and the B306 chaise longue. When they presented their new furniture and standardized storage units at the 1929 Salon d'Automne, the press immediately recognized them as radical and innovative. In this model apartment, Perriand's functionalist kitchen was of particular interest for its efficiency, transforming the kitchen from a space of service to one of enjoyment.

During the early 1930s, Perriand's growing interest in the Communist movement compelled her to turn her sights elsewhere, visiting the Soviet Union in 1930 and again in 1933 and returning to Paris in 1934 to immerse herself in the leftist political and cultural pursuits of the Popular Front.[5]

Perriand's designs, too, began to shift toward more organic and biomorphic forms and to make use of traditional materials, such as wood and cane, which were far more affordable than chrome. This more pragmatic and populist approach to design first became evident in her reinterpretation of the reclining chair in wood and rush featured at the 1935 Brussels International Exhibition and in her affordable, mass-produced folding-and-stacking chairs in the Living Room of Today exhibition at the 1936 Salon des Arts Ménagers.[6] The social turn in Perriand's work coupled with her newfound enthusiasm for collectivist and anonymous design ultimately led to her departure from Le Corbusier's atelier in 1937.

The day after the German invasion of Paris in 1940, Perriand departed for Japan at the invitation of the Japanese Ministry for Trade and Industry. For the next two years, Perriand acted as an industrial design consultant, traveling across Japan

Model kitchen for Le Corbusier's
Unité d'Habitation apartment
building, Marseille, France,
Charlotte Perriand, 1950. Photo
Charles-Édouard Jeanneret.
© The Museum of Modern
Art. Licensed by SCALA/Art
Resource, NY

LC2 Grand Confort armchair,
Le Corbusier, Pierre Jeanneret,
and Charlotte Perriand, 1928.
© The Museum of Modern
Art. Licensed by SCALA/Art
Resource, NY

with designer Sori Yanagi as her official guide and identifying furniture, household items, and materials she believed would be popular in overseas markets. She also began experimenting with bamboo and woven straw, which she adapted to some of her earlier designs. In 1941, Perriand presented the results of her research, alongside her own furniture prototypes, in an exhibition displayed at the Takashimaya department store in its Tokyo and Osaka locations.

In 1942, Japan labeled Perriand an "undesirable alien," forcing her to leave the Nazi ally empire and exiling her to French Indochina (present-day Vietnam), where she waited out the war. She returned home to Paris in 1946, and established herself once again as a visionary interior architect, this time drawing inspiration from Art Brut, vernacular design, and nature. She nevertheless remained committed to making quality design accessible to all. Her projects during the postwar production boom varied immensely, from fruitful collaborations with Jean Prouvé on a series of modular furniture systems and a kitchen prototype for Le Corbusier's renowned Unité d'Habitation in Marseille to workers' housing in the Sahara and airport lobbies for Air France in London and Tokyo. The pinnacle of Perriand's long career was a 40,000-person ski resort (1982) at Les Arcs in the Alps, which underscored her sensitivity to environmental conditions and her belief in equal access to *l'art de vivre*, the art of living. —**LFR**

Revolving Armchair, Charlotte
Perriand with Le Corbusier
and Pierre Jeanneret, 1928.
© The Museum of Modern
Art. Licensed by SCALA/Art
Resource, NY

GRETA MAGNUSSON GROSSMAN

BORN
Helsingborg, Sweden, 1906

DIED
Encinitas, CA, 1999

EDUCATION
Konstfack, 1932; Royal
Academy of Technology, 1940

PRACTICE
Studio, 1933–40; Magnusson-
Grossman Studio, 1941–60s

TEACHING
University of California, Los
Angeles (UCLA), lecturer,
1957–63

NOTABLE HONORS
Second Prize, Combination
Furniture category, Stockholm
Craft Association, 1933;
Second Prize, Combination
Furniture, Swedish Society
of Industrial Design, 1933;
Good Design Award, MoMA,
1950, 1952

Greta Magnusson Grossman was born into a family of furniture makers, carpenters, and house builders. After a woodworking apprenticeship with the Helsingborg-based furniture manufacturer Kärnans, she earned a scholarship to the esteemed Konstfack, Sweden's largest university of arts, crafts, and design in Stockholm, where she studied technical drawing, furniture, textiles, and ceramics.

In 1933, Magnusson Grossman garnered media attention after winning second prize in the Combination Furniture category for a competition sponsored by the Swedish Society of Industrial Design. With this achievement, she launched a successful furniture store and workshop called Studio with her former schoolmate Erik Ullrich. Over the next few years, Magnusson Grossman became one of the most prominent modernist designers in Sweden. She exhibited works at Galerie Moderne, a cultural mecca in Stockholm, inuring media coverage that celebrated her as the country's "first female furniture architect in action."

As war overtook Europe, Magnusson Grossman and her husband, British jazz musician Billy Grossman, immigrated to Los Angeles. Her arrival in the United States came on the heels of an influential exhibition of Swedish arts and crafts at the 1939 New York World's Fair. Magnusson Grossman opened her own furniture store in 1941 on the fashionable North Rodeo Drive, featuring pieces that adapted her brand of Swedish functionalism to the laid-back Los Angeles lifestyle.

In the late 1940s, she was the design consultant for the Barker Brothers' Modern Shop in downtown Los Angeles, known for its high-quality modern furniture at affordable prices. With Barker Brothers, Magnusson Grossman designed an innovative lighting series that included two of her most famous designs: the Grasshopper Lamp and the Cobra Lamp. They were among the first to employ directional shades and flexible arms and have since become icons of midcentury-modern interior design.[7] In 1950, the Cobra table lamp received the Good Design award from the Museum of Modern Art (MoMA), in New York, and was showcased in the prestigious Good Design Show, alongside the likes of Ray and Charles Eames and Alvar Aalto.

Though she is best known for her work as an interior designer, Magnusson Grossman simultaneously ran a successful architecture practice, designing fourteen houses in Los Angeles and one in San Francisco and one in Sweden. She frequently sited her glass-curtain houses on steep hillsides, taking full advantage of panoramic views. With expansive porches and courtyards, her houses integrated interior with exterior living spaces well suited to the warm Southern California climate. The widely published house she designed for herself and her husband (1957) on Claircrest Drive in Beverly Hills gained recognition for its open-plan layout and blend of comfort and functionalism.

By the mid-1960s, Magnusson Grossman was disillusioned with the design world and had a sense of having become stagnant. At the height of her career, she retired from architecture and moved with her husband to a house she designed in Encinitas, just north of San Diego, California, where she spent the next thirty years painting landscapes.[8] —*LFR*

9376 Claircrest Drive, Beverly
Hills, CA, 1957. Photo John
Hartley. Courtesy Estate of
Greta Magnusson Grossman,
R & Company Archives, New
York, NY

JANE DREW

BORN
Thornton Heath, South
London, England, 1911

DIED
Cotherstone, Durham,
England, 1996

EDUCATION
AA School of Architecture,
1934

PRACTICE
Joseph Hill, 1934–36; Alliston
Drew, 1936–39; Minister for
the West African Colonies,
assistant town planning
advisor, 1944–45; Office of
Maxwell Fry and Jane Drew,
1946–50; Fry, Drew and
Partners, 1950–52; Fry, Drew,
Drake and Lasdun, 1952–77

TEACHING
MIT, visiting professor, 1961;
Harvard University Graduate
School of Design (Harvard
GSD), visiting professor, 1970

NOTABLE HONORS
First woman elected to Royal
Institute of British Architects
(RIBA) Council, 1964–70;
Fellow, RIBA, 1971–74; Honorary
Doctorate, Open University,
Milton Keynes, 1973; Honorary
Fellow, AIA, 1978; Dame
Commander, Order of the
British Empire, 1996

Jane Drew was a leading proponent of the modern movement in postwar England and a pioneer of tropical modernism, a precursor of environmental design. The critical shift from art-for-art's sake to design incorporating nature's elements reflected her responsiveness to vernacular design. Through her work on housing, hospitals, and institutional buildings around the world, Drew advocated architecture as a tool for social reform rather than solely a medium for artistic expression.

Born in 1911, Drew grew up in a middle-class suburb on the outskirts of London. In 1929, she enrolled at the AA School of Architecture in London, where she trained in the Beaux Arts tradition (the modernist transformation of the school's curriculum did not occur until 1933).[9] She supported herself through school by teaching French in the evenings and also working part-time in the offices of Charles Holden and George Grey Wornum, where she worked on the design of the headquarters for the Royal Institute of British Architects (RIBA) in Portland Place.[10]

Drew graduated in 1934 and faced the economic fallout of the Great Depression, which was in full swing. Her inability to find work was exacerbated by the gender discrimination she experienced in a male-dominated field—she repeatedly had her job applications turned down for being a woman. She briefly worked with the architect Joseph Hill, before setting up an architectural practice in 1936 with her then-husband Jim Alliston. Drew's most notable projects during this time included the Putney Hospital (1937) in London, a winning competition entry for a cottage hospital (1939) in Devon, as well as modern houses in Cliftonville, Kent (1937), and St. Giles's Mount (1938) in Winchester. In 1937, Drew gave birth to twin daughters, Georgia and Jenny; after the separation from Alliston in 1939, she was sole caretaker for the girls.

During the war, Drew became involved with the modernist movement through her partnership with architect Maxwell Fry (who she married in 1942) and participation in the Modern Architectural Research (MARS) Group, a London branch of the Congrès Internationaux de L'Architecture Moderne (CIAM). In 1941, Drew became secretary of the RIBA Public Relations Committee and one of the main forces behind the Reconstruction Committee's efforts, for which she curated the Rebuilding Britain exhibition at the National Gallery in 1943.

Around this time, Drew established her own practice in St. James's, an exclusive neighborhood in London, with the initial intention of only hiring women architects. In 1943, she was appointed as consultant architect to the Domestic Commercial Heat Services Committee in order to study and develop ergonomic kitchens for the new prefabricated housing that replaced the homes bombed during the war. One outcome of her extensive research into modern building materials and labor-saving techniques was the development of the standard height of ovens that is still used today.[11] In 1945, while Drew was stationed in West Africa, a prototype of her prefabricated kitchen-bathroom unit was presented at the Kitchen Planning Exhibition at Dorland Hall in London. The following year, Drew contributed several kitchen models to the high-profile *Britain Can Make It* exhibition at the Victoria and Albert Museum.

Sultan Bello Hall, University
College, Ibaden, Nigeria, 1962.
RIBA Collections

Other major projects that Drew contributed to during the postwar years in England include the Chantry and Tanys Dell housing estates (1951) in Harlow; the Festival of Britain's New Schools Pavilion, Waterloo Entrance Tower, and Riverside Restaurant (1951); and the interior design for the ICA (1950) at Dover Street, London.

Drew and Fry are best known for the significant role they played in the migration of modern architecture and planning to British West Africa and India. Due to the short supply of architecture commissions during wartime, Drew and Fry were prompted to look abroad for building opportunities. In 1944, they were hired by the Colonial Office to supervise various infrastructure and urban planning projects in Nigeria, the Gold Coast (present-day Ghana), Sierra Leone, and the Gambia as part of a new colonial initiative to bolster economic development in overseas territories.[12]

In West Africa, Drew and Fry designed universities, hospitals, housing complexes, and dams that adapted their modernist agenda to meet the specific requirements of the tropical climate and cultural context. Drew developed an empirical, sociological approach that involved meeting with local residents, learning their language and customs, and organizing talks and exhibitions. Although the architectural duo was generally well intentioned and sympathetic to the needs of the local populations, they ultimately could not escape their own roles as unwitting agents of colonial hegemony.

Returning to London, Drew and Fry established their architectural partnership in 1946, while continuing their work in Nigeria and Ghana. Over the next ten years, they completed seventeen major educational commissions and twelve commercial ones in West Africa. One of their most notable projects, the University of Ibadan (1960) in Nigeria, demonstrated Drew and Fry's ability to incorporate visual variety on a limited budget. Featured throughout the campus is the use of reinforced-concrete screen walls that successfully responded to the climatic conditions by blocking out the sun while letting in natural light and ventilation.

Many of the building techniques implemented at Ibadan had been previously developed by Drew and Fry in the early 1950s in Chandigarh, India, where they worked alongside Le Corbusier and Pierre Jeanneret to plan a new Punjabi capital for the thousands of refugees arriving daily from Pakistan. Drew assumed leadership over the residential construction. Unlike the other members in their team, Drew and Fry consulted directly with workers and shopkeepers (albeit in limited numbers) and solicited feedback on their designs, which they then changed accordingly.

By the 1960s, Drew's architectural practice slowed as she focused her efforts on teaching and writing. While she was a visiting professor at MIT, she worked on the manuscript for *Tropical Architecture in the Dry and Humid Zones* (1964), a key text in the development of tropical modernism and a precursor to today's sustainability agenda.

Later in her life, Drew received numerous honors and awards for her substantial contributions to the field and to the greater public welfare. She was elected president of the AA School of Architecture in 1969 and became an honorary fellow of RIBA in 1971 and the AIA in 1978. Before her death in 1996, she was named a Dame of the British Empire by Queen Elizabeth, an honor bestowed for outstanding service to the arts and sciences and work with charitable organizations. Since 2012, the *Architects' Journal* annually awards the Jane Drew Prize to recognize the individuals who have advanced the status of women in architecture. —*LFR*

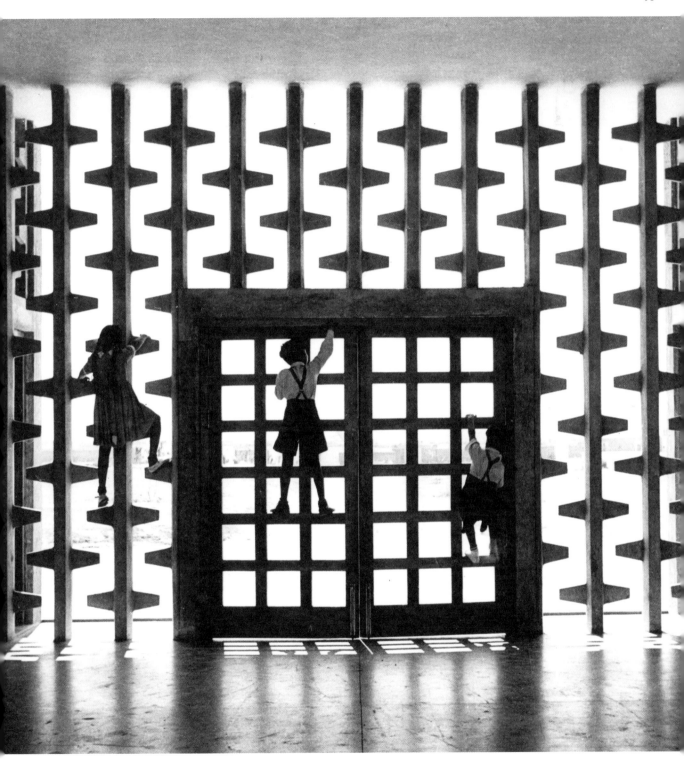

Higher Secondary School,
Sector 23, Chandigarh, India,
1956. RIBA Collections

SARAH PILLSBURY HARKNESS

BORN
Swampscott, MA, 1914

DIED
Lexington, MA, 2013

EDUCATION
Cambridge School of
Architecture and Landscape
Architecture for Women,
ca. 1938; Smith College,
MArch, 1940

PRACTICE
Peter and Stubbins, 1939–40;
Pillsbury and Vaughan,
1940–42; Dan Cooper, 1941–
43; Museum of Modern Art
Traveling Exhibitions, 1943–44;
The Architects Collaborative
(TAC), cofounder, 1945–87

NOTABLE HONORS
Boston Society of Architects,
1941; Honor Award, AIA, 1967;
Honorary Doctor of Fine Arts,
Bates College, 1974; Fellow,
AIA, 1979; Louis I. Kahn
Citation for Olin Arts Center,
Bates College, 1987; Award
of Honor in Education and
Research, Boston Society of
Architects, 1991; Women in
Design Award of Excellence,
2003

Sarah Pillsbury Harkness, generally known as Sally, studied art at Winsor School before pursuing architectural training in the mid-1930s at the Cambridge School of Architecture and Landscape Architecture, the country's pioneering graduate school for women.[13] After graduating with her master's degree from Smith College in 1940, Harkness and former schoolmate Louisa Vaughan Conrad opened an interior design office and showroom in Boston, where they sold furniture by Finnish designers Aino and Alvar Aalto.[14] During the war, Harkness and her husband, John Harkness, lived in New York City, where she worked as a designer for Dan Cooper and for Museum of Modern Art Traveling Exhibitions.[15]

In 1945, Harkness and her husband joined Walter Gropius and several Gropius protégés in founding TAC in Cambridge, Massachusetts, organized around a collectivist approach to design.[16] Their aim, in Harkness's own words, was "to remake the world."[17] In the 1950s and 1960s, TAC played an important role in promulgating American modernism and advancing the Bauhaus agenda for a socially responsible architecture. TAC created such large-scale projects as Baghdad University (1958) in Iraq, the Pan Am Building (present-day MetLife building) (1963) in New York City, the National Headquarters of the AIA (1972) in Washington, DC, and the Bauhaus Archive (1979) in Berlin.[18]

In both her professional and personal life, Harkness flouted gender conventions and challenged architecture's role in the perpetuation of the nuclear family unit. As the postwar era in the United States witnessed an influx of assembly-line suburban housing developments, the younger TAC members proposed an alternative approach to suburban living based on community engagement and collective decision-making. In 1947, the Harknesses and several other colleagues bought a twenty-acre plot of land in the countryside outside Lexington, Massachusetts, where they started the Six Moon Hill community made up of compact and affordable modern houses, shared neighborhood facilities, and open land.[19] Later home to more than thirty families, Six Moon Hill was described in a 1954 *Vogue* article as a "paradise for children."[20] With thirteen children between them, Harkness and colleague Jean Fletcher relied on this communal support system to maintain their architectural careers.

Later in her career with TAC, Harkness acted as principal designer on many award-winning educational and cultural buildings, including the Ladd Library (1973) and the Olin Arts Center (1986) at Bates College in Lewiston, Maine; Fox Lane Middle School (1967) in Bedford, New York; and Chase Learning Center at the Eaglebrook School in Deerfield, Massachusetts (1967).[21] Harkness's pioneering work on accessibility and sustainable design culminated in *Building without Barriers for the Disabled* (1976) and *Sustainable Design for Two Maine Islands* (1985).

In 1979, Harkness was elevated to the AIA College of Fellows, and in 1991 she was presented with an Award of Honor by the Boston Society of Architects. —*LFR*

Top
7 Moon Hill Road, Six Moon Hill,
Lexington, MA, Sarah Pillsbury
Harkness for The Architects
Collaborative, 1950. Photo Lara
Kimmerer

Bottom
Olin Arts Center, Bates
College, Lewiston, ME, 1986.
© Brian Vanden Brink

LINA BO BARDI

BORN
Rome, Italy, 1914

DIED
São Paulo, Brazil, 1992

EDUCATION
Liceo Artistico di Roma, 1934;
Rome University College of
Architecture, 1939

PRACTICE
Studio Bo e Pagani, 1940–42;
Lo Stile, graphic designer
and editor, 1941–43; *Domus*,
graphic designer and coeditor,
1944–45; Studio de Arte
Arquitetura Palma, 1948–51;
Habitat, cofounder and editor,
1950–53; Museu de Arte
Moderna da Bahia, founder and
director, 1958–64

TEACHING
University of Bahia, Salvador,
1958–64

NOTABLE HONORS
Pioneer of Brazilian Modern
art and architecture; Casa de
Vidro, Historic Heritage Site,
1987; major retrospective of
work, Venice Architecture
Biennale, 2009; Architectural
Fellowship, Brazil, British
Council, in collaboration with
the Instituto Lina Bo e P. M.
Bardi, 2013

Lina Bo Bardi was a prolific Italian-Brazilian architect and designer and a key figure in Brazilian postwar modernism. While her professional accomplishments are extensive and her oeuvre spans many different fields, she remains best known for designing two major, iconic public buildings in São Paulo, which serve as testaments to her belief in the social and cultural potential of architecture: the 1968 Museum of Art São Paulo (MASP) and the 1985 SESC Pompéia leisure center.

Bo Bardi described the ancient capital of Rome where she grew up as "one of the moldiest cities in the world; full of ruins."[22] In the 1920s and 1930s, the crumbling city was buttressed by a pervasive display of fascism under Benito Mussolini's regime. Against her parents' wishes, Bo Bardi enrolled at the Rome University College of Architecture in 1934, where she studied under Gustavo Giovannoni and Marcello Piacentini, who modeled the curricula after the fascist style of stripped classicism. When Bo Bardi graduated in 1939, Italian modern architecture was in crisis and the nation was about to enter World War II.

Bo Bardi moved to Milan in 1940, where she founded Studio Bo e Pagani, with architect Carlo Pagani. As bombs fell on the city, the studio struggled to find commissions and Bo Bardi turned to paper architecture. She worked as an editor and graphic designer for *Lo Stile*, a visually experimental though politically conservative design magazine, and later as coeditor and graphic designer of *Domus* magazine. *Domus* was forced to suspend its production in 1945.

The following year Bo Bardi married Pietro Maria Bardi, the influential art collector, journalist, and champion of Italian rationalism. The couple relocated to São Paulo, Brazil, where he was offered a position by media-mogul Assis Chateaubriand to create and direct a museum of modern art. Working alongside her husband, Bo Bardi conceived of the interior and exhibition design for MASP, initially located on the first floor of the Diarios Associados headquarters. Through its extensive programming initiatives and the magazine *Habitat*—cofounded by Bo Bardi in the early 1950s—MASP became a major cultural hub for modern art in the following decades.

Bo Bardi's first building (1950), a house she designed for herself and her husband in the Morumbi suburb of São Paulo, has since become an icon of Brazilian modern architecture. Built on a steep slope and raised high on slender pilotis, the Casa de Vidro (glass house) appears to float among the canopy of the surrounding trees. Bo Bardi's gift for placemaking differentiates her work from her European contemporaries, with interiors featuring sleek, mass-produced furniture, natural materials, and a heterogeneous collection of artworks and antiques from Italy and Brazil.[23] The house became a historic heritage site in 1987 and has since become the headquarters of Instituto Lina Bo e P. M. Bardi, preserving the legacy of the Bardis while promoting the study and research of Brazilian art and architecture.

With a growing permanent collection, MASP eventually outgrew its original location. In 1957, Bo Bardi was commissioned to design a highly visible museum on Avenida Paulista in the city center. Inaugurated in 1968, the reinforced-concrete and glass structure quickly cemented Bo Bardi's place in the history pages of architecture,

Museum of Art São Paulo
(MASP), Brazil, 1968. Photo
Wilfredo Rodríguez

Above
Glass House, Morumbi, São
Paulo, Brazil, 1950. Photo
Chico Albuquerque. © Chico
Albuquerque + Instituto Moreira
Salles Collection + Instituto
Bardi / Casa de Vidro

Opposite
SESC Pompéia, São Paulo,
Brazil, 1977. © Maria Gonzalez

influencing many Brazilian architects during the 1960s and 1970s.

Shortly after the military dictatorship came to an end in 1985, Bo Bardi completed the final stages of the SESC Pompéia leisure center in São Paulo, perhaps the most extraordinary work of her career. In 1977, Bo Bardi made her initial renovations to a former oil-barrel factory in the immigrant and working-class Pompeia neighborhood of São Paulo, which the local community had been using informally for various recreational activities. In a radical approach to historic preservation, Bo Bardi prevented the building's demolition and supervised the careful rehabilitation of the factory sheds and later added two concrete towers.[24]

In the late 1980s, Bo Bardi focused her efforts on the restoration of the historic city center of Salvador, the capital of the state of Bahia and the Afro-Brazilian culture center of Brazil, where she had previously founded and directed the Museu de Arte Moderna da Bahia. Although the restoration master plan was ultimately canceled, a handful of Bo Bardi's adaptive reuse projects were realized, most notably the Ladeira da Misericórdia Housing and Commercial Complex (1988) and Casa do Benin (1988), a museum dedicated to the cultural exchange between Bahia and Benin that resulted from the slave trade. Both buildings underscore Bo Bardi's visionary and socially conscious approach to design and how she viewed architecture "not as built work, but as possible means to be and to face [different] situations."[25] —*LFR*

FLORENCE KNOLL BASSETT

BORN
Saginaw, MI, 1917

DIED
Coral Gables, FL, 2019

EDUCATION
Cranbrook Academy of Art,
1935; Columbia GSAAP,
1935; Cranbrook Academy
of Art, 1937; AA School of
Architecture, 1939; Armour
Institute (now Illinois Institute
of Technology), 1941

PRACTICE
Walter Gropius and Marcel
Breuer, 1939–40; Ludwig Mies
van der Rohe, 1940; Raymond
Loewy; Herbert Bayer;
Richard M. Bennett; Harrison,
Abramovitz, and Fouilhoux,
1941–43; Hans G. Knoll
Furniture Company, 1940–46;
Knoll Associates, 1946–65

NOTABLE HONORS
Good Design Award, MoMA,
1950, 1953; Gold Medal for
Industrial Design, AIA, 1961;
International Design Award,
American Institute of Interior
Designers, 1962; Total Design
Award, American Society
of Interior Designers, 1977;
Athena Award for Creativity
and Excellence, Rhode Island
School of Design (RISD), 1983;
Hall of Fame, Interior Design,
1985; Honorary Degree,
Architecture, University of
Miami, 1995; National Medal
of Arts, National Endowment
for the Arts, 2002; Design
Excellence Award, Philadelphia
Museum of Art, 2004;
Honorary Degree, Design,
University of Minnesota, 2008

"Being a woman, I was given interiors," Florence Knoll Bassett told the *New York Times* in 1941, of her duties on being hired at the New York firm of Harrison, Abramovitz, and Fouilhoux. Nevertheless, she took what some might consider a professional limitation and turned it into a game-changing career. She brought a modernist ethos to office interiors, revolutionizing office design in the process.

Knoll Bassett was born Florence Schust in Saginaw, Michigan, in 1917, the only child of engineer Frederick E. Schust and his wife, Mina Schust. She lost both parents within a few years of each other, leaving her orphaned by the age of twelve. Her guardian, Emile Tessin, made arrangements for Knoll Bassett to attend boarding school. In 1932, she enrolled in the Kingswood School for Girls in Bloomfield Hills, Michigan, a part of the Cranbrook Educational Community. Under the tutelage of Rachel de Wolfe Rasman, the art director at Kingswood, Knoll Bassett undertook her first design project, a home that integrated interior and exterior designs. The project sparked the interest of architect Eliel Saarinen, then the president of the Cranbrook Academy of Art.

Saarinen and his wife, Loja, took Knoll Bassett under their wing. She spent summers with the Saarinen family in Finland and befriended their son, Eero, seven years her senior, who shared his love and knowledge of architectural history with her. After completing high school, she attended the Cranbrook Academy for two years, with Saarinen's advice and blessing.

Beginning in 1935, Knoll Bassett studied architecture at Columbia University before pursuing further studies at the AA School of Architecture in London. When war broke out in Europe in 1939, she moved to Cambridge, Massachusetts, where she worked for Walter Gropius and Marcel Breuer. Hoping to finish her degree, in 1940, she enrolled at Chicago's Armour Institute (later named the Illinois Institute of Technology), studying for a year under Ludwig Mies van der Rohe.

Knoll Bassett received her BA and moved to New York in 1941, where she worked for such architects as Herbert Bayer and Raymond Loewy before being hired at Harrison, Abramovitz, and Fouilhoux, the firm overseeing the construction of Rockefeller Center. Concurrently, she began completing side projects for furniture designer Hans Knoll. Her first assignment was designing the office of the Secretary of War, Henry L. Stimson, and in 1943 she became Knoll's full-time interiors specialist.

The scarcity created by World War II helped to foster the minimalism of her signature design aesthetic, placing an emphasis on bright colors and clean lines. In 1946, Knoll Bassett and Hans Knoll founded Knoll Associates, and two months later, they married. She became a full partner in the business the same year and spearheaded the operations of the Knoll Planning Unit, which brought architecture, fabric, furniture, and spatial planning together in a new and unprecedented way. The company expanded exponentially over the next decade, opening showrooms across the country and eventually in Europe. Knoll Bassett thought of the showrooms as "research labs," establishing an aesthetic model that could be sold to consumers.

Furniture, Florence Knoll and
Ludwig Mies van der Rohe.
Bassett Papers, Archives of
American Art, Smithsonian
Institution

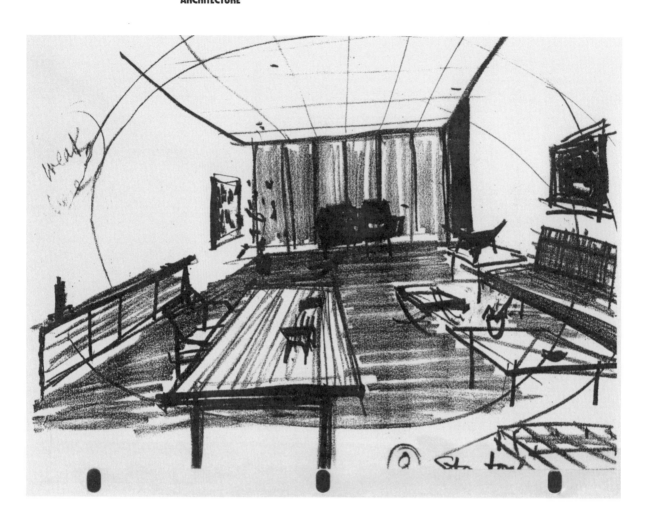

CBS Studios, Madison Avenue, New York, NY, sketch for photo shoot, ca. 1964. Bassett Papers, Archives of American Art, Smithsonian Institution

The Knoll Planning Unit model changed the field of interior design, effectively transforming it from mere decoration to the practice of spatial architecture. Knoll Bassett designed office interiors for CBS, GM, and IBM, some of the most prized corporate clients of the day. She also collaborated on furniture designs with architects like Eero Saarinen and Isamu Noguchi. She was an early advocate of the open-floor office plan. Another venture, KnollTextiles, filled what she perceived to be a gap in the market, and her use of fabric swatches in client presentations has since become an industry standard.

In 1955, Knoll was killed in an automobile accident, and Knoll Bassett continued to run the Knoll Planning Unit and all design-related aspects of the company. In 1958, she married the head of the First National Bank of Miami, Harry Hood Bassett, and commuted between Knoll's New York headquarters and Miami. She sold the company to Art Metal Construction Company in 1959, staying on as the design director until 1965, when she retired to private practice in Florida. She was awarded the National Medal of the Arts in 2002. She passed away in early 2019 at the age of 101. —KF

Top
Bertoia sculpture and chair
sketch, Florence Knoll Bassett,
1952. Bassett Papers, Archives
of American Art, Smithsonian
Institution

Bottom
Chair, table, credenza, and
light, Florence Knoll Basset,
Knoll International, ca. 1960s.
Bassett Papers, Archives of
American Art, Smithsonian
Institution

MINNETTE DE SILVA

BORN
Kandy, Ceylon (now Sri Lanka), 1918

DIED
Kandy, Sri Lanka, 1998

EDUCATION
Architectural Academy, Mumbai, India, private lessons, 1940, 1945; Sir Jamsetjee Jeejebhoy School of Art, 1941; AA School of Architecture, MArch, 1947

PRACTICE
Mistri and Bhedwar, Mumbai, 1940; Otto Königsberger, Bangalore, 1944–45; Studio of Modern Architecture, Kandy, Sri Lanka, 1948–73

TEACHING
University of Hong Kong, lecturer, 1975–79

NOTABLE HONORS
First woman to enroll at Sir Jamsetjee Jeejebhoy School of Art, 1940; first Asian woman to be elected to RIBA, 1948; Gold Medal, Sri Lanka Institute of Architects, 1996

Minnette de Silva was born and raised in Kandy, a large city situated around a central lake at the heart of Sri Lanka. Her parents were prominent figures in the fight for independence from British rule and her mother, Agnes de Silva, pioneered the campaign for women's suffrage, which was finally won in 1931.[26] Despite her father's progressive leanings, he did not support young de Silva in her pursuit of a formal education in architecture, so she appealed to her maternal uncle for funding.[27]

In 1941, she enrolled in the architecture program at Sir Jamsetjee Jeejebhoy School of Art but was expelled during her first year for participating in the student strikes sparked by Gandhi's arrest.[28] De Silva later joined her older sister, Anil, and Mulk Raj Anand in founding *MARG* (Modern Architectural Research Group), the first Indian magazine dedicated to modern art and design. The magazine became a highly influential platform in the development of a national identity following India's independence from British rule in 1947.

After earning her master's degree from the AA School of Architecture in London, de Silva returned home to a newly independent Sri Lanka, bound by a sense of duty to contribute to the nation's postcolonial identity.[29] Back in Kandy, de Silva established a pioneering architectural practice that grounded the International Style in local traditions and ecological contexts.

Her first project, the Karunaratne house (1951) in Kandy, served as a nascent experiment in what she came to call Regional Modernism. The open-plan layout of the house combined modern and local elements, such as glass bricks and woven Dumbara mats, and included two murals

by the distinguished Sri Lankan painter George Keyt. She developed these ideas further in the Ian Pieris House (1956) in Colombo, which was the first building in Sri Lanka to be built on pilotis—a decision she described as having been influenced by Le Corbusier's Villa Savoye.

During the remainder of her career, de Silva designed a handful of private residences and several larger-scale projects, including the Senanayake flats (1957) in Colombo, public housing (1958) in Kandy, and the Kandy Arts Centre (1984).

In the 1960s, de Silva's career began to decline, likely as the result of her abrasive character, prejudices against women, and her mixed ethnicity. In the early 1970s, she moved to London into a flat above the one shared by Maxwell Fry and Jane Drew, with whom she had mingled in her earlier days at the AA.[30] Through them, Scribner's commissioned her to write a section on Asian architecture in the eighteenth edition of Bannister Fletcher's *History of Architecture* (1975). Between 1975 and 1979, she lectured at the University of Hong Kong, developing a method of teaching a counterhegemonic history of Asian architecture.

In the 1980s, at the start of the Sri Lankan Civil War, de Silva attempted to revive her architecture practice, without success. Her contributions were largely forgotten by the world of architecture, eclipsed by the likes of Geoffrey Bawa, who was greatly influenced by de Silva's work and is frequently credited as the leading figure behind tropical modernism. —*LFR*

Above
Ian Pieris House, Alfred House
Gardens, Colombo, Sri Lanka,
1956. Photo David Robson, 2012

Right
Chandra Amarasinghe House,
Colombo, Sri Lanka, 1960.
*The Life and Work of an Asian
Woman Architect* (1998)

JADWIGA GRABOWSKA-HAWRYLAK

BORN
Tarnawce, Poland, 1920

DIED
Wrocław, Poland, 2018

EDUCATION
Wrocław University of
Technology, 1950

PRACTICE
Arkady Student Cooperative
of Architects, 1948–51;
Design and Research Studio
of General Construction
(Miastoprojekt), 1951–81

TEACHING
Wrocław University of
Technology, 1948–ca. 1980

NOTABLE HONORS
Mister Wrocław Award for
Researchers' House, 1960;
Minister of Construction and
Building Materials Industry,
1964, 1973; Wrocław Arts
Award, 1966; Gold Cross
of Merit, 1972; Honorary
Award, Polish Association of
Architects (SARP), 1974; Medal
of the Wrocław University
of Technology, 1977; best
architectural work, SARP, 1984;
Knight's Cross of the Order of
Polonia Restituta, 1989

Jadwiga Grabowska-Hawrylak was one of the first women to benefit from the Soviet propaganda effort to promote the image of worker emancipation, which admitted an unprecedented number of women into universities and employed them in the workforce.[31] At the close of World War II, she began her architecture education at the Wrocław University of Technology, surrounded by the city's ruins and attending classes in partially destroyed classrooms.[32]

Due to the controlled environment of state-owned architecture studios during the time after her graduation, the first phase of Grabowska-Hawrylak's architectural career was largely limited to restoration. In 1954, she was commissioned to rehabilitate two seventeenth-century tenement houses severely damaged during a wartime air raid. Her repairs were so true to their original form that the buildings were added to the register of historical monuments.

At the onset of de-Stalinization in the mid-1950s, increasing pressures to address the housing crisis forced city architects to abandon the state-sanctioned social-realist style and turn toward more efficient, industrial solutions. Grabowska-Hawrylak supervised and codesigned many residential and educational buildings that played a critical role in reshaping the city's new image, including the award-winning Scientist's House (1961) in Grunwaldzki Square, the nearby Gallery House (1962), and the Gajowice Housing Estate (1968).

In 1963, Grabowska-Hawrylak began collaborating with Zdzisław Kowalski and Włodzimierz Wasilewski on a large-scale residential and commercial complex in Grunwaldzki Square known as Wrocław's Manhattan Housing Complex. The estate features six high-rise apartment buildings linked by an elevated pedestrian platform with shops and services. Leveraging the morphological properties of concrete and new prefabrication technology, Grabowska-Hawrylak designed the tower facades of interlocking, curved patios (for which it earned its local nickname as the "toilet-seat buildings") as an acoustic barrier against noise. Blending form with function, the towers exemplified Grabowska-Hawrylak's humanistic approach to mass-produced housing. Although the towers were initially received with mixed reviews, their distinctive design quickly led Grabowska-Hawrylak to become the first female recipient of the prestigious Polish Association of Architects (SARP) honorary award in 1974.

As the era of stagnation set in and development slowed, Grabowska-Hawrylak's work took a futuristic turn, and her practice was largely relegated to paper. Her Eco-System project, designed for Stefan Müller's 1975 Terra-1 International Exhibition of Intentional Architecture, proposed a utopian city in the form of a massive, endless linear tube through the landscape.

It was nearly a decade before another one of Grabowska-Hawrylak's designs was realized. Her most notable projects included the home she built for herself and her husband, Henryk Hawrylak (1984), which won the 1984 SARP Home of the Year award, and the Millennium Memorial Church of the Wrocław Diocese (1990). In 2019, a year after Grabowska-Hawrylak passed away, a retrospective of her work was exhibited at the Center for Architecture in New York City, restoring the legacy of this pioneering architect. —*LFR*

Manhattan Housing Complex,
Wrocław, Poland, 1973.
Photo Arkadiusz Łojek, 2016

ANNE GRISWOLD TYNG

BORN
Lushan, Jiangxi, China, 1920

DIED
Greenbrae, CA, 2011

EDUCATION
Radcliffe College, BFA, 1942;
Smith College, Graduate
School of Architecture and
Landscape Architecture, 1942;
Harvard GSD, MArch, 1944;
University of Pennsylvania,
PhD, Architecture, 1975

PRACTICE
Konrad Wachsmann, 1944;
Van Doren, Nowland and
Schladermundt, 1944; Knoll
Associates, 1944–45; Stonorov
& Kahn, 1945–47; Office of
Louis I. Kahn, 1947–74; Anne
Griswold Tyng, FAIA, 1949–99;
Louis I. Kahn and Anne G. Tyng
Associated Architects, 1951–74

TEACHING
University of Pennsylvania,
1968–95

NOTABLE HONORS
Brunner Grant, AIA, 1963,
1983; Fellowship, Graham
Foundation for Advanced
Studies in the Fine Arts,
1965, 1979; Fellow, AIA,
1975; Academician, National
Academy of Design, 1975;
John Harbeson Distinguished
Service Award, AIA, 1991

Anne Griswold Tyng was a visionary architect, theorist, educator, and pioneer of habitable space-frame architecture. Through her research on innovative geometry, she played a central role in redefining modern architecture in the 1950s and 1960s.

Tyng, whose parents were American Episcopal missionaries, was born and raised in Jiangxi Province, China.[33] She studied fine arts at Radcliffe College, taking architecture courses in her senior year at the Smith College Graduate School of Architecture.[34] In 1942, Tyng joined the first class to admit women into the Harvard GSD, where she studied under Marcel Breuer, Walter Gropius, and Catherine Bauer Wurster.

In 1945, Tyng joined the Philadelphia-based office of Stonorov & Kahn.[35] When Louis Kahn and Oscar Stonorov parted ways in 1947, Tyng continued to work closely with Kahn at his independent practice. Once referred to by Buckminster Fuller as "Kahn's geometrical strategist," Tyng played an instrumental role in Kahn's famous Yale University Art Gallery (1953) and the Trenton Bath House (1956).[36]

Independent of her work with Kahn, Tyng maintained a successful design and research practice, gaining recognition in 1948 for her Tyng Toy prototype, a children's kit of modular pieces of plywood and dowel pins that could be assembled into anything from a wagon to a desk with stool. Tyng Toy was exhibited at the Walker Art Center, MoMA, and the Institute of Contemporary Art in Boston.

In the early 1950s, Tyng began exploring the potential uses of the octet-truss system developed by Fuller, which she applied to an addition to her parents'

farmhouse in Cambridge, Maryland. Tyng expanded on this tetrahedral framework for a cantilevered high-rise in Kahn's Civic Center project (1953) in Philadelphia. Tyng and Kahn later tripled the height of the City Tower, which was included in the 1960 *Visionary Architecture* exhibition at MoMA in New York. Kahn neglected to credit Tyng.

In the mid-1950s, Tyng took leave from her architectural practice, traveling to Rome to give birth to her and Kahn's child. Returning to Philadelphia in 1955 and continuing to work for Kahn as an independent contractor, she made significant contributions to Mill Creek Housing Project (1962) and Martin Marietta Baltimore Research Center (1957). Additionally, Tyng took on a leading role in the design of Clever House (1962) and Shapiro House (1962).

In the early 1960s, Tyng gradually departed from Kahn's office and began investigating the architectural possibilities of universal geometries, platonic solids, and mathematical sequences, such as nature's dynamic symmetries. In 1971, Tyng exhibited her Urban Hierarchy model for a spiral city as a part of *Metamorphology: New Sources of Form Making* at AIA Philadelphia.

Tyng fought hard to advance the status of women in architecture. She spoke out against the male-dominated profession in a handful of writings and exhibitions. Shortly before her death in 2011, Tyng was recognized by the University of Pennsylvania Institute of Contemporary Art with a retrospective of her work. —*LFR*

Above
Yale University Art Gallery and Design Center, New Haven, CT, Anne Griswold Tyng with Louis Kahn, 1953. Photo Samuel Ludwig, 2015

Right
City Tower project model, Philadelphia, PA, Louis Kahn with Anne Griswold Tyng, late 1950s. Louis I. Kahn Collection, University of Pennsylvania and Pennsylvania Historical and Museum Commission

NATALIE GRIFFIN DE BLOIS

BORN
Paterson, NJ, 1921

DIED
Chicago, IL, 2013

EDUCATION
Western College for Women,
1940; Columbia GSAPP, BArch,
1944

PRACTICE
Ketchum, Gina and Sharpe,
1944; Skidmore, Owings
& Merrill (SOM), 1944–74;
Neuhaus & Taylor (later 3-D
International), ca. 1975–80;
Graeber, Simmons & Cowan,
1980–94

TEACHING
University of Texas at Austin,
1980–93

NOTABLE HONORS
Fulbright Grant, France,
1951–52; Fellow, AIA, 1974;
Award for Outstanding
Educational Contributions in
honor of Edward J. Romieniec,
FAIA, Texas Society of
Architects, 1988

Natalie Griffin de Blois was a teenager when the New York World's Fair took over Flushing Meadows in 1939. Witnessing the fair's modern and futuristic designs, de Blois acquired a vision that shaped her career. Her father, a civil engineer, supported her chosen career path of architecture, and the mechanical drawing classes he placed her in paid off when she was able to work as a draftsperson to put herself through Columbia University.

Growing up in Paterson, New Jersey, de Blois had already decided to become an architect by the age of ten. Although her parents' ability to pay for her college education was stymied by the Great Depression, she was able to attend the Western College for Women in Oxford, Ohio, on scholarship for a year before transferring to Columbia, where she won two prizes and graduated in 1944, one of five women in a class of eighteen. After graduation, she worked at the firm of Ketchum, Gina and Sharpe, which drew her in with its commitment to modern design.

One of her biggest projects at Ketchum was designing prototype storefront components. In this role, de Blois experienced overt sexism for the first time in her career. De Blois told an interviewer of a fellow architect at the office: "He used to take me out dancing to hear Benny Goodman and Tommy Dorsey. I went out with him quite often. He was very fond of me, but he was not encouraged. So he went to Mr. Ketchum and told him that he just couldn't work with me there. Mr. Ketchum called me over to his desk. We were all in one room. He said he was sorry, I'd have to leave. Just like that. Of course, I hadn't experienced a shock like that before."[37]

Ketchum did put in a good word for her with Louis Skidmore, of SOM, whose offices were in the same building as Ketchum's on East Fifty-Seventh Street. At SOM, de Blois's talents were recognized immediately. She moved quickly from such tasks as technical lettering and designing the bathhouses at Jones Beach to contributing to some of SOM's most prominent New York commissions. Although SOM principal Gordon Bunshaft typically received credit for the design of SOM's most famous buildings, such as Lever House (1952), the Pepsi-Cola Building (1960), and the Union Carbide headquarters (1960), all in New York City, and the Connecticut General Life Insurance Company campus in Bloomfield, Connecticut (1957), de Blois was the senior designer or project designer. She handled much of the design process for these major structures, among others.

The structural complexity of the Union Carbide building at 270 Park Avenue emphatically raised de Blois's profile at SOM. The building, which covered a whole block on East Forty-Seventh Street, was the ninth-tallest structure in New York City when it was completed, and for decades, it remained a prime example of the postwar modernist building boom in New York— it was demolished in 2019.

Another project, the low-slung, modernist Connecticut General Life Insurance Company headquarters, was de Blois's first experience working with Isamu Noguchi, who had designed the building's outdoor terraces. Bunshaft didn't like one of the four courts designed by Noguchi, so he assigned the fourth to de Blois.

Of de Blois's relationship with Bunshaft, she said, "His treatment of me as a woman

was typical of that time." Before giving a presentation on the Kennedy International Airport, Bunshaft reportedly told her, "You can't come to the meeting unless you go home first and change your clothes. I don't like green."[38] On another occasion, he made her leave her children in the car in a parking lot while on a site visit. He did, however, recommend her for an architectural Fulbright grant to study in France, which she won in 1951 to research architect Auguste Perret, known for his postwar buildings.

Following a divorce in 1961, de Blois transferred to SOM's Chicago offices, becoming an associate partner in 1964 and working on designs for the Equitable Building, a thirty-five-story skyscraper along the north bank of the Chicago River. The 1970s found her taking a greater advocacy role for women in the profession, serving as a founding member of Chicago Women in Architecture in 1973. In 1974, after thirty years at SOM, she left the firm, taking a bicycle trip around France and Germany and eventually moving to Houston and working for Neuhaus and Taylor (later 3-D International). From 1980 to 1993, she taught skyscraper studios at the University of Texas at Austin, where a scholarship was created in her name. Her designs are still among some of the tallest woman-designed buildings in the world. —*KF*

Clockwise from left

Lever House, New York, NY, Natalie Griffin de Blois with Gordon Bunshaft for SOM, 1952. © Ezra Stoller

Union Carbide lobby, New York, NY, Natalie Griffin de Blois with Gordon Bunshaft for SOM, 1960. © Ezra Stoller

Pepsi World Headquarters, New York, NY, Natalie Griffin de Blois for SOM, 1960. © Ezra Stoller

HALINA SKIBNIEWSKA

BORN
Warsaw, Second Polish
Republic, 1921

DIED
Warsaw, Poland, 2011

EDUCATION
Noakowski Women's School
of Architecture, 1942; Warsaw
University of Technology, 1948

PRACTICE
Romuald Gutt, 1946–57;
Warsaw Housing Cooperative,
1958–65; PBM Center, 1965–75;
BPN Inwestprojekt, 1975–86

TEACHING
Warsaw University of
Technology, 1975–85,
Department of Housing,
Faculty of Architecture,
director, 1975–91; Warsaw
Housing Environment
Laboratory, 1991–2000

NOTABLE HONORS
First Prize, design contests for
Wrocław-Południe Housing
Project, 1962; Mister Warszawy
Award, 1972; Honorary Title,
Grand Officer of France's
Legion of Honour, 1972;
Honorary Award, Association
of Polish Architects, 1978;
Lenin Peace Prize, 1977–78;
Medal of the Warsaw University
of Technology, 2000

Halina Skibniewska was a Polish architect, urban planner, politician, and pioneer of accessibility in housing. Her original take on modern architecture prioritized social welfare above all else, advocating that design is the culmination of extensive interdisciplinary research, taking into account ecological, economic, sociological, and psychological factors.[39]

Born in 1921 in Warsaw under the Second Polish Republic, Skibniewska joined the Home Army of the underground Polish resistance organization during World War II and the Nazi occupation. She became an operative of the Żegota Council to Aid Jews, assisting an estimated thirty to sixty thousand Holocaust survivors.[40] She also began to study architecture at the Warsaw University of Technology during this time, continuing to operate underground during the war.

In the aftermath of the conflict, more than 85 percent of Warsaw was in ruins.[41] As a student, Skibniewska joined the reconstruction efforts and began working as a designer in the studio of Romuald Gutt, a prominent modernist architect. From Gutt, she learned to approach architecture as the combination of creativity, technical skills, and humanism. Skibniewska's notable projects included Warsaw's Central Statistical Office building and the reconstruction of the National Theater.

In the 1950s and 1960s, Skibniewska designed residential buildings for the Warsaw Housing Cooperative, working to address the urgent housing crisis caused by extreme overcrowding, poor sanitation, and a lack of basic amenities.[42] Her first major project, the Sady Żoliborskie Estate (1963), is widely recognized as one of the most successful housing complexes built in postwar Poland. Skibniewska introduced her model for an open, flexible apartment that could be adapted to the changing needs of its users.[43] At the center of the estate, five-story residential buildings were oriented around a central courtyard, while a school, kindergarten, childcare center, and commercial facilities were situated at the periphery. Located on the site of a former community garden, the spaces between the buildings were preserved as parks and green spaces. A harmonious blend of functionalism, comfort, and resourcefulness, the estate utilized ornamentation, brickwork, and wood from derelict historic structures found on site. The groundbreaking project influenced future modern housing standards.

Skibniewska's acute sensitivity to social needs was further encapsulated in her designs for Osiedle Sadyba (1975), the first independent living facility for the disabled and elderly. As part of the program for Sadyba, she proposed a decentralized social welfare system with two health centers located nearby.

Over the course of her long, accomplished career, Skibniewska designed and coauthored many other built works, including the Winogrady estate (1964) in Poznań; Environmental School (1971); a reclamation estate in Szwoleżerów known as Żoliborz Orchards (1974), balancing historic, ecological, and social elements; ZETO headquarters (1974); a kindergarten in Sokółka (1975); and the whole district of Białołęka in Warsaw (1986). She was bestowed with an Honorary Award from the Association of Polish Architects in 1978 and the Medal of the Warsaw University of Technology in 2000.

Her commitment to social betterment was not only reflected in her architectural career but also in her political and pedagogical activities. From 1975 to 1985, she was a professor at Warsaw University of Technology, her alma mater, where she also headed the Department of Housing. A committed member of the Communist party, she served in Poland's legislative body, the Sejm, from 1965 to 1985, and became the first woman to serve as the deputy marshal.[44] —*LFR*

Furnished interior, Sady Żoliborskie Estate, Warsaw, Poland, 1963. Photo Zbigniew Kapuścik for *Architecture Journal* 1 (1963)

BLANCHE LEMCO VAN GINKEL

BORN
London, England, 1923

EDUCATION
McGill University, BArch, 1945;
Harvard University, 1950

PRACTICE
Windsor Planning Commission,
1945; Regina City Planning
Committee, 1946; William
Crabtree, Architect, 1947;
Atelier Le Corbusier, 1948;
Mayerovitch and Bernstein,
1950–51; Blanche Lemco,
Architect, 1952–57; Van Ginkel
Associates, Montreal, 1957–66,
1968–77, Winnipeg, 1966–68,
Toronto, 1976–

NOTABLE HONORS
Woman of the Year,
Mademoiselle, 1956; Vienna
Grand Prix, International
Federation of Housing and
Planning Congress, 1956;
Massey Medal for Architecture,
1964; Queen Elizabeth II
Silver Jubilee Medal, 1977;
Service Award, Association
of Collegiate Schools of
Architecture, 1984; Order
of Canada, 2000; Ordre des
Urbanistes du Québec, 2003;
Queen Elizabeth II Diamond
Jubilee Medal, 2012; Chateau
Ramezay and Heritage
Montreal Achievement Award,
2013; Honorary Doctor of
Science, McGill University,
2014

Born in London in 1923, architect, educator, and urban planner Blanche Lemco van Ginkel moved to Canada with her family when she was fourteen. She attended McGill University on scholarship, graduating with an architecture degree in 1945. (McGill had only admitted its first female student the year before.)

After graduating, Blanche was a municipal planner in Canada before working as an architect for William Crabtree in London. In 1948, she was granted a summer job in Le Corbusier's Paris atelier, where she designed a rooftop kindergarten and gymnasium for the architect's brutalist Unité d'habitation in Marseille, a postwar housing project that Le Corbusier also called the *Cité radieuse*, or radiant city. It redefined high-density housing and remains one of Van Ginkel's most famous commissions.

Van Ginkel attended graduate school at Harvard University, studying under Walter Gropius and completing her degree in 1950. From 1951 to 1957, she served as a professor at the University of Pennsylvania, where many of her young students, close to her in age, were Korean War veterans. "They'd never had a woman teaching before or somebody with a funny accent. And when I wrote on the blackboard, I spelled wrong," she told the *Montreal Gazette* in 2012.

Van Ginkel met Dutch architect and planner Daniel (Sandy) van Ginkel at the International Congress of Modern Architecture (CIAM) in 1953. They married in 1956, and the following year they founded their Montreal-based architecture and planning firm, Van Ginkel Associates (it would later move to Winnipeg and Toronto). The van Ginkels built a reputation for bold, modernist design and nuanced urban planning.

Van Ginkel taught at the Harvard GSD in 1958, 1971, and 1975 and developed the first courses in urban design at the Université de Montréal and McGill University. She joined the faculty of the University of Toronto in 1977, becoming the first woman to serve as the dean of an architecture school in North America.

"Architecture is a cultural pursuit and those who practice it, or are allowed to practice it, reflect our culture, our mores, our attitudes, in Canada as elsewhere," she stated in a 1991 article.[45] The Van Ginkels' emphasis on walkable cities and public transportation was on the cutting edge of urban planning, predating the environmental movement (and such renowned planners as Jane Jacobs) by at least a decade.

Van Ginkel and her husband are known for their efforts to save Old Montreal, a heritage district in the city, which was threatened by an urban expressway in the late 1950s. After successfully convincing the city to run the expressway under the neighborhood and developing a comprehensive plan for the district's rehabilitation, Van Ginkel coauthored legislation for the first Quebec Provincial Planning Commission from 1963 to 1967. In 1962, the Van Ginkels drew up a preliminary master plan for Montreal's Expo 67, a world's fair that represented an important cultural moment for both Montreal and Canada. Van Ginkel helped to elevate the stature of Canadian women architects through her own high-profile work and published articles and by speaking about her own experiences. *—KF*

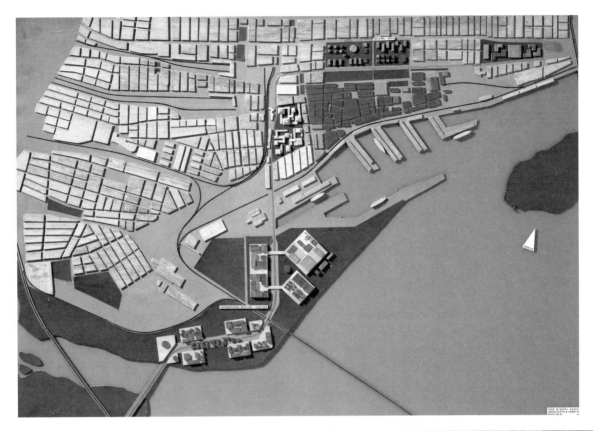

Above
Presentation model for the Canadian World Exhibition, Expo '67, Montreal, Quebec, Van Ginkel Associates, July 1962. Van Ginkel Associates fonds. Courtesy Canadian Centre for Architecture. Gift of H. P. Daniel and Blanche Lemco van Ginkel

Right
Bowring Park, St. John's, Newfoundland, Van Ginkel Associates, 1959

ZOFIA GARLIŃSKA-HANSEN

BORN
Kałuszyn, Poland, 1924

DIED
Warsaw, Poland, 2013

EDUCATION
Music Academy, 1943;
Noakowski Women's School
of Architecture, 1943; Warsaw
University of Technology, 1952

PRACTICE
Office for the Reconstruction
of the Capital, 1945–47;
Warsaw Housing Cooperative,
ca. 1948–51; Hydroproject
Office, 1952–59; Oskar Hansen
Studio

NOTABLE HONORS
Coauthor with Oskar Hansen
of the Open Form theory in
architecture and the Linear
Continuous System in urban
planning

Zofia Garlińska-Hansen came of age during the throes of World War II and the Nazi occupation of Poland. With Warsaw in shambles, Garlińska-Hansen joined the Office for the Reconstruction of the Capital and the Warsaw Housing Cooperative, where she assumed a leading role in the Rakowiec Housing Estate (1958).

While she was studying architecture at the Warsaw University of Technology, Garlińska-Hansen married fellow-student Oskar Hansen, with whom she later opened a studio.[46] Although Oskar frequently insisted upon the joint nature of their projects, crediting Garlińska-Hansen as the architectonic force behind them, to this day she is almost exclusively referenced in the context of her husband's achievements.[47] Regarding her own architectural pursuits and achievements, surprisingly little is known.

The Hansens were among the most radical thinkers in postwar Poland, with projects existing primarily on paper rather than built form. They championed an organic, humanist form of modernism predicated on indeterminacy, flexibility, and collective participation.

Throughout the 1950s, they leveraged commissions for international fairs as laboratories for their experimental ideas, designing pavilions in Stockholm (1953), Izmir (1955), and São Paulo (1959). Their hyperbolic paraboloid tensile structure comprising the Polish pavilion in Izmir was especially successful as a mutable "background" for the machines on display that would appear to shift in relation to the viewer's movement through the space.[48]

During the post-Stalin thaw, the Hansens wrote "Open Form in Architecture—The Art of the Great Number," which Oskar Hansen presented at the 1959 CIAM conference in Orrerlo, Netherlands. In addition to serving as a criticism of Le Corbusier's model of rigid modernism, Open Form advocated for the democratization of the design process. To varying degrees of success, Garlińska-Hansen and Hansen translated these ideas into built form through several housing estates, most notably those of Juliusz Słowacki (1966) in Lublin and Przyczółek Grochowski (1973) in Warsaw.

The most successful example of Open Form has endured in the Hansens' house in the village of Szumin (1970). Following the traditions seen in the Polish countryside, a bench and roofed terrace in the front of the house functioned as a semipublic space, encouraging passersby to sit and meet with the residents. Since 2014, the house has been under the care of the Museum of Modern Art in Warsaw.[49]

In the mid-1960s, the Hansens conceived of the Linear Continuous System (LCS), which transposed the concept of Open Form to an urban scale. The LCS strove to dissolve the hierarchical distinctions between center and periphery and between city and suburb. This was achieved through tiered, linear cities organized along waterways running from north to south, with distinct residential, social, industrial, and transportation zones.[50]

Though the full potential of Open Form and the LCS has never been realized, these visionary concepts were highly influential for an entire generation of Polish modernists. To this day, they continue to challenge architects and urbanists to think beyond the status quo and to reimagine lost futures.
—*LFR*

Top
Hansen House, Szumin, Poland,
1970s. © Zofia and Oskar
Hansen Foundation

Bottom
Juliusz Słowacki Housing
Estate, Lublin, Poland, 1966.
© Zofia and Oskar Hansen
Foundation

NORMA MERRICK SKLAREK

BORN
Harlem, New York, NY, 1926

DIED
Pacific Palisades, Los Angeles, CA, 2012

EDUCATION
Barnard College, Columbia University, 1945; Columbia University, BArch, 1950

PRACTICE
Department of Public Works, New York, 1950–55; SOM, 1955–60; Gruen Associates, 1960–80; Welton Becket Associates, 1980–85; Siegel Sklarek Diamond, 1985–89; Jerde Partnership, 1989–92

TEACHING
UCLA; University of Southern California (USC)

NOTABLE HONORS
First African American woman to graduate from Columbia University, 1950; first African American woman licensed to practice architecture in New York, 1954; first African American woman in AIA, 1959; first African American woman licensed in the state of California, 1962; first African American woman Fellow, AIA; Association of Black Women Entrepreneurs' Outstanding Business Role Model Award, 1987; Whitney M. Young Jr. Award, AIA, 2008; Gold Medal, AIA Los Angeles, 2019

Over the course of her long and prolific career, African American architect Norma Merrick Sklarek broke through many barriers and built many buildings. With extraordinary expertise, intellect, and determination, Sklarek overcame the prejudices of a white, male-dominated field, paving the way for a generation of architects from marginalized populations to follow.

Raised in Harlem and Brooklyn during the height of the Great Depression, Sklarek was nurtured by her parents, a doctor and a seamstress, who had immigrated to the United States from the West Indies. Sklarek attended Barnard College in New York City for one year before entering the architecture school at Columbia University in 1945.[51] Persevering in her studies despite the program's racial and gender homogeneity and atmosphere of hypercompetitiveness, Sklarek became the first African American woman to complete the program in 1950.[52]

Although she struggled to find work after school, having been rejected by nineteen firms, Sklarek was not deterred.[53] She secured a position as a junior draftsperson in the City of New York's Department of Public Works.[54] Craving more creative and challenging work, Sklarek took and passed the architects' registration exam on her first attempt in 1954, becoming the first licensed African American woman architect in the state of New York. The following year, SOM hired her, and she was routinely trusted with difficult jobs and tight deadlines.[55]

Sklarek moved to Los Angeles in 1960 and began a twenty-year tenure with Gruen Associates. Despite the challenges she undoubtedly faced as the only Black woman at the firm, her demonstrable expertise with complex, large-scale projects led her to quickly rise through the ranks. As director of architecture, she coordinated the technical aspects of such major commissions as the Fox Plaza (1966) in San Francisco, San Bernardino City Hall (1971), Commons-Courthouse Center (1973) in Columbus, the United States Embassy in Tokyo (1976), and the Pacific Design Center (1978) in Los Angeles.

In the early 1980s, Sklarek was vice president at Welton Becket Associates in Santa Monica, California, where she supervised the design and execution of Terminal One at Los Angeles International Airport in advance of the 1984 Olympics. The following year, she cofounded the women-owned firm Siegel Sklarek Diamond but soon abandoned the undertaking in pursuit of higher-profile commissions. She went on to serve as principal of the Jerde Partnership, where she worked on the Mall of America (1992) in Minneapolis.

Outside of her architectural practice, Sklarek left her mark on the field as an advocate, educator, and role model for minority architects. In addition to teaching at UCLA and USC, Sklarek helped make the profession more diverse by serving on many boards and committees, such as the AIA National Ethics Council, the California State Board of Architectural Examiners, and the National Council of Architecture Registration Boards (NCARB). In 2019, she was posthumously awarded the AIA Los Angeles Gold Medal, the chapter's highest honor.[56] —*LFR*

Left
US Embassy, Tokyo,
Japan, Norma Merrick Sklarek
for Gruen Associates, 1976.
Courtesy Gruen Associates

Below
Pacific Design Center,
Los Angeles, CA, Norma
Merrick Sklarek for Gruen
Associates, 1978. Courtesy
Gruen Associates

GERTRUDE KERBIS

Gertrude Kerbis grew up in a working-class family of German and Russian immigrants.[57] While a student at the University of Wisconsin–Madison, she became interested in architecture after reading about Frank Lloyd Wright. Mesmerized, she decided to hitchhike to Wright's legendary Taliesin estate in nearby Spring Green, where she climbed in through an open bathroom window and stayed the night. After this encounter, Kerbis transferred to the University of Illinois to study architectural engineering.

She pursued architectural training at the Harvard GSD with Walter Gropius. To finance her way through school, Kerbis worked in the studio of Carl Koch, a professor at MIT with whom she designed furniture for MoMA's Low-Cost Furniture competition.[58] She left Harvard after a year to study with Ludwig Mies van der Rohe at the Illinois Institute of Technology, where she received her master's degree in 1954.

She secured a position with SOM, where she worked as a designer on a handful of award-winning projects. At the US Air Force Academy in Colorado Springs, Kerbis led the design team for Mitchell Hall (1958). The first building to be constructed using computer calculations, the innovative structure features a steel truss and a cantilevered roof that allows for a column-free interior.

With the architectural firm Naess & Murphy, Kerbis designed the Jet Age–style Rotunda Building at Chicago's O'Hare International Airport (1963). Acting as a link between two major terminals, the rotunda became the social hub and visual centerpiece of the airport. A landmark of midcentury-modern design, the rotunda was also a feat of engineering, using an elaborate structural system of post-tensioning in order to create a column-free, continuous open space.[59]

Fatigued by the politics of large firms, Kerbis started her own practice in 1967, the first firm in Chicago to be owned and run by a woman.[60] She struggled to secure commissions and eventually decided to become her own client.[61] For the Greenhouse Condominium Project (1976) in the Lincoln Park neighborhood of Chicago, she was both designer and developer for the brick and black-glass modern apartment building.[62] It was her first solo project. The Greenhouse received AIA Chicago's Distinguished Building Award in 1976.

At the onset of the feminist movement in the early 1970s, Kerbis founded the Chicago Women in Architecture group in 1974 alongside seven other women, including Carol Ross Barney and Natalie Griffin de Blois. The organization remains devoted to challenging such issues as pay inequity, lack of recognition, lack of access to public projects, and lack of professional support for child-rearing or elder care.[63] Kerbis also went on to become a founding member of the Chicago Network in 1979. After being elevated to the AIA College of Fellows in 1970, she became the first female president of the AIA's Chicago Chapter in 1980.[64]

Through a combination of her advocacy work, mentorship, and architectural contributions, Kerbis left a lasting impact on the culture and landscape of Chicago, resulting in her reception of the AIA Chicago Lifetime Achievement Award in 2008. "Without her," Ross Barney remarked, "it would have taken a lot longer to make cracks in the ceiling." —*LFR*

Above
Mitchell Hall, US Air Force
Academy, Colorado Springs,
CO, Gertrude Kerbis for SOM,
1958. Courtesy US Air Force
Academy Special Collections

Left
O'Hare International Airport,
Rotunda Building, Chicago, IL,
Gertrude Kerbis for Naess &
Murphy, 1963. Gertude Lempp
Kerbis Archive, Ryerson and
Burnham Art and Architecture
Archives. Courtesy the Art
Institute of Chicago

III. ADVANCING THE AGENDA

Introduction by Doris Cole, FAIA

This generation, my generation, came of age as design professionals in tumultuous times. "Make love not war" was the slogan as young people protested the Vietnam War. Long hair, pot, and free love were among the lifestyle choices of the day. The pill enabled the sexual revolution. "Burn your bra," or never wear one, brought physical liberation to women. "Let it all hang out" was the informal, relaxed attitude, often without discretion. "Male chauvinist pigs," who thought they were superior to women, were not tolerated by the new feminists. The Civil Rights Act initiated by President Lyndon Johnson and passed by Congress in 1964 transformed the opportunities not only for minorities but also for women. Now we actually had the chance to work, progress, and contribute. It was a wonderfully exciting time to be young, skilled, enthusiastic architects.

Our architectural education had been supposedly gender neutral, but taught by men to men based upon their values and the goals of a primarily male profession. There were very few women professors or students in the architectural schools. The classical Beaux Arts curriculum had been replaced with a modern aesthetic based on the Bauhaus and similar philosophies. Some women architects did not find this education adequate for their professional and intellectual interests. On the East Coast, the Women's School of Planning and Architecture (WSPA) was founded in 1974 by seven women (Katrin Adam, Ellen Perry Berkeley, Phyllis Birkby, Bobbie Sue Hood, Marie I. Kennedy, Joan Forrester Sprague, and Leslie Kanes Weisman) to explore issues that they found relevant to women and architecture. And on the West Coast, the Woman's Building was established in 1973 by three women (artist Judy Chicago, art historian Arlene Raven, and graphic designer Sheila Levrant de Bretteville). As the decades progressed, the number of female students and faculty increased at university schools of architecture, and academic environments reflected the new gender realignment with considerably larger numbers of female students, faculty, and deans.

The AIA was the primary organization for architects in the 1960s and beyond. Women were accepted as members of the AIA, but it did not seem to meet our needs. Young women

Chicago Riverwalk, Chicago, IL, 2009 rendering, Carol Ross Barney, 2016. © Kate Joyce Studios

in architecture were finding their own voices, busy organizing, exploring, and talking with other female professionals. WALAP (Women in Architecture, Landscape Architecture, and Planning) in Boston (1972), Chicago Women in Architecture (1974), and AWA (Alliance of Women in Architecture) in New York City (1972) were just a few of the organizations that were formed or strengthened in the 1970s. Most of these organizations, and many other new groups, thrived during the subsequent decades: Women in Design groups at the Boston Society of Architects and at the Harvard GSD, and the Beverly Willis Foundation (BWF) in New York City are just a few newer groups in the 2000s. Finally, in 2015, the AIA held the first Women's Leadership Summit organized by women members.

We were a generation of firsts as we persisted in our careers. Phyllis Lambert was the first to found a museum and research center, the Canadian Centre for Architecture, in 1979; Beverly Willis was the first to found a nonprofit organization dedicated to changing the culture for women in architecture, the BWF, in 2002; Astra Zarina was the first woman to be awarded the Rome Prize in Architecture from the American Academy in Rome, in 1960; Doris Cole authored the first book on women in architecture in the United States in 1973; Judith Chafee was the first woman from Arizona to be named a Fellow of the AIA in 1983; Sharon Sutton was the first African American woman to become a full professor in an accredited architectural degree program, the University of Michigan, in 1995. The list goes on, as we actively advanced the agenda for women in architecture.

Our greatest legacy was the expansion and redefinition of architecture. We plunged beyond the traditional office practice. Phyllis Birkby was a practicing architect, feminist, filmmaker, and teacher; Eva Jiřičná was head of the Department of Architecture at the University of Applied Arts in Prague; Yasmeen Lari founded the NGO Heritage Foundation Pakistan; Susana Torre was a practicing architect, author, critic, and educator; Adele Chatfield-Taylor was the president and CEO of the American Academy in Rome; Carol Ross Barney founded her Chicago architectural firm to serve clients with social and cultural agendas; others became urban designers, artists, poets, and more. Certainly, our male colleagues had participated in some of these activities, but often apologetically for not being fully engaged in office practice. It was the women architects who brought the values and the freedom to all architects to allow them to explore the potential of our multifaceted profession.

PHYLLIS LAMBERT

BORN
Montreal, Quebec, Canada,
1927

EDUCATION
Vassar College, BA, 1948;
Illinois Institute of Technology,
MArch, 1963; Pratt Institute,
Honorary Doctorate of Fine
Arts in Architecture, 1990

PRACTICE
Mies van der Rohe and Philip
Johnson Architects, 1954–60;
Menkes & Webb Associate
Architects, 1963–68; Pier
Associates, 1970–71; Ridgeway,
1973–85; Peter Rose Architect
& Erol Argun, 1984–89

NOTABLE HONORS
Knight, National Order of
Quebec, 1985; Order of
Canada, 1985; Officer, Order
of Canada, 1990; Gold
Medal, Royal Architectural
Institute of Canada, 1991;
Officer, Ordre des Arts et des
Lettres, 1992; Hadrian Award,
World Monuments Fund,
1997; Companion, Order of
Canada, 2001; Grand Officer,
National Order of Quebec,
2005; Vincent Scully Prize,
National Building Museum,
2006; Golden Lion for
Lifetime Achievement, Venice
Architecture Biennale, 2014;
Wolf Prize in Arts, 2016

Phyllis Lambert's arrival to the public design scene is well known: As a twenty-seven-year-old, she wrote a passionate eight-page letter to her father, the head of the family distilling empire, Joseph E. Seagram & Sons, objecting to his choice of architect for the new headquarters building on Park Avenue in Manhattan. As she wrote in the *Architect's Newspaper (A/N)* in 2017, on the event of her ninetieth birthday: "'No, No, No, No, No, [the letter had begun]. You must put up a building which expresses the best of the society in which you live…You have a great responsibility.' For me the new building had to be a wonderful place to be, to work, for people passing by on the street, for buildings around it, for the neighborhood, for the city, for the world."

Entrusted with finding the right person to design what many later would believe to be the best modern building anywhere, Lambert met with ten or so architects in their offices to review the range of their work. She suggested Ludwig Mies van der Rohe to design the Seagram Building, citing the powerful effect of his articulation, proportions, and siting as among the deciding factors. Lambert later earned a master's degree at the school of architecture at the Illinois Institute of Technology (IIT), established by Mies van der Rohe. Her first commissioned work, by her family, the Saidye Bronfman Centre for the Arts at the YM-YHWA, was built in Montreal in the late 1960s and named for her mother. It is now home to the Segal Centre for Performing Arts.

An exhibiting sculptor by age eleven, Lambert was taught to be objective and also critical of her own work. "Art has always been for me the essence of existence,"

she noted in the same *A/N* article. During graduate school, she took up photography while on vacation in Turkey and Greece. Of her shooting, Lambert said, "It was a sort of notebook, a way of observing. Seeing the connections between things in the lens was exciting—land, sea, and flowers. And, of course, architecture was my focus."

Lambert then married her passion for photography with an interest in city building that had been sparked by a theory class at IIT. Her study, called Greystone, documented buildings in Montreal made from gray limestone. Focusing on how the stone was cut, surfaced, and laid revealed the era of the architecture and its economic, religious, political, and social contexts when considered with how they were sited, their locations, and the ambitions of their builders. Lambert doubled down on her efforts to fight against urban demolition, also heightening her desire for a more photographic mission. A nationwide study, "Court House: A Photographic Document," followed in 1978.

Her enterprising architectural investigations and preservation activism led to Lambert founding the Canadian Centre for Architecture (CCA), where she served as director from 1989 to 1996. She wrote in the *A/N* article: "It was crucial to establish a place where the many aspects of creating the built world could be discussed, a new type of cultural institution, with the specific aim of increasing public awareness of the role of architecture in contemporary society and promoting scholarly research in the field." The center's first exhibition and publication was *Photography and Architecture, 1839 to 1939*. It traveled to Cologne, Paris, New York, and Ottawa between 1982 and

Canadian Centre for
Architecture, Montreal,
Quebec, 1990. © CCA,
Montreal

Esprit-Généreux Warehouse
and Store, 1886; restoration
1974. © Richard Pare and Phyllis
Lambert

1984, even before the CCA's building was
designed. Lambert's final exhibition as
director, *Viewing Olmsted* (1996), was a
visual study of Frederick Law Olmsted's
work by three photographers who examined the various ecologies in his landscape
designs in every season. *Phyllis Lambert: 75
years at work*, for which the *A/N* piece was
written, was exhibited at the CCA in 2017.

Lambert's advice for architecture
students: "I would tell people considering

entering the field that architecture is not
one thing. In my practice, I built and con-
served older buildings, and I was involved
in urban design. Architecture is not about a
sector; it deals with life."[1] —*JSE*

Above
Seagram Building, New York,
NY, Ludwig Mies van der Rohe,
1958. Photo Iker Alonso

Right
*Imperfect Health: The
Medicalization of Architecture*,
exhibition, Montreal, Quebec,
2011. © CCA, Montreal

GAE AULENTI

BORN
Palazzolo dello Stella, Italy,
1927

DIED
Milan, Italy, 2012

EDUCATION
Milan Polytechnic School of
Architecture, 1954

PRACTICE
Gae Aulenti Studio, 1954–2012;
Casabella Continuità, 1954–62;
Lotus International, 1974–79;
FontanaArte, artistic director,
1979–early 1980s

NOTABLE HONORS
First International Prize, Milan
Triennale, 1964; Chevalier
de la Légion d'Honneur,
1987; Honorary Fellow, AIA,
1990; Imperial Praemium
for Architecture, Japan Art
Association, 1991; Knight
of the Grand Cross, 1995;
Honorary Degree, RISD,
2001; Gold Medal for Lifetime
Achievement, Milan Triennale,
2012

"Courage…you need a lot of it to intervene in the Guggenheim spiral," wrote Gae Aulenti in regard to the 1994 exhibition *Italian Metamorphosis*, in which the audacious Italian architect designed four points that projected into the center of the spiral atrium. As she discussed in the 1997 *Gae Aulenti* by Margherita Petranzan, the maneuver was interpreted as a challenge to Frank Lloyd Wright and an affront to modern architecture more broadly.

Aulenti was equally rebellious in her youth, choosing to study architecture in opposition to her parents' desire that she become "a nice society girl."[2] After the war, Aulenti moved to Milan, where she studied architecture at the Milan Polytechnic School of Architecture. She began her career as art director for *Casabella Continuità*, a leading avant-garde design journal during the 1950s and 1960s. Working alongside editor in chief Ernesto Nathan Rogers, Aldo Rossi, and Carlo Aymonino, Aulenti took part in the short-lived Neoliberty movement, which rejected modernism in favor of traditional building methods and individual stylistic expression, free from the constraints of a signature aesthetic.[3]

While working at *Casabella*, Aulenti had a successful freelance design practice—one of very few women to do so at the time. In the 1960s and 1970s, she produced furniture for such high-profile companies as Knoll, Zanotta, Kartell, and Poltronova, as well as lighting for Artemide, Martinelli Luce, and FontanaArte (of which she became artistic director in 1979).[4] Her two most iconic pieces are the Pipistrello Table Lamp (1965) and the postmodern industrial Table with Wheels (1980), both of which are part of the permanent collections at MoMA and the Centre Georges Pompidou.

Aulenti's diverse oeuvre demonstrated her ability to move fluidly between mediums and scales, from watches for Louis Vuitton (1988) to theater sets for La Scala Opera House in Milan (1994), and the Italian Institute of Culture in Tokyo (2005). She designed numerous stores for luxury brands, most notably the futuristic showrooms for Olivetti in Paris (1967) and Buenos Aires (1968) and for FIAT in Brussels and Zurich (1969–70). In 1972, an experiential installation by Aulenti was featured in the groundbreaking MoMA exhibition *Italy: The New Domestic Landscape*.[5]

In the 1980s and 1990s, Aulenti gained international prominence for her conversion of historic structures into museum spaces. Most famously, Aulenti supervised the conversion of a Beaux Arts train station in Paris into the Musée d'Orsay (1986), creating postmodern galleries within the historic structure.[6] In 1987, President François Mitterrand decorated her with the Chevalier de la Légion d'Honneur in recognition of her contribution to French culture.[7]

Aulenti's work went on to include the National Museum of Modern Art (1985) at the Centre Georges Pompidou in Paris, Palazzo Grassi (1986) in Venice, the National Museum of Catalan Art (1995) in Barcelona, and the Asian Art Museum (2003) in San Francisco. Weeks before her death in 2012, the Milan Triennale awarded Aulenti with the Gold Medal for Lifetime Achievement.[8] In December 2012, she was commemorated in Milan with a Piazza designed by Pelli Clarke Pelli Architects and named in her honor.[9] —*LFR*

Above
Musée d'Orsay, galleries, Paris,
France, 1986. © DeAgostini
Picture Library, 2020/Scala,
Florence

Right
Table with Wheels, model no.
2652, 1980. © The Museum
of Modern Art. Licensed by
SCALA/Art Resource, NY

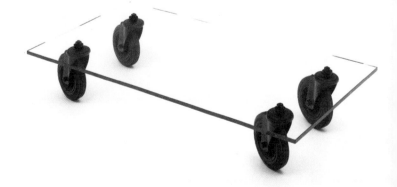

BEVERLY WILLIS

BORN
Tulsa, OK, 1928

EDUCATION
Oregon State University, 1948;
University of Hawaii, BFA, 1954

PRACTICE
Willis & Associates Architects,
1960–2020

NOTABLE HONORS
Fellow, AIA, 1980;
Lawrence Orton Award
for Excellence in City and
Regional Planning (with
Susan Szenasy), American
Planning Association, 2003;
Lifetime Achievement Award,
Professional Women in
Construction, 2003; AIA New
York Special Citation to Beverly
Willis Architecture Foundation
(BWAF), 2011; New York
Construction Award to BWAF
for Outstanding Public Service,
2015; Lifetime Achievement
Award, AIA California Council,
2017

Beverly Willis did not grow up wanting to be an architect; she wanted to be independent. From ages six to twelve, she and her brother were raised in an Oklahoma orphanage, until the Great Depression eased and her mother could afford to feed them again. Willis had to figure things out by herself. She credits her early life experiences with her willingness to take risks and push boundaries, traits that informed everything she would accomplish. The historical forces of circumstance, timing, and the economy, rather than preferences, directed her career. "Through constant learning and adaptation, I mastered many skills," she said.[10]

Willis, during her teen years, learned welding and carpentry and built a radio at the urging of the US government, which anticipated an invasion after the bombings of Hiroshima and Nagasaki. She became an artist, attending the San Francisco Art Institute and publicly showing her watercolors at twenty. While she was training with fresco painter John Charlot, people referenced her Buddhist sensibility, noting that she inverted the perspective of depth taught in the West. Willis's curiosity took her to the University of Hawaii to study Far Asian art history and where she supported herself by airbrushing newspaper images.

In 1954, Charlot recommended her to design four military officers' clubs in Honolulu, one for each branch of the US defenses—Army, Navy, Air Force, and Marines—returning from combat. Willis created the artwork and commissioned the rest of the work, from exterior to interior design and landscaping. When she critiqued an architect's efforts one day, he challenged her to become an architect and do better. She did just that, learning on the job and opening Willis & Associates Architects in San Francisco in 1960. During thirty-five years of practice, Willis worked on eight hundred projects, thirteen of which are noted in the Library of Congress. Her career mirrors the advancement of architecture as a modern profession that grew from single practitioners designing residences to firms designing multiuse structures on multiblock sites.

Willis's conversion of Barbary Coast sex trade houses into showrooms, the Union Street Stores (1965), won the Governor's Award. "It was novel at the time, adapting new uses to old buildings," she said. That project helped forge the relatively young city's identity and character, even though the client's motivation was to save money and to avoid a parking ordinance for new buildings.

Just after the nation's Environmental Protection Act was introduced in 1969, builders developing huge parcels of land for suburbs routinely bulldozed hills in the Bay Area, causing great environmental trouble. Willis recognized the need for a surveying tool to assess large land parcels to glean what should be protected. Her firm developed CARLA (Computerized Approach to Residential Land Analysis) by converting software used for dropping bombs accurately. (Willis received her pilot's license at eighteen and was aware of the program.) CARLA identified and saved environmentally sensitive land across the United States, and Willis & Associates was contracted to write new environmental impact reports for the state of California.

Willis's architectural practice also prospered. She was elected to the College of Fellows of the AIA in 1980, while she

San Francisco Ballet Building,
1982. Courtesy Beverly Willis

Beverly Willis Architecture
Foundation logo, black.
Courtesy Beverly Willis

completed the quintessential San Francisco Ballet Building in 1984 and the Manhattan Village Academy High School in Greenwich Village a decade later. When the slumbering economy prohibited many new building projects in the late 1980s, Willis spent two years on the northeast coast writing *Invisible Images: The Silent Language of Architecture and the Selected Works of Beverly Willis*. While there, she was exposed to New York City's rich culture of design organizations. "My own thinking focused on the people who live inside and outside the buildings," she said, noting that there was not a good understanding of urbanism at the time. Willis's humanistic architecture organically led to more pedagogical endeavors designed to make cities livable. A month after 9/11, she founded Rebuild Downtown Our Town (RDOT), with Susan Szenasy of *Metropolis* magazine. They made proposals to support people living in Manhattan's Financial District, a few of which were realized.

"It was later in my life, after I began to have some distance from the daily work of making architecture, that I discovered women were not in the history books, and I set about to change that," says Willis. She created the Beverly Willis Architecture Foundation (BWAF) with four others in order to evaluate the place of individual women in history. It was 2002 and Willis was seventy-five years old.

In advance of the Guggenheim Museum's fiftieth anniversary, the BWAF created programming (as it had done for MoMA and the National Building Museum) related to Frank Lloyd Wright. When Willis began researching the topic of women in Wright's firm, she found scant footnotes and no historical studies. *A Girl Is a Fellow Here: 100 Women Architects in the Studio of Frank Lloyd Wright*, a fifteen-minute documentary honoring the one hundred unsung women who had worked at Wright's firm, was born of her tenacious efforts to uncover their contributions. She has since directed four more short films.

As a coalition of architecture and its allied disciplines, BWAF and its members reflect the reality of what was happening in the profession, in which many other design-related jobs impact architecture. "Part of what I bring to an organization is history," said Willis. "It's a matter of understanding how developments occur in a discipline. My knowledge is based on having lived through several changes." She concludes, "Architecture is a part of something that's bigger." What she doesn't say is that she helped make it so. —*JSE*

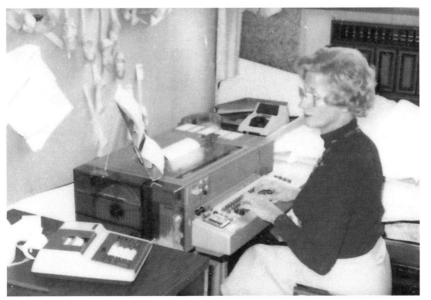

Above
Union Street renovation, San Francisco, CA, 1966. Courtesy Beverly Willis

Left
CARLA (Computerized Approach to Residential Land Analysis), Beverly Willis at paper tape punch machine, ca. 1970. Courtesy Beverly Willis

MARY OTIS STEVENS

BORN
New York, NY, 1928

EDUCATION
Smith College, BA, 1949; MIT, MArch, 1956

PRACTICE
The Architects Collaborative, 1956–57; Thomas McNulty Architects, cofounder, 1957–74; i Press Inc., cofounder, 1968–78; Architects for Social Responsibility, cofounder, 1973–2004; Design Guild, founder, 1975–92

NOTABLE HONORS
Fellowship, National Endowment for the Arts (NEA), 1975, 1976; NEA Grant; Blackstone Heritage State Park Visitor Center, Award for Excellence, AIA, 1990

Mary Otis Stevens grew up in rural Upstate New York, where a prevalence of Shaker culture influenced her later interest in New England vernacular. As a teenager, she attended Shipley boarding school in Pennsylvania, during which time she became active in the civil rights movement and adopted a vehement antiwar stance.

After earning a philosophy degree from Smith College, Stevens encountered Arthur Tuckerman's *The Five Orders of Architecture* (1891) and became determined to learn the architectural language she identified in its pages. Stevens took drafting lessons until she was encouraged by her instructor to pursue formal training at MIT. As a student, she lunched with Buckminster Fuller, a visiting lecturer, who happened to be a close family friend.

Upon graduating in 1956, Stevens earned a position working for Walter Gropius at The Architects Collaborative (TAC) but quickly became disillusioned with the culture of elitism. She left TAC after only four months and went on to cofound a studio with her then-husband, Thomas McNulty, an MIT faculty member. One of Stevens and McNulty's most important projects was the house they built for themselves and their three sons in Lincoln, Massachusetts (1965). Perhaps more remarkable than its novel use of exposed concrete and glass was the nonhierarchical, open layout predicated on the concepts of "movement and hesitation."[11] "Life is movement, flow," Stevens said. "And if life is about movement, then what is architecture? Architecture is setting the stage for movement."

In the late 1960s, Stevens, McNulty, and George Braziller founded i Press, which published a series of books focusing on the social, political, and economic dimensions of architecture. Stevens and McNulty's own work, *World of Variation* (1970), applies the framework of movement and hesitation to the scale of the city and proposes possible design solutions to the oppressive conditions of modern environments.

Later in her career, Stevens became a staunch advocate for a socially responsible architecture developed with input from the community. In 1975, Stevens founded Design Guild, an award-winning, Boston-based collaborative architecture practice dedicated to environmental, social, and historical sustainability. "There is no blank slate. One is never free from preconditions," remarks Stevens in a 1990 issue of *Design Spirit*. "What we're doing every day in our design work is dealing with the imperfect conditions we find and transforming them through the art of architecture."[12]

In 1975 and 1976, Stevens received two grants from the National Endowment for the Arts to study architectural traditions of early American settlers. She applied her knowledge in her design for the Wolf Trap performing arts center (early 1980s) in Vienna, Virginia, wherein two pre-Revolutionary barns—one German and the other English—were relocated from New York and joined together to form a music theater.

In 1990, Design Guild received an award for excellence in urban design from the AIA for the design of a visitor center for the Blackstone Heritage State Park. —*LFR*

Top
Lincoln House, Lincoln, MA,
Mary Otis Stevens and Thomas
McNulty, 1965. Mary Otis
Stevens and Thomas McNulty
Collection. Courtesy the
MIT Museum

Bottom
The Barns at Wolf Trap, Vienna,
VA, 1982. Mary Otis Stevens and
Thomas McNulty Collection.
Courtesy the MIT Museum

ALISON SMITHSON

BORN
Sheffield, England, 1928

DIED
London, England, 1993

EDUCATION
Durham University (now
Newcastle University), 1949

PRACTICE
London County Council School
Division, 1949–50; Alison and
Peter Smithson Architects,
1950–93

NOTABLE HONORS
Pioneer, New Brutalism and
Pop Art; Independent Group;
cofounder, Team 10

Alison Smithson enrolled at Durham University (now Newcastle University) to study architecture when she was only sixteen years old. In her final year at Durham, she married fellow student Peter Smithson. After graduating, the Smithsons briefly worked for the London County Council School Division before setting up their own practice.[13]

In 1950, the young couple gained prominence in architectural circles with their winning competition entry for a secondary school in Hunstanton, Norfolk.[14] Inspired by the Miesian school of modernism, their design's straightforward brick-and-glass facade and stripped interior with exposed infrastructure was described by Philip Johnson as a form of "anti-design."[15] Hunstanton School was the first building to be completed in the "new brutalist" style, a term Alison later coined in a 1953 issue of *Architectural Design* with reference to the "warehouse aesthetic" of her unbuilt Soho house.[16] The school was largely regarded as a critical success and touted as a stylistic declaration against the predominant new empiricism in architecture, even though it had many functional shortcomings.[17]

In collaboration with fellow Independent Group members Nigel Henderson and Eduardo Paolozzi, the Smithsons famously promulgated the aesthetic and ethical dimensions of new brutalism in the 1953 exhibition *Parallel of Life and Art* at the Institute of Contemporary Arts, London. By mounting a display of a hundred or so found photographs hung at random, the organizers strove to incite the viewer's unconscious, free-association skills rather than impose a set of didactics upon them.[18] For Alison and Peter, this "as found" approach declared that as with art, architecture could be the result of an act of choice rather than an act of design or authorship.

In 1956, the Smithsons displayed work in two historic exhibitions that marked the introduction of pop culture into art and architecture: *This Is Tomorrow* at Whitechapel Gallery and the *Daily Mail's Ideal Home Show*. For the latter, Alison conceived a House of the Future built from plastic and incorporating a system of automated housework.[19]

In 1953, the Smithsons began their seminal work with Team 10, which emerged out of the ninth Congrès International d'Architecture Moderne (CIAM) at Aix-en-Provence, France. Team 10 advocated for a popular approach to modernism, breaking down the barriers between the arts and the sciences and between high and low culture. With keen foresight, Alison played a critical role in documenting and disseminating the group's dialogues, frequently publishing her summaries in Monica Pidgeon's influential journal *Architectural Design*.[20] Several of Alison's major texts on the subject include *Team 10 Primer* (1964), *The Emergence of Team 10 out of CIAM* (1982), and *Team 10 Meetings: 1953–1984* (1991).

A handful of the Smithsons' designs were built, notably the Economist Cluster (1964) in Piccadilly in London, the Garden Building (1970) at St Hilda's College in Oxford, the Robin Hood Gardens housing estate (1972) in London, several buildings at the School of Architecture and Building Engineering, University of Bath (1988), and the Cantilever Chair Museum (2008) in Lauenförde, Germany. —*LFR*

Above
Robin Hood Gardens housing
estate, London, Alison and
Peter Smithson, 1972.
© Steve Cadmen

Right
Economist Cluster, Piccadilly,
London, Alison Smithson and
Peter Smithson, 1964. Photo a+t
research group

ASTRA ZARINA

BORN
Riga, Latvia, 1929

DIED
Civita, Italy, 2008

EDUCATION
University of Washington, BArch, 1953; MIT, MArch, 1955

PRACTICE
Paul Hayden Kirk, 1953; Yamasaki and Associates, 1955–57; Civita Institute, cofounder, 1981–2008

TEACHING
University of Washington, Architecture in Rome Program, 1970–84; University of Washington, 1984–2000; University of Washington, Rome Center, 1984–94

NOTABLE HONORS
First woman awarded Rome Prize in Architecture, American Academy in Rome, 1960; Fulbright Grant, Italy, 1960; Distinguished Teaching Award, University of Washington, 1979; Honorary Member, AIA Seattle, 1994

Born in 1929 in Riga, Latvia, Astra Zarina and her family immigrated to the United States shortly after World War II. In 1953, Zarina earned an architecture degree from the University of Washington, where she studied under Lionel Pries, Wendell Lovett, and Victor Steinbrueck. She briefly worked in the office of Paul Hayden Kirk before pursuing further architectural training at MIT. She subsequently worked in the Detroit office of Minoru Yamasaki, where she made significant contributions on such acclaimed projects as the Detroit College for Creative Studies (1957) and the First Methodist Church (1957) in Warren, Michigan. In a biography of the influential Japanese American architect, Zarina was described as "perhaps the most talented artist ever to work for Yamasaki."[21]

In 1960, Zarina became the first woman to be awarded the prestigious Rome Prize in Architecture by the American Academy in Rome, followed by a Fulbright grant that allowed her to continue her studies in Italy. During her time abroad, she worked on various restoration projects and designed several apartment towers in Mårkisches Viertel (1974), a large housing estate in West Berlin.[22]

She returned to Seattle and began lecturing at the University of Washington, where she collaborated with professor Tom Bosworth in founding the Architecture in Rome Program in 1970.[23] In recognition of the success of the programs and the cultural exchange they fostered, the University of Washington awarded Zarina with the Distinguished Teaching Award in 1979.[24]

In 1984, Zarina and her husband, Anthony Costa Heywood, expanded the study-abroad program into the Rome Center, a hub of multidisciplinary activity for University of Washington students and faculty. During the renovation of the Palazzo Pio, where the Rome Center was to be headquartered, Zarina helped discover and restore the remains of a medieval tower, which had been hidden behind the walls of the palazzo.

Undoubtedly the most significant project of Zarina's career was the restoration and revitalization of Civita di Bagnoregio, known as the "dying town" for its location on top of a crumbling hill of *tufa*, a soft volcanic rock.[25] Beginning in the late 1960s, Zarina and Heywood refurbished numerous buildings in Civita, including many homes for the families living there. In 1976, Zarina created the Italian Hilltowns summer residency as part of the Architecture in Rome Program, which later evolved into the Civita Institute, a Seattle-based organization dedicated to the preservation of the architecture, history, and culture of Italian hill towns through educational programs, residencies, and fellowships.[26] In 2006, the Civita Institute helped add Civita to the World Monuments Watch list of endangered sites and is currently working to earn Civita a place on the UNESCO World Heritage Site list.

In 1994, Professor Zarina was recognized for her many contributions to the field when she became an honorary member of AIA Seattle. She retired from teaching in 2000 and spent the remainder of her life in Civita. In 2019, renowned architect Steven Holl began construction in Civita on the Astra Zarina Belvedere, a public sculpture commemorating the life and work of his former professor.[27] —*LFR*

Above
Civita di Bagnoregio, Province of Viterbo, Italy, seventh century. Photo Paris Orlando

Right
Vicola delle Vaccha, Rome, Italy, pencil sketch, Astra Zarina, ca. 1970. The Civita Institute

VICOLO DELLE VACCHE

DENISE SCOTT BROWN

BORN
Nkana, Zambia, 1931

EDUCATION
University of Witwatersrand, BA, 1952; AA School of Architecture, 1955; University of Pennsylvania, Master of City Planning, 1960, MArch, 1965

PRACTICE
Venturi and Rauch, 1969–89; Venturi, Rauch and Scott Brown, 1980; Venturi, Scott Brown and Associates, 1989–2012

NOTABLE HONORS
Venturi, Rauch and Scott Brown, Firm Award, AIA, 1985; Distinguished Professor Award, Association of Collegiate Schools of Architecture, 1986–87; Vincent Scully Prize, National Building Museum, 2002; Athena Award, Congress for the New Urbanism, 2007; European Cultural Center Award, 2016; Gold Medal (with Robert Venturi), AIA, 2016; Jane Drew Prize, 2017; Sainsbury Wing, National Gallery of London, Twenty-five Year Award, AIA, 2019

Denise Scott Brown, recognized as one of the most influential architects of the twentieth century, in partnership with her husband, Robert Venturi, was born Denise Lakofski in Nkana, Zambia. She says that her earliest memory is of looking at blueprints for an early modern house her parents were building. Her mother had studied architecture and her father was a developer, providing Scott Brown insight into the field from a young age. Her upbringing in Johannesburg, South Africa, amid vibrant multiculturalism, despite racial segregation, later informed her approach to urban design and her theories about architectural postmodernism. She views herself as having one foot in architecture and one in urban planning, a difficult balance, she has learned.

After studying at Johannesburg's University of Witwatersrand, she traveled to London to work for modernist architect Frederick Gibberd, also pursuing a graduate degree at the AA School of Architecture. Scott Brown found it challenging to be away from home and to be one of only five women in a class of sixty-five. She gained encouragement from Arthur Korn, an architect and professor at the school, who mentored her and shared his wealth of knowledge on topics like the November Group, the German expressionist artists and architects.

Scott Brown graduated from the AA in 1955, the same year she married Robert Scott Brown, whom she had met at Witwatersrand. In 1958, the couple moved to Philadelphia to study at the University of Pennsylvania's planning department. Within the year, Robert Scott Brown died in a car accident. Denise, nevertheless,

completed her master's degree and joined the faculty following graduation. She even completed an additional master's degree in architecture while teaching.

When, in 1960, the University of Pennsylvania was considering demolishing the 1891 Library of Fine Arts by Frank Furness, Scott Brown protested. "It's what a modernist would do, you see," Scott Brown told the podcast *99% Invisible* in 2018. At her first Penn faculty meeting, she decided to speak up in support of preserving the library, convincing the rest of the faculty to vote for the same. After the meeting, a fellow faculty member and architect, Robert Venturi, introduced himself to her, saying that he agreed with everything she had said. Soon after, they began teaching classes together at Penn (from 1962 to 1964).

In 1965, Scott Brown accepted a teaching position at the University of California, Berkeley. Within months, she was named cochair of the Urban Design Program at UCLA where she became fascinated with the unique architecture and urbanism of Los Angeles and Las Vegas. In 1966, she invited Venturi to visit Las Vegas with her. He was equally intrigued. Scott Brown and Venturi married in Santa Monica in 1967, returning to Philadelphia to work together in Venturi's firm, Venturi and Rauch. Scott Brown became principal in charge of planning in 1969.

"I joined the firm first for no money at all," she said in the 2019 author's interview. "Then they thought I was bringing in money, because of [projects like] the South Street Project. They made me a partner in 1969." The South Street Project incorporated a new housing plan for the traditionally African American neighborhood

Venturi, Scott Brown and
Associates project montage
by Jeremy Tenenbaum, 2006.
Courtesy Venturi, Scott Brown
and Associates

National Gallery of London, Sainsbury Wing, London, Venturi, Scott Brown and Associates, 1991. Courtesy Venturi, Scott Brown and Associates

in Philadelphia, thwarting the city's plan for a new expressway that would have decimated the area. The expressway proposal was defeated a few years later.

Scott Brown published *Learning from Las Vegas: The Forgotten Symbolism of Architectural Form* with Venturi and Steven Izenour in 1972, incorporating student studies of the Las Vegas Strip from an architectural research studio. It was a counterpoint (and rebuke) to orthodox modernism and architectural elitism, touting the value of vernacular architecture and American sprawl.

In 1989, the firm was renamed Venturi, Scott Brown and Associates. The same year, Scott Brown published her essay "Room at the Top? Sexism and the Star System in Architecture," articulating the challenges she faced in being recognized as an equal partner of the firm in a male-dominated profession.

Punctuating this point, in 1991, Venturi was named winner of the Pritzker Prize. Scott Brown protested his singular limelight by not attending the ceremony. The fire continued.

In 2013, Harvard architecture graduate students started a petition to have Scott Brown recognized by the Pritzker Prize, ultimately signed by more than twenty thousand supporters. Although the prize was never amended, Scott Brown remarked, "The petition is my prize, and it's better than the Pritzker." In 2016, the AIA awarded both Venturi and Scott Brown their Gold Medal, the association's highest honor. —*KF*

Allen Memorial Art Museum,
Oberlin College, Oberlin,
OH, Venturi, Scott Brown and
Associates, 1977. Photo Tom
Bernard. Courtesy Venturi,
Scott Brown and Associates

PHYLLIS BIRKBY

BORN
Nutley, NJ, 1932

DIED
Great Barrington, MA, 1994

EDUCATION
Cooper Union, School of
Architecture, 1963; Yale
University, MArch, 1966

PRACTICE
Henry L. Horowitz, 1960–61;
Seth Hiller, 1961–63; Davis
Brody and Associates,
1966–72; Dober, Paddock &
Upton, 1973; Gary Scherquist
and Roland Tso, late 1970s;
Gruzen Partnership and Lloyd
Goldfarb, early 1980s

TEACHING
University of Detroit, Mercy
School of Architecture,
1968–73; Pratt Institute,
1974–78; City College of New
York, early 1970s; Southern
California Institute of
Architecture (SCI-Arc), late
1970s; New York Institute of
Technology, 1980s

NOTABLE HONORS
Key figure of New York City's
women's movement, 1970s;
cofounder, Women's School
of Planning and Architecture
(WSPA), 1974

After being dissuaded from pursuing architecture by her high school career counselors, who explained it was a profession for men, Noel Phyllis Birkby opted for an education in the fine arts. In 1950, she enrolled in the Women's College of the University of North Carolina, where she earned a reputation as a troublemaker. During her senior year, shortly after having openly expressed her affection toward a female classmate, Birbky was expelled.

While working administrative positions in the New York offices of the architects Henry L. Horowitz and Seth Hiller, she took evening classes at Cooper Union, earning a certificate in architecture. She later pursued a master's degree at the Yale University School of Architecture under the deanships of Paul Rudolph and Charles Moore. She graduated in 1966, one of six women in a class of two hundred. Subsequently, Birkby worked as a senior designer at Davis Brody and Associates, where she contributed to such notable projects as the Waterside Plaza (1974), a residential development on the Hudson River, and the Long Island University Library-Learning Center in Brooklyn.

In the early 1970s, Birkby became active in the women's liberation movement, adopting a lesbian feminist stance. Feeling as though her politics and principles no longer aligned with her professional life, Birkby left Davis Brody and established her own architectural practice in 1972. In collaboration with various firms and organizations, Birkby assisted in the designs for low-income housing units, the conversion of facilities for the disabled, and a number of other community residences, including halfway houses and women's communes.[28]

Birkby also helped found the Alliance of Women in Architecture and became involved in the lesbian consciousness-raising group known as CR One.[29]

In addition to her significant roles participating in and documenting the lesbian feminist culture in New York, Birkby fought to create a more diverse field through an architecture for and by women. In 1973, she collaborated with Leslie Kanes Weisman on a series of environmental fantasy workshops aimed at exploring "whether women have unique sensibilities that they bring to the process of designing their own environments."[30] The workshops invited women to abandon preconceptions from the male-dominated discipline in designing their ideal homes.

Birkby and Weisman later integrated these workshops into the curriculum at the WSPA, which they cofounded in 1974, alongside Katrin Adam, Ellen Perry Berkeley, Bobbie Sue Hood, Marie I. Kennedy, and Joan Forrester Sprague.[31] The WSPA's educational model was based on the concepts of nonhierarchical organization, consensus-based decision-making, and criticism of the patriarchal "star system" in architecture.[32] Birkby continued her research into the possibilities for a vernacular of women's architecture—which she called "herspace"—occasionally publishing her findings in the feminist magazine *Heresies*.

In 1994, at the age of sixty-two, Birkby died of breast cancer.[33] The Sophia Smith Collection commemorated Birkby's contributions in the 1997 exhibition *Amazonian Activity: The Life and Work of Noel Phyllis Birkby, 1932–94.* —*LFR*

Above
Waterside Plaza, New York, NY,
Phyllis Birkby for Davis, Brody &
Associates, 1974. Courtesy Davis
Brody Bond

Right
Women's School of Planning and
Architecture participants forming
the female symbol, 1975. Phyllis
Birkby Papers, Sophia Smith
Collection, Smith College

JUDITH CHAFEE

BORN
Chicago, IL, 1932

DIED
Tucson, AZ, 1998

EDUCATION
Bennington College, 1954; Yale
University, MArch, 1960

PRACTICE
Paul Rudolph, 1961–62; The
Architects Collaborative,
1962–63; Eero Saarinen,
1963–65; Edward Larrabee
Barnes, 1965–69; Judith
Chafee, Architect, 1965–98

NOTABLE HONORS
Yale University Fellowship
Award for Hospital Design,
1959; Excellence for House
Design, *Architectural Record*,
1970; Burlington House
Award, 1975; Excellence for
Design, *Architectural Record*,
1975; American Academy in
Rome Fellowship, National
Endowment for the Arts,
1977; Housing Award, AIA,
1978; Excellence in Concrete
Construction Awards,
American Concrete Institute,
1978; Tucson-Pima County
Historical Commission, 1978;
Fellow (first woman in Arizona),
AIA, 1983; Most Unique Use of
Concrete, American Concrete
Institute, 1984; renovation
of Ramsey Canyon Preserve,
AR, Nature Conservancy,
1986; Mortar Board Citation,
University of Arizona, 1988

Friends recalled in a 2016 film documentary about the life of Judith Chafee, "She smoked, drank, cursed, and built houses." Most of her designs were residential, although she won an award for a hospital design in 1959 during her time as a student at Yale University—the only woman in her class. Because the award ceremony was held in a men's club, she had to enter through the kitchen.

Born in 1932, Chafee came into the world four months after the death of her father, Dr. Percy Bernard Davidson. Her mother, Christina Affeld, newly widowed, returned to her home town of Chicago and remarried; the family moved to Tucson when Chafee was five. The adobe house that her family occupied inspired the path of young Chafee's career. Her mother's circle of friends in Arizona included Planned Parenthood founder Margaret Sanger, Eleanor Roosevelt, and Frank Lloyd Wright.

Chafee returned to Chicago for prep school at the Francis W. Parker School, majoring in visual arts. She attended Bennington College, again studying visual arts, and graduated in 1954. At Yale, she studied under Paul Rudolph, earning both bachelor's and master's degrees in architecture and graduating in 1960.

After completing her academic education, Chafee practiced for a decade in the Northeast with such preeminent modernists as Walter Gropius, Sarah Harkness, and Ben Thompson at TAC; Eero Saarinen; Edward Larrabee Barnes; and Paul Rudolph. Even working in the company of these rarefied artists, Chafee remained humble, telling *Mademoiselle* magazine in 1966, "As architects, our chief concern must not just be the relationship between buildings, but also the relationship between buildings and people."

In 1970, Chafee designed the Ruth Merrill residence in Guilford, Connecticut, which landed her the cover of *Architectural Record* for the coveted Record Houses edition. But even with her acclaim in the Northeast, Chafee felt a strong pull from the Southwest that was too strong to resist. She started her own private practice in Arizona that same year, purchasing several connected buildings in Tucson's historic downtown, now known as the Presidio neighborhood, where she lived for a time and housed her practice for the remainder of her life.

Chafee's work in Tucson combined an interest in Sonoran desert landscapes and endemic materials. Her first freestanding-house design was the Viewpoint Residence (1972), designed for her mother and stepfather, located on a four-acre desert site on the west side of the city. Chafee's Tucson work, as exhibited at Viewpoint, embodied environmental adaptation, a strong sense of place, and sensitivity to positioning of light.

"Chafee's work shows this influence of place and character—a kind of severe modernism that somehow roots itself in the forms and ideas of prehistoric Native American designs," wrote Christopher Domin for the Tucson Historic Preservation Foundation.

While Chafee never secured major public commissions during her career—scholars speculate that this was due to an attitude that was perceived as obstinate by potential clients, or simply gender bias—her residential projects in Tucson, including the Ramada House (1975), the Jacobson House (1975), the Finkel House

Ramada House, Tucson, AZ,
1975. Photo Bill Timmerman

Jacobson House, library stair, Tucson, AZ, 1975. Photo Bill Timmerman

(1984), and the Rieveschl House (1988), received recognition and acclaim. One controversial concrete design, the Blackwell House (1979), which Chafee described as the "least architecture possible" for its desert placement, was demolished during her lifetime, despite efforts by architectural students and faculty at the University of Arizona to save it.[34] The longtime smoker Chafee passed away of emphysema in 1998, months after the Blackwell House was demolished. —*KF*

Above
Centrum House, living room,
Tucson, AZ, 1983. Photo Bill
Timmerman

Right
Hydeman House,
Sonoita, AZ, 1982. Photo
Bill Timmerman

JOAN FORRESTER SPRAGUE

BORN
New York, NY, 1935

DIED
Cambridge, MA, 1998

EDUCATION
Cornell AAP, BArch, 1953;
Harvard University,
MEd, 1976

PRACTICE
Sprague Associates; Open
Design Office, cofounder,
1972–78; Women's School of
Planning and Architecture,
cofounder, 1974–78; Women's
Development Corporation,
cofounder, 1979; Women's
Institute for Housing and
Economic Development,
cofounder, 1981–88

NOTABLE HONORS
Woman of the Year Award,
Boston Business and
Professional Women, 1987;
Abigail Adams Award,
Massachusetts Women's
Political Caucus, 1988; *More
than Housing: Lifeboats
for Women and Children*,
International Book Award,
AIA, 1991

After receiving her bachelor's degree in architecture from Cornell University College of Architecture, Art, and Planning (Cornell AAP) in 1953, Joan Forrester Sprague designed furniture and worked as a consultant to a number of large design firms in the Boston area.[35] One of her designs was the Butcherboard Table (1953) commissioned by Benjamin Thompson's interior furnishing company Design Research.[36] In 1957, she married Chester Sprague, a professor of architecture at MIT, with whom she worked as a partner in Sprague Associates.[37] After nearly twenty years of working for other firms, Sprague grew frustrated by the limited opportunities afforded to her and went on to pioneer a handful of alternative architectural businesses.

In 1972, Sprague cofounded the Open Design Office (ODO), a nonhierarchical practice of women architects and planners. The ODO attempted to establish a viable business model for a feminist architectural studio predicated upon consensus-based decision-making, flexible work schedules, and equal distribution of both design and administrative responsibilities.[38] In a *New York Times* article from 1975, Sprague said, "The rule until now has been that if you don't make it as a designer in architecture, you've failed. To admit you can handle financial problems or comprehend the meaning of a contract is to admit you aren't a good designer. We don't agree."[39] In addition to challenging the star system that pervaded most architectural offices—a model that was regarded as quintessentially patriarchal—the ODO resisted profit motives and used any surplus to support research or community projects.[40]

Sprague also played an instrumental role in the formation of the WSPA, an experiment in feminist education that explored a collective model similar to the ODO.[41] From 1974 to 1978, the WSPA promoted consciousness and skill development in architecture, offering training and collaborations with grassroots women's movements.[42]

By the late 1970s, the economic crisis was in full effect, forcing the ODO to cease operations and the WSPA to lose enrollment. Sprague continued the visionary work she had begun with these organizations by cofounding the Providence-based Women's Development Corporation in 1979 and the Boston-based Women's Institute for Housing and Economic Development in 1981—both of which still exist today.[43]

Founded alongside Katrin Adam and Susan Aitcheson, the Women's Development Corporation (WDC) practiced community investment and participatory design, empowering their clients to take an active role in shaping and maintaining their own environments. The WDC's earlier projects focused on the adaptive reuse of abandoned historic properties, transforming them from housing largely built for nuclear families into cooperatively owned housing built around communal living, which created opportunities for shared household responsibilities, such as childcare and cooking.[44] The company later focused its efforts toward real estate management, development, and fundraising and diversified its target groups to include the elderly, disabled, homeless, and other marginal groups.[45]

Sprague was also the author of a handful of books and manuals addressing the

WOMEN SINGLE HEAD of HOUSEHOLD
IF YOU ARE INTERESTED IN
BETTER HOUSING & MAINTAINING HOUSING
COME TO A MEETING

at WEST END COMMUNITY CENTER
109 BUCKLIN AVE
TUESDAY JUNE 10
day - 12:30pm or evening - 7:00 pm
FREE CHILDCARE & TRANSPORTATION-CALL & REGISTER
•WOMEN'S DEVELOPMENT CORPORATION •
• 104 PRINCETON AVE • 751-4088 •

problem of homelessness and the lack of affordable housing for low-income women and children. Her book *More than Housing: Lifeboats for Women and Children* (1991), which received a Citation of Excellence from the AIA's International Book Awards, functions as a catalog of affordable housing prototypes called "lifeboats" and promotes communal living as a means of countering women's poverty issues.

For her outstanding work improving the lives of thousands of individuals and for empowering women both within and outside the profession to become part of

the design process, Sprague was awarded with the Woman of the Year Award from Boston Business and Professional Women in 1987 and the Massachusetts Women's Political Caucus's Abigail Adams Award in 1988. —*LFR*

Women's Development Corporation meeting notice for single mothers, "Better Housing & Maintaining Housing," n.d. Courtesy Schlesinger Library, Radcliffe Institute, Harvard University

ADA KARMI-MELAMEDE

BORN
Tel Aviv, Israel, 1936

EDUCATION
AA School of Architecture, 1959; Technion Israel Institute of Technology, BArch, 1963

PRACTICE
Dov Karmi Associates, 1962–65; Mitchell Giurgola Architects, 1967–69; Karmi Associates, 1984–92; Ada Karmi-Melamede Architects, 1992

TEACHING
Columbia GSAPP, adjunct professor, 1967–84

NOTABLE HONORS
Sandberg Prize for Israeli Art, Grant Research in Art and Architecture, 1985; Association of Architects and Engineers in Israel Award, 1998; Excellence in Architecture Award, Hadassah's Women of Distinction, 2000; Israel Prize for Architecture, 2007

Israeli architect Ada Karmi-Melamede asks herself many of the same questions at the beginning of each project. Her thought process is influenced by four principles: the architectural concept is in the space (especially the public space), the logic is in the structure, the tactility is in materials, and the mood is in the light.

It is this last element that ignites the design process for Karmi-Melamede: "The white sun is very harsh here in Israel, and you need to harness and tame it. I work to bring the light into spaces indirectly, and I look for ways to channel the light so it ricochets until it becomes soft and awakens the materials. Light can change the spacing and mood of the same sequence of built elements, just as in spoken language pacing and tone can change the meaning of the same sequence of words."[46] Her perspective results in enduring buildings that can appear carved rather than constructed.

Karmi-Melamede and her brother, Ram Karmi, designed the Supreme Court Building (1993) in Jerusalem, Israel, winning an international competition that revealed their diverse form-making languages. Karmi was into new brutalism while Karmi-Melamede favored modernism. The project's extraordinary jury included Charles Moore, Cesar Pelli, and philosopher Isaiah Berlin, among others. Karmi-Melamede especially appreciated Berlin's understanding of architecture's value extending far beyond function. "It's not what is quantified but also what is not quantified that's important," said Karmi-Melamede. "Architecture should address human needs that don't have a name."

During the construction of a recent project, the Wailing Wall Heritage Center, Roman and Jewish artifacts from more than two thousand years ago were unearthed. In response, she designed the building as a floating steel structure, allowing the public to descend and view the archaeological discovery below. "Buildings without a memory are uninteresting, like people," she said. "In Jerusalem, there's always been someone there before. Antiquities are everywhere."

Karmi-Melamede enjoys the collaborative nature of the profession, which she treasured while teaching at Columbia. "My teaching experience was my best education," she said. "The students inspired me to think more broadly about architecture." In recent years, she has found herself working closely with landscape architects. Her Ramat Hanadiv Visiting Center (2008) is Israel's first certified Green Building. The structure provides an entry to the Rothschild family memorial gardens, dating from the 1950s, creating a long and gentle edge covered in greenery. The center has become an integral part of the gardens even though they were built at different times.

Predicting an end to the demand for glass towers, Karmi-Melamede said, "Don't give up the idea that building is textile… When glass buildings take over the urban landscape, we lose the opportunity to express our sense of identity, of self, and of community." —*JSE*

Above
Supreme Court Building,
Jerusalem, Israel, Ada Karmi-
Melamede with Ram Karmi, 1993.
Photo Richard Bryant

Right
Ramat Hanadiv Visiting Center,
Zikhron Ya'akov, Israel, 2008.
Photo Amit Giron

SUSAN JANE "SU" ROGERS

BORN
London, England, 1939

EDUCATION
London School of Economics,
BS, Sociology, ca. 1960; Yale
University, BArch, 1963

PRACTICE
Team 4, 1963–67; Richard + Su
Rogers, 1967–72; Colquhoun,
Miller and Partners (later John
Miller + Partners), 1986–2011

TEACHING
AA School of Architecture,
1972; Royal College of Art,
1972–86; visiting professor
at University of Cambridge,
Columbia GSAPP, University
College Dublin, and University
of Toronto

NOTABLE HONORS
Royal Scottish Academy
renovation (with John Miller),
international competition, 1999

Susan Jane "Su" Rogers was born in 1939 to Marcus and Irene Brumwell. Marcus, a British advertising pioneer, designer, businessman, and political activist, was also the managing director of Stuart Advertising Agency and later founded Design Research Unit, one of the first generation of British design consultancies that combined expertise in architecture, graphics, and industrial design. Su Rogers attended Frensham Heights School, continuing on to earn a degree in sociology at the London School of Economics (LSE). She met architect Richard Rogers at the LSE, and they married in 1960, having three sons together.

Su decided to pursue a degree in architecture at Yale University, which she completed in 1963, when she and Richard started an architectural practice with two other partners, Norman Foster and Wendy Cheesman (Foster), calling it Team 4. One of the firm's first projects was Creek Vean, a new house in Feock, Cornwall, for Su's parents. The modernist structure was made of concrete blocks and situated on a steep hillside overlooking Fal Estuary. Another early commission, a 120-unit housing development called the Water Homes at Coulsdon, Surrey, Richard later said was "probably the most important project of our Team 4 period."

Team 4 dissolved in 1967, with Richard and Su founding an eponymous firm of their own. Their design of the conceptual Zip-Up House, conceived for a House of Today competition sponsored by the DuPont chemical company, was featured in the 1969 Ideal Home Exhibition, London. The design was for a factory-built house, quick to assemble, with relatively inexpensive insulation panels used on refrigeration trucks. The goal was rapid construction at a low cost. Its design later inspired a commission given to Richard and Su by Richard's parents at 22 Parkside in Wimbledon, London.

In 1971, the Rogerses' firm joined forces with Renzo Piano to design the Centre Georges Pompidou in Paris, a mixed-use structure that now houses the Public Information Library, the Musée National d'Art Moderne, and IRCAM, a center for music and acoustic research. In 1972, Su left the partnership to work at London's AA and teach at the Royal College of Art until 1986. She and Richard divorced in the early 1970s.

Rogers married architect John Miller in 1985, becoming a partner in the firm Colquhoun, Miller and Partners the following year. This firm specialized in designs for universities, affordable housing, and art galleries. (It became John Miller + Partners in 1990.)

In 1999, the firm won an international competition to design a refurbishment of the Royal Scottish Academy, which included additional exhibition space and a lecture theater and education suite. In 2001, they redeveloped the Tate Britain, referred to as the Centenary Development, which provided improved access and public amenities. In 2004, they completed the renovation of the Fitzwilliam Museum in Cambridge.

Rogers continued teaching throughout her design career. —*KF*

Above
Creek Vean House, Feock,
Cornwall, England, Su Rogers
for John Miller + Partners,
2010. Photo James O. Davies.
Courtesy Heritage Image
Partnership/Alamy Stock Photo

Right
Dr. Rogers House, Wimbledon,
England, Richard Rogers and Su
Rogers for Rogers Stirk Harbour
+ Partners, 1969. Photo Richard
Bryant/Arcaid Images

EVA JIŘIČNÁ

BORN
Zlin, Czechoslovakia (now
Czech Republic), 1939

EDUCATION
Technical University, BA, 1960;
Prague Academy of Fine Arts,
MA, 1962

PRACTICE
Greater London Council, 1968;
Louis de Soissons, 1969–80;
David Hodges, 1980–85; Jiřičná
Kerr Architects (now Eva
Jiřičná Architects), 1985–

TEACHING
Academy of Arts, Architecture
and Design, Prague, 1996–

NOTABLE HONORS
Royal Designer for Industry,
1991; Commander of the Order
of the British Empire, 1994;
RA Council, Royal Academy of
Arts, 1997; Honorary Doctorate,
University of Nottingham
and London Metropolitan
University, 2008; Jane
Drew Prize, 2013; Honorary
Doctorate, Royal College of
Art, 2013

Eva Jiřičná developed an early fondness for chemistry. Yet her love of the subject soured after a teacher discouraged her from pursuing it because she was a woman. "I just started thinking, 'What else can I do?'" she recalled.[47] At the time, she felt that her options were limited by the Communist regime. She knew about architecture because her father was an architect. She had always loved looking at buildings and learning about the history of architecture, but she never saw it as a viable option.

"It wasn't really something that I ever thought would be my profession, because I always thought, like everybody else, that it was a profession for a man," she said. When she told her family that she was planning on studying architecture at the university, her father speculated that she would end up as an architect's wife rather than an architect.

She first studied at Prague's Technical University before earning her MA in engineering and architecture at the Prague Academy of Fine Arts in 1962. All of her professors, she notes, were modernists, of the same generation as the Bauhaus. In 1965, she took part in a design competition in Paris, marking the first time she had crossed the Iron Curtain. This taste of Western freedom fueled her interest in leaving Czechoslovakia. In 1968, she moved to London to work as an architect for the Greater London Council, three weeks before Russia invaded her country. Because Jiřičná was not a member of the Communist party in Prague, she was told she could not return. "I had two little bags when I came to London, because I thought I would be back by Christmas," she says.

Her answer to this personal and political turmoil was to throw herself into her work. In 1969, she joined the Louis de Soissons Partnership and started work on Brighton Marina, a harbor, housing, and retail development in Brighton, England, completed in 1980. That same year also found Jiřičná forming her own practice with David Hodges.

Through an introduction to fashion designer Joseph Ettedgui, Jiřičná took on the project of designing several of the Joseph retail shops. Interior designs for Harrods and other department stores followed. Jiřičná had become known for her use of glass as a structural material, especially in staircases, first using it in a Joseph store to encourage people to go down to the basement. Her retail designs demonstrated that this commercial genre could be treated as architecture, with spaces maximized in a way that was innovative.

In 1985, she formed Jiřičná Kerr Architects with Kathy Kerr, which at this writing operates under the name Eva Jiřičná Architects. She was able to go back to Prague in 1989 and has been the head of the Department of Architecture at the University of Applied Arts in Prague since 1996.

"I have worked all my life on something I've loved doing," she says today. "I hope I have encouraged women in my profession."
—*KF*

Left
Cultural and University Centre,
Tomas Bata University, Zlín,
Czech Republic, Eva Jiřičná
Architects with A.I Design,
2008. Photo Ivan Nemec

Below
Canada Water Bus Station,
London, Eva Jiřičná Architects,
1998. Photo Peter Cook

SHARON E. SUTTON

BORN
Cincinnati, OH, 1941

EDUCATION
Manhattan School of Music,
1959; University of Hartford,
Hartt College of Music, BA,
1963; Parsons School of
Design, ca. 1965; Columbia
GSAPP, MArch, 1973; City
University of New York (CUNY),
PhD, Psychology, 1982

TEACHING
Brooklyn public school,
1973; University of Michigan,
Taubman College of
Architecture; University of
Washington, 1998–2016;
Parsons School of Design,
2019; The New School, 2019

NOTABLE HONORS
Fellow, AIA, 1995; ASCA
Distinguished Professor Award,
1995–96; Life Recognition
Award, Michigan Women's
Hall of Fame, 1997; Whitney
M. Young Jr. Award, AIA, 2011;
Medal of Honor, AIA Seattle,
2014; Medal of Honor, AIA New
York, 2017

Dr. Sharon Egretta Sutton's most ambitious project may be her ongoing interrogation of the practice of architecture. In an article for *Progressive Architecture* in 1992, she argued that the profession was exclusionary for recognizing only licensed practitioners and denigrating the contributions of everyone else, represented (in part) by interior designers, landscape architects, teachers, and scholars, a fact she sees as unrealistic and unjust, and which holds back the field, its adherents, and those it serves. In contrast, as Sutton states, "many licensed architects, for instance, are horrible teachers."[48] In her view, the future of the four-hundred-plus-year-old architecture profession depends on a realignment of values, a construction of a vision that's inviting, egalitarian, and hopeful. Her professional efforts claim two goals: helping people help themselves and amplifying the voices of disenfranchised communities.

Sutton describes her path as being shaped by her personal and political views "plus a lot of serendipity." She believes in actively giving back the gifts she received along the way. Her background as a child growing up in Appalachia was worlds away from the Broadway stage, where she played the French horn in the original cast of *Man from La Mancha*, after being chosen to study music at the Manhattan School of Music at age eighteen. A subsequent exploration of interior design at Parsons School of Design positioned her to receive an affirmative action scholarship to study architecture at Columbia University, at a time when the school was being protested for its lack of diversity. Sutton's 2017 book *When Ivory Towers Were Black: A Story about Race in America's Cities and Universities* describes

that experience. At Columbia, her mentor was Max Bond Jr., in whose firm she later worked.

Graduating in 1973, during the Arab oil embargo, meant that architecture jobs were scarce. She turned to teaching underserved children at a Brooklyn school while earning a PhD in psychology. As the first female African American full professor of architecture at an accredited institution, the University of Michigan, she expanded her doctoral work to found a national outreach program for K–8 teachers, helping them to engage their students in design activities.

In 1995, she became the second African American woman to attain an AIA Fellowship. Sutton's next academic post, at the University of Washington (1998–2016), centered on her research about teenagers' placemaking efforts.

She was among a few architects to receive a Kellogg Foundation fellowship, equipping her to work across disciplines on social justice issues, solidifying her commitment to "encouraging design for everyone, including the most disenfranchised."

Moving back to New York City in 2016, Sutton participated in the 2018 Center for Architecture panel discussion, "Unsung Protagonists: The Power of Women in 21st Century Architecture." When the moderator asked her all-female respondents whether it was necessary to call out one's gender by way of identification or whether they consider themselves part of "one big design community," Sutton answered, "Men's leadership is validated by the patriarchy; women's leadership is validated by themselves and their conversations, by their awareness of their position in society. We need to set ourselves apart *because we're*

Urban Youth Programs in America

A STUDY OF YOUTH, COMMUNITY, AND SOCIAL JUSTICE
CONDUCTED FOR THE FORD FOUNDATION

Sharon E. Sutton in collaboration with
Susan P. Kemp, Lorraine Gutiérrez, and Susan Saegert

set apart. It's different to be in the margins than to be at the center. It requires a different strategy."

Currently, Sutton is an ethnographic consultant to design studio instructors at Parsons School of Design and the New School. She is also writing a book on youth activism: "It's about young people developing tolerance in a socially disabled country, about using placemaking to negotiate

a shared vision," she says. The kids she profiles live in Michigan, Hawaii, and New York, all in a "state of emergency," where they're hard at work transforming their own circumstances. Their storyteller, an accomplished architect, artist, professor, and musician, knows a thing or two about that. —*JSE*

Urban Youth Programs in America: A Study of Youth, Community, and Social Justice, by Sharon E. Sutton, with Susan P. Kemp, Lorraine Gutiérrez, and Susan Saegert, 2006

YASMEEN LARI

BORN
Dera Ghazi Khan, Pakistan, 1941

EDUCATION
Oxford School of Architecture (now Oxford Brookes University), 1963

PRACTICE
Lari Associates, 1964–2000; Heritage Foundation of Pakistan, 1980–

NOTABLE HONORS
President, Institute of Architects Pakistan, 1978; cofounder, Heritage Foundation of Pakistan, 1980; Chair, Pakistan Council of Architects and Town Planners, 1983; United Nations Recognition Award, 2002; Pakistan Star of Distinction, 2006; Pakistan Crescent of Distinction, 2014; Fukuoka Prize, 2016; World Heritage Makli Trophy, 2018; Jane Drew Prize, 2020

Architects often begin their careers with a small project like a parent's house, ramping up gradually in scale and complexity. Yasmeen Lari's path as the first woman architect in Pakistan followed a different trajectory. She became a member of the Royal Institute of British Architects in 1969; president of the Institute of Architects Pakistan in 1978; and the first chairperson of Pakistan Council of Architects and Town Planners (PCATP) in 1983. She distilled the lessons learned from designing her celebrated brutalist buildings over three decades into a single powerful belief: architecture's primary role is to instill pride and dignity in its users.

Lari's gurus are Vesuvius ("for line") and Hassan Fathi ("for earth"). They aptly speak to her transition from designing expensive buildings, like the multistory Finance and Trade Centre (1989) and Pakistan State Oil House (1991), both in Karachi, to creating homes made of bamboo, mud, and lime in the country's rural provinces. Lari's fundamental philosophy as a good designer is to help people. "Things must be well put together," she says.[49]

In 1980, Lari cofounded the Heritage Foundation of Pakistan with her husband, historian Suhail Zahar Lari. The UNESCO-supported conservation organization combines architecture and social justice, with a focus on training people to value and safeguard Pakistan's cultural heritage. The conservation work and Lari's humanitarian efforts inform one another, with native building techniques aiding in the preservation of religious structures, and traditional Pakistani arts, like tile-making, being taught to villagers.

The big idea is to train people to build their own houses so that they can, in turn, train others. Since the devastating 2005 earthquake in Northern Pakistan that killed eighty thousand people, more than forty thousand of Lari's mud, lime, and bamboo homes have been housing families in safe structures that survive regular flooding. Circular, elevated bamboo community centers provide social services and also offer higher ground when needed.

"Doing this with very little money is the only way to grow," says Lari. "There's so much corruption in the country that money never reaches the poor. Too many architects are working for the 1 percent. We need more working for the 99 percent." An especially impressive example of Lari using design to give people dignity and pride is her development of a smokeless stove called the Pakistan Chali. Lari designed an earthenware vessel that burns biowaste and placed it up onto a platform away from frequent flooding. To her astonishment, that consequential elevation also raised these women's status in their communities because they no longer sit on the floor. There are sixty thousand of these critical innovations in use.

Lari is also focused on housing for the mendicant community in Makli, a UNESCO-recognized necropolis spanning 6.2 miles with more than five hundred thousand tombs dating from the fourteenth through the eighteenth centuries. Thanks to her dwellings there, and in other areas, that are constructed from the simplest materials, Pakistan can now claim the world's largest zero-carbon shelter program. Lari's books include *The Dual City: Karachi During the Raj.* —*JSE*

Right
A decorated chulah stove,
Pakistan. Courtesy Heritage
Foundation of Pakistan

Below
Zero Carbon Cultural
Centre, Makli, Pakistan,
2019. Courtesy Heritage
Foundation of Pakistan

MIMI LOBELL

BORN
Champaign-Urbana, IL, 1942

DIED
New York, NY, 2001

EDUCATION
Middlebury College, 1961;
University of Pennsylvania, BA,
1963, MA, 1966

PRACTICE
Kahn and Jacobs; Marcel
Breuer; Johansen & Bhavnani;
Mimi Lobell Studio

TEACHING
Pratt Institute, 1972–2001

NOTABLE HONORS
Cofounder (with Regina
Goldberg Weile), Alliance
of Women in Architecture,
Architectural League, 1972–85;
cofounder, Archive of Women
in Architecture, 1973; Board,
Architectural League of New
York, 1970–76; established
Myth & Symbol in Architecture
Study Center, Pratt Institute,
1980–2000; Advisory Board,
Sacred Sites International
Foundation 1998–2000

Architect, professor, author, mythologist, and spiritualist feminist, Mimi Lobell studied architecture at the University of Pennsylvania with some of the leading architects of her time, including Edmund Bacon, Denise Scott Brown, Robert Geddes, Romaldo Giurgola, Louis Kahn, Ian McHarg, and Robert Venturi.

At Penn, she married John Lobell, a fellow student. They moved to New York City, where she worked in the architectural offices of Kahn and Jacobs and also of Marcel Breuer. For Breuer, she worked on the brutalist Grand Coulee Dam's Third Power Plant (1974). When asked if she designed houses after telling someone that she was an architect, Lobell replied, "No, I am working on the Grand Coulee Dam Third Power Plant," the largest powerhouse at the dam.

An early pioneer of the pushing the role of women in architecture, Lobell was among the originators of the 1977 exhibit *Women in American Architecture* at the Brooklyn Museum. She also cofounded the Alliance of Women in Architecture (AWA) with Regi Goldberg Weille and the International Archive of Women in Architecture at Virginia Tech.

Through her coincident spiritual studies of Buddhism, the works of Carl Jung, and neolithic and ancient cultures, Lobell became interested in the spirituality of architecture. She described her widely published design, a contemporary Goddess Temple (1975), as spiritual feminism, rooted in ancient cultures and Jung's psychology.

She began teaching at Pratt's school of architecture in 1972, gaining tenure in 1983, the second woman to receive the full-time appointment. In her teaching and research, Lobell never stopped exploring, pursuing archaeoastronomy and playing the harp. She died after a short illness in 2001. Her students remember her as an important influence in their lives. —*JL*

Section

Left
Goddess Temple, design
sketch, 1975. Architectural
Archives, University of
Pennsylvania

Below
Third Power Plant, Grand
Coulee Dam, Grant/Okanogan
Counties, WA, design by Marcel
Breuer; project architect Mimi
Lobell, 1974. Courtesy US
Department of Energy, Energy
Technology Visuals Collection

MERRILL ELAM

BORN
Nashville, TN, 1943

EDUCATION
Georgia Institute of
Technology, BArch, 1971;
Georgia State University,
MBA, 1982

PRACTICE
Mack Scogin Merrill Elam
Architects, 1984–

TEACHING
Harvard GSD, 1993; University
of Illinois at Chicago, 1994;
Yale University, 1996;
University of Texas at Austin,
2003; University of Toronto,
2005; City College of New
York, 2006; UVA, 2010; SCI-
Arc, 2014; Georgia Institute of
Technology, 2015

NOTABLE HONORS
National Design Award,
Architecture, Cooper Hewitt
2012; Silver Medal Award,
AIA Atlanta, 2012; Shutze
Medal, Georgia Institute of
Technology, 2013; Women in
Architecture, *Architectural
Record*, 2014; Design
Excellence Award, University
of Florida, 2015; Distinguished
Leadership Award, Connecticut
Architecture Foundation, 2017;
National Academician, National
Academy of Design, 2018;
Resident, American Academy
in Rome, 2020

Growing up in a small Georgia town with a father who was a tinkerer, Merrill Elam learned how to nail and saw and pull a wall together at an early age. Her mother saved a childhood drawing she made of looking down the train tracks before she was familiar with the word *perspective*. As a teenager, she reconfigured sewing patterns to invent other clothing designs, foreshadowing the practice of translating two-dimensional drawings into three-dimensional objects, which characterized her career as an architect of buildings.

Merrill remembers watching Edward R. Murrow interview Frank Lloyd Wright on a black-and-white television in the 1950s, when she was a child, and finding it interesting. She also recalls attending the presentation of a beleaguered local architect on career day at school; he advised the students not to enter the field. Instead, Merrill chose architecture school so that she could earn a college degree, and was among the two women in her group at Georgia Institute of Technology. "No one ever said to me, 'You can't be an architect.' But if the men hadn't been nice, or if we weren't mutually interested," she says, "I wouldn't have made it."[50] A number of Merrill's enlightened instructors had studied at the Bauhaus and the École des Beaux-Arts.

Her first architecture job was for a firm that designed "simple industrial buildings that offered practical lessons like scoring concrete so it doesn't crack." Merrill and Mack Scogin, her partner of over forty years, opened their own firm in 1984. After decades of practice, she is still drawn to the uncertainty of how a project will ultimately take shape. "Architecture is complex and scale is always surprising," she reasons.

"I think you are greatly affected by the conditions and environment around you," Merrill says. "I'm not likely to put a large screened porch on a house, for example." For Merrill, the big question about the environment is how to advance the design dialogue. And she's found that it's likely through teaching: "I'm invigorated by the students. They often do something you would never expect that grew out of a conversation you had." Her visiting professorships include stints at Georgia Tech, SCI-Arc, University of Virginia (UVA), City College of New York, University of Toronto, Ohio State University, University of Texas at Austin, Yale University, Harvard GSD, and the University of Illinois at Chicago.

As the architects for the new Gathering Place in Tulsa, Oklahoma, Mack Scogin Merrill Elam Architects (MSME) worked with landscape architect Michael Van Valkenburgh, who planned the park. MSME designed a lodge and a boathouse. Merrill values the fact that the buildings are completely open and free to the public. "Little shards of buildings that are extensions of the landscape," is how she sees their work there. She likes their incompleteness.

Another recently completed project brings three high-rise residential towers to Long Island City, New York. On the boards is a courthouse in Des Moines, Iowa, and the firm will soon create its first freestanding museum for a vibrant fellowship of artists called the Goat House, as part of the new MOCA Georgia facility. "There's always something different to dive into and try to understand, endless questions to be asked." —*JSE*

Left
Lulu Chow Wang Campus
Center, Wellesley College,
Wellesley, MA, Mack Scogin
Merrill Elam Architects, 2005.
Photo Timothy Hursley

Below
Ernie Davis Hall, Syracuse
University, Syracuse, NY, Mack
Scogin Merrill Elam Architects,
2010. Photo Timothy Hursley

REGINA GOLDBERG WEILE

BORN
New York, NY, 1943

EDUCATION
Pratt Institute, BA, 1966

PRACTICE
Philip Johnson, 1960s; Ulrich
Franzen & Associates, 1960s;
Regina Goldberg Weile,
1970s–2004

TEACHING
Cooper Union, adjunct
professor, 1975–2004

NOTABLE HONORS
Cofounder, Alliance of Women
in Architecture, Architectural
League, 1972–85; cofounder,
Archive of Women in
Architecture, 1973

Early in her career, Regina "Regi" Goldberg Weile hit a professional barrier. Her boss did not think there was any precedent for women architects supervising construction and refused to send her to the site of a project she designed. Weile began researching former and current female practitioners and focused on the dearth of published architectural projects by women, the underrepresentation of female students and faculty in architecture schools, a lack of awareness of women's historic contributions to architecture, the prejudices women faced at the individual and institutional levels, and the need for women to win more awards and competitions. Weile's efforts led to the formation of the Alliance of Women in Architecture (AWA) in 1972. Its first meeting was held on May 4, 1972, at the Architectural League of New York. It was among several women's professional organizations in architecture formed in the early 1970s that continued to support women in practice until the early 1990s.

Weile grew up in the Bronx and attended the High School of Music and Art in Manhattan, where she studied art and architectural history and learned drafting. She entered Pratt Institute in 1961, one of only a handful of female students. Sibyl Moholy-Nagy hired her as a research assistant and was an important role model. Similar to many women at the time, Weile wasn't able to articulate how her gender shaped her experiences in the mostly male environments of architectural school and practice until the emergence of the women's liberation movement.

Weile began teaching at Cooper Union in 1975, one of the first women hired. She was an important role model to both female and male students, who were rarely exposed to women in the profession. Like many adjunct teachers who had no pedagogical training, it took some time for her to develop as an educator. While students' reactions were mixed, she developed a loyal following from those who appreciated her theoretical rigor and her encouragement of developing ones own ideas.

Weile worked for Philip Johnson, Ulrich Franzen, and others before opening her own office in the mid- or late 1970. As a women-owned business, her firm was able to compete for projects from public clients, such as New York City's Metropolitan Transportation Authority (MTA). Her small practice took on a range of projects, from renovations and house designs to institutional and public works. She was an early pioneer of promoting accessible design, even before the Americans with Disabilities Act passed in 1990. In 2004, Weile retired from teaching and moved her practice to Long Island, New York. —*AJM*

NOVEMBER 16, 1972
VOLUME ONE   No: 2

Above
Cover of Alliance of Women in Architecture, *Newsletter* 1, no. 2 (November 16, 1972). Courtesy Regina Weile

Left
Forty-second Street A, C, E Subway Station ramp, New York, NY, Regina Goldberg Weile, ca. 1985. Photo Andrea J. Merrett

SUSANA TORRE

BORN
Puan, Buenos Aires, Argentina,
1944

EDUCATION
University of Buenos Aires,
School of Architecture, 1967;
Columbia GSAPP, MArch, 1968

PRACTICE
The Architectural Studio,
1978–85; WASA Architects and
Engineers, 1985–88; Susana
Torre Raymond Beeler and
Associates, 1988–90; Susana
Torre and Associates, 1990

TEACHING
SUNY, Old Westbury, New York,
assistant professor, 1972–76;
Columbia GSAPP, associate
professor, 1981–89; Barnard
College, 1982–85; Parsons
School of Design, Architecture
and Environmental Design,
1991–94; Cranbrook Academy
of Art

NOTABLE HONORS
Houses Award of Excellence,
Architectural Record, 1981,
1988; Fellowship, National
Endowment for the Arts, 1973,
1979, 1986, 1990; Fellowship,
National Endowment for the
Humanities, 1986, 2005; first
woman invited to design a
building in Columbus, Indiana,
1987; Fulbright Senior Scholar,
1990; Ailsa Mellon Bruce
Senior Fellow, National
Gallery, 2003; The Graham
Foundation, 2002

Born in Puan, a small town near Argentina's fertile lowlands, or Pampas, Susana Torre is an American architect, educator, and critic, the daughter of an economist father and a schoolteacher mother. "Architecture is my profession but also it is my passion," Torre says of her work. "It has encompassed a series of practices at different scales: building design, master planning, exhibition design, teaching, lecturing, and writing. The framework has been a life-long interest in the tension between the 'completeness' of objects and the 'incompleteness' of design as a process."[51]

As a feminist, she believes that the program of a project must aim to improve the experience of all its users. In 1977, she edited *Women in American Architecture: A Historic and Contemporary Perspective* and curated the influential exhibition of the same name. In 1987, she was the first woman invited to design a building in Columbus, Indiana, a city well known for its collection of modern buildings designed by prominent American architects. There, to facilitate the integration of women in her Fire Station Five (1987), she replaced the then-typical open dorms and locker rooms that assumed an all-male firefighting force with spaces to promote bonding among all colleagues, setting the precedent for the "gender-neutral" fire stations that have been built since.

Torre pursued her personal and professional life in North and South America and in Europe. While a student at the University of Buenos Aires, she designed and built a small house and a six-story apartment building. In 1968, she studied and taught at Columbia University and began practicing in New York. Torre's professional practice has ranged from a small office of three to five people to being one of seven partners in a 150-person office (WASA Architects and Engineers). Her work spans residential and institutional projects, graphic and exhibition design, and urban design. Her designs include homes in the Hamptons, Long Island, New York; interior renovations, such as the Ivory Coast Consulate in New York; and a community of seven dwellings in Carboneras, Spain, which includes her studio and a residence that she shares with her husband, writer and sociologist Geoffrey Fox. This project was based on her concept of "space as matrix," first published in the 1970s.

Other projects have included the Montauk Library on Long Island and the renovation of Schermerhorn Hall at Columbia University. Her graphic and exhibition designs include the cover of Lucy Lippard's book *From the Center: Feminist Essays on Women's Art (1976)* and the exhibition installation of *Women in American Architecture* at the Brooklyn Museum.

Torre's work as a scholar on feminism and architecture, Latin America, and the representation of collective memory has been supported by grants and fellowships from the National Endowments and other institutions. Since 1973, she has lectured assiduously at international universities and professional organizations. —*KF*

Above
Fire Station Five, Columbus,
IN, Susana Torre with WASA
Architects and Engineers, 1987.
Photo Charles Budd

Left
*Women in American
Architecture: A Historic and
Contemporary Perspective*,
Brooklyn Museum, New York,
NY, exhibition, 1977–78.
© Norman McGrath

ADELE CHATFIELD-TAYLOR

BORN
Washington, DC, 1945

EDUCATION
Manhattanville College,
BA, 1966; Columbia GSAPP,
MArch, 1974

PRACTICE
New York City Landmarks
Preservation Commission,
1973–80; New York Landmarks
Preservation Foundation,
1980–84; National Endowment
for the Arts, 1984–88;
Columbia GSAPP; American
Academy in Rome, 1988–2013

NOTABLE HONORS
Rome Prize, American
Academy in Rome, 1983–84;
fellow, American Academy of
Arts and Sciences, 1996; Order
of the Italian Republic, 2002;
Vincent Scully Prize, National
Building Museum, 2010

"As a society, we're terrified of oldness," says Adele Chatfield-Taylor, implicating both new buildings and face-lifts in her assessment.[52] Over forty years of leading architectural preservation efforts, she worked to keep aging and the enrichment it offers "visible and tangible." She grew up in Virginia with a mother and grandmother who loved old buildings and inherited that sensibility from them.

Chatfield-Taylor held positions with the New York Landmarks Preservation Foundation, the National Endowment for the Arts (NEA), the New York City Landmarks Preservation Commission (LPC), and Columbia University—"When I had the good luck to discover the preservation department there fifty years ago, it was becoming part of a larger discussion about the environment"—and as the president and CEO of the American Academy in Rome for twenty-five years. She retired from that post in 2013.

While working on the Percent for Art legislation at the NEA, Chatfield-Taylor and a colleague from another department recognized that artists were being commissioned only after a building was already built. "It's a typical example of what plagues society today, when people are in their silos," she says. "It's more useful and more meaningful when those things are part of the conversation from the beginning. It's also important to work with someone who has a different take than you do."

Chatfield-Taylor fondly remembers attending public hearings for the LPC during the 1970s and 1980s. The process required justifying a building's value based on historical, architectural, or cultural significance. As she explains it, in the first case if, for instance, George Washington had slept there, that structure would not be sacrificed; the second section, artistic uniqueness in terms of architecture, usually had to be explained; cultural merit, the last category, was hardest to pin down and the aspect that impressed her strongly. She admired neighborhood residents who felt compelled to stand up and share their personal stories: "Dylan Thomas used to sit here and recite his poetry," someone said of a building in question. "This is where my child took his first steps," a mother testified. "These things are fabulous, and they meant so much to them," she says. "Where else can you say what something means to you?" Chatfield-Taylor admired the courage that it took to go into the Board of Estimate Chambers in City Hall, "that big, beautiful building." Today, she champions the efforts of Sites of Conscience, the group that landmarked the prison where Nelson Mandela spent thirty years (an otherwise undistinguished building) and changed his country as a result.

During her generation of leadership at the American Academy in Rome, Chatfield-Taylor oversaw the renovation of the main building, designed by McKim, Mead & White and dating from 1912. It was rewarding to lead a like-minded team that accomplished their goal with restraint, ultimately leaving more of the existing building than originally planned. She was also proud of raising the money for the effort ahead of time instead of borrowing it. The storied building lives up to its reputation, with many quirky and beloved attributes retained in the renovation. Notable among them, for Chatfield-Taylor, is a tiny hallway leading to the scholars' cubbyholes above

Above

Wesleyan Methodist Church, Women's Rights National Historic Park, Seneca Falls, NY, National Park Service, 1980. Photo Kenneth C. Zirkel

Opposite

American Academy in Rome, Italy, McKim, Mead & White; renovation stewarded by Adele Chatfield-Taylor, president, 1994. Photo Jonathan Wallen. © American Academy in Rome, Institutional Archive

the library: "It's like being inside a business envelope," she says of the odd dimensions (twenty-four inches wide and very tall). "Everyone asks why it looks like that," she says. (The space was designed for balconies that were ultimately too expensive to install.) "Anything that makes a person ask a question about a building is valuable."

When the academy's library considerably expanded, the card catalog was computerized. "We had a rebellion," she remembers. As a result, the original was also kept as an archive, with the many notes scrawled on the cards about various books throughout decades of use.

All interior doors were retained, their surfaces scraped and doorknobs realigned, and the floor still squeaks whenever someone walks in late to a meeting or presentation in the *salone*. Chatfield-Taylor insisted on the preservation of a portion of a railroad track in the basement that once transported coal to heat the building "because it's a fact about its age." She believes that the changes the group made to the building, such as adding elevators to make handicap access

manageable and improve the working conditions for the cleaners, didn't subtract from the place at all.

In 2016, President Barack Obama appointed Chatfield-Taylor to the Cultural Property Advisory Committee at the Bureau of Educational and Cultural Affairs. Her current project is a book about "what preservation really is, and what it isn't." She's also keenly concerned about the need for conversations about cities, especially affordable housing and homelessness. "There are so many unexplored territories," she says hopefully. —*JSE*

CHRISTIANE SCHMUCKLE-MOLLARD

BORN
Chambery, France, 1946

EDUCATION
Technical University of Munich, 1977; School of Chaillot, Heritage Architecture, 1979

PRACTICE
Agence Christiane Schmuckle-Mollard, 1980–2012; Historic Monuments in France, chief architect, 2012–16

TEACHING
National Architecture School, Paris, professor, 1985–87

NOTABLE HONORS
Council of the Academy of Architecture, 1993; Founding Member, ICOMOS International Scientific Committee on Structures, 1996–2005; Chevalier de l'Ordre des Arts et des Lettres, 2002; Chevalier de l'Ordre de la Legion d'Honneur, 2008; World Monuments Fund/Knoll Modernism Prize, 2018

Christiane Schmuckle-Mollard was the first woman to fulfill the role of Chief Architect of Historic Monuments in France (2012–16). She came to the job prepared, having spent forty years strategically restoring significant architecture in her country, from Gallo-Roman archaeological sites and the fifteenth-century Strasbourg Cathedral to seventeenth-century chateaux and twentieth-century concert halls, as well as historic gardens, parks, and public spaces. Schmuckle-Mollard is a founding member of the ICOMOS International Scientific Committee on Structures and served as its vice president from 1996 to 2005. Representing ICOMOS together with UNESCO, Schmuckle-Mollard oversaw the World Heritage site evaluations, internationally, from 2006 to 2014.

The decade-long restoration of the iconic Karl Marx School in Villejuif, a formerly Communist suburb of Paris, earned Schmuckle-Mollard a 2018 World Monuments Fund/Knoll Modernism Prize. Designed and built by functionalist architect André Lurçat in 1933, the school was long admired for its clean lines and considerable access to natural light; in 1996, the by-then-distressed educational complex was recognized as a national historic monument in France, improving its chances for survival. Schmuckle-Mollard's firm, Agence Christiane Schmuckle-Mollard, had consulted on the restoration of two of Lurçat's houses and was familiar with the complex. She was delighted that the structure had not been altered in significant ways and spent seven years studying the buildings and their users' needs, after which she spent three years on preservation and reinvention.

The school's new wing, designed to accommodate contemporary needs, takes the form of a glass capsule beneath a canopy. In the older portion, Schmuckle-Mollard communicated its value to the public by fixing exterior cracks, conserving interior ceramic sandstone tiles, resealing the structure's windows, restoring frescoes by Lurçat, and reemploying the school's original colors. "The success of Lurçat's design should teach us that school buildings can be much more than just functional," said Schmuckle-Mollard in a conversation with the World Monuments Fund (WMF). "The change of behavior of the students at the Karl Marx School before and after the restoration shows us how much architectural quality and beauty impact the well-being of its users, and how it can positively inspire respect, a keystone for social work at schools."

As a former professor at the National Architecture School in Paris, Schmuckle-Mollard is proud that her work has ignited interest among teachers about the social relevance of architecture, who have organized class trips to the Fondation Le Corbusier as a result. She says, "We need to preserve the best examples for the future."

Columbia art history professor and MoMA design curator Barry Bergdoll agrees. As jury chair for the World Monuments Fund/Knoll Modernism Prize in 2018, he noted, "The Karl Marx School in Villejuif is one of the landmark school designs of the 20th century…It resonates today with the idealism and optimism of its original creators, the municipality and the architect through this sensitive and erudite restoration." **—JSE**

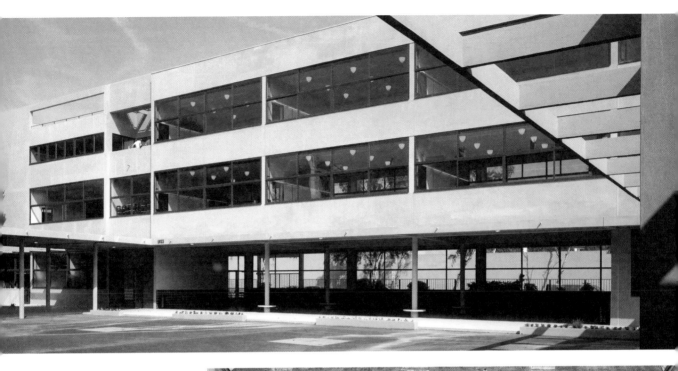

Above
Karl Marx School, Villejuif,
France, André Lurçat, 1933;
restoration and preservation,
Christiane Schmuckle-Mollard,
2018. Photo Priska Schmückle
von Minckwitz

Right
Hôtel Carnavalet courtyard,
Paris, France, sixteenth
century; restoration, Christiane
Schmuckle-Mollard, 2015.
Photo Priska Schmückle von
Minckwitz

JULIE SNOW

BORN
Grand Rapids, MI, 1948

EDUCATION
University of Colorado,
BArch, 1970

PRACTICE
Hammel, Green & Abrahamson,
1970–87; James/Snow
Architects, 1989; Julie Snow
Architects, 1995; Snow Kreilich
Architects, 2014–

TEACHING
University of Michigan,
Taubman College of
Architecture, 2001; University
of Oklahoma, Bruce Goff
Creative Chair, 2001;
University of Arkansas, 2003;
Washington University,
2005, 2010; Harvard GSD,
2006–8; Syracuse University,
2011; University of Southern
California (USC), 2013; Yale
University, 2018

NOTABLE HONORS
Ralph Rapson Distinguished
Teaching Award, University
of Minnesota, 1999; Design
Excellence, US General
Services Administration, 2000;
Architect of Distinction, AIA/
Midwest Home Magazine, 2011;
American Academy of Arts
and Letters, 2011; Gold
Medal, AIA Minnesota 2014;
Firm Award, Snow Kreilich
Architects, AIA, 2018

Julie Snow realized her passion for architecture while at the University of Colorado, joining a love for art with strong science and math skills. "What was really compelling to me, once I started down the path, was [architecture's] effect on every part of our lives," she says. "It really was amazing; it just seemed like everything I learned in every class, even outside of architecture, was about architecture."[53]

After completing her undergraduate degree, Snow was hired by the Minnesota-based firm of Hammel, Green & Abrahamson, where she stayed until 1987. In 1989, she founded James/Snow Architects with Vincent James. In 1995, she opened her own firm, Julie Snow Architects, while also teaching at the University of Minnesota. The firm tackled projects on a variety of scales, from private single-family residences to institutional and public buildings.

Snow says that when she founded her firm, it was considered the norm to develop expertise in one project type and build on that. It was less typical to focus on a diverse array of work. "[It] was not about creating expertise in a single project type, but about elevating architecture across all project types," she says. "We were very interested in mining each project for its potential." At its start, the firm primarily focused on projects in the private sector.

Because many of the firm's early clients were private and no selection committees were involved, Snow was able to jump into projects without previous experience with similar works in her portfolio. "I basically would pursue projects that had some visionary leader at the helm, and that was the way that we would pursue work," she says. "If you had a vision, if you had an idea of what architecture needed to do, then I would make it happen." Eventually, the firm was able to expand into the public sector, and in 2011, Julie Snow Architects won an AIA Honor Award for the US Land Port of Entry in Warroad, Minnesota.

In 2014, Snow named Matthew Kreilich, a ten-year veteran of the firm, as coprincipal, and the firm became Snow Kreilich Architects. About half of Snow Kreilich's employees are women or minorities. In 2018, it was awarded the AIA Firm award.

Snow has shared her expertise with architecture students at Harvard GSD, USC, and the University of Minnesota College of Design (from which she received the Ralph Rapson Award for Distinguished Teaching), among others.

One of Snow's favorite projects to date is the CHS Field, the home of the minor-league baseball team the Saint Paul Saints. She calls the field's opening day "a wonderful place to be as an architect."

"There were families, there were hipsters and large crowds, there were older folks that have been longtime fans, new fans—it was just so much fun," she says. "To see that diversity of people enjoying the same thing and enjoying each other's company was marvelous. We've become this kind of tribal culture, and our public spaces are about breaking down the boundaries." —*KF*

Above
Weekend House, Schroeder, MN, 2009. © Corey Gaffer

Left
Great Plains Software, Fargo, ND, 2004. © Don Wong

CAROL ROSS BARNEY

BORN
Chicago, IL, 1949

EDUCATION
University of Illinois, Urbana-Champaign, BArch, 1971

PRACTICE
Holabird and Root, 1972–79; Ross Barney Architects, 1981–82; Ross Barney + Jankowski, 1982–2005; Ross Barney Architects, 2005–

TEACHING
University of Illinois Chicago; Illinois Institute of Technology

NOTABLE HONORS
Cofounder, Chicago Women in Architecture, 1973; Thomas Jefferson Award, AIA, 2005; Jewish Reconstructionist Congregation Synagogue, World Architecture Category Commendation, 2009; COTE Top Ten Green Project Award, AIA, 2013; first woman to design a Federal building, Oklahoma City Federal Building, 2015; Gold Medal, AIA Illinois, 2015; Lifetime Achievement Award, AIA Chicago, 2017

"I have always been really susceptible to space," Carol Ross Barney says. "When I look at things, I see light, I see space."[54]

Born in Chicago, Ross Barney distinctly remembers hearing a mandate from President John F. Kennedy as a child about the importance of helping one's country. A self-described "child of the sixties," she felt that the profession of architecture was a way to improve the quality of urban life and make city spaces "delightful to be in."

After graduating from the University of Illinois in 1971 and facing a recession that would certainly impact architecture, Ross Barney decided to enter the Peace Corps with her husband. They were assigned to Costa Rica, which she calls "the first place I was thrust into sustainability." The work she did for the Costa Rican National Park Service gave her a strong background for her later design work in the public realm.

Upon returning to Chicago after the Peace Corps, Ross Barney joined Holabird and Root, where she was mentored by John Holabird until his death. Her work there included the 1979 restoration of the Chicago Public Library, which won a 1979 AIA Institute Honor Award. Of Holabird, she says, "You need to have a sponsor or a mentor. You have to have someone who's working with you and more or less on your side."

In 1973, Ross Barney cofounded Chicago Women in Architecture and served as the group's first president. The group's primary purpose was to be a sounding board and a welcoming place for women in architecture in Chicago.

Ross Barney started a solo practice in Chicago in 1981 and then partnered with her college classmate James Jankowski

in 1982 to form Ross Barney + Jankowski. Because she had worked extensively on public and government projects during her time at Holabird and Root—what she jokingly calls the "noble projects" assigned to her by Holabird—those were the clients she initially took on at her own practice.

Ross Barney became the first woman to design a federal building when she was chosen as the lead designer for the Oklahoma City Federal Building, following the 1995 terrorist bombing. Due to her firm's work on two schools in port-of-entry communities in Chicago, which garnered attention for her small firm, she was able to make a strong case for why the firm was a good choice for the job.

In 2016, Ross Barney's firm completed the Chicago Riverwalk, along Wacker Drive, opening up 3.4 miles for public amenities and concessions. Her love of Chicago has also manifested in her designs of intramodal stations for the Chicago Transit Authority. In addition to her design work, she has taught at the University of Illinois Chicago, and serves as an adjunct at the Illinois Institute of Technology.

Carol Ross Barney says, "This is a really hard profession, and I eventually did learn that being a woman in architecture is part of the hill you have to climb, but I never regretted the choice." —*KF*

Above
University of Minnesota,
Swenson Civil Engineering
Building, Duluth, MN, Ross
Barney Architects, 2010.
© Kate Joyce Studios. Courtesy
Ross Barney Architects

Right
Chicago Riverwalk, Chicago, IL,
Ross Barney Architects, 2016.
© Kate Joyce Studios. Courtesy
Ross Barney Architects

IV. ROCKING THE WORLD

Introduction by Margaret Birney Vickery

The "rocking the world" generation built on the progress of its predecessors, wrangling with what feminist architecture could be and recognizing the complexities involved in choosing architecture as a career. Their contributions lie less in deconstructing the history of women in architecture and more in successfully navigating the winding avenues of success and gaining respect and admiration for their achievements.

These women, mostly born in the 1950s, came of age in the late 1960s and early 1970s, a period of dramatic civic and social unrest in the United States, Britain, and Europe. While the Beatles and the Rolling Stones shook up popular music, student protests demanded institutional and educational change; the Vietnam War drew heavy criticism and debate; and figures from Martin Luther King to Betty Friedan called for racial and gender equality. Free love and recreational drug use, together with Timothy Leary's explorations of hallucinogenic drugs, exploded the domestic and societal norms associated with the 1950s. By 1972, when the National Organization for Women was founded and Gloria Steinem produced her first edition of *Ms.* magazine, the second wave of feminism was firmly established in the public arena and helped push new ideas about birth control, abortion, women's bodies, and their career opportunities.

By the late 1970s, when some members of this generation were graduating with MArch degrees from the likes of Columbia, Cooper Union, Yale University, and the AA in London, these women knew of the work of early women architects such as Eileen Gray and Theodate Pope Riddle. But they also benefited from the efforts of Susanna Torre and Denise Scott Brown, who not only designed buildings and wrote extensively but also questioned the traditional assumption of the male architectural genius and his lonely, Roarkian quest for architectural novelty. Such questioning paved the way for women, such as Billie Tsien, Francine Houben, Patricia Patkau, and Deborah Berke, to carve out highly successful careers based on collaboration and flexibility.

Indeed, in cultural historian Anna Lebovic's 2019 article "Refashioning Feminism: American *Vogue*, the Second Wave, and the Transition to Postfeminism," she points to the rise of "choice feminism," which "posited that the overriding goal of the women's movement was to facilitate women's ability to choose in *all* areas of their lives, be it marriage, motherhood, sexual orientation, or occupation. This more expansive and inclusive ethos quickly found footing in activist and non-activist women alike."[1] The women of this generation can be understood as heeding artist Rochelle Martin's 1989 call:

> If real change is to occur, it will have to come from outside—from marginal people, men and women, who question the standards and assumptions and practices of the profession. A new kind of professional must be envisioned, one who can balance a desire for professional excellence with an ability to pursue personal interests and commitments. Restructuring of professional career paths is not a concession to women. Men also need second careers, re-training periods, and the redefinition of goals making possible a more balanced and rewarding life.[2]

By and large, the results of this restructuring in architecture produced collaborative partnerships and offices with female architects. Most of them are partners, either in smaller, though highly respected firms, such as Yvonne Farrell and Shelley McNamara of Grafton Architects and Julie Eizenberg of KoningEizenberg, or in larger firms, such as Sylvia Smith of FXFowle or Shirley Blumberg of KPMB. Upon receiving the Woman Architect of the Year award from the *Architect's Journal*, Francine Houben spoke for many of the women of this generation when she said, "I feel privileged to be a woman, a mother and an architect. Architecture is about teamwork, about being supportive and visionary at the same time. Women are especially good at that."[3] The collaborative nature of many of the women of this generation has made possible their professional success to coexist with personal life choices, such as marriage and children.

Support of the collaborative model has its detractors. Many say such structural changes to the profession are moving too slowly and that women in partnership with men are still not taken seriously. Zaha Hadid addressed the issue, arguing, "Even if the woman is the lead person, they're always seen as the second fiddle, no matter how good they are. There are many people whose partners or husbands are taken more seriously than they are, almost automatically."[4] And Despina Stratigakos reported in her 2012 essay, "Why Architects Need Feminism," that others see that "the declining status of the discipline is reflected in the growing presence of women in architecture schools."[5] Such cynicism attempts to undermine the hard-fought equal and collaborative efforts of most of the women in this section.

Of the women here, only Hadid stands out as a Roarkian starchitect, a mainly misunderstood, lone genius of dramatic vision. Certainly, the world has room for Hadid's expressive work. In general, though, the architecture of this generation eschews the starring role in favor of thoughtful, progressive partnerships that further a refreshing new approach to the profession. As Peggy Deamer describes, "Collaboration, open-source networking, non-hierarchical practices, entrepreneurialism, streamline production and profit-sharing do away with the singular author. We need to focus on how our buildings perform socially, environmentally, and economically over the long term. We are ready to fly under the radar to infiltrate larger spheres of influence."[6] The women of this generation, through their architecture, their teaching, and their examples have exerted deep and meaningful influence throughout the profession, broken through glass ceilings, and established themselves as vital players in the architectural landscape.

BILLIE TSIEN

BORN
Ithaca, NY, 1949

EDUCATION
Yale University, BFA, 1971;
UCLA, MArch, 1977

PRACTICE
Tod Williams Billie Tsien
Architects, 1986–

TEACHING
City College of New York,
2005; Yale University, 2003,
2005, 2010, 2012, 2014, 2016,
2019–21; Cornell AAP, 2013;
Harvard GSD, 2013, 2016

NOTABLE HONORS
Arnold Brunner Memorial
Prize, 1996; Chrysler Award
for Innovation in Design,
1998; President's Medal,
Architectural League of New
York, 2003; National Design
Award, Cooper Hewitt, 2003;
Architecture Firm Award, AIA,
2013; National Medal of Arts,
presented by President Barack
Obama, 2013; Praemium
Imperiale, Architecture, 2019

When Billie Tsien was majoring in art at Yale University, she remembers her drawing instructor, painter William Bailey, telling his students, "It's not about the line but what's between the lines"—words she took to heart.[7] That kind of very considered indirectness has informed both the architect's process and her buildings since the late 1970s.

"Architecture is very much for me not an object but an experience," says Tsien. "It's important that I look at many things for inspiration, not just architecture." She cites as influences food writer M.F.K. Fisher's focus on the senses, on taste and smell, and Trisha Brown's dancing and choreography, how it's "rebellious but also working within a structure." In terms of architects, the "weight and timelessness" of Louis Kahn's work is a significant touchstone for Tsien.[8]

The design for the upcoming US Embassy in Mexico City by Tod Williams Billie Tsien Architects (TWBTA) references Colonial architecture—thick walls and patios—as well as the solidity of Mayan buildings, conferring a sense of groundedness. The six-story building features two levels below grade, which is ideal for security reasons. A sculptural metal screen makes a cryptic presence on the building's front, enlivening the repetitive window scheme. For Tsien, it recalls the Trisha Brown dance "If you could see me," during which her back is turned to the audience. She also thinks the design gesture references her Chinese background, reflecting the slowness in letting others know her, speaking to a desire "not to be known," to be silent. She admires architecture that does not immediately announce

its intentions, that is quiet and becomes richer as an experience over time.

According to Tsien, her husband and partner, Tod Williams, has been her most significant mentor. "Our partnership/marriage works because we're diametrically different," she explains. "We supply things that are missing for one another. Tod has a certain relentlessness about looking for what is right in order to make work with integrity that continues to inspire me." The revisions to the Obama Presidential Center in Chicago, for example, benefited greatly from that kind of single-mindedness.

The summer of 2019 was very exciting for the couple because they worked closely with President Barack Obama and radically reshaped the complex: "It's the project of a lifetime…After three years of working together, I admire him even more, perhaps, for wanting to make a place that's right for the people coming to see it, for being respectful of their journey…It needs to be warm and welcoming but also convey that something important—the country's first Black president—happened." Through the center's architecture, she explains, "he wants to honor other people's stories and enable those stories." Like the former president, Tsien doesn't shy away from generously sized ideals.

Tsien considers TWBTA a relationship-based practice, with clients whose values are aligned with theirs. For her, the word *service* is very important in architecture. "Not servile," she's quick to explain, but the pursuit of "doing something for someone else in a deep way has the potential of being noble."

Childcare, Tsien says, is the biggest challenge for women in architecture. "It's

Phoenix Art Museum, Phoenix,
AZ, Tod Williams Billie Tsien
Architects, 1996/2006. © Bill
Timmerman

up to those of us in a position to make decisions to understand how critical this is for young women." Her intimate studio of thirty-eight people is like a family, and if anyone—mothers and fathers—needs to leave at any time for a family reason, they are encouraged to. One of the benefits of having parents in the demanding profession: "People who have limited time tend to be very efficient."

Teaching is a key aspect of practice for Tsien, and she says that it keeps her connected to what the students are seeing: "Students are generally people who have not yet developed a language and are coming from places other than architecture." She advises young people: "You don't have to be a specific kind of person to be an architect. Dive in! It's an incredible career with a real, physical result. Sometimes there's even rare joy." —*JSE*

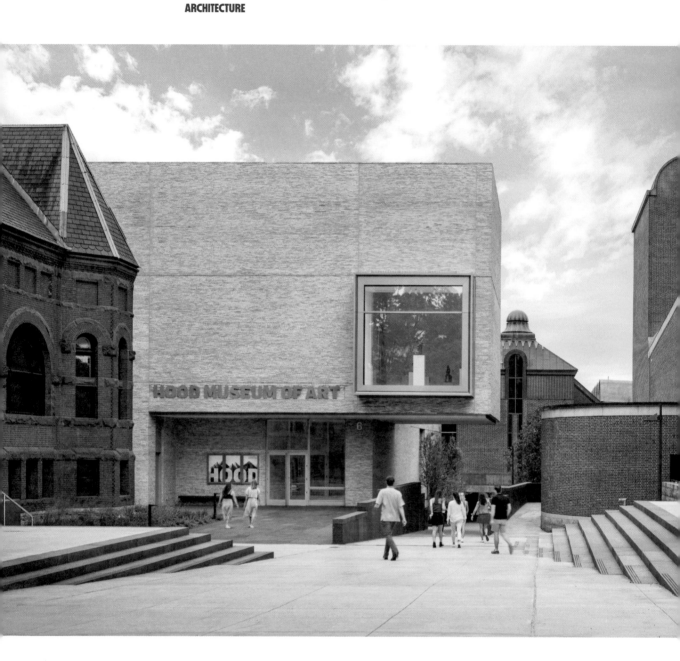

Above
Hood Museum of Art, Hanover,
NH, Tod Williams Billie Tsien
Architects, 2019. © Michael
Moran

Opposite
American Folk Art Museum,
New York, NY, Tod Williams
Billie Tsien Architects, 2001.
© Giles Ashford

ZAHA HADID

BORN
Baghdad, Iraq, 1950

DIED
Miami, FL, 2016

EDUCATION
American University in
Beirut, 1972; AA School
of Architecture, 1977

PRACTICE
Office for Metropolitan
Architecture, 1977; Zaha Hadid
Architects, 1980–2016

TEACHING
AA School of Architecture,
1980–87; Columbia University;
Harvard GSD; Yale University;
University of Applied Arts
Vienna

NOTABLE HONORS
Gold Medal, British
Architecture, 1982; Erich
Schelling Architecture
Award, 1994; Pritzker Prize,
2004; Designer of the Year,
Design Miami, 2005; Austrian
Decoration for Science and Art,
2005; Phaeno Science Centre,
Royal Institute of British
Architects (RIBA) European
Award, 2006; Thomas
Jefferson Foundation Medal in
Architecture, 2007; Nordpark
Cable Railway, RIBA European
Award, 2008; Praemium
Imperiale, 2009; MAXXI, RIBA
European Award, 2010; Jane
Drew Prize, 2012

Born in Baghdad to a wealthy Iraqi family, Zaha Hadid was captivated by architecture since childhood. "When I was six years old, my aunt was building a house in Mosul in north Iraq," she told the *Guardian* in 2012. "The architect was a close friend of my father's, and he used to come to our house with the drawings and models. I remember seeing the model in our living room and it triggered something."[9] Exploring Sumerian ruins in the South of Iraq as a teenager with her family further fueled her fascination.

Hadid's father was a cofounder of the National Democratic Party in Iraq, and her mother was an artist from Mosul. Of the political climate of her childhood, she says, "there was an unbroken belief in progress and a great sense of optimism. It was a moment of nation building…The ideas of change, liberation, freedom and social reform were so important to me."[10] Her family left their native Iraq after the rise of Saddam Hussein and the outbreak of war with Iran.

Hadid studied mathematics at the American University in Beirut, Lebanon, before transferring to London's AA School of Architecture, a center for experimental design, where she studied with architectural giants such as Elia Zenghelis, Rem Koolhaas, and Bernard Tschumi. After graduating in 1977, Hadid went to work for Koolhaas and Zenghelis at the Office for Metropolitan Architecture (OMA) in Rotterdam, the Netherlands. She opened an office of her own in London in 1980, in addition to teaching courses at the AA. In 1988, her international reputation grew when she was chosen to show her drawings and paintings as part of the

Deconstructivist Architecture exhibit at MoMA, in New York, curated by Philip Johnson and Mark Wigley.

Hadid entered a number of design competitions in the 1980s and early 1990s, receiving interest and acclaim from her fellow architects while remaining relatively unknown to the public at large. Her family's affluence allowed her to pursue some projects that weren't necessarily lucrative up front. A prize-winning design in a competition for the Peak, a sports club jutting out from a mountain slope in Hong Kong, was never built.

After several smaller projects, the first major commission of Hadid's to be built was a small fire station commissioned by the Swiss furniture company Vitra, constructed between 1993 and 1994 in Weil am Rhein, Germany. In 1994, her design for the Cardiff Bay Opera House in Wales won a design competition but was never built after the project's funder, Britain's National Lottery, withdrew support.

Her designs continued to draw attention and acclaim, however, and in 1998, she was awarded the Lois and Richard Rosenthal Center for Contemporary Art in Cincinnati, her biggest commission to date. Her next significant American project was designing Price Tower Arts Center, a museum adjoining Frank Lloyd Wright's Price Tower in Bartlesville, Oklahoma. "I started out trying to create buildings that would sparkle like isolated jewels; now I want them to connect, to form a new kind of landscape, to flow together with contemporary cities and the lives of their peoples," she told the *Guardian*.[11]

In 2004, she won architecture's highest honor, the Pritzker Prize, becoming the

Opus, Dubai, United
Arab Emirates, Zaha Hadid
Architects, 2020.
© Laurian Ghinitoiu

Heydar Aliyev Center,
Baku, Azerbaijan, 2012.
Photo Iwan Baan

first woman to receive the award. In the mid-2000s she received a commission for her first permanent structure in the United Kingdom, a cancer-care center in Fife, Scotland, called Maggie's Centre.

Hadid's structures are characterized by concrete, steel, and glass and by swooping facades juxtaposed with stark angles. She found ninety-degree angles uninteresting, avoiding them at every opportunity. Patrik Schumacher, her partner at Zaha Hadid Architects, helped the firm's most extravagant concepts become reality through computer-based approaches he called "parametricism."

In addition to such triumphs as the Aquatics Building for the 2012 Olympics in London and the 2012 Heydar Aliyev Center in Baku, Azerbaijan, Hadid's career experienced moments of controversy. The $250 million cultural center in Baku forced the eviction of families from the site, and a commission for the 2020 Tokyo Olympics was scrapped in 2015 due to rising costs. Hadid and her firm also came under fire for collaborating with Qatar's government

on a proposed stadium for the 2022 World Cup, despite the country's alleged human-rights abuses.

Nevertheless, Hadid continued to create architectural designs without precedent and received highest honors in the United Kingdom and elsewhere: the Stirling Prize from the Royal Institute of British Architects (RIBA) in 2010 and 2011; designation as of one of the *Time* 100: The Most Influential People, in 2010; and Britain's Royal Gold Medal in February 2016.

Hadid died of a massive heart attack in a Miami hospital in March 2016. She was being treated for bronchitis and was just hours short of heart surgery. "She was bigger than life, a force of nature," Amale Andraos, the dean of Columbia University's architecture school, told the *New York Times* in an obituary. "She was a pioneer."[12] Her firm, Zaha Hadid Architects, continues to work on designs internationally. —*KF*

Left
One Thousand Museum, Miami, FL, Zaha Hadid Architects, 2019. © Hufton+Crow

Below
Riverside Museum, Glasgow, UK, Zaha Hadid Architects, 2011. © Hufton+Crow

PATRICIA PATKAU

BORN
Winnipeg, Manitoba, Canada,
1950

EDUCATION
University of Manitoba, BA,
Interior Design, 1973; Yale
University, MArch, 1978

PRACTICE
Patkau Architects, 1978–

TEACHING
UCLA, assistant professor,
1988–1990; University of
British Columbia, School
of Architecture, professor,
1990–2010

NOTABLE HONORS
Fellow, Royal Architectural
Institute of Canada, 1994;
Royal Canadian Academy of
Arts, 1995; Honorary Fellow,
AIA, 1999; Honorary Fellow,
RIBA, 2002; Order of Canada,
2004

Walking past the architecture studios every day while studying interior design at the University of Manitoba, Patricia Patkau was seduced. Fred Koetter was her mentor in architecture at Yale University. "He had a great depth of knowledge of both architecture's history and currency," she remembers.[13]

Practicing for over forty years with her husband and partner, John Patkau, Patricia describes their fruitful working style as "fighting it out," finding common ground to move forward. "The love of architecture and landscape, along with a curiosity as to how they reside in the world in various places and times, has redefined 'work' as 'life' for us," she says. The role of the architect, for her, is establishing beneficial relationships between things. "Intuitively, our tendency has been *not* to put human beings at the generative center of the endeavor," she says, "but to try and build sustainable and enduring relationships between places, natural systems, other species and life forms, and our own needs and desires as communities and individuals."

Patkau values the process of looking, a series of formal "investigations" the firm pursues as research. Whether they're using metal or wood, the critical thing is the form-finding: "Watching the force on a material and allowing it to find its way." The new, blossom-shaped Temple of Light (2018), designed for the Yasodhara Ashram Society, offers an example of results of their research. The firm has exhibited its large-scale sculptural endeavors, seen in their 2017 monograph, *Material Operations*, by Princeton Architectural Press.

"Early in my career being a woman was actually a benefit," Patkau says, citing the growing awareness of the inappropriateness of the male domination of academic faculties. At the behest of UCLA's dean of Architecture and Urban Design, she was an assistant professor there for two years. Then, she returned home to practice in Vancouver and to teach at the University of British Columbia (UBC), where she has been a professor emerita for more than twenty years.

Patkau views construction that addresses the grave health of the environment of the greatest value. "Our work has produced a growing awareness about the things that construction can do," she says. "It points to a place where the act of construction can help a community gain a sense of pride in its accomplishments and architecture can act as a vehicle of repair." Ideally for Patkau, "construction leads to a condition where a site and a building are bound culturally, environmentally, and physically."

Yet in much of the developed world, Patkau sees destructive construction. She is critical of architects who "sell themselves and the job instead of doing it." She is also wary of technology: "Because digital tools are capable of just about anything, just about anything gets built." What about place, people, and the environment, she asks?

Patkau's favorite part of her architectural practice is sitting at her desk designing, which is what she does a large portion of every day. "John and I decided very early on that we would keep the practice at a scale where we could remain principal designers on all the work, not default to the position of management." —*JSE*

Fort York National Historic Site,
Toronto, Ontario, Patkau Architects,
2014. Photo Tom Arban

Opposite
Audain Art Museum, Whistler, British Columbia, Patkau Architects, 2016. Photo James Dow

Below
Cottages at Fallingwater, Mill Run, PA, Patkau Architects, 2018. Courtesy Patkau Architects

Right
La Grande Bibliothèque du Quebec, Montreal, Patkau Architects, 2005

PEGGY DEAMER

BORN
San Francisco, CA, 1950

EDUCATION
Oberlin College, BA,
Philosophy, 1972; Cooper
Union, BArch, 1977; Princeton
University, MA, Architecture
History, Criticism, and Theory,
1983, PhD, Architecture
History, Criticism, and Theory,
1988

PRACTICE
Deamer+Phillips, 1986;
Deamer, Architect, 2003–

TEACHING
Barnard College, Architecture,
program director, 1992–96;
Yale University, Advanced
Studies, director, 1995–2000,
School of Architecture,
2001–19

NOTABLE HONORS
Emerging Voices Honoree,
Architectural League of
New York, 1993; Women in
Architecture Award, Activism,
Architectural Record, 2018; 16
Women Breaking New Ground
in Architecture, *Visual Culture/
Artsy*, 2018; Cooper Union
Alumni Association, Hejduk
Award, Cooper Union, 2021

Peggy Deamer started her academic career at Oberlin College as a philosophy major. Yet in her architecture and history courses, she discovered academic disciplines that felt more immediate. "Philosophy seemed hard and endless, and my courses in architecture seemed concrete and delightful," she says. One assignment required her to analyze a house, any house, in the town of Oberlin. "I liked looking, I liked considering it," she says.[14]

Oberlin didn't have an architecture major, so she finished her philosophy degree in 1972 and interned at the Institute for Architecture and Urban Studies in New York before pursuing a BArch at Cooper Union. There, she received a design education that instilled social and ethical values.

The history and theory of architecture represented a gap in her knowledge, and she decided to pursue a PhD rather than a master's degree in architecture. After completing her doctorate at Princeton, she taught part-time at Parsons School of Design, Barnard College, Princeton University, and Yale University, while also starting a new firm, Deamer+Phillips, with her husband, Scott Phillips.

Deamer's position at Yale started in 1993 and eventually became a full-time position. After 9/11, business at Deamer+Phillips slowed down, encouraging Deamer to place more of her focus on academia: "I began to see that high-end residential did not offer the opportunity to think about significant things, and I began to feel like we were taking projects just to be able to pay for the staff."

This distancing from the practice allowed Deamer to explore and weave together questions of design with questions of theory, which led to the founding of the Architecture Lobby, a group that advocates for "the value of architecture in the general public and for architectural work within the discipline." Deamer was concerned about whether architects could feel creative in the profession as it was currently available to them. She was also concerned about the public's perception of architects as purveyors of aesthetics. "I think the more that we've identified ourselves as aestheticians, the more elite, expensive, and trivial we look to the public," she says—an image that the Architecture Lobby seeks to counter.

In 2007, the University of Auckland in New Zealand recruited Deamer for a teaching position. While she eventually went back to Yale, Deamer visited New Zealand frequently and decided to build a house in the area of the Kaiwaka settlement, in a move that she has said "still feels brave to this day."

Of her most impactful career accomplishments, Deamer is proud of how she has placed well-designed projects in the larger context of the economy and cultural discourse. "What architects are asked to do—and how we have described our design problems to ourselves—[is] not of our making, and we need to understand why we're handed the problems we're handed and why we're asked to consider the things we're asked to consider," she says. "So I'm proud of that contextualization." —*KF*

Above
Kaiwaka House, Kaiwaka,
New Zealand, 2016. Courtesy
Peggy Deamer

Right
Protest at AIA National
Convention, Philadelphia,
PA, 2016. Courtesy The
Architecture Lobby

ELIZABETH PLATER-ZYBERK

BORN
Bryn Mawr, PA, 1950

EDUCATION
Princeton University, BA, 1972;
Yale University, MArch, 1974

PRACTICE
Arquitectonica, 1977; Duany
Plater-Zyberk, 1980–

TEACHING
University of Miami, School
of Architecture, associate
professor, 1979–90, professor,
1990–, dean, 1995–2013;
Matheson Distinguished
Professor, 2006–; Prince of
Wales Institute, 1993; Harvard
University GSD, 1990, 1984;
Yale University School of
Architecture, Bishop Chair
(with Andrés Duany), 1987

NOTABLE HONORS
Vincent Scully Prize (with
Andres Duany), National
Building Museum, 2001;
Arrow Honor Society,
University of Miami, 2008;
Richard H. Driehaus Prize
for Classical Architecture,
2008; appointment to US
Commission of Fine Arts,
2008; Arts and Culture Award,
Coral Gables Community
Foundation, 2014

As a child, Elizabeth Plater-Zyberk was enchanted by the pencil drawings that her father, Josephat Plater-Zyberk, an architect, left on his worktable at home. "We were a family of modest means, as immigrants, so my father was always puttering with the old house," she says. "I had a lot of construction around me, so many things conspired to push me in this direction." Her father left Poland in 1947, and Plater-Zyberk was born in Bryn Mawr, Pennsylvania, in 1950. Her mother, Maria Meysztowski, was a French professor at Villanova University.

"I was always growing up with a great admiration for the early American architecture that surrounded me in Pennsylvania, the modest but elegant farm houses," she says. "My father was among the architects helping people turn them into modern-day country homes."[15]

Plater-Zyberk graduated from Princeton University with a degree in architecture and urban planning in 1972 and a master's degree from Yale University in 1974. In 1977, she cofounded the firm Arquitectonica with her husband, Andrés Duany, and partners Bernardo Fort-Brescia, Hervin Romney, and Laurinda Spear. The firm's Atlantis Condominium (1982), a shining postmodern structure on Brickell Avenue, south of downtown Miami, was featured in the opening credits of *Miami Vice*.

In 1980, Plater-Zyberk and Duany founded Duany Plater-Zyberk (DPZ), based in Miami. In 1985, their design for Seaside, Florida, a planned urban community with 350 dwellings on an eighty-acre beachfront parcel, won acclaim upon first occupancy for the way in which it evoked traditional urbanism by utilizing walkable streets and a more traditional form for its dwellings. "Seaside was about dignifying something that was going on for a long time in American culture: Americans prefer traditional forms for their houses, for their residences," Plater-Zyberk says. "Seaside was making a place for that. It was recognizing that part of the popular culture. It has served as an example of how to make transit-friendly, less vehicle-dependent communities."

Following the success of Seaside and similar urban planning projects that shaped existing suburbs into livable downtown hubs, such as Kentlands in Gaithersburg, Maryland (1988), DPZ became a leader in the burgeoning New Urbanism movement, prioritizing traditional neighborhood design and transit-oriented development. In 1993, Plater-Zyberk cofounded, with Duany, the Congress for the New Urbanism, a nonprofit organization dedicated to promoting the movement's principles: "It was an intention to have a larger influence both in terms of educating the public, and in terms of changing public education and policy."

Since 1995, Plater-Zyberk has served as the dean of the University of Miami's School of Architecture, where she is proud of fostering a community-based approach that prioritizes placemaking and urbanism as a matrix for architecture. "[It] was about architecture being a part of a bigger picture rather than just the individual artistic or branded effort," she says. In 2008, she was appointed to the US Commission of Fine Arts, the principal stewards of building design in the nation's capital and of historic Georgetown in Washington, DC. —*KF*

Above
Seaside, Florida, DPZ
Architecture, 1985. Photo
Alex McLean

Left
*Suburban Nation: The Rise
of Sprawl and the Decline
of the American Dream*,
Andrés Duany, Elizabeth
Plater-Zyberk, and Jeff
Speck, 2000

The Rise of Sprawl

and the Decline of

the American Dream

Andres Duany, Elizabeth Plater-Zyberk, and Jeff Speck

LAURINDA SPEAR

BORN
Rochester, MN, 1950

EDUCATION
Brown University, BA, 1972;
Columbia GSAAP, MArch, 1975;
Florida International University,
Master of Landscape
Architecture, 2006

PRACTICE
Arquitectonica, 1977–;
ArquitectonicaGEO, 2005–

NOTABLE HONORS
Rome Prize, American
Academy in Rome, 1978;
Silver Medal Award for Design
Excellence, AIA Miami,
1998; Hall of Fame, *Interior
Design*, 1999; American
Prize Architecture, Chicago
Athenaeum and European
Center for Architecture, Art,
Design, and Urban Studies,
2019

"My mother mentioned to me when I was really little—maybe age eight—'Oh, you can be an architect,'" says Laurinda Spear.[16] She embraced this suggestion and obtained her architecture degree from Columbia University and later cofounded the architecture firm of Arquitectonica in 1977 with fellow architects Bernardo Fort-Brescia, Andrés Duany, Elizabeth Plater-Zyberk, and Hervin Romney. In its early years, the Miami-based firm created a number of colorful, geometrically inspired structures that have become iconic, including the Pink House (1979) and the Atlantis Condominium (1982). Spear also introduced a new style of interiors emphasizing vibrant colors and tactile surfaces into many of the Arquitectonica buildings. This move spurred her line of products for international firms, such as Brayton, Wolf Gordon, and Hunter Douglas, among others.

"I was interested in architecture, as well as in color. It seemed that, in Miami, we were another one of the islands," she says of the design of the Atlantis Condominium and other early work. "Now, with sea-level rise, we are even more like an island." Later, Arquitectonica's work evolved to include subtly dramatic stylistic elements, though less colorful, like the crinkled facade of the Icon Bay residential tower (2015) and the curving concrete roof of the Thomas P. Murphy Design Studio Building (2019) at the University of Miami School of Architecture.

After two decades of architectural practice, Spear's interest shifted to nature and the interaction between a building and its site and context: "I felt there was something unconscionable about the way architecture was often ignoring the site, even thinking that it wasn't necessary to visit. About fifteen years ago, I thought, to do it right, you'd have to be a landscape architect as well." She returned to school and obtained her master's degree in landscape architecture, founding GEO in 2005, an extension of Arquitectonica. GEO is a collaborative studio with the main purpose of creating resilient landscapes that address the current climate crisis. GEO embraces and encourages the blurring of the line between building architecture and landscape architecture in every project.

Spear works differently now than she did during the early days of Arquitectonica. "I prioritize how the building fits into the site, and I prioritize the site over the building." Her book *Geo Bio Miami* (2020) addresses green infrastructure, climate change, stormwater management, and the value that landscape architecture contributes to a building's value. "Planting more trees is what will make a difference," she says. "Every project that we do in GEO is about elevating landscape—we're always thinking of resilience, things that will work in the years to come." —*KF*

Above
Miami Children's Museum,
Miami, FL, Arquitectonica,
2003. © Robin Hill

Right
Atlantis Condominium,
Miami, FL, Arquitectonica,
1982. © Norman McGrath

TOSHIKO MORI

BORN
Kobe, Japan, 1951

EDUCATION
Cooper Union, BArch, 1976;
Harvard GSD, Hon. MArch,
1996

PRACTICE
Edward Larrabee Barnes and
Associates, 1976–81; Toshiko
Mori Architect, 1981–

TEACHING
Harvard GSD, 1995–

NOTABLE HONORS
Bernoudy Visiting Architect
Fellowship, American Academy
of Rome, 2002; inaugural John
Hejduk Award, Cooper Union,
2003; Award in Architecture,
American Academy of Arts
and Letters, 2005; Medal of
Honor, AIA New York, 2005;
Fellow, American Academy
of Arts and Sciences, 2016;
AD100, *Architectural Digest*,
2019, 2018, 2017, 2016, 2014;
Women in Architecture Award,
Architectural Record, 2019;
ACSA Topaz Medallion for
Excellence in Architectural
Education, 2019

During her childhood in Japan, Toshiko Mori's grandmother often took her to visit historic temple grounds and gardens and to see traditional Japanese arts and crafts. Although her grandmother's dreams of becoming a doctor were not possible as a woman of her generation, she encouraged Mori to pursue academics and a fulfilling career. As a teenager, Mori was passionate about the sciences, engineering, arts, and philosophy, and she chose to study architecture because it could combine those subjects in a fascinating way. While at Cooper Union during the 1970s, she found a generous mentor in Dean John Hejduk.

Upon graduation, Mori worked for modernist Edward Larrabee Barnes, who she describes as "one of the last gentleman architects."[17] Barnes had been a student of Walter Gropius and Marcel Breuer and lived in a house very similar to Breuer's. Mori spent time there with Barnes and his wife, becoming familiar with its placement of terraces and trees and of modernist proportions. Mori later renovated and created an addition for a Breuer house and studio that reflected on that experience.

Mori values architecture as the product of a dialogue, with listening and observation being fundamental components. Her own dialogues also continue with deceased twentieth-century masters, sometimes as exercises in contrast or contradiction. These are among the lessons she shares with her students at the Harvard GSD, where she teaches studios and seminars and advises thesis students. In 1995, Mori became the GSD's first tenured female professor.

Perhaps, Mori suggests, because she was fortunate enough to be mentored by "men who shared similar values," she only recently became fully conscious of herself as a "woman" architect. "Architecture is about originality and having a unique vision," she says, and she is excited to see women's "fresh and creative" viewpoints influencing the profession more broadly. She wonders if being a woman may be an advantage now to architects for the first time.

One of Mori's recent, award-winning projects is Thread, an artist's residency and cultural center in rural Senegal, from 2015. Relying exclusively on local materials, construction techniques, and project management, the project establishes ownership and belonging. She began its design by looking at African-hut vernacular and, in particular, its traditional pitched roof. The voluptuous curvature of her own building's bamboo roof is a kind of inversion of that model, featuring openings that function as compression rings to make it stronger. Its design drives rainwater into a cistern that satisfies a substantial amount of the community's domestic and agricultural water requirements. It also uses prevailing wind directions to help cool the building's inhabitants with breezes during extreme heat. Mori has designed several canopies; this one's highly sophisticated geometry recalls two earlier ones her firm designed for Manhattan's No. 7 subway extension and Hudson Yards Subway Station at 34th Street.

Mori perceives architecture as a dynamic system of checks and balances that usually works, "unlike financial and political systems, which break down a lot. The architectural system as a way of working is much more robust." —*JSE*

Left
Peter Freeman Gallery, New
York, NY, Toshiko Mori Architect,
2013. © Michael Moran

Below
Thread, Artists' Residency
and Cultural Center, Sinthian,
Senegal, Toshiko Mori Architect,
2015. © Iwan Baan

YVONNE FARRELL & SHELLEY McNAMARA

YVONNE FARRELL / BORN
Tullamore, Ireland, 1951

SHELLEY McNAMARA / BORN
Lisdoonvarna, Ireland, 1952

EDUCATION
University College Dublin,
BArch, 1974

PRACTICE
Grafton Architects, 1978–

TEACHING
University College Dublin,
1970s; Kenzo Tange Chair,
Harvard GSD, 2010; École
polytechnique fédérale de
Lausanne, 2020

NOTABLE HONORS
Fellow, RIBA, 2009; Silver
Lion Prize, Venice Biennale,
2012; Fellow, Royal Institute of
Architects Ireland, 2013; Jane
Drew Prize, 2015; Co-curator,
Venice Architecture Biennale,
2018; Gold Medal, RIBA, 2019;
Pritzker Prize (with Yvonne
Farrell), 2020

"Good neighbors" is the way the Pritzker Prize jury describes the exemplary buildings by 2020 laureates Yvonne Farrell and Shelley McNamara, cofounders of Grafton Architects. The contributions of their thoughtful architecture consistently leave the communities where they're located in better shape than when they found them. Perhaps equally refreshing in this profession is that the architects' generosity extends to how they run their own office and their generosity toward their colleagues, things cited as additional criteria in their selection for the prize. Labeled by the Pritzker jury as "pioneers in a field that has traditionally been and still is a male-dominated profession, they are also beacons to others as they forge their exemplary professional path." Farrell and McNamara are the fourth and fifth women (after Zaha Hadid, Kazuyo Sejima, and Carme Pigem) to be honored with the Pritzker Prize and the first architects based in Ireland.

Educational work is a significant part of the partners' professional identities as well as their portfolio: they have led design studios for over forty years at University College Dublin, where they met and from which they both graduated. They also held the Kenzo Tange Chair at Harvard GSD in 2010. Farrell and McNamara currently teach at the École polytechnique fédérale de Lausanne in Lausanne, Switzerland.

Their outstanding architecture for educational institutions includes the University of Engineering and Technology (2015) in Lima, Peru, and the economics department at the Bocconi University (2008), recipient of the World Building of the Year Award. In a 2014 video interview, Farrell described their delight in designing the University of Limerick Medical School (2013): "The idea behind this new medical school was to reform the way that medicine was taught in Ireland." It was apparently based on the model of a teacher of medicine in Canada, who had been inspired by the pedagogy of a school of architecture. The theory goes something like this: "Knowledge is absorbed consciously and unconsciously. It's absorbed accidentally. Sometimes it's consumed; sometimes it's discovered. If you put students into a certain kind of space, they will expect to be fed; if you put them in another kind of space, they will expect to be challenged. So space prepares you to receive or to respond." Both women received honorary doctoral degrees from Trinity College Dublin.

Curating the 2018 Venice Architecture Biennale, McNamara and Farrell chose the theme of "Freespace." "We are interested in going beyond the visual, emphasizing the role of architecture in the choreography of daily life," the team declared. "We see the Earth as client. This brings with it long-lasting responsibilities." The event showcased exemplary work, much of it created by women in this book.

In a 2014 exhibition at the Royal Academy of Arts, *Sensing Spaces: Architecture Reimagined*, the Grafton cofounders revealed an earlier exploration into the experiential qualities of architecture. "How does the room you're sitting in make you feel?" was the show's simple yet provocative premise. McNamara and Farrell made this statement: "Buildings tell the stories of our lives in built form… We walk through and feel spaces with our whole bodies and our senses, not just with our eyes and with our minds. We are fully

involved in the experience; this is what makes us human."

Those words are given form in the creators' outstanding buildings, such as the Offices for the Department of Finance (2009) in Dublin. Liberating examples of spaces for education and work, they manage to make stone appear at once monumental and humanizing with the play of light on its surface. By all accounts, light is an extraordinary tool in their hands.

The Pritzker Prize jury noted that the architects' sophisticated understanding of designing sections of buildings allows interior spaces to connect with the outdoors, permitting natural light to penetrate and animate spaces deep inside a building. "Often light streams from skylights or upper-story windows throughout the interiors…providing warmth and visual interest, helping the inhabitants easily orient themselves in the spaces."

McNamara views the quality of light in a place as one of the cultural aspects of architecture. "Light is free; everyone can have it," she said in the 2014 video interview. "How can we move it and change it and capture it so that for a short time in your life you say, 'Hmm, this is something lovely here.'" With that generous thought, she lights the way for a more promising future for the profession.

"Each project is both beginning again and continuing," Farrell told the *New York Times* after she and McNamara were the first two women to win the Pritzker Prize together. "Architecture is the silent language that speaks," she added, likening them to inventors. "We're really saying that, when people need something, they don't just need a building that will keep the rain out. They need something we need to find expression for."[18] —*JSE*

Bocconi University, Milan, Italy, Grafton Architects, 2008. © Frederico Brunetti

Left
University of Limerick, Piazza, Ireland, Grafton Architects, 2013. © Denis Gilbert

Below
University of Engineering and Technology (UTEC) Campus, Lima, Peru, Grafton Architects, 2015. © Iwan Baan

Opposite
The Marshall Building, London School of Economics, London, rendering, Grafton Architects, 2021. Courtesy Grafton Architects

SHIRLEY BLUMBERG

BORN
Cape Town, South Africa, 1952

EDUCATION
University of Cape Town, 1972; University of Toronto, MArch, 1976

PRACTICE
Barton Myers Associates, 1977; KPMB Architects, 1987–

NOTABLE HONORS
International Award, RIBA, 2012; Order of Canada, 2013; Governor General's Medal of Excellence, 2014; cofounder, Building Equality in Architecture, Canada, 2015–

Shirley Blumberg describes the Cape Town, South Africa, of her childhood in the 1960s as a country "hardly on the cutting edge in terms of women's liberation."[19] Although she loved drawing, science, and art in high school, she didn't see architecture as a career path that was available to her, even after her sister suggested that she consider enrolling in architecture school. She decided to pursue architectural studies, however, and she graduated from the University of Cape Town in 1972. Soon after, she left the country for England.

Because of the oil crisis of 1973, the job market in London was poor, and she left the following year to pursue a degree in architecture at the University of Toronto. Even with all of her relocations, her experience growing up in apartheid-era South Africa never left her, shaping much of her career.

Blumberg began working at Barton Myers Associates in Toronto in 1977, where she remained for a decade. In 1987, Myers announced his decision to move his office to Los Angeles, and Blumberg and the firm's other three partners—Bruce Kuwabara, Thomas Payne, and Marianne McKenna—stayed in Toronto and formed Kuwabara Payne McKenna Blumberg Architects (KPMB).

An early competition in Blumberg's career was the complex and ambitious one for Toronto's Design Exchange (1994)—KPMB beat out forty other interviewees to win the job. Blumberg became partner-in-charge of the $8 million redesign and expansion of the city's historic Stock Exchange building (1994), incorporating a 1960s Mies van der Rohe structure next door.

In addition to designs for museums, theaters, and medical and educational buildings, such as Canada's National Ballet School (2005) and the Centre for International Governance Innovation (2011) in Waterloo, Ontario, the recipient of the RIBA International Award in 2012, Blumberg has placed a strong emphasis on housing and community building through the prism of pluralism.

In 2012, KPMB completed work on Blumberg's Toronto Community Housing Block 32, providing family-centered rental housing in the city's Railway Lands West precinct. The adjacent Fort York Branch Library (2014) of the Toronto Public Library, also designed by Blumberg, offers a central gathering place within the community. She is a member of the Toronto Community Housing Design Review Panel and has served on the City of Toronto Design Review Panel. In 2013, the Order of Canada invested Blumberg as a member, particularly for her "commitment to creating spaces that foster a sense of community."

Blumberg is a cofounder of Building Equality in Architecture in 2015, an organization with multiple chapters around Canada, promoting the visibility and achievements of women and minorities in the architectural profession. —*KF*

Left
150 Dan Leckie Way, Toronto
Community Housing Block
32, Toronto, Ontario, KPMB
Architects, 2012. © Tom Arban

Below
Fort York Branch Library,
Toronto, Ontario, KPMB
Architects, 2014. © Riley
Snelling

KATHRYN FINDLAY

BORN
Finavon, Scotland, 1953

DIED
London, England, 2014

EDUCATION
Edinburgh College of Art; AA
School of Architecture, MArch,
1979

PRACTICE
Arata Isozaki, 1980–82; Ushida
Findlay Architects, 1986–2004;
Kathryn Findlay, 2004–14

TEACHING
University of Tokyo, mid-
1980s–2001; University of
Dundee Architecture and
Urban Planning, honorary
professor, 2004–9

NOTABLE HONORS
First female professor at
the University of Tokyo;
Development in Scotland for
Flagship building, Glasgow,
Regional Award, 2000; first
female architect elected to
Royal Scottish Academy, 2006;
Jane Drew Prize, 2014; Royal
Incorporation of Architects in
Scotland, 2013–14

When Kathryn Findlay was a student at Edinburgh College of Art, she visited the Glasgow School of Art, where the eponymous Mackintosh building profoundly influenced her. The "alchemy of space, light, shadow and materials" and "the idea of combining something poetic with something practical" inspired her to pursue architecture.[20] She trained at London's AA School of Architecture, where she was mentored by Peter Cook and Leon van Schaik.[21] After graduating in 1979, she traveled to Japan on a scholarship and worked with Arata Isozaki, one of the leading figures of the Metabolist movement. In Japan, Findlay learned the importance of smells, sounds, and textures in the design of the built environment.[22]

In 1986, Findlay set up an architectural practice with her then-husband Eisaku Ushida. The couple achieved international acclaim in the 1990s for their eccentric homes on urban plots that went against the dominant style of Japanese minimalism. The futuristic Truss Wall House (1993) in Tokyo exemplifies the duo's interest in movement and morphology. Composed of a series of curves and folds—where walls, floors, ceilings, and furniture merge into one continuous surface—the house appears less constructed than sculpted.[23]

Following Japan's economic recession in 1997, Findlay and Ushida gradually relocated their practice to London. Shortly thereafter, they separated yet maintained their collaborative efforts from a distance. In 2002, Findlay and Ushida won a competition from the RIBA for a "country estate of the future" in Cheshire, England.[24] The glass and sandstone house features four cone-shaped wings that stretch into the surrounding landscape.[25] It envisioned a radical approach to provincial English living.[26]

Prior to declaring bankruptcy in 2004, Ushida Findlay Architects completed a handful of significant projects: an inner-city Homes for the Future (1999) in Glasgow, Pool House 1 (1999) in London, Graveney School (2002) in London, and the Kasahara Culture and Amenity Hall (2006) in Gifu, Japan.[27]

Findlay made a comeback with her vernacular-busting Poolhouse 2 (2008) in Chilterns, England. Collaborating with David Miller Architects, the indoor swimming pool proposed an innovative solution to the challenge of joining a sixteenth-century farmhouse with a seventeenth-century barn while complying with local preservation codes. The steel and glass structure's roof elegantly mixed technology with craftsmanship, as well as British and Japanese vernaculars.[28]

The following year, Anish Kapoor and Cecil Balmond commissioned Findlay to realize the architectural elements of their ArcelorMittal Orbit Tower for London's 2012 Olympic Park, an "anti-tower" conveying a sense of instability and motion similar to Findlay's early houses.[29] Before the completion of Findlay's final project, the renovation of the York Art Gallery (2016), she passed away from a brain tumor at the age of sixty. Just days after her death, the *Architects' Journal* announced she had won the 2014 Jane Drew Prize for her "outstanding contribution to the status of women in architecture."[30] **—LFR**

York Art Gallery, York, England,
2015. Photo Giles Rocholl

JILL N. LERNER

BORN
Mamaroneck, NY, 1953

EDUCATION
Cornell AAP, BArch, 1976

PRACTICE
Norman Rosenfeld Architects,
mid-1970s–1994; Kohn
Pedersen Fox Associates (KPF),
1994–

TEACHING
University of Chicago Booth
School of Business; Walter
B. Ford College for Creative
Studies; UCLA, Semel Institute
and Center for Health Sciences

NOTABLE HONORS
CUNY Baruch College,
Honor Award, AIA, 2003;
President, AIA New York, 2013;
Keystone Award, Beverly Willis
Architecture Foundation, 2018

Jill Lerner loved art, math, and science as a child, yet she had not considered a career in architecture until her twelfth-grade guidance counselor steered her in that direction. This was the push she needed to pursue an architecture degree at Cornell University. Lerner graduated from Cornell AAP in 1976. While in school, she interned at a small firm near her New Jersey hometown. She joined Kohn Pedersen Fox Associates (KPF) in New York City in 1994. Just five years later, in 1999, Lerner became the first woman partner in the firm's history. KPF's principals valued her experience with large educational projects.

"When I joined, KPF had pretty much only done corporate and commercial work, and they were very much wanting to expand and diversify," Lerner says. "In my case, they said, 'Well, we really want to do these building types and we haven't had any luck getting them, so maybe we should hire you.'"[31] Lerner's experience allowed her to jump in for a design for Baruch College, an 800,000-square-foot campus for the CUNY system in downtown Manhattan. The project won an AIA Honor Award.

"We were off to the races, and we did a big building for Wharton Business School after that, and a number of other really diverse buildings," Lerner says.

A new area of practice that Lerner and KPF are now exploring is the overlap between developers and academia, where developers work with colleges and universities to build academic and research buildings. This brings "research from ideas to reality and from the strict research stage into incubating businesses, creating tech campuses, creating jobs," Lerner says. She has led master planning for the graduate school of business at the University of Chicago, as well as the Walter B. Ford College for Creative Studies in Detroit and the Semel Institute and Center for Health Sciences at UCLA.

Lerner is particularly proud of the civic projects she has overseen in recent years, including the New York City Housing Authority (NYCHA) Red Hook Houses (in conjunction with FEMA and NYCHA) in Red Hook, Brooklyn (2020), an area that suffered extensive damage from the deadly Hurricane Sandy in 2012.

Lerner's involvement with the architectural community has extended to her serving as president of the New York chapter of the AIA in 2013. She also emphasizes the importance of mentorship in the architectural profession, particularly for women, who have fewer role models. Recognizing her own responsibility as an architect of stature, she identifies as being among "a fairly rare group within the major firms in New York City," she says. "The more women that really persevere and take on more and more responsibilities, the more role models there are." —*KF*

Left
William and Anita Newman
Vertical Campus, Baruch
College, New York, NY,
Jill N. Lerner for KPF, 2001.
© Michael Moran

Below
New York University Shanghai,
Shanghai, China, Jill N. Lerner
for KPF, 2021. Courtesy KPF

SYLVIA SMITH

BORN
Chicago, IL, 1954

EDUCATION
Dickinson College, BA, 1973;
UVA, MArch, 1978

PRACTICE
Michael Graves Architecture
& Design, 1980; Fox & Fowle,
1982; FXFOWLE Architects,
2000; FXCollaborative, 2018–

TEACHING
Yestermorrow Design Build
School

NOTABLE HONORS
Fellow, AIA, 2008; Bernard
Baruch Medal for Business
and Civic Leadership, 2010;
Kea Distinguished Professor,
University of Maryland School
of Architecture, 2014; panelist,
Venice Architecture Biennale,
2014; Woman of Distinction,
Girl Scouts of Greater New
York, 2016

"I have always thought in three dimensions and always thought spatially," Sylvia Smith says of her natural inclination toward architecture. Her father was an amateur pilot, and Smith was able to see the "logic of the landscape" from the air while flying with him around the Chicago suburbs.[32] This shaped her understanding of, and passion for, the built environment.

Smith was constantly building and making things as a child, manifesting what ultimately became her career as an early interest in art. Yet she had little knowledge of the creative genius of architects. "I don't think I met an architect or understood what an architect did until I was in my art classes in college, and those architects were Brunelleschi and Bramante and Alberti," she says. During her time at Dickinson College, where she studied studio art and art history, she was involved in theater and set design. Here is where she first learned how to make scale drawings.

After receiving her bachelor's degree, Smith took a job at the Fine Arts Library at UVA, where she interacted with graduate architecture students and architecture faculty. This contact facilitated her interest in the field. "I realized that here were all the things that I thought about, plus my interest in aesthetics, my interest in social issues, making the world better."

She continued her education at the University of Virginia, where she designed and built two houses in the Charlottesville area and received her master's degree in architecture. Smith subsequently moved to New York and worked for Michael Graves before joining Fox & Fowle (what is now FXCollaborative) in 1982. In 1986, the firm won the assignment to design the new American Craft Museum on Fifty-Third Street in Manhattan.

Mixed with her practice, Smith spent summers teaching two-week courses on the concepts of basic design and building techniques at Yestermorrow Design Build School in Vermont. At Yestermorrow, she focused on sustainability in the built environment.

Promoted to partner in 1996 and founding the firm's Cultural/Educational Studio, Smith concentrated on cultural and educational design work, which she found more fulfilling than commercial high-rises. "I thought if I could create an esprit de corps around that work, others would share the passion," she says of building the studio's team designing museums, schools, and similar types of buildings.

Working in a male-dominated profession, Smith says she retained a dominating voice in her head telling her not to give up: "I just sucked it up and said, 'I'm going to do this.'"

Recent projects include the Lion House (2008) and the Center for Global Conservation (2009) at the Bronx Zoo, the Lincoln Center North Plaza (2011), New York's Statue of Liberty Museum (2019) on Liberty Island, a new Business School for Columbia University (2022, in collaboration with Diller Scofidio + Renfro), and the new Children's Museum of Manhattan (2023).
—*KF*

Left
WCS Center for Global
Conservation, Bronx Zoo, New
York, NY, FXCollaborative,
2009. © David Sundberg/Esto

Below
Alice Tully Hall, Lincoln Center,
New York, NY, FXCollaborative
with Diller Scofidio + Renfro,
2011. © Iwan Baan

DEBORAH BERKE

BORN
Queens, NY, 1954

EDUCATION
RISD, BFA, BArch, 1977; CUNY,
MUP, Urban Design, 1984

PRACTICE
Deborah Berke Partners, 1982–

TEACHING
Yale University School of
Architecture, instructor,
1987–2016, dean, 2016–

NOTABLE HONORS
Hall of Fame Inductee, *Interior
Design*, 2002; Honorary
Doctorate of Fine Arts, RISD,
2005; Berkeley-Rupp Prize,
University of California,
Berkeley, 2012; Sackler
First Award, Sackler Center
of Feminist Art, Brooklyn
Museum, 2017; National Design
Award, Interior Design, Cooper
Hewitt, 2017; Medal of Honor,
AIA New York, 2019

Deborah Berke is widely considered a minimalist. Yet accepting that label misses the extraordinary care that she puts into choosing the materials and creating the details that make up every gesture of her firm's buildings. "I worry that minimalism may be shorthand for things being spare," she says. "My idea behind the understated nature of the work is that you can find something new each time you visit."[33] That's a very different definition. "Enduring" may be a more apt description of the architecture Berke has created over the past forty years.

While re-envisioning the Rockefeller Arts Center at SUNY Fredonia, originally designed in 1968 by I .M. Pei & Partners, Berke's team made an effort to connect its new classrooms, studios, and performance spaces to the site's history. Their research revealed that the sons and grandsons of the concrete workers who made the original walls were still doing that type of work. Informing the new design, concrete details by these craftsmen augmented Deborah Berke Partners's (DBP) metal- and glass-wall additions.

In 2016, Berke became dean of the Yale University School of Architecture, where she had been teaching since 1987. Her leadership has shaken off the long shadow of former dean Robert A. M. Stern. Billie Tsien, who also teaches in the department, credits Berke with creating an environment where students, female and male, can test out ideas with a sense of confidence. (Singling out Berke's mentorship of women, the 2012 Berkeley-Rupp Prize highlighted this as one of her strengths.)

She's familiar with the challenges women face. She also sees the much larger issue that students and architects point to: the numbers of unrepresented people in the profession—by race, gender, or socioeconomic background, as well as the narrow profile of those typically served by buildings designed by architects. To the last point, DBP's "mission-driven" work focuses on housing organizations like the Gay Men's Health Crisis (2011) and the Wallace Foundation (2020). A recent groundbreaking project is the exhibition, coworking, and black-box theater space for NXTHVN (2019), an experimental artists' collective in New Haven, Connecticut.

Artists have always figured prominently in Berke's life. She says, "It's my world." Berke's mother was a fashion designer and professor at Fashion Institute of Technology in New York City. As a teenager, Deborah knew that she wanted to attend an arts school rather than a traditional liberal arts college. She studied fine arts and architecture at RISD. Little-known fact: Berke also briefly worked in construction at Arcosanti in the 1970s, Paolo Soleri's experimental community in the Arizona desert.

Berke's design for the Irwin Union Bank (2006) in Columbus, Indiana, was unique enough to have earned it a role in the 2017 film *Columbus*. DBP also conceived a new distribution headquarters in Indianapolis for the Cummins Engine Company (2016), whose financial commitment to architecture since the 1950s catalyzed Columbus's unparalleled collection of great buildings. "Today Columbus feels active and vital," she says. Speaking of J. Irwin Miller and his family, who created an architectural destination of their hometown, Berke says, "They've done a great job bringing it into the twenty-first century." —*JSE*

Top
Cummins Indy Distribution
Headquarters, Indianapolis, IN,
Deborah Berke Partners, 2016.
Photo Chris Cooper

Bottom
North Penn House, Indianapolis,
IN, Deborah Berke Partners,
2016. Photo Glint Studios

ELIZABETH DILLER

BORN
Łódź, Poland, 1954

EDUCATION
Cooper Union, BArch, 1979

PRACTICE
Diller + Scofidio, 1981–2003;
Diller Scofidio + Renfro, 2004–

NOTABLE HONORS
MacArthur Fellowship,
1999; James Beard Award
for Outstanding Restaurant
Design, 2000; National Design
Award, Smithsonian, 2005;
100 Most Influential People,
Time, 2009; Centennial Medal
of Honor (with Ricardo Scofidio
and Charles Renfro), American
Academy in Rome, 2013;
Architecture Innovator of the
Year Award, *Wall Street Journal*
magazine, 2017; *Time 100*: The
Most Influential People of 2018;
Jane Drew Prize, 2019; Royal
Academy Architecture Prize
(Diller Scofidio + Renfro), 2019

Elizabeth Diller was born in Poland in 1954 to a Jewish family heavily impacted by the Holocaust. "I grew up never knowing aunts, uncles, or grandparents," she told *Architectural Digest* in 2018. She moved to New York City with her parents when she was six.

Diller initially studied art at Cooper Union, particularly film and multimedia installations. Her interest shifted and her curiosity was piqued when she saw a class called Architectonics in the course catalog. Becoming interested in the discourse around architecture, rather than the profession of architecture, Diller's own thinking shifted to three dimensions. She decided to get an architecture degree, even while she still wasn't committed to the idea of being a practicing architect

While at Cooper Union in the 1970s, Diller began collaborating with one of her professors, Ricardo Scofidio. "When Ric and I started working together, we imagined an alternative practice: not an architecture practice, but a practice where we could teach, write, and make installations," she says. "We wanted to create agendas that followed our curiosity, independent of the profession which we felt was intellectually bankrupt at the time. We had little interest in making buildings." She says that during this time, she and Scofidio realized that it was possible for an architect to work on issues of "everyday space" without a client and without a budget, and even without a potential site.

Diller graduated from Cooper Union in 1979, and she and Scofidio founded their firm, Diller + Scofidio, in 1981. The couple eventually married. Much of the firm's work in the 1980s and 1990s was theoretical and experimental.

The firm's 1989 design for the Slow House on Long Island was conceptualized as "a house with a view," but not in the traditional sense. A long passage from the entrance door to a window opposite culminated in a view of the water. The view was enriched by a TV camera mounted on a boom angled up and away from the house, which recorded the vista and showed it on a monitor that was suspended in front of the sea-facing glass. The house, Scofidio and Diller said, was conceived as a passage, a door that leads to a window,…a physical entry to an optical departure."[34] The foundation was poured, but construction was never finished. Nevertheless, the house strengthened Diller and Scofidio's reputations as design visionaries.

In 1999, the MacArthur Foundation awarded Diller and Scofidio with a MacArthur Fellowship "Genius Grant," allowing them to create some of their most notable built works, including the Blur Building, a temporary pavilion built for the 2002 Swiss Expo in Yverdon-les-Bains, Switzerland. The project started as a critique of high-end media. A man-made cloud encompassed a metal framework, creating the illusion of a vaporous building measuring 300 feet wide and 65 feet high. "The project used sensing and real-time computing. We were reading and detecting weather conditions and responding with a smart system in real time. It was growing artificial intelligence."[35] Once inside, visitors could immerse themselves in white noise and whiteout visual conditions.

Since the early 2000s, Diller + Scofidio (which became Diller Scofidio + Renfro [DS+R] in 2004, with the addition of partner Charles Renfro) has cemented a

Roy and Diana Vagelos
Education Center, New York, NY,
Diller Scofidio + Renfro, 2016.
Photo Iwan Baan. Courtesy Diller
Scofidio + Renfro

The Shed, New York, NY, Diller Scofidio + Renfro, 2019. Photo Iwan Baan. Courtesy Diller Scofidio + Renfro

spot at the highest echelon of designers of public and cultural spaces. "The idea of working in the public realm was always part of the ethos of our work," Diller says. This ideology drove the firm's work on projects like the Institute of Contemporary Art in Boston (2006), a cantilevered structure on Boston Harbor, housing dynamic space for public programs and an intimate context for viewing art.

This ethos also carried through to DS+R's work on the High Line, New York's 1.45-mile elevated park built on a former rail line, some of their most notable to date. The park, completed in phases between 2000 and 2019, receives an estimated eight million visitors annually. It terminates at Hudson Yards, featuring the DS+R-designed Shed, a cultural center featuring a U-shaped moving roof that was completed in 2019.

DS+R's work often incorporates surrounding vistas. "In many of our projects, we claim more space than we have,

optically," Diller says. "What's strong and unusual about the High Line, and one of the reasons it became so popular, is that it opened up more than the surface of the High Line. It opened up new, unofficial vistas of New York."

Diller taught at the Cooper Union's Irwin S. Chanin School of Architecture from 1981 to 1990, and currently serves as a member of the architecture faculty at Princeton University. In 2018, she was the only architect named in *Time* magazine's list of the 100 Most Influential People.

Diller still considers herself an artist, a fact that helped shape her perspective working on the MoMA project, developing the museum space to interact with the art on display. In October 2019, MoMA reopened following a two-year renovation and expansion designed by DS+R and Gensler. "It's the obligation of the museum architect—almost their moral imperative—to add to the culture of architecture through the design of the building," she says. —*KF*

Blur Building, Swiss Expo,
Yverdon-les-Bains, Switzerland,
Diller Scofidio + Renfro, 2002.
Photo Beat Widmer. Courtesy
Diller Scofidio + Renfro

CARME PINÓS

BORN
Barcelona, Spain, 1954

EDUCATION
Escola Tècnica Superior
d'Arquitectura de Barcelona,
BArch, 1979

PRACTICE
Pinós-Miralles, 1981–91;
Estudio Carme Pinós, 1991–

NOTABLE HONORS
First Prize, Spanish Biennial of
Architecture, 2008; Honorary
Fellow, AIA, 2011; International
Fellow, RIBA, 2013; Creu de
Sant Jordi Medal, 2015; Richard
Neutra Award, California
Polytechnic State University,
Pomona, 2016; Berkeley-
Rupp Professorship and
Prize, University of California,
Berkeley, 2016

Carme Pinós views the future of architecture as problematic. "I am a little afraid," she says. "The current direction is for big offices that do not take risks or make buildings with personality. They express luxury but no poetry."[36] Her work over the past four decades, typically produced by an office of less than twenty people, makes an outstanding case for an alternative.

Working in all scales—from furniture and product design to district planning—and in very different places—Mexico, Australia, and Spain among them—Pinós leaves her signature everywhere she goes. Reading about history and cultures helps her to stay informed and to sharpen her perception of scale and monumentality in Mexico, for instance, versus a smaller, more contained site in Europe. Uniting her designs, however, are a few consistent choices she makes: "It's difficult to find symmetry in my architecture because it's very fluid." Pinós explains her preference for dynamic, "never static," forms and always considers the human scale. She values movement and the relationships between people. Robust, sculptural words like *soaring*, *hovering*, *colliding*, *anchoring*, and *tethering* come to mind when viewing Pinós's most celebrated recent works: MPavilion (2018) in Melbourne; Escola Massana, Art and Design Center (2017) in Barcelona; and CaixaForum Cultural and Exhibition Centre (2014) in Zaragoza, Spain.

Pinós established her first practice, Pinós-Miralles in 1981 with her former husband, Enric Miralles, whom she met in architecture school. They traveled together throughout Europe to visit the buildings of the masters of the 1950s. "We were autodidacts and taught ourselves," she says. "His energy helped me to discover myself."

Some of the working processes the couple implemented in their firm carried over to Pinós's own practice, which she established in 1991: "Everything starts with diagrams," she says, referencing the compelling drawings on her site. "I'm first looking at structure and the rules to develop the project and find a final shape." She then shares her ideas with her team. Regarding materials, she prefers "natural materials that express time in a dignified way," like concrete.

Pinós completed a set of buildings in the historical center of Barcelona in 2019, after winning an urbanism competition. The center-city intervention includes Gardunya Square, La Massana Fine Arts Center, a housing block, and the legendary La Boqueria Market. "We must offer a sense of the relationships that make up a community, provide a dialogue between old and new. Context is also memory and culture."

"The idea of the city should come first, before architecture. Public space, commonality, places where we can be social and experience freedom, is more important than fantastic architecture. The square is a place where different people can meet."

Pinós looks forward to the future work of women architects, believing that "architecture requires operating from a position of flexibility, not seclusion…Women are better at this. For millennia, women have listened and tried to understand others, which is so important for architecture."
—*JSE*

Above
Cube 2 Office Tower, Zapopan,
Mexico, Estudio Carme Pinós,
2014. © Jordi Bernadó

Below
MPavilion, Melbourne,
Australia, Estudio Carme Pinós,
2018. © John Gollings

JULIE EIZENBERG

BORN
Melbourne, Australia, 1954

EDUCATION
University of Melbourne,
BArch, 1978; UCLA, MArch II,
1981; University of Melbourne,
Honorary PhD, Architecture,
2016

PRACTICE
Koning Eizenberg Architecture,
1981–

NOTABLE HONORS
Emerging Voices Award,
Architectural League of
New York, 1990; Firm of the
Year, Residential Architect
Leadership Awards, 2004;
Firm Award, AIA California
Council, 2009; Gold Medal,
AIA Los Angeles, 2012; Gold
Medal, Australian Institute of
Architects, 2019

Los Angeles–based Julie Eizenberg designs both houses and housing. "We don't distinguish between people with means and those without," she says of the eponymous firm she cofounded with her partner and husband, Hank Koning. (The firm now also includes partners Nathan Bishop and Brian Lane.) "What gives light to one gives light to another; we just have a different toolkit available to work with."[37]

Eizenberg remembers when, in the mid-1980s, social impact work was not seen as legitimate. Eizenberg, who served as a frequent advisor to the Mayor's Institute on City Design, has helped to raise the status of this effort. Speaking of Koning Eizenberg's practice, she says, "We approach these designs with the belief that design can and should benefit all and, moreover, that a client's means is no measure of design opportunity."

According to Eizenberg, uniformity is the biggest problem in housing today. The operating principles, scale, and speed, she says, are the drivers, the same as they were in the 1960s, the era of the soulless, mass-produced high-rises. "I believe design should be based first on the residents' experience." Informal shared space is the biggest contribution her firm makes to all its residential projects, whether an outdoor common space in housing or an indoor family space.

In 2020, *Architecture Australia* published an article by the architects describing their working philosophy. Briefly, it stated: "Trust is engendered by empowering and valuing the user. A spatial sequence that offers choice cedes power to the user and discovery further consolidates a sense of control."[38]

For the Geffen Academy (2018), a progressive secondary school on the UCLA campus, Eizenberg and her team honed a building program for a renovation fostering a "community of learning" in an existing 75,000-square-foot building designed sixteen years earlier by Steven Ehrlich. Rethinking how kids master knowledge resulted in two transformative concepts: an open library that replaces traditional circulation and features a changing, unsecured book collection designed to build curiosity and a lounge and work spaces for students and faculty. This open and inviting configuration serves as an educational prototype with a philosophy that also resonates with its architects: exploration of ideas and conventions.

The education niche is a growing focus for Koning Eizenberg. Eizenberg has a suggestion for improving this type of work: "I wish school districts would understand the need to invest in an ongoing relationship with their architects instead of commissioning a one-off building. Education is changing rapidly. That deeper relationship could produce greater cultural value."

Similarly, she notes that women's influence in architecture will continue to grow as the cultural norms of childcare grow. "I believe the acceptance of flexible schedules and family leave is a direct consequence of women's impact in the workplace," says Eizenberg. "Think about what might be if we had universal daycare—we could really see how women redefine practice and the aspirations of the profession." —*JSE*

Above
Twenty-Eighth Street
Apartments, Los Angeles, CA,
Koning Eizenberg Architecture,
2012. © Eric Staudenmaier

Right
Geffen Academy, Los Angeles,
CA, Koning Eizenberg
Architecture, 2018. © Eric
Staudenmaier

FRANCINE HOUBEN

BORN
Sittard, Netherlands, 1955

EDUCATION
Delft University of Technology,
MSc Architecture/Urban
Planning, 1984

PRACTICE
Mecanoo, 1984–

TEACHING
Yale University School of
Architecture, 2020–

NOTABLE HONORS
Honorary Fellow, RIBA, 2001;
Curator, First International
Architecture Biennale,
Rotterdam, 2003; Honorary
Fellow, AIA, 2007; Honorary
Fellow, Royal Architectural
Institute of Canada, 2007;
Woman Architect of the Year,
Architects' Journal, 2014;
Honorary Doctorate, Utrecht
University, 2016; International
Honorary Fellow Award,
Architecture Institute of
Taiwan, 2018; International
Prize, Prix des Femmes
Architectes, 2019

Francine Houben is lending her somewhat invisible expertise to the New York Public Library system. "Libraries are the most important public buildings," she told Amy Frerson for *Dezeen* in 2013. Both the city's most heavily used branches, the Mid-Manhattan Library and, across Fifth Avenue, the 1911 Beaux Arts Stephen A. Schwarzman Building, are greatly benefiting from her watchful eye. "Although the floor plan is very simple, it's not easy to find your way around," she notes about the beloved older structure.[39]

The vastly improved circulation plan of the library will improve the experience of millions of visitors—a new entrance on Fortieth Street, a new elevator and staircase, and the relocation of staff and support spaces from ground- and street-level floors to allow for more public programs and exhibitions. Researchers will occupy the quieter upper levels. Other libraries designed by Mecanoo, the thriving practice Houben founded in 1984, include the Delft Institute of Technology Library (1997); England's Library of Birmingham (2013), Europe's largest public library; the KRONA Knowledge and Cultural Centre (2015) in Norway; and the renovation of the Mies van der Rohe–designed Martin Luther King Jr. Memorial Library (2020) in Washington, DC.

The name Mecanoo refers to a building toy set that many architects discovered as children, as they did with Trix, Arckit, and Lego. "Architecture should touch all the senses," she says. Mecanoo employs people from twenty-five countries, 40 percent of whom are women. This diversity, says Houben, "helps us understand and reconsider the world," she told *Architect* magazine. "We don't have a formal style because that would block me. In every project we have the same attitude, but what exactly we'll be making is a kind of adventure or surprise." Mecanoo's interdisciplinary approach integrates architecture, landscape, interior design, and urban planning. A model workshop in the office engages traditional timberwork methods alongside 2D and 3D techniques: "The combination of traditional crafts and cutting-edge technology is essential to understanding the world around us."

Colorfully illustrating her statement is Delft City Hall and Train Station (2017), which received an Architizer+ Jury Award in 2016. The hybrid structure sits atop a new train tunnel, replacing a viaduct that had bisected the city since the 1960s. A massive vaulted ceiling that connects the building's two functions displays an 1877 map of Delft printed on hundreds of beams. Halls, walls, and columns are adorned with a contemporary interpretation of Delft Blue tiles, while the view outside the slick glass structure recalls a painting by Johannes Vermeer.

Houben likens her multifarious role at her firm to that of a symphony conductor. "Architecture is never a solo act," she says. "It's all about teamwork, being visionary, sensitive, and supportive at the same time." Her recent interdisciplinary teaching efforts at Yale University School of Architecture in 2020 involved leading an advanced studio for the 2024 Olympic Games in Paris. Yale's schools of drama and music collaborated with the architecture students to envision the Opera House of the Future, an ambitious project advancing the shared values of Paris and the Seine Saint-Denis suburb to a global audience. —*JSE*

Above
Delft City Hall and Train Station, Delft, Netherlands, Mecanoo, 2017. Courtesy Mecanoo

Right
St. Mary of the Angels Chapel, Rotterdam, Netherlands, Mecanoo, 2001. Photo Christian Richters

DORIANA MANDRELLI FUKSAS

BORN
Rome, Italy, 1955

EDUCATION
Sapienza University of Rome, BA, 1979; École Spéciale d'Architecture, 2000

PRACTICE
Studio Fuksas, 1985–

NOTABLE HONORS
Officier de l'Ordre des Arts et des Lettres de la République Française, 2002; Award for Excellence Europe, Urban Land Institute, 2006; Commandeur de l'Ordre des Arts et des Lettres de la République Française, 2013; Chevalier de l'Ordre de La Légion d'Honneur Française, 2020

Born in Rome in 1955, Doriana Mandrelli Fuksas attended the Sapienza University of Rome. She graduated with a degree in the history of modern and contemporary architecture in 1979, earning an additional degree in architecture from ESA, the École Spéciale d'Architecture, Paris. Upon meeting architecture professor Massimiliano Fuksas at Sapienza, "It was love at first sight," she told the blog *An American in Italia* in 2009. She completed her degree in architecture, and the two began collaborating. Mandrelli Fuksas joined Fuksas at his firm in 1985.

Fuksas founded his architecture studio, Studio Fuksas, in Rome in 1967. The work of Studio Fuksas has progressed over the decades, from schools and residential complexes to large-scale public buildings and spaces. Mandrelli Fuksas, herself, has contributed to a wide-ranging body of modern and brutalist designs around the world, serving as director of Studio Fuksas since 1997. Today, the firm's work, and Mandrelli Fuksas's contributions, are defined by versatility, incorporating art, architecture, town planning, landscape architecture, and interior design. Innovative creations, like the Shenzhen Bao'an International Airport Terminal 3 (2013), use original techniques, such as the inclusion of thousands of hexagonal skylights, to create grand designs that are nonetheless friendly and inviting at a human scale.

Studio Fuksas's work in Rome and elsewhere seamlessly blends a reverence for history with a modern, avant-garde sensibility, as most recently exemplified by the duo's design for Sveta Nedelya Square (2022) in Bulgaria, which finds its roots in the historical definition of the place but will also serve as a modern space for social interaction at the heart of the community. Of the responsibility of designing public buildings and spaces, Mandrelli Fuksas says "You have never to forget that you are doing something very important that will have an influence on the people that will stay there, that will live there, that will work in these spaces."[40]

In 2018, after Massimiliano Fuksas alone was awarded the Premio alla Carriera Architettura (the Gold Medal for Italian Architecture) from Italy's Istituto Nazionale di Architettura, more than 250 architects, designers, writers, and academics, including Bjarke Ingels, Rem Koolhaas, and Denise Scott Brown, signed a letter calling for "equal recognition for equal work." The open letter was backed by campaign groups RebelArchitette and Voices of Women Architects, which had launched a petition demanding the Pritzker Prize committee retrospectively recognize Denise Scott Brown for her contributions to husband Robert Venturi's prize, awarded in 1991. The open letter read: "It's important to correct the record now so that young architects can look up to their incredible work and know the whole story—that the work is strong because of joint creativity and collaboration." At this writing, the Istituto Nazionale di Architettura has failed to include Doriana Fuksas in the award. —*KF*

Above
Shenzen Bao'an International
Airport, Terminal 3, Shenzhen,
China, Studio Fuksas, 2013.
© Archivio Fuksas

Left
New Rome/EUR Convention
Center and Hotel ("The Cloud"),
Rome, Italy, Studio Fuksas,
2016. © Roland Halbe

ANNE LACATON

BORN
Saint-Pardoux-la-Rivière,
France, 1955

EDUCATION
School of Architecture of
Bordeaux, BArch, 1980;
University of Bordeaux, Urban
Planning, 1984

PRACTICE
Lacaton & Vassal, 1987–

TEACHING
University of Madrid, visiting
professor; MCH (Master
in Collective Housing),
2007–13, 2017–19, 2021; EPFL
Lausanne (Federal Institute
of Technology in Lausanne),
2004, 2006, 2010–11; Ivan
Smith Studio, University of
Florida, 2012; Clarkson Chair,
University of New York-Buffalo,
2013; Harvard GSD, 2011, 2015;
Sassari University, 2014–15;
Delft University of Technology,
2016–17; Swiss Federal
Institute of Technology,
emeritus associate professor,
2017–21

NOTABLE HONORS
Grand Prix National
d'Architecture, France, 2008;
Simon Architecture Prize/
Fundació Mies van der Rohe
(with Frederic Druot), 2016;
Lifetime Achievement, Trienal
de Arquitectura de Lisboa,
2016; Grand Parc Bordeaux,
EU Mies Award, 2019; Pritzker
Prize (with Jean-Philippe
Vassal), 2021

Born in 1955 in Saint-Pardoux-la-Rivière, France, Anne Lacaton attended the School of Architecture of Bordeaux, graduating in 1980. During her time as an architecture student, Lacaton met and eventually developed a design and personal partnership with Jean-Phillipe Vassal, who had grown up in Casablanca, Morocco. Vassal wanted to return to Africa to work as a civil servant. He moved to the former French colony of Niger, where Lacaton frequently visited him. The local Niger architecture exhibited a design value system that was radically different from what the two had experienced in France. One of their earliest collaborations was a straw hut, inspired by the area's Tuareg nomads, which they used as their Niger home for two years. It formed a model for the way Lacaton and Vassal worked in the future.

By 1984, Lacaton had received a diploma in urban planning from the University of Bordeaux. She and Vassal founded their firm, Lacaton & Vassal. The majority of the firm's work has focused on cultural buildings, housing, and urban projects at a city scale. Beginning in 1993, with a residence they designed for a local Bordeaux family on a tight budget, Lacaton and Vassal started to incorporate adaptable and inexpensive techniques often found in greenhouses in many of their projects. Lacaton and Vassal's design for the expansion and rehabilitation of the Palais de Tokyo in Paris, a deteriorated 1937 building, emphasized raw materials and a stripped-down aesthetic. The rehabilitated building reopened in 2002, and the architects orchestrated a further expansion in 2012.

The Transformation of 530 Dwellings in Bordeaux (2016) consisted of converting three buildings of 530 units. Built in the early 1960s, the buildings and the units desperately needed upgrading. Lacaton and Vassal's transformation started from the interior, creating airy, full-width greenhouse patios on each unit, offering more space, more light, and more view.

Regardless of how green the replacement building is, Lacaton and Vassal maintain that demolition is not an environmentally friendly option—90 percent of what is required is generally already available on-site. "Buildings are beautiful when people feel well in them," Lacaton said in a 2017 speech at the VELUX Daylight Symposium in Berlin. In addition to her design work, Lacaton has had an active role in the academic community, teaching at the University of Madrid, the University of Florida, the University of New York-Buffalo, and the Federal Institute of Technology in Lausanne, among others.

Lacaton and Vassal's work "reflects architecture's democratic spirit," said the Pritzker Prize, proving "that a commitment to a restorative architecture that is at once technological, innovative, and ecologically responsive can be pursued without nostalgia." The Pritzker committee commended the team's work for being "at once beautiful and pragmatic, they refuse any opposition between architectural quality, environmental responsibility, and the quest for an ethical society." This is epitomized in the FRAC Nord-Pas de Calais in Dunkirk (2013), where the team chose to keep the 1949 hall, attaching a second one echoing the original structure, creating transparency, openness, and luminosity throughout the spaces. —*KF*

Above
Transformation, 530
Dwellings, Bordeaux, France,
Lacaton & Vassal, 2016. Photo
Philippe Ruault

Left
Palais de Tokyo, Paris, France,
2002, Lacaton & Vassal. Photo
Philippe Ruault

ODILE DECQ

BORN
Laval, France, 1955

EDUCATION
École d'Architecture de Paris,
BA, 1978; Institut d'Etudes
Politiques, 1979

PRACTICE
ODBC, 1985–98; Studio Odile
Decq, 1998–

TEACHING
École Spéciale d'Architecture,
professor, 1992–2007, director,
2007–12; Confluence Institute
for Innovation and Creative
Strategies in Architecture,
cofounder, 2014–

NOTABLE HONORS
Golden Lion, Venice
Architecture Biennale (with
Benoît Cornette), 1996;
Commander, Order of Arts
and Letters, France, 2001;
International Fellowship, RIBA,
2007; Women in Architecture
Prize, ARVHA (Prize of
Women Architects, France),
2013; Jane Drew Prize, 2016;
Architizer A+Awards, Lifetime
Achievement, 2017; European
Cultural Centre Architecture
Award, 2018

Odile Decq grew up in the small town of Laval, in western France. She initially studied art history at university in Rennes, but after meeting a group of female architecture students, she decided it was architecture that she wanted to pursue. However, not everyone in her family agreed with Decq's career choice. "My father didn't believe it was a profession for a woman," she says.[41]

In France, it was only after educational reforms in 1968 that women began to seriously pursue architectural studies. The director of the architecture program in Rennes told Decq that she lacked the right "spirit" to pursue architecture. Nevertheless, she was allowed to continue on to her second year of architecture studies. After that, she left for Paris.

In order to pay for her education, Decq worked for theorist Philippe Boudon, who was writing about the theory of architecture. "At that time, it was a kind of freedom where I had to learn to manage my life by myself," she says. While studying at the École d'Architecture de Paris, many of her teachers were involved in political action and frequently on strike, requiring her to teach herself much of what she needed to know—"I was at school without being at school." She completed her undergraduate studies in 1978 and went on to study urbanism at the Institut d'Etudes Politiques, completing her degree in 1979. She started her own eponymous firm the same year.

London and Paris influenced Decq during her early career. After she met her romantic and, eventually, professional partner, architect Benoît Cornette, she traveled with him to London every other weekend to see music and look at architecture. London's music scene had a strong influence on Decq's personal style and her design aesthetic. In 1985, she and Cornette earned architecture degrees, establishing the architecture firm ODBC.

The first design to bring Decq and Cornette international recognition was the Banque Populaire de l'Ouest et d'Armorique (1990) in Rennes. Drawing inspiration from deconstructivist architecture popular during the mid-1980s to early 1990s in the UK, the partners designed the building with a steel-frame structure and modular industrial components. Similar high-tech projects followed, including a housing project in Rue Ernestine (1995) and a master plan for the Port de Gennevilliers (1995). The pair won a Gold Lion award for the interior of the French pavilion at the 1996 Venice Architecture Biennale.

In 1998, Cornette died in a car accident that also injured Decq. She has continued her work under the name Studio Odile Decq. In 2010, her high-profile addition for the Museum of Contemporary Art of Rome was inaugurated, and her design for Le Cargo, Europe's largest business incubator space, opened in 2016.

Decq has also interwoven teaching into her decades-long career. After leaving her position as director of the École Spéciale d'Architecture in Paris in 2012, she cofounded the Confluence Institute for Innovation and Creative Strategies in Architecture. The institute's goal is to promote "architecture thinking," or interdisciplinary problem-solving with the goal of reconsidering architecture in the world. —*KF*

Left
TWIST, Paris, France, Studio Odile Decq, 2015. © Roland Halbe

Below
Fangshan Tangshan National Geopark Museum, Nanjing, China, Studio Odile Decq, 2015. © Jinri & Zhu Jie

AMANDA LEVETE

BORN
Bridgend, Wales, 1955

EDUCATION
AA School of Architecture, 1980

PRACTICE
Richard Rogers Partnership, 1984–88; Future Systems, 1989–2009; Amanda Levete Architecture (AL_A), 2009–

NOTABLE HONORS
Lord's Cricket Ground, Stirling Prize, 1999; Workplace of the Year, *Architectural Journal*, 2017; Museum of Art, Architecture and Technology, The Design Prize, 2017; Jane Drew Prize, 2018; Fellow, AIA, 2019; Board of Trustees, Victoria & Albert Museum, 2020

"Architecture as a medium has a built-in resistance that forces you to question, challenge, and sometimes divert in order to get to where you want to get," says Amanda Levete. "I work best when I come up against resistance. When I understood that, I knew I wanted to be an architect."[42]

Aesthetic and technological breakthroughs are a hallmark of Levete's remarkable shape-shifting designs over the past thirty years. Her partnership at Future Systems with her husband, the late Jan Kaplický, transformed the United Kingdom's architectural landscape with two iconic buildings: the Media Centre at Lord's Cricket Ground (1999) and Selfridges (2003) in Birmingham.

The watershed moment in her own firm, AL_A, established in 2009, was its competition-winning design for the new galleries, courtyard, and entrance at the Victoria & Albert Museum (V&A) in London, winning the building of the year of the RIBA London Awards in 2018. "It had always been my dream to work on a public project in my hometown."

The key to the success of all Levete's work is collaboration: "We always start with a conversation rather than a sketch— a sketch commits too much too soon, but a conversation allows us to interrogate the purpose before finding the opportunities… It enables us to focus on the right questions as much as the right solutions. Put simply, conversations are inherently collaborative, while sketches are not."

In addition to collaborating with the three codirectors in her office, all of whom work on every project, Levete reaches out to talented people in different disciplines. Her proudest achievement may be the creation of an exceptional office, "one where I love working every day," she says. "I learnt from Richard Rogers the importance of creating spirit and culture in an office and we recently agreed that this is far more difficult than architecture."

For the V&A project, Koninklijke Tichelaar, the oldest company in the Netherlands, brought an artistic sensibility to produce the tiles for the first porcelain courtyard in the world. "Constructing the Exhibition Road Quarter was a huge structural challenge requiring extensive excavation. Cambridge University, working closely with ARUP, were so taken with the challenges that they installed fiber optic cables in the 50-meter-long (164 feet) tension piles because they believe the movements that will be recorded may disprove aspects of the elastic theory."

In Levete's view of the future, ambition and restraint are not mutually exclusive. "Demolishing a building is very energy-intensive and polluting, so instead of constructing new buildings, we need to find more imaginative ways to repurpose and reimagine what we have." She calls this "the new sobriety," using resources responsibly. "Sometimes, the most radical thing is not to build." —*JSE*

Above
Central Embassy, Bangkok,
Thailand, AL_A, 2017.
© Edward Barnieh

Right
Victoria & Albert Museum,
gallery for temporary
exhibitions, London, AL_A,
2017. © Hufton+Crow

KAZUYO SEJIMA

BORN
Mito, Ibaraki, Japan, 1956

EDUCATION
Japan Women's University,
BA, 1979, MArch, 1981

PRACTICE
Toyo Ito and Associates,
1981–87; Kazuyo Sejima and
Associates, 1987–95; Sejima
and Nishizawa and Associates
(SANAA), 1995–

TEACHING
Princeton University School
of Architecture, Jean Labatut
Professor, 2005–8; University
of Applied Arts Vienna,
Institute of Architecture,
2015–19; Tama Art University,
2019–; Japan Women's
University, 2019–

NOTABLE HONORS
Young Architect of the
Year, Japanese Institute of
Architects, 1992; Kenneth
F. Brown Pacific Culture
and Architecture Design
Award, 1995; Erich Schelling
Architecture Prize, 2000;
Golden Lion Award, Venice
Architecture Biennale, 2004;
Rolf Schock Prize, 2005;
director, Venice Architecture
Biennale, 2010; Pritzker
Prize, 2010; World Jury, Prix
Versailles, 2019

In 2010, as the first woman to direct the 12th International Architecture Exhibition in Venice, Kazuyo Sejima said, "I have a dream that architecture can bring something to contemporary society. Architecture is how people meet in space." Sejima evoked the experience and sensation of exceptional buildings. "I try to make architecture that is free from hierarchy and space that lets people choose their own paths through it," she says.[43]

Sejima, who goes by her surname, has professionally partnered with Ryue Nishizawa since they met as employees in Toyo Ito's practice more than thirty years ago. They eventually opened SANAA in 1995. The thirty-member studio has been compared to a monastery, where "endless contemplation and focus eventually lead to enlightenment: architecture as devotion… This is slow architecture."

The duo's curved glass buildings for viewing art are legendary, among them the 21st Century Museum of Contemporary Art (2004) in Kanazawa, Japan; the Glass Pavilion for the Toledo Museum of Art (2006); and the Louvre Lens (2012), a sister to the Parisian icon. Approaching these structures, the visitor's senses are heightened by surfaces that become transparent or reflective depending on weather and what they contain. The invitation to notice things continues inside, revealing the two most vital features of contemporary museums: circulation and natural light.

Sejima's attraction to architecture was originally ignited by an image: "One day when I was a child, I saw a picture of a house in a book, *Sky House*, by Kiyonori Kikutake. Sometime after that, I remembered this feeling and got interested in architecture." In turn, Sejima's buildings inspire childlike wonder, regardless of their sophistication, which extends to a playful element in the text of the firm's projects: "The architects wanted to bring to mind boats on a river coming together to dock gently with each other" (Louvre Lens's five buildings); "a semi-transparent dress for the shifting body of the building" (the anodized aluminum mesh covering the New Museum, in Manhattan's Bowery).

Sejima is a visiting professor at the Tama Art University and Japan Women's University. Between 2015 and 2019, she taught at the Institute of Architecture at the University of Applied Arts Vienna. She was the Jean Labatut Professor at Princeton University between 2005 and 2008.

In 2010, Sejima was the second woman, after Zaha Hadid, to receive the Pritzker Prize (along with Ryue Nishizawa). On that occasion, she shared some advice regarding the role of women in architecture: "Be patient," she answered. "When I was young it was hard and I almost gave up." —*JSE*

Top
The Louvre Lens, Lens, France,
SANAA, 2012. Photo Hisao
Suzuki

Bottom
Osaka University of Arts, Arts
and Science Department,
Osaka, Japan, SANAA, 2018.
Courtesy Kazuyo Sejima

LENE TRANBERG

BORN
Copenhagen, Denmark, 1956

EDUCATION
Royal Danish Academy of Fine
Arts, School of Architecture,
1977

PRACTICE
Lundgaard & Tranberg, 1976–

NOTABLE HONORS
Eckersberg Medal (with Boje
Lundgaard), 1994; Dreyer
Honorary Award (with Boje
Lundgaard), 2002; Nykredit
Architecture Prize, 2005;
C. F. Hansen Medal, 2005;
Honor Prize, National Bank of
Denmark Jubilee Fund, 2008;
Honorary Fellow, AIA, 2010;
Danish Business Woman of the
Year, 2010

Lene Tranberg studied under the renowned Danish architect Erik Christian Sørensen at the Royal Danish Academy of Fine Arts, School of Architecture. A year before graduating in 1977, Tranberg founded Lundgaard & Tranberg Architects with fellow architect Boje Lundgaard. The two eventually married.

"We won a competition drawing at the kitchen table in the evenings," Tranberg told Vikram Prakash of ArchitectureTalk in 2018. These drawings were a comprehensive design for a former fruit orchard being transformed into a suburban district emphasizing green spaces and a communal ideal of living. Tranberg and Lundgaard designed approximately one hundred residences, community houses, and a day care center.

After their first successful competition, Tranberg and Lundgaard began to develop a particular emphasis on museum design, starting with the Trapholt Museum of Modern Art (1996) in Kolding, Denmark. More recent projects include the Sorø Art Museum and the Danish Castle Center in Vordingborg (2011) and the Workers Museum (2014) and Freedom Museum (2015) in Copenhagen.

In 1989, the firm won another open design competition, this time for a combined heat and power production (CHP) plant in Horsens, Denmark. Engaged in this particular building typology, Tranberg and Lundgaard diversified into technical plants and infrastructure, continuing to work into the 1990s with several more CHP plants around Denmark, as well as a wastewater treatment plant and industrial laundry facility.

Sustainable and energy-efficient solutions have been a recurring theme throughout Tranberg's career, starting with a 1992 project that included infill, courtyard design, building renovation, and new construction in the Copenhagen district of Vesterbro. It incorporated passive and active solar heating via solar panels and rainwater collection. Throughout the 1990s, the firm focused on developing an innovative design approach through collaborations with Danish Building Research and other organizations on projects that promoted sustainable construction. Projects like Charlottehaven, which combines private houses with shared communal facilities, were the first of their kind in Denmark, combining energy efficiency with social living.

The early 2000s found Tranberg and the firm embarking on three ambitious design projects that heightened their profile and placed them on the international stage: the Wedge building for the Copenhagen Business School (2005), the Tietgen Dormitory (2006) at the University of Copenhagen, and the Royal Danish Playhouse (2008). The firm has been instrumental in shaping the development of modern Copenhagen over the past several decades.

Although Tranberg and Lundgaard divorced in 1994, they remained partners in the firm until Lundgaard's death in 2004. Tranberg then extended partnership to six longtime employees, a structure that remains today. Tranberg began teaching at the Royal Danish Academy of Fine Arts in 1986, serving as a lecturer. She has also taught at the University of Washington as a visiting professor, and served as the CEO of the Danish Architecture Center from 1998 to 2002. "I think that the profession has such a wonderful ability to connect," she told ArchitectureTalk in 2018.[44] —*KF*

Top
Tietgen Dormitory, University
of Copenhagen, Sweden,
Lundgaard & Tranberg, 2006.
Photo Jens Markus Lindhe

Bottom
Royal Danish Playhouse,
Copenhagen, Sweden,
Lundgaard & Tranberg,
2008. Photo Maria Eklind/
CC BY-SA 2.0

MARION WEISS

BORN
Palo Alto, CA, 1957

EDUCATION
UVA, BArch, 1979; Yale
University, MArch, 1983

PRACTICE
Mitchell Giurgola Architects,
1979–89; Weiss/Manfredi,
1989–

TEACHING
Harvard GSD; Cornell AAP;
Yale University, Eero Saarinen
Visiting Professor; Graham
Professor of Practice in
Architecture, University of
Pennsylvania

NOTABLE HONORS
Honor Award (with Michael
Manfredi), AIA, 2003; Harvard
University Veronica Rudge
Green Prize in Urban Design,
2007; Distinguished Alumni
Award, UVA, 2014; Women in
Architecture Design Leader
Award, *Architectural Record*,
2017; National Design Award,
Architecture (with Michael
Manfredi), 2018; National
Honor Award (with Michael
Manfredi), American Society of
Landscape Architects, 2019

Growing up in the hills south of San Francisco, Marion Weiss spent her childhood designing and building dollhouses. She estimates that by the time she was in sixth grade, she had built twenty-three of them. "There was a predisposition to building and creating these environments that were perfect fantasies of what an ideal way to live might be," she says.[45] Later, she became intimately familiar with Northern California's topography when she competed as a distance runner in school. Ascending and descending the hills around her home made her conscious of the interplay between built structures and the land surrounding them. Her later designs interweave landscape and architecture with one another.

"The awareness of the land as the biggest protagonist and the buildings being something that might complement them was very much embedded," she says. "It was kind of this networked system of architecture and landscape together that inspired me to pursue a kind of education that would do both."

Weiss went to architecture school at the suggestion of Ernest Kump, who had designed Foothill College in Los Altos, California. Graduating in 1979 from UVA, where she received the AIA Scholastic Award and the SOM Traveling Fellowship, Weiss went to work at the New York City firm of Mitchell Giurgola Architects. Her first assignment was drawing twenty-six staircases for an executive education center at IBM, a project that took eight-and-a-half months. "I was honestly devastated," she says upon initially receiving her instructions. "What emerged was that I developed the most profound passion for stairs in architecture and what it means to craft the topography that connects buildings together."

While working at Mitchell Giurgola, Marion met Michael Manfredi, her future husband and business partner. "[Michael and I] both had felt that there was a real need to do architecture in the public realm for an audience that couldn't afford architecture," Weiss says of the shared ethos that formed the basis for their partnership

They entered design competitions for pro bono projects in Harlem, discovering in the process that they were both left-handed and their drawings could be indistinguishable from one another's. A signature part of their partnership ever since has been intentionally obscuring who designs which components of their projects.

In 1989, Manfredi and Weiss entered a competition to design a memorial and museum for Women in Military Service for America at Arlington National Cemetery. Even though both she and Manfredi were "more academics than architects" at the time, they won. The structure's curvilinear design, abutting an original historic hemicycle retaining wall and constructed out of glass, created a distinctive new gateway to Arlington National Cemetery and garnered national media attention. It marked the start of their official partnership, and the Weiss/Manfredi firm.

The awe of seeing her first, large-scale design become reality, Weiss says, hasn't grown smaller in the years since. "There's still something indescribable about being an architect—hunches and approximations become incredibly precise, and you see them realized," she says. "[All of this] comes from the very beginning of

Brooklyn Botanic Garden
Visitor Center, Brooklyn, NY,
Weiss/Manfredi, 2012. © Albert
Večerka/Esto

Women's Memorial and
Education Center, Arlington,
VA, Weiss/Manfredi, 1997.
© Jeff Goldberg

somebody trusting you enough with their money and their dreams to be able to give it measure," Weiss says.

For Weiss and Manfredi, there was no slow development from small to large projects: they've been designing world-class public spaces ever since. Projects like the Olympic Sculpture Park for the Seattle Art Museum (2007), which overlooks the city's Elliott Bay and dramatically zigzags through the natural landscape, and a new visitor center for the Brooklyn Botanic Garden (2012) incorporate natural elements in surprising and unexpected ways. Hunter's Point South Waterfront park (2018), a recent design, transforms a postindustrial area in Long Island City into a welcoming public amenity.

Throughout her career, Weiss has continued to teach. She is currently the Graham Professor of Practice in Architecture and a tenured faculty member at the University of Pennsylvania and has taught design studios at Cornell University, Harvard University, and Yale University as the Eero Saarinen Visiting Professor. She has resisted being pigeonholed exclusively as an academic, architect, or landscape architect: "The idea of the Renaissance notion of what an artist and designer is, I would say, is an underpinning of what propels me forward—which is not staying within the guardrails of what, traditionally, architecture has been captured within." —*KF*

Olympic Sculpture
Park, Seattle, WA,
Weiss/Manfredi, 2007.
© Benjamin Benschneider

V. RAISING THE ROOF
Introduction by Julia Gamolina

Writing the introduction to this group of women originally led to the thought that these women do not belong to the same group, or to any group at all. All the architects of the "Raising the Roof" generation are known as singular figures, each unique and extraordinary. There is no one else like Maya Lin, or Jeanne Gang, or Annabelle Selldorf. Thinking of them as peers, as contemporaries, and belonging to a certain guild or common identity is new for me. They are ageless, iconic, and each strongly defined by what makes her different.

Returning to the years during which they came of age in the industry begins to inform what *does* unite them. These women all started to practice in the late 1980s and early 1990s, at the dawn of the internet and digital technology, the fall of the Berlin Wall, and a new age politically in the United States. Unity, not division, was on people's minds, and the internet allowed connection, in every which way, to happen more easily and eventually almost immediately—across borders, oceans, languages, and, in general, different worlds.

What then unites these architects most significantly is the idea of unity itself, unity that stems from connection, and unity that eventually leads to the transcending of boundaries—between architecture and landscape, between architecture and art, between old and new, interior and exterior. This unity then, goes a step further. By blurring boundaries, these women, these architects, began to completely redefine what architecture is and can be—not architecture and landscape, but architecture *as* landscape. Not art and architecture, but art *as* architecture. And finally, by redefining what architecture can be, they then also redefined what architects, what architects who are women, can be as well.

The blurring of disciplinary boundaries came first. Twenty-one-year-old Maya Lin's Vietnam memorial of 1981–82 was the first of its kind—public art, landscape, sculpture, and architecture all in one—setting the tone for the next few decades in architecture. Katherine Chia, who worked for Maya Lin on numerous art and architecture commissions, has continued such thinking. For Annabelle Selldorf, those boundaries are blurred in the context of new and old, historic and contemporary, art and architecture. Claire Weisz sets an example for bringing together architecture and urbanism; Karen Fairbanks, practice and academia. Brigitte Shim advocates for how lessons in academia shape the future of cities. The internet enabled the connections to be made faster, especially across disciplines.

Cross-pollination then led to redefinition. Selldorf and partner Sara Lopergolo gave dignity to a public work with the Sunset Park Material Recovery Facility of 2013. Weisz and her peers at Dattner Architects set the tone with the Spring Street Salt Shed of 2015, dignifying a type of architecture that had often been overlooked, not considered worth celebrating. Alison Brooks has advocated for the role of housing in civic building, and Sharon Johnston has defined and redefined the idea of house and home in general. Lisa Iwamoto's use of digital tools and technologies bring new ideals that elevate workplace design. Mónica Ponce de León has been frequently highlighted as redefining the nature of the architectural license as it exists within the United States. Mabel O. Wilson spearheaded necessary and overdue conversations about race and architecture. With this came many firsts and also the spotlighting of architecture that was much more public and accessible, redefining the notion of who this architecture is for.

In 2018, Dorte Mandrup publicly proclaimed, "I am not a female architect; I am an architect."[1] However, even acknowledging her gender in this way, and speaking up with regard to gender, makes her an architect of her time, a feminist one. The prior generation didn't remark on their gender, on family life, on motherhood. And now this generation doesn't want to be called female architects, but they have been acknowledging their gender. Weisz said it best when she called herself a feminist architect. These women, growing up amid women's lib, are truly the first generation of feminist architects, ones that acknowledge their gender, the issues that come with it, and that are explicitly and publicly for equity. Jeanne Gang announced her equal pay initiative; Selldorf's firm is majority woman-owned; and Wilson and Dina Griffin have personified the significant contributions and drive of Black architects.

Every generation redefines the field in which they inhabit, making their own what they inherited from the generation before. In this case, in asking questions about what architecture is, who it is for, and who makes architecture what it is today, these women have truly raised the roof of possibilities—so much so that the seeds they've planted are full-blown focal points for those of us at the beginning of our careers today. This generation of women truly defined that architecture is for everyone and that we, men included, can all be feminist architects.

KAREN BAUSMAN

BORN
Allentown, PA, 1958

EDUCATION
Cooper Union, BArch, 1982

PRACTICE
Bausman Gill Associates,
1982–95; Karen Bausman +
Associates, 1995–

TEACHING
Harvard GSD, Eliot Noyes
Chair, 1994; Yale University
School of Architecture, Eero
Saarinen Chair, 2001

NOTABLE HONORS
Rome Prize, American
Academy in Rome, 1994;
Progressive Architecture
Award, Performance Theater,
1998; Hall of Fame, Cooper
Union, 2009; Design
Excellence Award, City of New
York, 2010, 2012, 2014, 2016

When Karen Bausman was six years old, she decided that her calling in life was architecture. "My mother was describing to my older brother during breakfast what an architect was and how they worked," she says. "I interrupted to ask, 'Can a girl be an architect?' 'Of course,' came the reply. And that was it."[2] Understanding what an architect did helped her formalize all the topics she was already deeply interested in, and in the fifth grade, she decided that she would apply to Cooper Union in New York to study architecture.

Bausman was born and raised in southeastern Pennsylvania, a culture she describes as committed to stewarding the natural environment. She sources her design ethos, rooted in nature's sustainable structures, to her upbringing. "I have always had a consuming interest in boundaries, natural and man-made," she says. "Within all of my work, I am preoccupied with the concept of 'line'—how to locate it, how to notate it, how to occupy it."

Bausman graduated from Cooper Union in 1982, and she credits John Hejduk, Cooper Union's dean, as having a powerful influence on her architectural education. Her thesis project, One-Way Bridge, was featured in the 1988 Rizzoli book *Education of an Architect*.

In 1982, Bausman founded the firm Bausman Gill Associates with fellow architect Leslie Gill. One of Bausman's first building commissions as a practicing architect was for Warner Brothers' Performance Theater (1999) in Burbank, California, sited on what had been a 150-car parking lot surrounded by the company's global headquarters and its movie-studio back lots.

She says that her response to the constraints and unique demands of the site was to "cultivate" the parking lot surface, designing a theater that "bursts through the Earth's crust in the form of a giant flower, allowing vibrant urban light to slip beneath the building's base." She received a Progressive Architecture Award for the theater, the first female architect leading a design studio to do so.

Bausman has held academic positions since 1987, starting at the Parsons School of Design. She is the only American woman to hold both the Eliot Noyes Chair at the Harvard GSD and the Eero Saarinen Chair at Yale University School of Architecture. In 2001 and 2002, Bausman's work was featured in *Karen Bausman: Supermodels*, a solo exhibition of her building designs and working methods at Harvard University.

In 1995, Bausman founded her own practice, Karen Bausman + Associates. Early in 2005, the firm was one of only twenty-four named to a roster of preferred architects for New York City projects costing up to $10 million as a part of the city's Design + Construction Excellence program under Mayor Michael Bloomberg. Bausman says that the design projects that most excite her are the ones for the City of New York, concentrating on urban coastal research and issues of sustainability impacting the city's populated waterfronts, including sites along the Hudson, Harlem, and Bronx riverfronts. —*KF*

Left
Hamlin Library and Chapel, model, Hamlin, PA, Karen Bausman + Associates, 2020. Photo Jock Pottle

Below
Warner Bros. Headquarters, lobby, New York, NY, Karen Bausman + Associates, 1992. Photo Scott Frances/ESTO

BRIGITTE SHIM

BORN
Kingston, Jamaica, 1958

EDUCATION
University of Waterloo, BS, 1981, BArch, 1983

PRACTICE
Arthur Erickson Architects, 1981–87; Baird/Sampson Architects, 1987–94; Shim-Sutcliffe Architects, 1994–

TEACHING
University of Toronto, professor, 1988–; Yale University, Eero Saarinen Visiting Professor, 2005, 2010, 2014

NOTABLE HONORS
Member and Fellow, Royal Architectural Institute of Canada, 2005; Royal Canadian Academy, 2005; Honorary Fellow, AIA, 2008; Queen Elizabeth II Diamond Jubilee Medal, 2013; Order of Canada, 2013

The contemplation of time is essential to Brigitte Shim's approach to design and building: the heavy, geological time of the Earth's development informed her weekend home (2006) in Canada's Georgian Bay region; the fleeting, ephemeral time of a live musical event was inspirational to the Integral House (2012), for a mathematician and musician. Both endeavors represent time spent in discovery, collecting and experimenting and ultimately providing evidence of how we live our lives. The work of Shim-Sutcliffe Architects, founded with her husband and partner, Howard Sutcliffe, in 1994, is a reminder of architecture's capacity to enfold all of these.

Shim's desire to create ambiguous spaces that oscillate between inside and out—aligning nature and constructed nature—is realized in a meticulously crafted weekend "camp" for the architects. "We are camping in an ancient landscape, which will be around for much longer than we will be."[3] It evokes an awakening of the spirit, a place where one could expect to be reintroduced to the water, the wind, and perhaps one's own thoughts.

Shim also made a conscious decision, shortly after architecture school in 1983, to make furniture as an ongoing research project. Decades later, the firm's award-winning plywood HAB Chair (2004) embodies an experimental approach and nods to the iconic chair designed by Charles and Ray Eames, another architectural partnership devoted to investigation.

Teaching is another passion. Shim was the Eero Saarinen Visiting Professor at Yale University School of Architecture (2005, 2010, and 2014) and has been a professor at the University of Toronto since 1988.

"Lessons in schools should shape future cities, not exist as mere exercises," she says.

Shim's primary home is located in a "laneway," or alley, a service artery that originally housed stables for horses in the 1700s. Conceived twenty-five years ago and dissected in *Shim-Sutcliffe: The Passage of Time* (Dalhousie Architectural Press, 2014), the house reflects the densification of the city, where, for instance, garages are transformed into guest suites and residences, allowing people to age in their own neighborhoods. Shim considers these villages within the city, which allow people and communities to be self-sufficient, a kind of micro-urbanism, which remains relatively untapped.

The firm's most ambitious residential project is the Integral House, from 2009. Two years of meetings in the studio followed by four years of construction, resulted in a 7,000-square-foot showpiece. The architects, their client, and his house were the subjects of the documentary *Integral Man* (2017), in which the client describes the architectural process as, "going on a journey, elevating the world, not knowing what we're going to get."

In another meditation on time, Shim speaks to building in our cities: "Sustainability was once a topic, and now it permeates everything we do. Architects are huge consumers. To make a huge difference, we better make buildings that can stay around awhile. Our buildings speak about who we are and what we value." **—JSE**

Left
Sisters of Saint Joseph, Toronto,
ON, Shim-Sutcliffe Architects,
2014. Photo James Dow

Below
Integral House, Toronto, ON,
Shim-Sutcliffe Architects, 2009.
Photo James Dow

MARY-ANN RAY

BORN
Seattle, WA, 1958

EDUCATION
University of Washington,
BFA, 1981; Princeton University,
MArch, 1987

PRACTICE
Studio Works, 1985–

TEACHING
SCI-Arc, 1988–2009; BASE
Beijing, 2005–; University of
Michigan, Centennial Professor
of Practice, 2007–; University
of California, Berkeley, College
of Environmental Design,
Visiting Esherick Professor in
Architecture, 2017

NOTABLE HONORS
Rome Prize, American
Academy in Rome, 1987–88;
Chrysler Design Award, 2001;
Stirling Prize, Memorial Lecture
on the City, 2008

Mary-Ann Ray's art-school teachers were abstract expressionists, color field painters, and Bauhaus-trained designers. "I was set on abstraction as a powerful language," she says.[4] After graduation, her work, which was already large in size, became even larger, moving from the canvas to the wall and becoming three-dimensional. During a European trip to look at paintings in the early 1980s, Ray found herself instead drawn to the spaces of the cities, courtyards, and buildings, resulting in "a desire to work in a medium that was spatial and abstract and that had a visceral effect on the viewer, who was also an inhabitant."

Michael Graves became Ray's mentor when she worked in his office while studying at Princeton. Her thesis advisors, Graves and Peter Eisenman, "were like brothers at two ends of the architectural spectrum," she says, which challenged her to make independent decisions on how to move forward.

In 1985, Ray joined Studio Works, the practice of her partner, Robert Mangurian. Interdisciplinary in nature, the practice worked in scales ranging from as small as a postage stamp to the expanse of the city and the phenomena of global migrations. In addition to architecture, Studio Works engages in archaeology, documentary work, and endeavors more like research or art, for which they have collaborated with artists Joe and Emily Pulitzer, Mary Miss, Vito Acconci, Eric Orr, James Turrell, Ai Weiwei, and others.

Each summer between 1985 and 1995, Ray and Mangurian worked with one hundred fifty students from schools around the world to document Hadrian's Villa, north of Rome. "Through our work with students, we have been able to develop thoughts and design strategies that we believe can nudge and provoke practice," says Ray. And in the early 2000s, they established BASE Beijing as a platform and laboratory for issues of design, urbanism, and ruralism in China. "While the time away from our 'real' practice prevented us from producing a huge body of built work, we remain grateful for the experiences and work that our teaching and independent research allowed us to engage," she says.

Designed for inner-city Los Angeles students, Studio Works' West Adams Preparatory High School (2009) particularly "considered our clients," says Ray, the students. The architects produced a performing arts hall, athletic facilities modeled after a fitness and health club, a dining facility after an urban café, and playfields, which included a park, garden, swimming pool, and stepped theater. Ray says, "It was meaningful for us to be able to do this for a group of kids who didn't have any of these things even within many miles of their communities."

A lifelong student in spirit, Ray's example inspires creativity and deep admiration for the profession by others. "We hope that a large part of architecture will return to essentials, to engaging work that might benefit the other 98 percent that cannot afford architecture as it exists now. We see a future where a model of practice returns to the slow evolution of architecture, that is, a vernacular process." —*JSE*

Above
West Adams Preparatory High
School, Los Angeles, CA,
Studio Works, 2009. Photo
Grant Mudford

Left
BASE Beijing, China, exhibition
of works in progress, Studio
Works. Courtesy Mary-Ann
Ray, 2015

MAYA LIN

BORN
Athens, OH, 1959

EDUCATION
Yale University, BA, 1981,
MArch, 1986

PRACTICE
Maya Lin Studio, ca. 1985–

NOTABLE HONORS
Rome Prize, American
Academy in Rome, 1999; Finn
Juhl Prize, 2003; National
Women's Hall of Fame, 2005;
American Academy of Arts
and Letters, 2005; National
Medal of Arts, 2009; Dorothy
and Lillian Gish Prize,
2014; Presidential Medal
of Freedom, 2016

Maya Lin's Vietnam Veterans Memorial (1982) forever altered the landscape of memorial design. It rejects the didactic example of older tributes and instead embodies the dark, abstract nature of grief. Perhaps because Lin's profound design rises above politics and morality, the black granite slabs, engraved with the names of the 58,318 US soldiers who died in Vietnam, now also bear witness to those lost in Afghanistan and Iraq, in a separate collection of objects deposited before them since those wars began. In 2007, the AIA ranked the memorial #10 on its list of Favorite American Architecture.

Maya was a twenty-one-year-old senior at Yale University when her competition submission was selected anonymously from 1,421 designs. And, although she was envied widely, in a recent video interview she calls the experience a "crazy trial by fire" that she wouldn't wish on anyone. "I think being a woman and being very young made it extremely difficult," she said. "It was very, very prejudiced, and I don't just mean my race. What people have said to me and how I've been treated was very demeaning at times." But Lin also notes that she's seen a shift over the past decade, to "real discussions about race, gender, and equity in the creative fields."

Lin comes from an immigrant Chinese family of educators and artists. Her father was a ceramist, her mother and older brother poets; her aunt was likely the first female architect in modern China. Lin also works as a sculptor, and her art, both large and small and which focuses on the environment, can be found in the permanent collections of the Metropolitan Museum of Art, MoMA, the Smithsonian,

the Nelson-Atkins Museum, Crystal Bridges Museum of American Art, and the California Academy of Sciences. President Barack Obama honored her with both the National Medal of Arts (2009) and the Presidential Medal of Freedom (2016). Her husband, the late Daniel Wolf, was a visionary art and photography collector until his death in 2021.

Maya Angelou and Toni Morrison attended the dedication of the Langston Hughes Library (1999) in Clinton, Tennessee, designed by Lin for a retreat center owned by the Children's Defense Fund.
The building sits on a farm once owned by Alex Haley and contains a noncirculating collection of five thousand reference volumes relating to the Black experience, mostly written by African American authors and illustrators. The 1,200-square-foot library sits in an 1860s-era barn; two glass-encased corncribs serve as a base for the refurbished cantilevered structure and glow like a lantern at night. Lin also designed the Riggio-Lynch chapel (2004) on the same 157-acre parcel of land, surrounded by the Appalachian Mountain ridges.

Subsequent buildings include the 2009 Museum of Chinese in America, near Manhattan's Chinatown. Lin's interest in promoting that institution, in part, stems from a desire that her two daughters learn to be familiar with that part of their heritage. As a child growing up in Ohio, she didn't think of herself as Chinese.

Memorials continue to hold a special appeal for Lin. "I've never seen myself as a political artist and yet, obviously, I am," she says. "But in order to really advocate for

Vietnam Veterans Memorial,
National Mall, Washington, DC,
Maya Lin, 1982. Photo Terry
Adams. Courtesy National Park
Service

Vietnam Veterans Memorial.
Photo Victoria Sambunaris.
Courtesy Maya Lin Studio

change I'm doing it through the memorials, through that hybrid creature between the architecture, which is a functional art form, and the art, which I think is much freer and about who you personally are."

Following the Vietnam Veterans Memorial came the Civil War Memorial (1989) in Montgomery, Alabama. Sponsored by the Southern Poverty Law Center, it honors forty-one people who were killed in the Civil Rights struggle between 1954 (when the Supreme Court ruled that segregation in schools was unlawful) and 1968, the year Martin Luther King Jr. was assassinated. The fountain, an inverted cone made of black stone, gives form to a passage in MLK's "I Have a Dream" speech: "We will not be satisfied until justice rolls down like waters."

Four years later, Lin designed the *Women's Table* (1993) at Yale University, her alma mater, commemorating the role of women at the university. The *Confluence Project* (2002) explored history, culture, and ecology through outdoor installations and interpretive artworks located at several public parks that follow the path of Lewis and Clark through the Columbia River basin in Washington and Oregon. Its decentralized configuration is exploited with even more latitude in her *What Is Missing?* (2009), an ongoing memorial to the planet's decreasing biodiversity. Available

for viewing on Lin's website, as well as the "What Is Missing" website, the memorial specifically addresses the crisis surrounding biodiversity and habitat loss.[5]

True to their creator's vision, each of Lin's memorials elevate their subjects while also conferring grace on their visitors. "I'm not going to overtly force an opinion on you," she says. "I need you to come to your own conclusions and your own experiences with it." Lin also has generous, poignant words, this time for other creators: "Never be intimidated. Never let anyone tell you that you can't do what you know you need to do. It might sound kind of corny, but you have to follow an inner truth as to who you are, and how you enjoy the exploration."

Lin's recent contributions to the Novartis Institutes for BioMedical Research complex (2015) in Cambridge, Massachusetts, is especially admired for its biomorphic exterior screen, inspired by "microscopic views of organic coral or bone structure." Toshiko Mori designed the adjacent building to Lin's; together, they wrap a courtyard designed by landscape architect Michael Van Valkenburgh. In total, one thousand pharmaceutical researchers work at the complex, located near MIT. Lin's redesign for the Neilson Library at Smith College (2021) opens to the site's natural light while building on environmental design principles. —*JSE*

Novartis Institutes for BioMedical
Research, Cambridge, MA, Maya
Lin Studio, 2015. Photo Iwan Baan.
Courtesy Maya Lin Studio

KAREN FAIRBANKS

BORN
Mesa, AZ, 1959

EDUCATION
University of Michigan, BArch, 1981; Columbia GSAPP, MArch, 1987

PRACTICE
Gund Partnership, 1981–84; Alexander Cooper & Partners (Cooper Robertson), 1987–89; Marble Fairbanks, 1990–

TEACHING
Barnard and Columbia College, Department of Architecture, professor and chair, 2002; UVA, Michael Owen Jones Memorial Lecturer, 2007; University of Michigan, Charles and Ray Eames Lecturer, 2004

NOTABLE HONORS
40 Under 40, *Building Design + Construction*, 1996; Emerging Voices, Architectural League of New York, 1998; Fellow in Architecture, New York Foundation for the Arts, 1988, 1994, 2004; American Libraries Association Committee, 2012–; Distinguished Alumna Award, University of Michigan Taubman College of Architecture, 2013; Educator of the Year, AIA New York, 2015; Board of Directors, AIA New York, 2017–; Oculus Award, Beverly Willis Architecture Foundation, 2018; Fellow, AIA, 2021

Karen Fairbanks is professor and chair of architecture at Barnard and Columbia College, and with Scott Marble, the chair of the School of Architecture at Georgia Tech, cofounded Marble Fairbanks. "As teachers we're at the forefront of digital technologies," says Fairbanks. "We're always talking about the future of education, and we bring that expertise to our practice."[6]

Information is at the core of their practice. Marble Fairbanks's award-winning Glen Oaks Library (2013) in Queens evolved from research revealing the tremendous diversity of the neighborhoods it serves: twenty thousand residents from fifty countries who speak thirty languages. The community-centered building functions as an archive of a changing population. On the facade, the word *SEARCH* is projected by the sun and morphs according to the changing light and weather.

The firm designed a library (2020) in Greenpoint, Brooklyn, that doubles as an environmental education center, reflecting the concerns of its local community. Using the $5 million awarded from a settlement following an oil spill there in the 1970s, a community-driven initiative gave rise to its hybrid uses. The building works on multiple scales, including as a hub across the city for educating librarians about how to communicate environmental issues; a design contributing to the local ecosystem, with exterior landscapes welcoming people, plants, and animals; and a repository for the remediation reports documenting the site's resilience story. The Brooklyn Navy Yard fabricated the structure's major facade features.

"Reenvisioning Branch Libraries," their interdisciplinary research project focusing on libraries as social infrastructure, operated as a metaphorical bridge between the two buildings. The design team viewed the various branches as three connected systems that could fill social gaps for their neighborhoods. With that in mind, Fairbanks's mapping process for a site goes something like this: "Where is the industry? The green spaces? What are the mixed-use opportunities? Could affordable housing be a component? How about twenty-four-hour coworking spaces or meeting places?"

Collaboration in her practice is second nature to Fairbanks. This approach is embedded in her students' projects at Barnard, working with the Climate Museum in the fall of 2019 on-site near Socrates Sculpture Park and with the Apollo Theater during the college's Harlem Semester later that spring. Collaboration also informs her firm's pro-bono work for organizations like FC Harlem, a soccer club of a sports-based charter high school, and Girl Be Heard, a spoken-word nonprofit with offices in the same building as Marble Fairbanks. Both efforts are aimed at creating more inclusion and equity in practice, which Fairbanks views as architecture's greatest challenge.

Fairbanks says her choice to teach at a women's college is key to her mindset. She lists Peggy Deamer and Donna Robertson, both former directors of the architecture curriculum at Barnard, as mentors who gave her the teaching opportunities that she was able to parlay into a role shepherding the program into a full-fledged department.
—*JSE*

Above
Slide Library, Columbia
University, New York, NY,
Marble Fairbanks, 2005.
Courtesy Marble Fairbanks

Right
Greenpoint Library and
Environmental Education
Center, Brooklyn, NY, Marble
Fairbanks, 2020. Courtesy
Marble Fairbanks

ANNABELLE SELLDORF

BORN
Cologne, Germany, 1960

EDUCATION
Pratt Institute, BArch,
1985; Syracuse University,
MArch, 1985

PRACTICE
Selldorf Architects, 1988–

NOTABLE HONORS
Award in Architecture,
American Academy of Arts
and Letters, 2014; Medal
of Honor, AIA New York,
2016; American Academy
of Arts and Letters, 2017;
Alumna Award, University of
Michigan Taubman College of
Architecture, 2013; Educator of
the Year, AIA New York, 2015;
Board of Directors, AIA New
York, 2017–; Oculus Award,
Beverly Willis Architecture
Foundation, 2018

"When architecture is successful, it elevates the experience of people," says Annabelle Selldorf. "When you see that happen, talk about it, encourage thought and consciousness."[7] In 2001, Selldorf Architects designed the Neue Galerie New York, her first public space in New York City. The firm's renovation of a Beaux Arts mansion into a museum for displaying early twentieth-century German and Austrian masterpieces brings the modernity of the period in Europe to life.

Selldorf's seventy-person practice is currently at work on another project along Manhattan's Museum Mile: the expansion and garden restoration of the Frick Collection. An addition to the rear of the library will allow the Frick to bring the art collection and the library together, fulfilling its educational mission.

The German-born architect is guided by the belief that context, history, and precedent matter: "Architecture is always determined as a set of conditions…I don't think we can invent very much. I look at the past to address the future because I have respect for the intelligence in these older buildings."

In Brooklyn, Selldorf's master plan and design for the eleven-acre Sunset Park Material Recovery Facility (2013) celebrates the context of the industrial site. "We wanted to make a difference on the waterfront, to create human-scale spaces," she says. "It was important to figure out how it works for the people who work there." Awards from the Public Design Commission and the Beverly Willis Architecture Foundation honored her solution. From the striking, open-air Education Center terrace, both employees and schoolchildren visiting the processing site for the city's curbside recycling are treated to framed views of Manhattan and the Statue of Liberty. Flood-protection initiatives ensured protection from natural disasters, like Hurricane Sandy, while under construction.

The firm's Mwabwindo School and Community Center (2019) in Zambia takes another approach to climate challenges, harvesting rainwater and employing a solar roof. The experience reminded Selldorf of why she wanted to be an architect, but it also raised concerns: "When Western architects come to places where the development of infrastructure is rudimentary, the goal is to produce positive projects that let communities thrive on their own terms. But we also impose certain values about how to educate others. I am a stranger in that culture so I want to understand who these people are and where they're coming from. Am I doing the right thing? Is there enough cross-cultural exchange? I have more questions than answers, but I know that we need to be inclusive, not condescending. It's true in everything we do."

To those considering architecture, Selldorf calls it "the best profession" and stresses that a willingness to listen is among the skills that truly matter. "You never stop learning, and it's never done. You need stamina to stay with it, and it comes with a huge responsibility. Be prepared to participate: from the smallest to the biggest details, they all matter. To me it always comes down to being in the service of people." —*JSE*

Left
Mwabwindo School, Mwabwindo, Zambia, Selldorf Architects, 2019. Photo Chosa Mweemba

Below
The Frick Collection, New York, NY, expansion rendering, Selldorf Architects, 2023. Courtesy Selldorf Architects

SUSAN T. RODRIGUEZ

BORN
New York, NY, 1960

EDUCATION
Cornell AAP, BArch, 1982;
Columbia GSAPP, MArch, 1985

PRACTICE
Polshek Partnership Architects,
1985–2010, renamed Ennead
Architects, 2010–16; Susan T.
Rodriguez Architecture and
Design, 2016–

TEACHING
Design studios at Cornell AAP;
Columbia GSAPP; City College
of New York, Spitzer School of
Architecture

NOTABLE HONORS
Polshek Partner Architects,
Firm Award, AIA, 1992; Fellow,
AIA, 2003; Polshek Partnership
Architects, Firm Award,
Cooper Hewitt, 2004; Ennead
Architects, Medal of Honor,
AIA New York, 2012; Women
in Architecture, *Architectural
Record*, 2016

"I was always, from a very young age, very interested in design and drawing," Susan T. Rodriguez says.[8] She was also a strong math student, and the combination of those skills took a more concrete shape when she went to Cornell for a summer architecture program during her junior year of high school. She earned an architecture degree from Cornell in 1982.

Of her undergraduate days at Cornell, Rodriguez says, "We were exposed to a balance between abstraction and history." She earned a master's degree in architecture from Columbia because she wanted to teach and because she thought that the curriculum would offer a perspective different from Cornell's. One of her mentors at Columbia was James Stewart Polshek, who had a humanistic impact on the curriculum. After graduating, Rodriguez worked for Polshek Partnership Architects.

"He had great faith in me and enabled me to lead the effort of making public architecture, and really developing my own voice," she says of Polshek. Her projects with Polshek Partnership include the National Museum of the National Indian Cultural Resources Center (2003), the Smith College Brown Fine Arts Center (2003), and the Elizabeth A. Sackler Center for Feminist Art at the Brooklyn Museum (2009).

Rodriguez is driven by the power of architecture to effect change, an ethos that's evident throughout her work designing cultural, educational, and civic institutions. "It's not just about the artifact we're making, but it's so much about the experience," she says. "I think I value equally the making of the experience to the making of the artifact. I think they really go hand-in-hand."

In 2010, the Polshek Partnership renamed itself Ennead Architects (Polshek had given up his partnership five years earlier). Rodriguez continued to work on public buildings, including projects like Schermerhorn House (2009) in Brooklyn, an affordable and supportive housing project; the Pfizer Research Laboratory at the New York Botanical Garden (2006); and the Westmoreland Museum of American Art (2015) in Greensburg, Pennsylvania.

In 2016, Rodriguez started her own self-named practice, where she continues to work on design in the public realm in New York City and elsewhere. She has a second home in Maine, where she has worked on projects such as an evolving network of modular buildings on Fiddlehead Island, the College of the Atlantic's Center for Human Ecology, and summer camp cabins at Camp Chewonki for Girls. "Working in the public realm, in such a wide variety of projects and places, means that I can hover above it all and then get very targeted toward the specifics and the unique circumstances that intersect at a particular space and time," Rodriguez says.

Rodriguez's commitment to education and the public realm has extended to teaching design studios at Cornell AAP, Columbia GSAPP, and City College of New York's Spitzer School of Architecture, as well as being a longtime board member of the Architectural League of New York since 1999, and a founding board member of Art Works Projects: Art + Design for Human Rights in 2008. —*KF*

Top
Westmoreland Museum of
American Art, Greensburg, PA,
Susan T. Rodriguez, 2015. Photo
Roy Engelbrecht

Bottom
Frank Sinatra School of the Arts
High School, Astoria, NY,
Susan T. Rodriguez, 2009.
Photo Jeff Goldberg/Esto

CLAIRE WEISZ

BORN
Rochester, MN, 1960

EDUCATION
University of Toronto,
BArch, 1984; Yale University,
MArch, 1989

PRACTICE
Urban Innovations Group (with
Charles W. Moore), 1985–88;
Hayne, Winkler, Weisz,
1988; Agrest & Gandelsonas
Architects, 1989–93; Weisz and
Warchol 1993–98; WXY, 1998–

NOTABLE HONORS
Winner (with Mark Yoes),
Architectural League of New
York, 1994; Cofounder, Design
Trust for Public Space, 1995;
Firm of the Year, AIA New
York, 2016; Medal of Honor,
AIA New York, 2018; World's
Most Innovative Companies,
Fast Company, 2019; Women
in Architecture Award,
Architectural Record, 2019;
Architizer A+ List, 2020

The issue of waste has long featured prominently in Claire Weisz's work. She tries to avoid it, whether it is in the form of materials or an opportunity. Working on public projects for New York City government authorities over the past twenty years, WXY (W times Y), the firm she cofounded with Mark Yoes in 1998, creates design methodologies that don't sacrifice design excellence.

In 2020, WXY collaborated with BIG on the Downtown Brooklyn Public Realm Action Plan, designed to enhance pedestrian access through improved sidewalks, furniture, and street crossings. At its core was the question, "Can we move away from car-dominated places?"

Weisz admits that working for the public sector is challenging. With so many stakeholders, approvals are complicated, the environments are constrained, and the work commands lower fees than those for institutions or the private sector. But she has praise for the city's strong mayoral system and admires the people she works with, the "best and brightest" public servants who are attracted to New York City government unlike many other places.

As the mother of three girls, Weisz says that parenthood has not directly impacted her work but for two striking conditions. The first was decisions about how to spend one's time. The second touches on her refusal to waste anything. Not wasting resources extends to valuing everyone's contribution at WXY. Weisz's firm has ensured pay equity on an annual basis since 2015.

SeaGlass Carousel (2015) in Lower Manhattan is one of WXY's most beloved efforts. The carousel references the New York Aquarium, employing digital projection and environmental noise made by the structure's moving parts. Nearby, the firm's striking West Thames Bridge (2019) allows pedestrians to safely cross over a car tunnel to Manhattan's Battery Park City. Weisz describes it as a gateway and a greeting moment. "That passage is a way to create people sharing space," she says, adding that the fritted glass and mesh sides make you feel like you're floating, especially when a breeze moves through. Weisz wonders if the bridge is the last of its kind or if it is auspicious, whether the infrastructure below will someday be raised. "It's the architect's responsibility to think about the past *and* the future of any project," she says.[9] —*JSE*

Top
West Thames Bridge,
New York, NY, WXY, 2019.
Photo Albert Vecerka/Esto

Bottom
Brooklyn Navy Yard, New
York, NY, master plan, WXY,
2018. Bloomimages, 2017

DORTE MANDRUP

BORN
Aarhus, Denmark, 1961

EDUCATION
School of Arts and Crafts, 1989; Aarhus School of Architecture, MArch, 1991

PRACTICE
Henning Larson, 1991–96; Fuglsang & Mandrup-Poulson Architects, 1996–99; Dorte Mandrup, 1999–

TEACHING
Cornell AAP, 2018; Mendrisio Academy of Architecture, 2021

NOTABLE HONORS
Eckersberg Medal, Royal Danish Academy of Fine Art, 2004; Nykredit Architecture Prize, 2007; C. F. Hansen Medal, Royal Danish Academy of Fine Art, 2008; Art, Design and Architecture Award of the Year, Hansen Foundation, 2017; Finn Juhl Architecture Award, 2018; Berlin Art Prize, Architecture, 2019; AZ Award, *Azure Magazine*, Environmental Leadership, 2020

Dorte Mandrup identifies herself as an architect and a humanist. She's quick to add, "In many ways, I don't feel like a traditional Scandinavian architect. There's a certain backward thinking that I don't relate to that reflects a very pristine lifestyle—protestant, minimal, restraining thought and experimentation, hiding things."[10]

Mandrup's values are evident in the nuanced approach to her project choices. For instance, the design for the Trilateral Wadden Sea World Heritage Partnership Center (2018) engages an emotionally loaded site: a World War II German submarine harbor on Denmark's West Coast. A leftover bunker incorporated into the new building represents her desire to "work with history in a way that you can embrace it without rejecting it." At night, the lighted, five-story glass facade beckons like a lighthouse; outside, a series of natural pools fill and drain with rainwater, alternately concealing and revealing pathways and alluding to the building's purpose, a home for a global organization that preserves the surrounding UNESCO-protected ecosystem.

Two hundred fifty kilometers (155 miles) north of the Arctic Circle lies another UNESCO-protected area in Greenland. Mandrup's Icefjord Centre (2021) was the competition winner for a meeting place to study the massive Sermeq Kujalleq glacier being impacted by climate change. The dramatic, rugged landscape has been withdrawing for twenty years. Her aerodynamic building, amid this beautiful landscape, features an accessible, double-curved roof and viewing platform covered in wood.

Many of Mandrup's building forms reflect her preoccupation with sculpture, beginning from the time she studied art in Georgia on a Rotary scholarship after high school. As a professor at Cornell AAP in 2018, Mandrup introduced her students to the mountainous Caucasus region to consider its design promise for the tourism industry.

Mandrup believes that architects have a responsibility to give back to the public in a way that shapes the physical framework around people's lives, "to make things possible for them rather than being oppressive. We can influence the ways we meet each other and have lots of impact on social interactions."

Mandrup has famously objected to being considered a female architect, a statement firmly engraved in *Dezeen* in 2017. "In the beginning I didn't realize the invisible borders I would meet," she says. "It's still a boys' club." It's an invisible structure. "In the end, the extraordinary requires nerve!" Mandrup states on her website, as she advocates improving the position of women in the profession. —*JSE*

Top
Trilateral Wadden Sea
World Heritage Partnership
Center, Esbjerg, Denmark,
Dorte Mandrup, 2018. Photo
Adam Moerk

Middle
Culture House and Library,
Karlskrona, Sweden, Dorte
Mandrup, 2021. Image MIR

Bottom
Icefjord Centre, rendering,
Ilulissat, Greenland, Dorte
Mandrup, 2021. Image MIR

ALISON BROOKS

BORN
Welland, Ontario, Canada, 1962

EDUCATION
University of Waterloo, BArch, 1988, Honorary Doctorate of Engineering, 2016

PRACTICE
Ron Arad Associates, 1989–96; Alison Brooks Architects, 1996–

NOTABLE HONORS
Stephen Lawrence Prize, Royal Institute of British Architects (RIBA), 2006; Manser Medal, RIBA, 2007; Stirling Prize, RIBA, 2008; BD (Building Design) Architect of the Year, 2012; Woman Architect of the Year, *Architects' Journal*, 2013; Alumni Achievement Award, University of Waterloo, 2014; Contribution to the Profession Award, *Architects' Journal*, 2017; *Dezeen*, Architect of the Year, 2020

When Alison Brooks became a founding partner of Ron Arad Associates in 1988, it represented for her a newfound sense of architectural possibility. The foray into the unknown continues to impact the way she views architecture. "Living in a global metropolis and working alongside a super inventive designer and furniture-maker was really liberating," she recalls. "It gave me the opportunity to broaden my architectural repertoire and do work that was 100 percent off the spectrum. [For example,] we broke every convention when we built our studio in Chalk Farm."[11]

Brooks's attraction to working outside convention and her commitment to sustainable building are abundantly evident in The Smile, a project she conceived for the 2016 London Design Festival. "I wanted to make something enigmatic, a super-sized sculpture that you could inhabit," she says, describing the experience of feeling the curved floor beneath the feet and the immersive smell of tulipwood, an elemental sensation. The bespoke result was a rare synthesis of material, form, geometry, and structure that is difficult to achieve in more complex building programs. The Smile was carbon negative, having sequestered forty tons of CO_2 emissions, and is helping hardwood cross-laminated timber (CLT) achieve certification as a structural product. Brooks regularly advocates for the use of responsibly sourced timber as a building material. Pledging to protect the environment, she is a founding signatory of Architects Declare, a collective of Stirling Prize–winning firms.

The far-ranging, site-specific work of Alison Brooks Architects (ABA) is known for having an unapologetic point of view. "Without subjectivity the architect loses authority," states Brooks in the introduction to ABA's 2017 catalog, *Ideals then Ideas*. She also poses an alternative narrative to modernism's functionalist mandate by citing four alternative ideals espoused by her firm over twenty-one years: authenticity, generosity, civicness, and beauty. Among her projects that demonstrate the wisdom of engaging such an ethical approach are Ely Court (2015), an integrated housing scheme in London that was a finalist for the 2017 Mies van der Rohe Award, and the nuanced Cohen Quadrangle at Exeter College (2017) in Oxford.

Brooks's offering for the 2018 Venice Architecture Biennale, *ReCasting*, presented a direct, physical experience of architecture with facsimiles of actual spaces from ABA's housing projects. Four inventive "totems" represented places with potential for meaningful, subjective experiences: Passage (a monumental, "dematerialized arch"); Inhabited Edge; Threshold; and Roofspace, all featuring enigmatic apertures inviting people in. Sitting together on a plinth in the Arsenal building, the totems formed a simulacrum of an urban condition. Brooks believes urban housing to be the most important type of civic architecture, as it "frames everyday life and forms people's world view."

Reinforcing her thoughts about existential reality in design, in a 2019 lecture called "This Is Not a Fake," Brooks said, "Although we are operating in a maelstrom of information and disinformation, the work of the architect is *not* a fake. Problem solving, designing, detailing, producing instructions for building; these acts, although sometimes dreamlike, are commitments to the real, the solid, the permanent, the instrumental."
—*JSE*

Above
The Smile, London, England,
Alison Brooks Architects, 2016.
Photo Paul Riddle

Left
Exeter College, Cohen
Quadrangle, Oxford, England,
Alison Brooks Architects, 2017.
Photo Paul Riddle

CARME PIGEM

BORN
Olot, Girona, Spain, 1962

EDUCATION
Escuela Técnica Superior
de Arquitectura del Vallès,
Architecture, 1987

PRACTICE
RCR Arquitectes, 1988–

NOTABLE HONORS
National Culture Award,
Catalonia Government, 2005;
Honorary Fellow, AIA, 2010;
International Fellow, RIBA,
2012; Gold Medal, Academy
of Architecture, France, 2015;
Officers and Knights of the
Order of Arts and Letters of
the French Republic, 2008
and 2017; Pritzker Prize, 2017;
Gold Medal from Catalonia
Government, 2018; Foreigner
from Academy of Architecture,
France, 2020

Carme Pigem's professional story is one of relationships: "Us to each other, our buildings to their places, and architecture to the disciplines beyond it that we explore."[12] She appreciates design critic William Curtis's allusion to a jazz trio when he described RCR Arquitectes' method of collaborating. "It's about participation, not my idea against yours but talking together to reach a resolution. We discuss not only with words but with sketches, models, and referential images."

The Catalonian practitioners and partners of RCR, Pigem, Rafael Aranda, and Ramon Vilalta, believe it's fundamental to understand a place, whether in nature or in the middle of a city. Their approach is to establish a strong, powerful relationship between a place and any structures they introduce to it. "Ideally, the architecture is contaminated by the place and the place by the architecture," she says. "The boundaries and edges are blurred but not unclear or undefined."

Clarity, in fact, is one of the strengths of the 2017 Pritzker Prize–winning practice. Consider the Bathing Pavilion (1998), located along a river in Olot, Spain, and surrounded by trees. Pigem describes how they designed views from inside the building: "We created a series of voids, each related to an individual tree to allow it to appear when framed, thereby increasing its value in the realm of perception."

The firm's design process, whether for a restaurant, kindergarten, park, or museum, in France, Belgium or Spain, is the same: "Our way is to first understand the place and why we have to do something new there…The shapes and forms arise from that understanding. We try to find a good way to propose conditions for doing activities in a specific place."

The team's material selection is intentionally narrow. "Our goal is to use as few materials as possible to ensure that users are not distracted by lots of materials and colors." The versatility of steel helps them to accomplish this. La Lira Theater Public Space (2011) exemplifies this immersion in materials. On the site of a demolished theater in Spain stands a covered, open-air space that frames views along the river in the historic district of Ripoli. Weathering steel used as pavement, latticework walls, and the roof circumscribe an urban stage and meeting place, a versatile alternative to the traditional town square.

The ultimate honor bestowed on RCR Arquitectes by the 2017 Pritzker Prize jury acknowledges the trio's mastery: "They create buildings that are both local and universal at the same time…help us to see, in a most beautiful and poetic way…that we can, at least in architecture…aspire to have both our roots firmly in place and our arms outstretched to the rest of the world."

Indeed. Each summer, students descend on the studio, a former foundry that once cast bronze sculptures, for a three-week laboratory and workshop, creating new kinds of relationships with architecture. The focus has included audiovisual and photography, scenography, and, more recently, dance. Pigem says, "Architecture is about movement. It's important to understand space with your body. —*JSE*

Top
Soulages Museum, Rodez,
France, RCR Arquitectes
with Gilles Trégouët, 2014.
© PepSau

Bottom
Bathing Pavilion, Olot, Spain,
RCR Arquitectes, 1998. © Clara
Pardo Gromaches

YOLANDE DANIELS

BORN
Queens, NY, 1962

EDUCATION
City College of New York, BA,
1987; Columbia GSAPP, MArch,
1990; Whitney Museum of
American Art, 1999

PRACTICE
Smith-Miller + Hawkinson,
1990–95; Studio SUMO, 1995–

TEACHING
CUNY; Columbia GSAPP; MIT;
USC, 2019–

NOTABLE HONORS
MoMA PS1 Young Architects
Program Finalist, 2001; Rome
Prize, American Academy
in Rome, 2003–4; Design
Vanguard, *Architectural
Record*, 2006; Emerging
Voices Award, Architectural
League of New York, 2010;
Award of Excellence, AIA New
York, 2012

Yolande Daniels became acquainted with architecture while shadowing her father on construction sites as a child. She didn't realize she wanted to pursue it until she visited Howard University's school of architecture while moving her younger sister onto campus. "That was the first time I understood what architecture as a field might offer. The way that I saw it was [as] a place where I could combine interests that I had in writing and research and art in a built thing that affected society," she says.[13] A faculty member at CUNY encouraged her to apply for a summer internship in architecture after she completed her undergraduate environmental science degree. She highlights the invaluable learning experience she acquired in the late 1980s in the office of Steven M. Davis (later of the New York City firm Davis Brody Bond).

The beginning of her career was firmly rooted within small firms, including Smith-Miller + Hawkinson. "Working in an office that was kind of a design boutique helped me see architecture in a different way," she says, one that was less rigid and formal. After honing her design and theoretical skills, Daniels decided to pursue a master's degree in architecture at Columbia GSAPP, which she completed in 1990. Additionally, Daniels's time studying at the Whitney Museum of American Art, from 1997 to 1999, allowed her to follow what she calls "an art model," to work on architecture as a theoretical practice. Teaching architecture was a natural next step, first at CUNY and Columbia GSAPP and eventually at MIT.

In 1995, Daniels cofounded Studio SUMO with fellow architect and academic Sunil Bald. The two drew on their academic expertise to enter a competition for the New York City MTA Arts for Transit and Urban Design. They designed the Museum for African Art (2001) in Queens, and later, the Museum of Contemporary African Diasporan Arts in Brooklyn invited Studio SUMO to design its building (2006). They have also designed commercial, institutional, and cultural spaces in Japan and Brazil.

The firm's work ranges from art installations to institutional buildings. More recent designs include lofts and apartment buildings, such as the Mitan Housing apartments in Miami's Little Haiti. Daniels and Bald's design incorporates a series of blocks made up of shotgun and Creole manor–style apartments.

In August 2019, Daniels began teaching at USC and established a West Coast branch of Studio SUMO. "My practice [explores] work across a range of scales—from societal patterns that inform the designs of objects, to the forming of objects, to the patterning of object-surfaces," she told USC Architecture's blog in July 2019. —*KF*

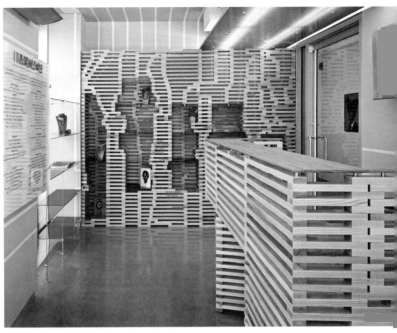

Top Left
iHouse Dormitory, Josai
University, Togane-shi,
Chiba-ken, Japan, Studio
SUMO, 2016. Photo
Kawasami Kobayashi

Top Right
Museum of Contemporary
African Diasporan Arts,
Brooklyn, NY, Studio SUMO,
2006. Photo Frank Oudeman

Bottom
Mizuta Museum of Art,
Josai University, Sakado-shi,
Saitama-ken, Japan, Studio
SUMO, 2012. Photo Daici Ano

MABEL O. WILSON

BORN
Neptune, NJ, 1963

EDUCATION
UVA, BArch, 1985; Columbia
GSAPP, MArch, 1991; New
York University (NYU), PhD,
American Studies, 2007

PRACTICE
6Ten Studio, 2007–

TEACHING
Columbia GSAPP, 2007; Rupp
Professor, director of Institute
for Research in African
American Studies, codirector
of Global Africa Lab, 2007;
visiting faculty at University
of California, Berkeley;
California College of the Arts;
Princeton University; Ohio
State University; University
of Kentucky

NOTABLE HONORS
American Academy of Arts
and Letters, 2019; Women
in Architecture Design
Leadership Program,
Architectural Record, 2019

As a scholar, designer, and artist, Mabel O. Wilson has taken a theory-driven approach to architecture; her work examines the impact of social inequalities on the built environment. "Architecture seemed like a happy medium between something that was intuitive and also analytical," she says.[14]

During her time as an undergraduate in architecture at UVA, she struggled to see herself and her own cultural and familial experiences in the classes she was taking. "I felt like I was a vampire, like I was looking into this mirror, and I could not see myself," she says. Regarding the places she studied, Wilson says, "I learned the language, but fundamentally, I never saw the neighborhoods I grew up in, where my grandparents were from. [I never saw] my own sense of Blackness and the spaces in which Black lives unfold—or even an understanding of anti-Black racism. It never came up in this work."

During a semester at London's AA School of Architecture, she gained a different perspective on the architectural discipline, one made possible, she says, by a different pedagogical approach. "People were coming from around the world with their own traditions, histories, spaces, conflict, and bringing that into their work. And I [thought], oh, that's what I want to be able to do," she says.

She realized she was going to have to look beyond the ways in which architecture was being presented in her own education. Cultivating what she calls a transdisciplinary practice in order to examine race in the built environment, Wilson excavates the influence of race and slavery on African American and Native American dispossession in American architecture.

After earning an MArch from Columbia GSAPP and a PhD in American Studies from NYU, she joined the faculty of Columbia University in 2007 as a professor of architecture, where she is a codirector of the university's Global Africa Lab and the associate director at the Institute for Research in African American Studies. Her work has been exhibited at the Venice Architecture Biennale, Art Institute of Chicago, Storefront for Art and Architecture, and the Cooper Hewitt Smithsonian Design Museum's Triennial. Her published books include *Begin with the Past: Building the National Museum of African American History and Culture* (2016) and *Negro Building: Black Americans in the World of Fairs and Museums* (2012).

"For me to explore these questions about Black life, Black space, I really had to expand how we work and think about architecture," she says.

Wilson was designer and historian on the architectural team designing the Memorial to Enslaved Laborers at UVA (2020), a monument to those who both built the university and then maintained it until Emancipation and the end of the Civil War. Meejin Yoon and Eric Höweler are leading the team. "It's been a really profound experience, but a very challenging one," Wilson says. —*KF*

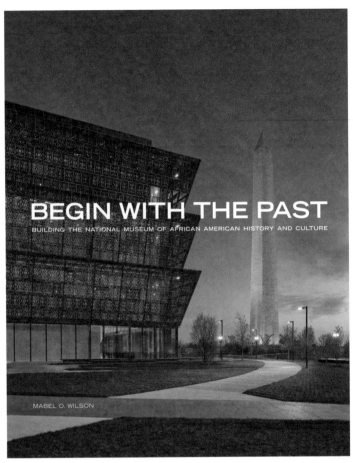

Left
Begin with the Past: Building the National Museum of African American History and Culture, Mabel O. Wilson, 2016

Below
Memorial to Enslaved Laborers, University of Virginia, rendering, Meejin Yoon, Mabel O. Wilson, Gregg Bleam, Frank Dukes, and Eto Otitigbe, 2020. Courtesy Höweler + Yoon Architects

BENEDETTA TAGLIABUE

BORN
Milan, Italy, 1963

EDUCATION
Istituto di Architettura di Venezia, BA, 1989; Cooper Union, MArch, 1990

PRACTICE
Miralles Tagliabue EMBT, 1994–

TEACHING
Escola Tècnica Superior d'Arquitectura de Barcelona; visiting professor at Harvard GSD and Columbia GSAPP

NOTABLE HONORS
Premi Nacional de Catalunya, 2001; Stirling Best Building Award for Scottish Parliament, RIBA, 2001; Catalan National Prize, 2002; Stirling Prize, RIBA, 2005; National Spanish Prize, 2006; Best International Building, Spanish Pavilion at World Expo, RIBA International, 2011; AIT-Award, Health/Care, Second Prize, 2020

Milan-born Benedetta Tagliabue describes architecture as "the first passion I had, imagining that being an architect would be like building a fantastic type of society."[15] She studied architecture at the Istituto di Architettura di Venezia in Venice, graduating in 1989.

Tagliabue met Spanish architect Enric Miralles while pursuing a master's degree in architecture at Cooper Union in New York. "We were fond of each other, and I decided to try to go to his city, which was Barcelona," she says. At first an experiment, Tagliabue ended up staying. Miralles's design process involved talking with and bouncing ideas off of someone else, and even though Tagliabue initially intended to work independently when she came to Barcelona, the two very quickly became creative partners as well.

Tagliabue and Miralles married and founded the firm Miralles Tagliabue EMBT in 1994, working closely on public and private projects, both in Spain and internationally. "It was like a complete world where it was very difficult to separate from whatever domestic and everyday actions we were doing, and the projects," she says. Their design projects include the Gas Natural Building (2005) in Barcelona, the headquarters of the Spanish energy company, since renamed Naturgy Energy Group S.A. Designed in high-tech architectural style, the structure holds a distinctive place in the Barcelona skyline.

In 2000, Miralles died of a brain tumor at the age of forty-five, and Tagliabue took over the operation of EMBT. From 1997 to 2005, she worked on a redesign of Barcelona's first covered food market, Santa Caterina, originally built in 1845, a significant project for the city and also for Tagliabue. In 2001, she received the Premi Nacional de Catalunya for the project.

Tagliabue's first large solo project, without any contributions from Miralles, was for the Spain Pavilion at the 2010 World Expo in Shanghai. Once her ambitious design won, she had to figure out exactly how to execute it. The finished product incorporated elements of wickerwork, creating an undulating woven shell representing the Spanish climate.

Tagliabue balances teaching and practice, something she recommitted to following Miralles's death. In 2010, Miralles Tagliabue EMBT opened an office in Shanghai, designing projects like the Chinatrust Tower (2017) in Taichung, Taiwan, and the Zhang Daqian Museum (2016) in Neijiang.

One of the recent projects that Tagliabue found the most rewarding was the design of Kálida Sant Pau Centre (2019) in Barcelona, a part of the Maggie's Centres network of facilities for cancer patients and the first one located outside of the United Kingdom. The emphasis is on creating a welcoming domestic environment in contrast to clinical hospital buildings.

In his citation for the 2013 Royal Institute of British Architects Jencks Award, architectural critic Charles Jencks wrote of Tagliabue: "While other architects [in Barcelona] have rejected, or been frightened of, extending some lessons of its master, Antoni Gaudí, EMBT has honored this tradition without letting it down. Of no other practice can that be said." —*KF*

Above
Gas Natural Building, Naturgy
Energy Group S.A., Barcelona,
Spain, Miralles Tagliabue EMBT,
2005. Photo Jordi Miralles

Right
Kálida Sant Pau Centre,
Barcelona, Spain, 2019.
© Duccio Malagamba

DINA GRIFFIN

BORN
Chicago, IL, 1963

EDUCATION
University of Illinois, Urbana-Champaign, BArch, 1986

PRACTICE
Interactive Design Architects (IDEA), 1999–

NOTABLE HONORS
Alan A. Madison Fellow/Alan Madison Award for Diversity, AIA Illinois, 2006; Advance: Legacy of INOMA Women Honoree, Illinois Chapter of the National Organization of Minority Architects, 2016; *Ebony Magazine* Power 100, "Women Up" Awards Gala, 2017; Fellow, AIA, 2018; Star Award, International Interior Design Association, 2018; Women in Design Award, 2018

The only African American woman in her engineering class at the University of Illinois, Urbana-Champaign, Dina Griffin was discouraged by a professor from pursuing a degree in architecture. However, the experience only fueled Griffin's conviction to break barriers in the field, paving the way for the increased representation of minorities among the next generation of practicing architects.

In 1999, Griffin became president of Interactive Design Architects (IDEA), a certified minority- and women-owned firm in Chicago. With interactivity as its guiding philosophy, IDEA prioritizes a collaborative practice within and outside of the office, an inclusive design process that incorporates diverse perspectives critical to the success of any project. "At IDEA, we all have an opportunity to express creativity and that's what we encourage here," says Griffin.

With a team of ten licensed architects, the small and "decidedly not corporate" firm has a remarkably extensive portfolio, which includes projects for the University of Chicago, the Chicago Public Schools, the Catholic Charities, Chicago's Lincoln Park Zoo, and the General Services Administration. IDEA is best known for their collaboration with the Renzo Piano Building Workshop on the award-winning Modern Wing of the Chicago Art Institute (2009).[16] Currently, IDEA is working with Tod Williams Billie Tsien Architects on the Obama Presidential Center (2023) on Chicago's South Side, a 19.3-acre plan that will include a museum, forum building, library, athletic center, and public green space.

Griffin recently designed the new Bruce D. Nesbitt African American Cultural Center at her alma mater, the Illinois Urbana-Champaign campus, becoming the first female graduate of the school of architecture to design a building there. Prior to its completion in 2019, IDEA sought feedback from students, faculty, staff, and alumni on the design and programming of the new center. Responding to the frequent requests that the building "wear its identity," the center's exterior features a multicolored brick facade, representing the many skin tones of the diverse student body. Through a combination of multipurpose activity rooms and private spaces for studying on the second floor, IDEA effectively realized the center's stated mission of "inclusion and openness while at the same time being a sanctuary of learning and support"—echoing Griffin's aspirations for the field more broadly.[17]

As an extension of her pioneering practice, Griffin is a dedicated advocate and mentor for minority architecture students and emerging professionals, serving on numerous professional boards and giving lectures and talks across the country. She is the former president of the Illinois Chapter of the National Organization of Minority Architects and a former member of the board of directors for the Illinois chapter of the AIA. Additionally, she serves on the Illinois Architect Licensing Board as committee chair. For her work "making the profession of ever-increasing service to society," Griffin was elevated to the College of Fellows of the AIA in 2018.[18] —*LFR*

Top
University of Chicago,
Media Arts, Data, and Design
Center (MADD), Interactive
Design Architects (IDEA), 2019.
Photo IDEA

Bottom
Bruce D. Nesbitt African
American Cultural Center,
University of Illinois,
Urbana-Champaign, IL,
Interactive Design Architects
(IDEA), 2019. © Interactive
Design Architects (IDEA)

RÓISÍN HENEGHAN

BORN
Castlebar, County Mayo,
Ireland, 1963

EDUCATION
University College Dublin,
BA, 1987; Harvard GSD,
MArch, 1992

PRACTICE
Heneghan Peng Architects,
1999–

TEACHING
Yale University School of
Architecture; MIT; Harvard
GSD; University College
Dublin; Cornell AAP

NOTABLE HONORS
Young Architects Forum,
Architectural League of New
York, 1999; Irish Pavilion,
Venice Architecture Biennale,
2011; Aga Khan Award for
Architecture, 2019

It's not enough to say that Heneghan Peng's work is site specific. Rather, the buildings are of their sites, heightening one's awareness of these special places without hiding what is concealed by the structure. Having seen the buildings, it's hard to imagine them not being there. In 2019, Róisín Heneghan gave a lecture in New York City, during which she discussed the Giant's Causeway Visitor Centre (2012) in Northern Ireland and the Palestinian Museum (2016) in the West Bank. In both cases, a simple gestural idea about how they inhabit the land gave way to highly engineered buildings.

The Giant's Causeway, a UNESCO World Heritage Site, sees a million visitors annually. Forty thousand hexagonal basalt columns rise there from the sea as a result of volcanic activity. Heneghan, her partner, Shih-Fu Peng, and their team began by carving two L-shaped cuts into the cliff side and establishing a walkway between them with a view to the sea. One cut obscures a sizable car park and the second cradles the visitors' center. "We wanted to get people to refocus from the object of the causeway to the entire landscape," explained Heneghan. They built with basalt, despite its lack of structural integrity, and every piece required tension rods for support. The resulting striated glass and stone facade is haunting. It's at home in the ancient locale while also appearing modern.

The Palestinian Museum at Birzeit University is cloaked in limestone from Bethlehem and faces west, toward the Mediterranean Sea. It received the Aga Khan Award for Architecture in 2019, cited for both its aesthetic and environmental (LEED Gold) eminence. The heavily terraced hilltop site was formerly used for agriculture, which suggested to the designers a series of cascading gardens as an extension of the small museum. Divided by long fieldstone walls, the pomegranates, figs, grapes, and oranges planted nearest the building "talk about the centrality of the area to trade routes over time," explained Heneghan. Lara Zureikat, a Jordanian landscape architect who wasn't allowed access to the West Bank, collaborated remotely with the architects. In keeping with the low building's acute geometries, finlike projections intersect the glass facade on the western side to reduce the summer heat gain. Water runoff from the roof is collected and stored for irrigation.

Heneghan Peng refurbished the historic wings in the National Gallery of Ireland in 2017. The long-awaited Grand Egyptian Museum (2021), faced in black onyx, now sits comfortably on the Giza plateau, not far from the Pyramids. Future projects include the visitors' center for the city's Botanic Garden and Botanical Museum (2022) and the Canadian Canoe Museum (2024) in Ontario. Like all their monumental work, these projects inspire awe and are thoroughly unapologetic. —*JSE*

Left
National Gallery of Ireland
courtyard, Dublin, Ireland,
Heneghan Peng Architects,
2017. © Marie Louise Halpenny

Below
Giant's Causeway Visitor Centre,
County Antrim, Northern Ireland,
Heneghan Peng Architects, 2012.
© Hufton+Crow

LISA IWAMOTO

BORN
Berkeley, CA, 1963

EDUCATION
University of Colorado, BS,
Structural Engineering, 1984;
Harvard GSD, MArch, 1993

PRACTICE
Bechtel Corporation;
Schwartz Silver Associates;
Thompson and Rose;
IwamotoScott, 2002–

TEACHING
University of California,
Berkeley, College of
Environmental Design,
professor of architecture

NOTABLE HONORS
Emerging Voices Award (with
Craig Scott), Architectural
League of New York, 2011; Hall
of Fame inductee (with Craig
Scott), *Interior Design*, 2018;
Women in Architecture Award,
Architectural Record, 2018;
National Design Award, Interior
Design (with Craig Scott),
Cooper Hewitt, 2019

Starting in high school, Lisa Iwamoto began to see architecture as a possible career that could allow her to be both creative and analytical. Her father, however, a civil engineer, wasn't confident that architecture would be a lucrative endeavor and encouraged her to study engineering.

At the University of Colorado, Iwamoto studied architectural engineering while also pursuing ballet, her other passion. She graduated with a degree in civil engineering and worked for several years as a structural engineer at Bechtel Corporation in San Francisco. Yet she knew she wanted to pursue a degree in architecture.

Iwamoto met her future husband and business partner, Craig Scott, in San Francisco in the late 1980s, and in 1989, they both matriculated at Harvard GSD, where Iwamoto studied with Rafael Moneo and Mohsen Mostafavi. In 2002, Iwamoto and Scott founded their firm, IwamotoScott Architecture, in the Bay Area. Iwamoto was offered and accepted a teaching position at the University of California, Berkeley.

Iwamoto is known as a pioneer in the field of digital fabrication, which involves the transfer of design from a computer to the machinery that creates building components. She constructed the first digital fabrication lab at UC Berkeley in the early 2000s. Her book *Digital Fabrications: Architectural and Material Techniques* was published in 2009.

Digital fabrication "is a way to leverage design in new ways, but…it's important to have the design present so that it has a purpose," she says.[19] Her use of digital fabrication reflects IwamotoScott's larger ethos of straddling the line between the theoretical and the concrete. Not surprisingly, the firm

has won several awards for its speculative work. In 2008, IwamotoScott beat out seven other local firms to win the grand prize in the City of the Future design competition for the History Channel. Called Hydro-Net, the design "provides a new subterranean regional infrastructure for transportation, water, and power" based on the projected needs of the city of San Francisco one hundred years into the future. Another speculative project, the Jellyfish House, was designed to coexist with its environment as a set of networked senses and responses. It won a number of awards, including the AIA San Francisco Design Award in 2007 and induction into *Interior Design*'s prestigious Hall of Fame in 2018.

IwamotoScott has also triumphed in art installations and interiors, designing the offices of a number of Bay Area tech companies, including Pinterest, Twitch, and JUUL. Their designs frequently include elements that are sculptural and abstract. The firm's ethos is strongly informed by creativity and experimentation. "Engineers always talk about optimization—'oh, this one thing can be perfect,'" she says. "That's not architecture at all. Architecture is trying to take all these varied elements and bring them together to form a cohesive whole." —*KF*

Above
Goto House, Napa County,
CA, IwamotoScott, 2017. Photo
Bruce Damonte

Right
University of California, San
Francisco, 3rd Street Garage,
facade, IwamotoScott, 2020.
Courtesy IwamotoScott

JEANNE GANG

BORN
Belvidere, IL, 1964

EDUCATION
University of Illinois, Urbana-Champaign, BArch, 1986; Harvard GSD, MArch, 1993

PRACTICE
OMA/Rem Koolhaas, 1993–95; Booth Hansen Architects, 1995–97; Studio Gang, 1997–

NOTABLE HONORS
John D. and Catherine T. MacArthur Fellow Genius Grant, 2011; Chevalier de l'Ordre National de la Légion d'Honneur, 2015; Woman Architect of the Year, *Architectural Review*, 2016; Marcus Prize, University of Wisconsin-Milwaukee, 2017; Louis I. Kahn Memorial Award, Center for Architecture and Design, 2017; American Academy of Arts and Sciences, 2017; International Fellow, RBA, 2018; *Time* 100: The Most Influential People, 2019

"It's kind of a breakthrough," said Jeanne Gang of the high-rise buildings her Chicago-based firm is increasingly known for.[20] Indeed. "When I began practicing, not much attention had been paid to tall buildings for quite a while, beyond the realm of corporate architecture," explains Gang. "I thought they deserved to be considered in a new way, and there seemed to be a lot of fertile territory not yet explored." Beginning with the eighty-two-story Aqua Tower (2010), Studio Gang's sculptural skyscrapers have rejected the traditionally hermetic environment of their predecessors by, for instance, extending the indoor/outdoor threshold of each unit with terraces that stand in for traditional porches.

Gang enjoys merging engineering and architecture in these projects and the pleasure of bringing variation and pattern to them, made possible by their size. "We initially focus on the spatial experience of the interior and exterior for the building's inhabitants and build up from that, as opposed to beginning with the overall silhouette of the form," she says of subsequent designs such as City Hyde Park, also in Chicago. "But these buildings also try to be good neighbors by giving the public something active at ground level and visually engaging at the urban scale."

Chicago architect Stanley Tigerman, whom Gang considered her mentor, invited Gang's participation in a number of competitions and exhibitions, including one at the National Building Museum in 2003, sponsored by the International Masonry Institute, for which she built the astonishing *Marble Curtain*. Gang's tenure as president of the Chicago Architecture Club (2000–01) cemented their professional relationship.

Studio Gang is currently at work on another conceptual breakthrough: the competition-winning design for a new terminal at Chicago's O'Hare International Airport, a 2.2 million-square-foot structure, with a projected completion date of 2028. "We're bringing a totally different vision of the airport," Gang says, noting that while traditional approaches to airport design have focused on the "glorification of flight," the bulk of a passenger's journey is actually spent on the ground. "We want to make it an experience that's part of everyday life: where you can interact, work, or find some quiet, and at the same time easily connect to other modes of transport. We see it as the seed of an urban territory that will blossom into part of the future city." Among other changes, she envisions the time when cars won't be stored at airports and the former parking areas will open to other uses.

Gang is drawn to the complexity of this type of project, the logistical and efficiency constraints, and "finding solutions that seem effortless in the final building." She believes strongly that design knowledge is not only transferable but also that it brings innovation: "We can learn from completing one project type and introduce that knowledge to another type. It's one of the reasons we take on projects of different programs and sizes."

Over the past twenty years, Studio Gang has grown to more than 130 people and four offices, in Chicago, San Francisco, New York, and Paris. A deep appreciation for—and inventive take on—context remains one of its calling cards. Gang's desire to make the O'Hare design "of this place" is visible in the atypical selection of wood for the terminal's interior spaces. The firm opted

Aqua Tower, Chicago, IL,
Studio Gang, 2010. Photo Steve
Hall © Hall + Merrick

to use trees from Chicago streets that, because of age, storms, or disease, would otherwise have been destroyed. "The wood will lend a warm feeling to the space and, as a local, renewable resource, it will speak to this city's specific history and ecology." The designers' decisions about materials also specify a local workforce to make these elements.

Each of Studio Gang's architectural achievements relies heavily on research, which happens at the firm in a number of ways: research into a project's issues to get a strong grounding in its context; design research when taking on a competition; and research about a prospective building type, material, or independent idea.

Baleinopolis: The Secret Societies of Cetaceans (2019–20), a Studio Gang–designed exhibition at the Tropical Aquarium of the Palais de la Porte-Dorée in Paris, illustrated this last type of research. Projects combining science and art, culture and education, are of great interest to Gang, who is a professor in practice at the Harvard GSD. "At a time when the humanities are being downplayed, the combination of art and science helps the public engage with and understand complex issues, like those facing our oceans and its inhabitants," she says of the firm's Parisian effort.

At Spelman College in Atlanta, the firm is working with the Black women's college to create the Center of Innovation & the Arts, bringing together art and technology disciplines and blurring their boundaries. Sited just outside the walls of the historic campus, the building offers performance and exhibition spaces on the ground floor, which extends into a generous outdoor "porch." Another innovative educational endeavor, a unified campus for the California College of the Arts, uses a two-level, indoor-outdoor "double ground" to metaphorically pull the well-loved natural environment of the old Oakland campus into the industrial San Francisco environment, explains Gang. The bottom level features a series of interdisciplinary workshops that are separated by glass to control heat and noise while still making it possible to see what's happening in those spaces. The project's carbon-neutral design employs a wood structure, natural ventilation, and waste-heat recovery from activities like glass blowing.

In an op-ed for *Fast Company* in 2018, Gang detailed how her firm discovered and fixed its small but unexpected pay gap between men and women, and called on other leaders to do the same. "Equal pay puts you at the same level. It's the key to being respected by your peers," says Gang. *—JSE*

MÓNICA PONCE DE LEÓN

BORN
Caracas, Venezuela, 1965

EDUCATION
University of Miami, BArch, 1989; Harvard GSD, MArch, 1991

PRACTICE
Office dA, 1991–2010; MPdL Studio, 2011–

TEACHING
Northeastern University; USC; RISD; Georgia Institute of Technology; Harvard GSD, professor, 1996–2008; University of Michigan, Taubman College of Architecture and Urban Planning, dean, 2008–16; Princeton University School of Architecture and Planning, dean, 2016–

NOTABLE HONORS
Young Architects Award, Architectural League of New York, 1997; Academy Award in Architecture, American Academy of Arts and Letters, 2002; National Design Award, Architecture, Cooper Hewitt, 2007; Teaching Award of Excellence, Association for Computer Aided Design in Architecture, 2018; Women in Architecture Award for Educator/Mentor, *Architectural Record*, 2020

"I am told by my family that I was drawing plans at age seven," says Mónica Ponce de León, who was born in Caracas, Venezuela, in 1965. "We were in a dentist's office, and I drew the plan of the waiting room, and then I drew a plan of the lobby, and I drew a plan of the whole building. And everybody in the waiting room was looking over my shoulder and asking my mother, 'What is this girl doing?'"[21]

Although Ponce de León showed an early aptitude for drawing floor plans, she didn't remember how much architecture had held her interest as a child until she was asked to consider three career options during secondary school. Her first two choices were computer science and mechanical engineering, with architecture being the third. After attending an orientation and hearing professional architects speak about their careers, and after visiting several concrete residential buildings in Caracas's Sabana Grande district, she understood the power of architecture to shape people's lives.

Ponce de León immigrated to Miami with her family from Caracas after graduating from high school. She worked in a millwork shop before enrolling at the University of Miami, completing her architecture degree in 1989. She then pursued graduate studies at Harvard, receiving a master's degree in architecture in urban design in 1991.

For the duration of her career, Ponce de León has taught and practiced architecture simultaneously. She first taught at the University of Miami and subsequently moved to the Boston area to teach at Northeastern University and eventually the Harvard GSD, where she was a faculty member for twelve years. She cofounded Office dA, based in Boston, with Nader Tehrani in 1991 and founded her current firm, MPdL Studio, in 2011.

A major focus of Ponce de León's career has been the application of robotic technology to building fabrication, and the exploration of the potential that it holds for the architecture and construction industries. "I was educated at a time when the discipline was transitioning from drawing by hand to using digital tools," she says. "I was part of the first digital wave, the first digital revolution…Digital fabrication was really dominating [the construction industry], but academia was completely oblivious to it," she says. "I became very interested in this blind spot."

At Harvard, Ponce de León directed the school's first robotic fabrication lab and served as the graduate program coordinator. She has also utilized fabrication in her own practice in projects such as new study spaces, a reading room, and a circulation island inside the Fleet Library at RISD (2006) and the interior design of the Conrad NY Conference and Events Center in the Conrad New York Downtown Hotel (2012).

Ponce de León's other work includes the Banq (2008) restaurant and the residential Macallen Building (2008), both in Boston for Office dA, and the Helios House (2007) in Los Angeles, a green gas station, in collaboration with JohnstonMarklee. In addition to her full-time academic positions, she has also held teaching appointments at the SCI-Arc, RISD, and Georgia Institute of Technology. In 2007, she became the first Latina to win the Cooper Hewitt National Design Award in Architecture.

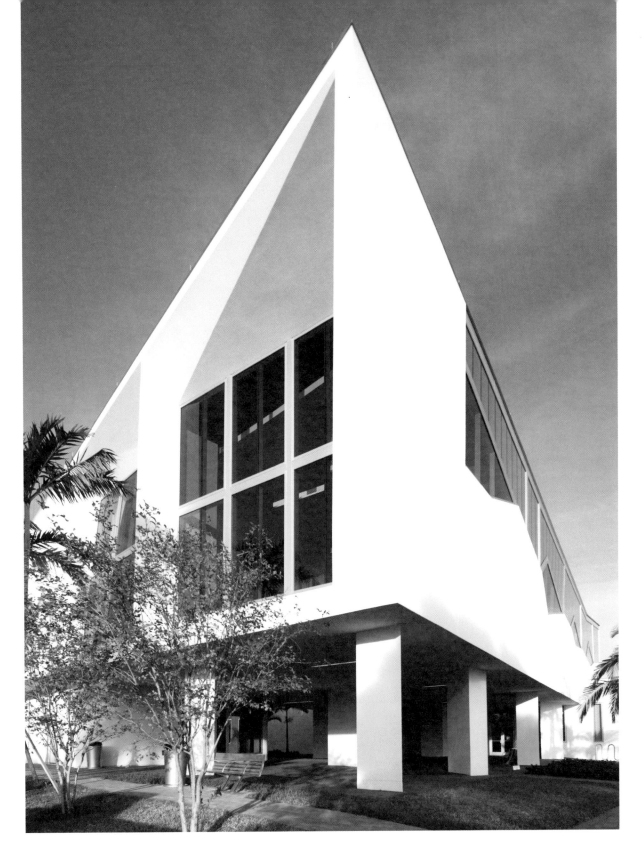

Pompano Beach Library, Cultural
Arts and Media Center, Pompano
Beach, FL, MPdL Studio, 2017.
Photo Josh Reynolds

From 2008 through 2015, Ponce de León was the dean of the Taubman College of Architecture and Urban Planning at the University of Michigan, where she developed the largest robotic fabrication facility in any school of architecture in the United States. The student-run lab's purpose was to be available to both students and faculty for learning, teaching, and research. Since then, this model has become standard for other schools of architecture in the country. Aside from computer numerical control (CNC) machines and laser cutters, the resource has expanded to include automation tools, rapid prototyping machines, and a CNC knitting device.

In 2016, Ponce de León became the first woman dean of the Princeton University School of Architecture while also continuing to practice at MPdL Studio. The studio has offices in New York, Boston, and Ann Arbor, Michigan. —*KF*

KATHERINE FAULKNER

BORN
Boston, MA, 1965

EDUCATION
Dartmouth College, BA, 1987;
Harvard GSD, MArch, 1993;
Boston University, MBA, 2010

PRACTICE
James Cutler Architects,
1993–96; Herault-Arnod
Architectures, 1996; Graham
Gund Associates, 1997;
Centerbrook Architects, 1998–
2001; Ai, 2001–4; Shepley
Bulfinch Richardson Abbott,
2004–11; NADAAA, founding
principal, 2011–19

NOTABLE HONORS
Top 50 US Design Firms, No.
1, *Architect Magazine*, 2013,
2015; Women in Design Award
of Excellence, Boston Society
for Architecture, 2017; Fellow,
AIA, 2020

After studying history at Dartmouth College and architecture at Harvard GSD, in 1993, Katherine Faulkner found an economy recovering from recession. The majority of her schoolmates struggled to find architecture work. "I feel I am part of a generation that got 'lost' in the profession. Of my female friends in my class, there are few that are still conventionally practicing," says Faulkner.[22]

Despite these trying circumstances, Faulkner moved to Seattle, where she juggled multiple part-time jobs before landing a position with Herault-Arnod Architectures in Grenoble, France. She returned to New England in 1997 and eventually joined the woman-owned and women-run Shepley Bulfinch Richardson Abbott in Massachusetts. (She became associate principal in 2008.)

After earning an MBA from Boston University, Faulkner founded the award-winning architecture and design firm NADAAA with former schoolmates Nader Tehrani and Dan Gallagher. Since 2011, the Boston-based studio has gained international recognition for its command of a diverse range of typologies and scales, from furniture to architecture and urban design.

In addition to contributing to the everyday operations of NADAAA, Faulkner has helped the firm expand its portfolio to include various institutional and educational projects, a speciality. Faulkner oversees the on-site fabrication facilities, which are central to the firm's innovative research and development initiatives. For her work with NADAAA, Faulkner has received a 2014 Holcim Award, three Green Good Design Awards, six Progressive Architecture Awards, and several AIA and Boston Society for Architecture awards.

Faulkner has acted as managing principal on many of the firm's most significant, large-scale commissions, including the Raemian Model Home Gallery (2012) in Seoul, South Korea, and the Research and Design Center at the Beaver Country Day School (2018) in Newton, Massachusetts.

At the University of Toronto, the Daniels Building (2017) won numerous accolades for NADAAA's bold juxtaposition of the original neo-gothic building with a new addition made of metal, concrete, and black glass in addition to its success in reconnecting the site to the rest of the campus—a substantial challenge considering its location on an island in a traffic circle.[23] The Daniels Building represents one of Faulkner's many contributions to the sustainability agenda in architecture.

Though Faulkner departed NADAAA at the end of 2019, she continues her work with the firm on several active projects, including the MIT Kendall Square Residential Tower (2020, with Perkins + Will), the student residence North Hall at RISD (2020), the Beacon Cleveland apartment tower (2021), and the Adams Street Branch Library (2021) in Dorchester, Massachusetts, for the Boston Public Library. In recognition of her design excellence, Faulkner received the Boston Society for Architecture Women in Design Award of Excellence in 2017 and was elevated to the AIA College of Fellows in 2020. —*LFR*

Above
Daniels Building, University
of Toronto, Ontario, NADAAA,
2017. © Nic Lehoux

Right
Raemian Model Home Gallery,
Seoul, South Korea, NADAAA,
2012. © John Horner

SHARON JOHNSTON

BORN
Santa Monica, CA, 1965

EDUCATION
Stanford University, BA
History, 1988; Harvard GSD,
MArch, 1995

PRACTICE
Johnston Marklee, 1998–

TEACHING
Princeton University; UCLA;
Rice University, Cullinan Chair
of Architecture; University
of Toronto, Frank Gehry
International Chair; Harvard
GSD, 2018–

NOTABLE HONORS
Presidential Board Honoree
for Emerging Practice, AIA Los
Angeles, 2013; Fellow, AIA,
2015; Award for Excellence,
Public Engagement with the
Built Environment, Society
of Architectural Historians,
2017; American Academy
in Rome, 2017; codirector,
Venice Architecture Biennale,
2017; New Generation Leader,
Women in Architecture Design
Leadership, *Architectural
Record*, 2019

The Johnston Marklee website home page features small, two-dimensional collages that communicate a lot with very little. The same may be said of the buildings they represent. "The collages began early in our practice and have become a touchstone in our design process and part of our search for irreducible conditions," says Sharon Johnston.[24]

Consider the recent UCLA Margo Leavin Graduate Art Studios (2019) in Culver City, conceived as a factory to make art. The industrial neighborhood lent the designers a subtle palette of material systems: tilt-up concrete walls and curved glulam beams. "Our design created continuity with the fabric of the city. We were not interested in a monumental, institutional structure," Johnston says. "The exceptional norm" is her term to describe a situation in which a viewer's initial reaction might be familiarity, before it transforms into something new and unfamiliar with time—a moment of discovery. With its pillowed column facade, Johnston Marklee's building beckons in a way the neighboring warehouses don't.

"Living in Los Angeles is part of who we are," explains Johnston. "In terms of architecture, that translates to a sensibility about building porosity, relations of interior and exterior space, shaping light as a material, and the importance of gardens," she says. "At the same time, the fabric of Los Angeles and the background quality of the urban boulevards is also important to us and informs how we think about context and the continuity of buildings with the city."

Johnston Marklee's client list reads like a Who's Who of significant arts organizations: its first project was designed for the Lannan Foundation, a residence for writers and poets in Marfa, Texas. "We studied with art historians and artists while students at Harvard GSD, and within our practice we have created an ecosystem of collaborators around the arts," says Johnston. The partners' relationship with their alma mater remains close; Mark Lee has served as the chair of the architecture department since 2018, where both Johnston and Lee are professors in practice. She has also taught at Princeton, UCLA, Rice, and the University of Toronto.

In 2018, the firm completed the Menil Drawing Institute on a thirty-acre arts campus in Houston. A masterful roof made of white steel plate spans sixty feet, gathering buildings and courtyards beneath its winged profile. "The idea was to stretch into the landscape to embrace the garden as prelude before entering the building," says Johnston. The enigmatic roof appears both heavy and light from underneath the canopy, which caps the sixteen-foot-tall buildings that relate to the modest scale of the surrounding bungalows.

Johnston has watched the role of museum and cultural spaces evolve over the past decade into places that are more diverse and inclusive. She especially admires the organizations that partner locally and establish close ties with their neighbors while also engaging with artists from around the world. "Cultural institutions hold more meaning for the advancement of cities today as there's an understanding that culture can bring people together and lift everybody up." —*JSE*

UCLA Margo Leavin Graduate Art
Studios, Culver City, CA, Johnston
Marklee, 2019. Photo Iwan Baan

NATHALIE DE VRIES

BORN
Appingedam, Netherlands,
1965

EDUCATION
Delft University of Technology,
1990

PRACTICE
Mecanoo, 1990–93; MVRDV,
1993–

NOTABLE HONORS
Fritz Schumacher Preis Award,
MVRDV, 2003; Finalist, Mies
van der Rohe Award, 2003;
Firm of the Year, Architizer,
2018; Chair, Royal Institute of
Dutch Architects, 2015–19;
Honorary Fellow, AIA, 2019

Nathalie de Vries first discovered modernism at age seventeen. Her investigation of artist Constant Nieuwenhuys and his New Babylon project eventually provided an ethos for the forward-looking firm she cofounded in 1993, MVRDV. "We consider ourselves to be an extension of these," she says of interdisciplinary art movements with a social consciousness, such as De Stijl. MVRDV's blurring of architecture, landscape architecture, and urbanism and the firm's merging of tech with hard and soft materials complement those precursors.[25]

The chair of the Royal Institute of Dutch Architects, de Vries noted that just 20 percent of registered architects in the Netherlands are women. "I was astonished to learn that it had not improved at all from the time I was in school," she says. "I thought I was part of a wave, that we would be seen as equals." De Vries posited challenges to the organization's member firms: "How can we chart the future if we don't look like the future? Look at the management of your company. How is the culture in your firm? Are there minorities? Is there a place for young people with families?" To the few other women present leading firms, she insisted that sharing and supporting the perspective that being a woman should not distinguish them was not serving the profession. "Be there, show yourselves," she encouraged.

For an exhibition at the Tyrolean Architecture Centre, Innsbruck, Austria (2019), de Vries prepared *Architecture Speaks: The Language of MVRDV* to illuminate the firm's creative process: "Our methods allow us to research the questions surrounding our projects, in terms of program, context, and typology…They reveal our strategies for creating and organizing volumes, voids, and building elements, which ultimately become the containers of life, spaces for action, surfaces of representation and production." Large, aggregated forms in saturated colors depicted terms like *Village* (the future is social), *Activator* (the future is productive), *Stack* (the future is collective), and *Pixel* (the future is diverse).

Densification is also a driving force in MVRDV's design work. "We can't let the public life be only at the street level," says de Vries. "We must build up." MVRDV's competition-winning Vanke Headquarters building (2009) in Shenzhen, China, illustrates that thinking: a cluster of eight interlinked blocks of offices, houses, and culture rise from four separate bases to converge into one tower. "It's a 3D world, with everything interacting…We use different scales and make them intertwine."

The firm has taken care in its growth, with staff organized in studios of fifteen to twenty people led by partners and studio directors. Digitalization has made supervising easier for de Vries. Even so, MVRDV depends on a humanistic approach to practice. "We always think about who we want to be," she says. "How to keep the same DNA was of great concern to us. We're a horizontal organization and we wanted to retain our spirit in the face of changing economics. We wanted to preserve the way we talk to each other." The Rotterdam-based firm founded the NL Resilience Collective (2018), which partners with other local firms to bring their time-tested hydrological methods to areas like Miami and other coastal cities. —*JSE*

Left
Architecture Speaks exhibition,
Tyrolean Architecture Centre,
Innsbruck, Austria, MVRDV,
2019. Courtesy MVRDV

Below
Book Mountain, Spijkenisse,
Netherlands, MVRDV, 2012.
© Daria Scagliola & Stijn
Brakkee

KATHERINE CHIA

BORN
Bedford, NY, 1966

EDUCATION
Amherst College, BA, 1988;
MIT, MArch, 1991

PRACTICE
Prentice & Chan; Ohlhausen
Architects; Stephen Tilly
Architect; Maya Lin Studio,
1992; Desai Chia Architecture,
1995–

TEACHING
The New School of Design;
Van Alen Institute, Program
Leadership Council, co-chair;
United Nations International
School, trustee; Parsons
School of Design, 2019

NOTABLE HONORS
Top 20 US Houses, Dezeen,
2017; Top 50 Ranking for
Design, *Architect*, 2017;
Honor Award for Interior
Design, AIA, 2018

Even as a child, Katherine Chia made things with her hands: dresses, three-dimensional art projects, paintings, and drawings. Her childhood home, built in the 1940s, was designed by Edgar Tafel, an apprentice to Frank Lloyd Wright. "It [makes] you aware of materials, and how powerful materials can be in their raw state," she says of the ways in which growing up in the house impacted her future design work. The home had stone walls crafted by a local mason, and the windows were handmade. "I was always attuned to that [level of] finite or very finessed detail because I grew up in that environment, I lived in it every day."

When Chia's parents enlisted Tafel to design an addition to their house, he recognized potential in Chia. She had developed dual passions for mathematics and art, and as she was heading into her undergraduate studies at Amherst College, Tafel guided her to pursue coursework that would eventually allow her to become an architect.

After spending her junior year abroad in Denmark and graduating in 1988, Chia pursued graduate studies at MIT, completed in 1991. Subsequently, she worked in the New York office of designer, architect, and artist Maya Lin, on both architectural and artistic projects. She cites the *Wave Field* (1995), an earthen sculpture project at the University of Michigan; a Bronx Recycling facility (1998); and the *Eclipsed Time* sculptural project at New York's Penn Station (1995) as invaluable learning experiences during her time with Lin: "The process and the effort to really remain very clear and true to a strong vision was [great] for me to experience through her."

Lin's emphasis on artistic projects also helped Chia craft her future design ethos.

"It was an opportunity to continue with architecture, but to still stay very connected to the making and conceptualization of art," she continues. "That's continued to be a thread through our practice."

In 1996, Chia cofounded the firm Desai Chia Architecture with her husband, fellow architect Arjun Desai, whom she met at MIT. The firm focuses on interiors and landscape design, with importance placed on integrating light as a unifying theme.

Throughout her career, Chia has threaded teaching appointments with her architectural practice and is currently an adjunct faculty member at Parsons School of Design. Through her involvement with the New York chapter of the AIA and her elevation to the AIA's College of Fellows, Chia, who is a first-generation Chinese American, feels that she is making contributions to moving the traditionally white, male-dominated profession forward. "One of the biggest challenges, I think, is visibility," she says. "To see more women involved, and to see us all participating and fully involved and…bringing in a younger cohort who's much more diverse and balanced gender-wise is a really great thing." —*KF*

Above
Michigan Lake House, Leelanau County, MI, Desai Chia Architecture, 2016. Photo Paul Warchol

Left
FloodLAB, New York Restoration Project, Inwood, NY, Desai Chia Architecture, 2013. Photo Desai Chia Architecture

SANDRA BARCLAY

BORN
Lima, Peru, 1967

EDUCATION
Universidad Ricardo Palma, Architecture, 1990; École d'Architecture de Paris-Belleville, Architecture, 1993; Universidad Diego Portales, Santiago de Chile, Master of Territory and Landscape, 2013

PRACTICE
Barclay & Crousse, 1994–

NOTABLE HONORS
Hexágono de Oro National Architecture Prize, XVIII Peruvian Architecture Biennale, 2018; Architect of the Year, Women in Architecture Awards, *Architectural Review* and *Architects' Journal*, 2018; Mies Crown Hall Americas Prize, Edificio E, University of Piura, 2018

The practice that Sandra Barclay cofounded with Jean-Pierre Crousse designed one of its most important projects in their home country of Peru in 2013. The Place of Remembrance in Lima is stitched into a bayside landscape of cliffs and ravines. It's a significant building for the city, both in terms of form-making and purpose. "The building has a very important role in society," says Barclay. "It is an educational and cultural institution open to all, the exhibitions of which talk about the period of terrorism in Peru between 1980 and 2000, to make new generations aware of our history and avoid this happening again."[26]

Apart from honoring the more than seventy thousand people who died at the hands of the Shining Path, the revolutionary terrorist organization, the partners were additionally challenged with trying to redefine the meaning of architecture in a society disinterested in it. Along with their beliefs in defining space by the building's structure and eliminating any unnecessary elements, the notion of memory could be manifested in various ways. Accepting imperfections in buildings and leaving a trace of the construction process registers the participation of the people who helped make the structures. Barclay employed the movement of light to reveal the time of day in her architecture.

Barclay's father is an architect who designed and built the home she grew up in, from the time she was five. "I found the construction process magical!" she remembers. "Only after starting my career did I realize that architecture also has a role that can improve living conditions, which gave more meaning to my choice."

Her own learning curve in architectural practice has been a work in progress. In 2018, Barclay received the Women in Architecture Award from *Architectural Review*. "It felt like the first time I received a concrete award especially for me," she says. "I came from a society where men were more important and had the last word. Then I went to France and realized that wasn't the case there." The partners opened Barclay & Crousse in Paris in 1994 and subsequently opened a second office in Lima in 2006.

During the early years of their practice, Barclay raised the children she shared with Crousse while also working. The more extroverted Crousse lectured widely. Eventually, she, too, began traveling at his urging and values the opportunity "to become a reference for my students."

Both Barclay and Crousse trained as landscape designers as well as architects. In a 2019 studio at Yale University on climate and infrastructure, they inquired of the students, How can architecture help to be more resilient to these situations? "Buildings should help to solve problems in a permanent way and be able to support the community in these crisis situations, acting also as an infrastructure and no longer an isolated building," says Barclay. "It's architecture's responsibility to be attentive to place, climate, and people." —*JSE*

Left
Place of Remembrance, Lima,
Peru, Barclay & Crousse, 2013.
Photo Jean Pierre Crousse

Below
Paracas Museum, Paracas,
Peru, Barclay & Crousse, 2012.
Photo Jean Pierre Crousse

VI. INNOVATING FOR A BETTER WORLD
Introduction by Lori Brown

The generation of women born between the late 1960s and the early 1980s, often referred to as part of the Gen-X cohort, came of age during a time when society was still grappling with women's emergent power and their expanding positions within a rapidly evolving world. As young women, they were completely unencumbered by being female because during their youth and early adulthood, gender was not perceived as an inhibitor. These women were able to pursue any career located anywhere in the world. However, once into their careers, they have become more aware of how social and cultural constructions of gender and their associated biases impede women's advancement.

Culturally and politically, these decades experienced significant upheaval of establishment norms that had inscribed and perpetuated strict heteronormative expectations and performances of gender, race, and class and also ongoing economic disenfranchisement of people of color and women. The 1960s and 1970s witnessed the overturn of some of these practices through major legislation and political action. This period of radical transformation is better contextualized through highlighting several key policy and juridical moments, including the Civil Rights Act (1964); the Voting Rights Act (1965); the Fair Housing Act (1968); the establishment of the Environmental Protection Agency (1970); the FDA approval of the birth control pill (1960); the legalization of contraception for married couples (1965) and for all Americans (1972); the decriminalized of abortion (*Roe v. Wade*, 1973); and the Public Health Service Act's Title X (1970), as part of family planning, and Title IX (1972), prohibiting federally funded educational institutions from discriminating on the basis of sex.

Although second-wave feminism was instrumental in advancing women's rights and control over their own bodies, the legacy of the baby boomer generation has considerably shaped the evolution of this generation of women and how they take action in the world. These younger women made significantly different choices—in regard to the types of architectural practices they create and the scales of contributions they make. They seek paths that provide more autonomy and flexibility. Within this section's time period, the demise of the welfare state was fully underway, co-led by Margaret Thatcher and Ronald Reagan. Neoliberal economics became the basis of policy decisions with severe reductions of state services, producing a global conservative turn. These women entered adulthood during this cultural backlash of the late 1980s and 1990s and the pivotal swing away from the monumental gains of the previous two decades.

Although larger numbers of women began to be admitted into architecture schools during the 1970s, there was little within existing architectural educational paradigms supporting and educating more diverse student populations. Albeit somewhat better, this remained the case when these young women entered higher education. In response to the change in student demographics, significant feminist scholarship emerged during the 1970s and 1980s as more women began to teach and become professors. Research, practice, and teaching by a number of these soon-to-be prominent women during this time dramatically altered the discipline and its future trajectories. These women excelled despite the structural inequalities they encountered, creating openings that Gen Xers fully embraced. Yet today, much more progress for equity remains to be made, and the women in this section are at the forefront, significantly changing the direction and scope of architecture.

Women born between the late 1960s and early 1980s are now partners in firms, deans and full professors in schools across the globe, and industry innovators. Importantly, these women have dramatically expanded modes of architectural practice and for whom and how architecture can be practiced—they take into account intersections of sociopolitical contexts, environmental conditions, and ways in which design can contribute more broadly to the built environment. Beyond the construction of buildings, this generation continues to discover ways to test and apply their expertise, opening up more diverse and broader avenues for design's critical engagement. Some of these areas include environmental and ecological research, material innovation, robotic labs, publicly engaged design build, research and writing, curation and exhibition, and urban design.

Many included here occupy multiple positions—within the academy and practice, practice and industry, academy and public engagement—and these nexuses provide opportunities for increased potential for impact and agency, working with students and being affiliated with institutional partners. These relationships enable greater scaled opportunities for research and collaboration, working between education and public and private sectors. Through the myriad practices, this generation of women is invested in expanding architecture's significance and relevance for the future of a better world.

SADIE MORGAN

BORN
Kent, England, 1969

EDUCATION
Kingston Polytechnic, BA, 1991;
Royal College of Art, MA, 1993

PRACTICE
dRMM, 1995–

NOTABLE HONORS
Stirling Prize Winner, RIBA
Awards, 2017; Sustainability
Award, RIBA North West, 2018;
Contribution to the Profession,
AJ100 Awards, 2019; Female
Architectural Leader of the
Year, BD Design Awards, 2019;
Order of the British Empire
Award, 2020; Honorary Fellow,
RIBA, 2020

Sadie Morgan was raised on a commune with a deep sense of social responsibility and a "compulsion to make the world a better place." Her role as a public servant is an intuitive part of her twenty-six-year-old architectural practice, dRMM. As cofounder and director of the London-based firm, she says it has always had a social purpose: transforming people's lives.

The reinvention of Kingsdale Foundation School that dRMM completed nearly twenty years ago still impacts how the firm approaches design. Kingsdale's boys and girls represent widely diverse youth who require nontraditional approaches to learning, discipline, behavior, and communicating. "We had to find a way to make twelve hundred kids with low self-esteem feel important," says Morgan.[1] "They needed a place to inspire them." Instead of tearing the building down, dRMM removed the surveillance cameras and provided connection and passive surveillance along with an enclosed courtyard where everyone could walk and be seen. The kids felt ownership because they were part of the process, and Kingsdale became the best-performing school in the borough. "It was all about showing the kids you believed in them." Morgan reasoned, "So why stop with just buildings? Take on the environment as a whole."

In 2013, Morgan became the youngest president of the AA School of Architecture and the fourth woman to hold that position. A Commissioner on the National Infrastructure Commission (NIC) since 2014, Morgan chairs the Independent Design Panel for High Speed 2 (HS2), the country's rail initiative and the biggest infrastructure project in the United Kingdom. The group's goal is to improve the understanding of the value of design. "I am there to help the government think through people, place, and time in terms of this legacy," she explains. "HS2 will have a massive effect on our built environment and designing it well is absolutely crucial." Among Morgan's contributions are: a chapter on good design in the NIC's five-year National Infrastructure Assessment; insisting that projects are subject to design review; and the creation of a young professionals panel that includes people twenty-five to thirty years old, who will be inheriting these projects. She is also one of the Mayor of London's design advocates.

Morgan has recently set up the Quality of Life Foundation, an initiative to encourage developers to promote quality of life. "Everyone is focused on aesthetics—a pitched roof or a flat roof?" she laments. "What about safety, community, connection, affordability, and physical distance from key resources?" Morgan prompts.

In 2017, dRMM won the Stirling Prize for Hastings Pier. "I think of it as having a soul," Morgan says of the reimagined Victorian pleasure pier, designed with sustainability as a priority.

As for the future of architecture, Morgan emphasizes redefining what designers do, making it useful in a world where tech is transforming the practice. "We owe it to people to take on bigger things. Architects are great at problem solving. It's what we're trained to do but we're also trained to lock it into buildings. That skill can be applied to any scale of project." —*JSE*

LORI BROWN

BORN
Atlanta, GA, 1969

EDUCATION
Georgia Institute of
Technology, BS, 1991;
Princeton University,
MArch, 1994

PRACTICE
Pei Cobb Freed & Partners,
1995; Gwathmey Siegel
Associate Architects, 1996;
Polshek and Partners, 1997;
Hali Weiss Architects, 1998;
Lab Practices, 2005–

TEACHING
Syracuse University, professor
and director of diversity,
equity, and inclusion, 2001–

NOTABLE HONORS
New York Merit Award,
Unbuilt Project for the Upstate
University Hospital Chapel
renovation, AIA Central, 2005;
Chancellor's Award for Public
Service, Syracuse University,
2006; Milka Bliznakov
Research Prize Commendation
for *Feminist Practices*
exhibition, 2008; Diversity Best
Practices Honorable Mention,
AIA, 2008; Tribune Award
to ArchiteXX, Beverly Willis
Architecture Foundation, 2016;
New York State Buildings of
Excellence, 2021

Born and raised in Atlanta, Lori Brown studied at the Georgia Institute of Technology and received a master's of architecture from Princeton University. Brown's experience of being educated in an overwhelmingly male-dominated environment greatly influenced her later interest in architecture's responsibility to matters of gender and social justice. After graduating, Brown worked as an architect in New York City for several award-winning firms, including Pei Cobb Freed, Gwathmey Siegel, and Hali Weiss. In these workplaces, she grew frustrated with architecture's overall lack of engagement with political issues.

In 2001, Brown began teaching at Syracuse University School of Architecture, where she is currently a tenured professor, the director of diversity, equity, and inclusion, and a faculty advisor for the student-run organization Women in Design. At Syracuse, Brown's educational and organizational activities address the minority and gender gaps in architecture by creating networks of support, solidarity, and mentorship that span professional and academic spheres. "If we want to change the discipline, we have to begin to model what we hope that would look like in the academy," she says.[2] Her studios and seminars have focused on topics such as the US border conditions, the politics of public space, waste, climate change, and the housing crisis in New York City. In 2006, Brown and Alison Mountz received the Syracuse University Chancellor's Award for Public Service for the class they taught, Boundaries in Syracuse: Gender Architecture Geography.

Brown's design practice—a veritable spatial manifestation of her feminist values—demonstrates how architecture can improve people's everyday lives. In Syracuse, she has worked on the Library of Feminism for the Matilda Joslyn Gage Foundation (2005), the unbuilt Upstate University Hospital chapel (2005–6), low-income housing for single mothers recently released from incarceration (2006), and renovations for the Ver House Women's Shelter (2012). Brown has also consulted for abortion clinics in Alabama and Mississippi and a birthing center in Texas. Her extensive research on abortion clinics in North America has resulted in numerous exhibitions, lectures, and publications, including *Contested Spaces: Abortion Clinics, Women's Shelters and Hospitals* (2013), revealing how clinics can be designed in order to improve access to abortion.

As an extension of her own research and design, Brown is active in numerous feminist initiatives. From 2007 to 2009, she curated and participated in *Feminist Practices*, a traveling exhibition and public talk series that resulted in a book of the same name (2011). In 2012, Brown cofounded ArchiteXX with Nina Freedman, fostering intergenerational collaborations among women architects through exhibitions, publications, and various other forms of programming. Since 2015, ArchiteXX has collaborated with the Melbourne-based group Parlour and the Berlin-based group n-ails to address the exclusion of many women from the history of architecture through the collective writing of Wikipedia articles.

ArchiteXX's groundbreaking 2018 exhibition, *Now What?! Advocacy, Activism & Alliances in American Architecture since 1968*, examines the overlooked history of the civil rights, women's, and LGBTQ movements

in architecture and design.[3] Currently, Brown and Karen Burns are coediting *The Bloomsbury Global Encyclopedia of Women in Architecture 1960–2015*, an ambitious work that will make a major contribution toward increasing the visibility of women practitioners, educators, and writers in the field. —*LFR*

Top
Alabama Women's Center for Reproductive Alternatives, Huntsville, AL, rendering, Lori Brown with Patricia Cafferky, 2021; project on hold. Courtesy Lori A. Brown

Bottom
ArchiteXX promotion, 2012, organization cofounded by Lori Brown and dedicated to transforming the architecture profession for women

GEORGEEN THEODORE

BORN
Rockville Centre, NY, 1969

EDUCATION
Rice University, BArch, 1994;
Harvard GSD, MArch, 2002

PRACTICE
Eric R. Kuhne & Associates,
1995–2002; Peterson/
Littenberg Architecture &
Urban Design, 2002; Interboro
Partners, 2002–; Ehrenkrantz
Eckstut & Kuhn Architects,
2003–5

TEACHING
New Jersey Institute of
Technology, director of
Infrastructure Planning
Program, 2011–

NOTABLE HONORS
Young Architects Award, The
Architectural League of New
York, 2005; New Practices
Award, AIA New York, 2006;
Emerging Voices Award,
Architectural League of New
York, 2011; Urban Design Merit
Award, AIA, 2012; Alliance
Spotlight Award, Rice Design
Alliance, 2013; Design Prize,
Social Design Circle, Curry
Stone Foundation, 2017

Georgeen Theodore is architect, urbanist, theorist, and advocate for accessibility and resilience in urban design. She is the cofounder of Interboro Partners and professor at the New Jersey Institute of Technology, where she directs the Infrastructure Planning Program.

Following her architectural education at Rice and Harvard, Theodore worked as project manager for Eric R. Kuhne & Associates in London, where she oversaw the planning and design of large-scale retail projects in Europe and the Middle East. Later, as a senior designer for Ehrenkrantz Eckstut & Kuhn Architects, Theodore participated in mixed-use and waterfront projects, such as Governors Island Development Framework Plan (2006) in New York and San Pedro Waterfront Plan (2005) in Los Angeles.

In 2002, Theodore cofounded the Brooklyn-based Interboro Partners with former schoolmates Tobias Armborst and Daniel D'Oca, focusing on architecture, urban design, and planning. The firm has since become one of the leading voices for inclusive urban design and community engagement. Its hallmark is a participatory, place-specific approach to public-space interventions, neighborhood planning, and resilience projects.

Interboro first gained recognition in 2003 for its project In The Meantime: Life with Landbanking, as part of LA Forum for Architecture and Urban Design's Dead Malls competition. In the Dutchess County Mall in Fishkill, New York, officially closed, Interboro discovered a hub of informal activities and businesses, which they responded to by proposing a handful of temporary, economical solutions to bolster the site's preexisting uses. "We believe that all the hints about how to make a place better are there already," says Theodore.

The firm furthered its reputation for imaginative, resourceful urban interventions with projects such as LentSpace (2009), an art space and sculpture garden in Lower Manhattan, and Holding Pattern (2011), the winning-entry to the MoMA PS1 Young Architects Program. For the latter, Interboro asked more than fifty local organizations if there was something they needed that the firm could design for them.[4] These requests, including benches, ping-pong tables, and trees, were used in the courtyard at PS1 during its outdoor music series, Warm Up, and later distributed to the various organizations in the fall.

As part of their work promoting accessibility in the built environment, Interboro has developed landscape and waterfront projects investigating the complex interrelationship between social and ecological systems. In the aftermath of Hurricane Sandy in 2012, Theodore led an international, multidisciplinary team in a comprehensive resilience plan for the southern shore of Long Island, where 35,725 residents had been displaced. One significant facet of the Living with the Bay project aimed to improve stormwater management in order to mitigate flooding and environmental degradation.[5] Additionally, Interboro proposed to develop the public space along the river's banks, thereby improving the quality of life for the local population.

Currently underway are a number of large-scale neighborhood planning

initiatives, including the DTE Energy
Campau Campus and Neighborhood Master Plan
and the Campau/Davison/Banglatown
Neighborhood Framework Plan, both in
Detroit, Michigan. The latter project won
a 2020 AIA Award for Regional & Urban
Planning. —*LFR*

Above
Holding Pattern, Courtyard,
MoMA PS1, Long Island City, NY,
Interboro Partners, 2011. Photo
Dean Kaufman

Below
Campau/Davison/Banglatown
Neighborhood Framework Plan,
Detroit, MI, Interboro Partners,
2019. Courtesy Interboro
Partners

MEG GRAHAM

BORN
Toronto, Ontario, Canada, 1971

EDUCATION
University of Waterloo, BS, 1995, BArch, 1997; Harvard GSD, MArch, 2003

PRACTICE
KPMB Architects, 1997–2004; superkül, 2005–

TEACHING
University of Toronto, adjunct assistant professor, 2001–

NOTABLE HONORS
Design Excellence, Ontario Association of Architects, 2009, 2014; Toronto Urban Design Award of Excellence, 2009; International Green Interior Award, 2015; Fellow, Royal Architectural Institute of Canada, 2015; CaGBC Greater Toronto Chapter, LEED Award, 2016; Architecture MasterPrize, 2018; *DesignLines Magazine*, Designer of the Year, superkül, 2020

Meg Graham's commitment to sustainable design can be traced back to her time at the University of Waterloo. During her thesis year, she was awarded the AIA Award for Excellence for her design of a therapeutic bath complex built into a ravine adjacent to an existing rehabilitation hospital in Toronto. Later, in 2003, Graham graduated with distinction from Harvard GSD.

During the late 1990s and early 2000s, she worked as project designer for the firm KPMB, where she met her husband and future-collaborator, Andre D'Elia. During this time, Graham contributed to various educational projects, such as the Sprague Memorial Hall at Yale University (2003), Raether Library & Information Technology Centre at Trinity College (2004), Charles R. Walgreen Jr. Center at the University of Michigan (2007), and the Munk School of Global Affairs at the University of Toronto (2012).

In 2005, she joined D'Elia as coprincipal of superkül, a Toronto-based architecture practice founded on the criteria of constructability, durability, and sustainability. At superkül, Graham has led numerous residential, institutional, and retail projects, from innovative interiors for Steelcase Worklife in Toronto (2013) and New York City (2017) to an ongoing collaboration on the master plan for Pier 8 in Hamilton, Ontario.

Though superkül has a diverse portfolio of project types, the firm is best known for its award-winning, innovative homes that sensitively and creatively respond to their local context. In rural Ontario, the all-white Compass House (2016) either complements or blends in with the landscape, depending on the season, underscoring the firm's belief that architecture should establish a deep connection with its climatic, geographic, and social environs. This connection verges on the cosmological for Graham, who says, "Architecture is about designing both for the individual and for the collective, creating a kind of space that transcends the individual—I want to be able to stand in a space and feel connected to the sky, the land and the people around me."[6]

Making use of Toronto's urban lanes, where residential use is complicated by privacy concerns and zoning restrictions, projects like Gradient House (2012) and 40R Laneway House (2008) demonstrate the firm's ability to navigate the complexity of the urban fabric. More recently, Graham and D'Elia have been concerned with questions of affordability and are currently working with R-Hauz in designing a series of prefabricated, energy-efficient laneway houses for Toronto.[7]

As part of her work advancing sustainability and affordable housing agendas in architecture, Graham recognizes that advocacy is a critical component of transforming the built environment and insists on incorporating design at the level of city policy. Between 2005 and 2006, Graham acted as a special advisor to the mayor's Beautiful City initiative to improve the city's green standards and is currently working with the city on exploring how to improve Toronto's architecture. Additionally, she is a former chair of the Toronto Society of Architects and cochair of the City of Toronto Design Review Panel and serves on the advisory committee of Building Equality in Architecture Toronto. —*LFR*

Compass House, Mulmur,
Ontario, superkül, 2016.
Photo Ben Rahn

J. MEEJIN YOON

BORN
Seoul, South Korea, 1972

EDUCATION
Cornell AAP, BArch, 1995;
Harvard GSD, MAUD, 1997

PRACTICE
MY Studio, 2001–4; Höweler +
Yoon Architecture, 2004–

TEACHING
MIT, 2001–18; Cornell AAP,
dean, 2018–

NOTABLE HONORS
Rome Prize, American
Academy in Rome, 2005;
Design Vanguard Award,
Architectural Record, 2007;
United States Artists Award,
2008; Audi Urban Future
Award, 2012; New Generation
Leader Award, *Architectural
Record*, 2015; American
Academy of Arts and
Letters, 2021

J. Meejin Yoon moved to the Washington, DC, area with her family when she was a child. School field trips to the East Building of the National Gallery of Art and the Hirshhorn Museum sparked her interest in architecture. "[I appreciated] having exposure to these super unusual buildings," she says.[8] "[The] more abstract buildings were surprising to me, and I was very curious and intrigued by them and what made them different from 99 percent of the other buildings."

After completing her formal studies in architecture at Cornell AAP and then Harvard GSD, she received a Fulbright grant to study architecture and urbanism in Seoul. She was interested in the period of Japanese occupation of the city, from 1910 to 1945, and the impact it had on the city's built environment. Her time in South Korea still informs her current work, which includes a strong interest in organizational systems, exemplified through work like the 2004 *Aztec Empire* show at the Guggenheim, which involved setting up relationships between the artifacts, the museum itself, and a mediating wall.

Yoon became a professor at MIT in 2001. She established MY Studio the same year, to create work at the intersection of art, technology, and architecture. In 2002, she and partner Eric Höweler married, and in 2004, they founded Höweler + Yoon Architecture. The firm is currently based out of Boston.

Höweler + Yoon designs are often cited for their innovative use of new and emerging technologies in design and fabrication. Through pioneering integration of responsive technologies and architecture, the firm has created a number of interactive environments in public spaces.

"I've always been interested in both the limits and opportunities of emerging technologies, and I have always embraced building and architecture as a way of testing these limits," Yoon says. She cites the Sean Collier Memorial at MIT, unveiled in 2015, as "a project that looks at old technologies and new technologies simultaneously." The memorial, dedicated to a campus police officer killed in the wake of the 2013 Boston Marathon bombing and inspired by the gesture of an open hand, is composed of thirty-two solid blocks of granite that form a five-way stone vault. The design creates an unprecedented form by combining age-old structural techniques for spanning masonry vaults with new digital fabrication and structural computation methods to create an interlocking, self-supporting edifice. Another Höweler + Yoon design hailed for its innovative use of digital technologies is the interactive installation for the 2004 Athens Olympics, titled *White Noise White Light*. A luminous, responsive sound and light field filled with fiber-optic stalks changed according to the movement of the visitors walking through.

Höweler + Yoon work on a variety of project types—institutional and residential, public and private. The firm's design versatility has translated to a number of innovative residential projects, such as the Bridge House (2015) and the Oblique House (2019), both in McLean, Virginia. Both houses blur the boundaries between indoors and outdoors and are informed by specific site conditions. Yoon says that it is not the type of project as much as the connections that they engender that she finds the most rewarding.

Sean Collier Memorial, MIT,
Cambridge, MA, Höweler +
Yoon Architecture, 2015. Photo
Iwan Baan

"I have a preference for projects that allow for a lot of meaningful engagement with people," she says. "Whether it's residential, institutional, or commercial, I think it's those projects that ask hard questions that I feel lucky to get to work on."

Yoon spent almost two decades on the faculty at MIT. During her time leading the department of architecture, Yoon's accomplishments included the establishment of a design minor open to all MIT undergraduates, the relaunch of a bachelor of science in art and design, and an increase in cross-disciplinary studios within the graduate program. In 2018, Meejin was named dean of the Cornell AAP. —*KF*

Oblique House, McLean, VA,
Höweler + Yoon Architecture,
2019. Photo Jeff Wolfram

Left
Chengdu Wide Horizon
Hotel, Chengdu, China,
Höweler + Yoon Architecture,
2021. Courtesy Höweler + Yoon
Architecture. Rendering by
Luxigon

Below
White Noise White Light,
2004 Olympics, Athens,
Greece, Höweler + Yoon
Architecture. Photo Andy Ryan

TATIANA BILBAO

BORN
Mexico City, Mexico, 1972

EDUCATION
Universidad Iberoamericana,
BArch, 1998

PRACTICE
LCM, 1999–2004; MX.DF,
2004; Tatiana Bilbao Estudio,
2004–

TEACHING
Harvard GSD; AA School
of Architecture; Rice
University; Yale University;
Peter Behrens School of Arts;
Columbia GSAPP; Andrés
Bello University; Universidad
Iberoamericana

NOTABLE HONORS
Top 10 Emerging Firms
Award, Design Vanguard,
2007; Emerging Voice Award,
Architecture League of New
York, 2009; Kuntspries Berlin
Award, 2012; Global Award
for Sustainable Architecture,
LOCUS Foundation, 2014;
Cité de l'Architecture et du
Patrimoine of Paris, 2014;
Marcus Prize, 2019; Tau Sigma
Delta, Gold Medal, 2020

Born into a family of architects, Tatiana Bilbao also studied architecture at university, joining the Urban Housing and Development Center of Mexico City after graduation in 1998, while also working as an advisor to the government agency that oversees urban development and housing in Mexico City.

A year later, in 1999, Bilbao cofounded the firm LCM with architect Fernando Romero, mostly designing houses for wealthy clients and for public libraries and museums. In 2004, she cofounded MX.DF, a Mexico City–based urban research center, in partnership with architects Derek Dellekamp and Michel Rojkind and managing director Arturo Ortiz. She founded her practice Tatiana Bilbao Estudio the same year to work on projects in China, Europe, and Mexico.

The first project built by Bilbao's studio was an interdisciplinary exhibition pavilion in Jinhua Architecture Park (2007), an effort led by Chinese artist Ai Weiwei, who selected a group of young architects from around the world to design a large park in China, which was organized by a network of pavilions. Bilbao's design, one of her most-published works, features multiple levels and strategic blocking made of bold, intersecting geometric forms of raw concrete and stone.

One of Bilbao's earliest high-profile commissions came in 2006, when artist Gabriel Orozco hired her to help design and build the Observatory House (2009) in Roca Blanca, Mexico. Based on Orozco's original design—inspired by the Jantar Mantar Astronomical Observatory, built in Delhi in 1724—Bilbao developed the architectural plans. Built around a central pool, the house has sweeping views of the surrounding coastline.

For another coastal initiative in northwest Mexico, Bibao regenerated the Culiacán Botanical Garden (2013) with art installations, an auditorium, and orientation center. Describing her work here, Beatrice Galilee wrote in *ICON* magazine in 2011, "Bilbao operates with architecture rooted in strategy, aiming at unlocking public space and opening unused and unloved parts of the city." She also applies theories of how people circulate through space. "Our studio is not about the form or the shape of the building," Bilbao said in a 2017 interview with PLANE—SITE. "It's about making places and spaces by people, for people."

Another design by Bilbao in Culiacán is the Biotechnological Park Building on the campus of Tecnológico de Monterrey (2012), featuring a series of glazed boxes. Although the university asked for a traditional stacked structure, Bilbao convinced the board that separating the building's different levels and shifting them to create cantilevered forms for a distinctive and iconic structure would also be more practical. (The colored glass and deep overhangs cut glare and save on air conditioning costs.)

Marked by a fondness for brutalist forms and a commitment to sustainable solutions, Bilbao's body of work veers between public and private spaces, which the *New York Times* described as "eclectic." Her efforts to create low-cost housing to address Mexico's social housing problem has resulted in a prototype design to aid low-income individuals afford their own home, one which she presented at the 2015 Chicago Architecture Biennial.

Bilbao has balanced design work with academia throughout her career, and has

served as a visiting professor at Andrés
Bello University, Rice University, Yale
University School of Architecture, and
Peter Behrens School of Arts. She has also
taught at Columbia GSAPP, and served as
a professor of design at her alma mater,
Universidad Iberoamericana. —KF

Top
Pavilion, Jinhua Architecture
Park, Zhejiang, China, Tatiana
Bilbao Estudio, 2007. Photo
Iwan Baan

Bottom
Los Terrenos, Monterrey,
Nuevo León, Mexico, Tatiana
Bilbao Estudio, 2016. Photo
Rory Gardiner

ROZANA MONTIEL

BORN
Mexico City, Mexico, 1972

EDUCATION
Universidad Iberoamericana, BArch, 1998; Universitat Politècnica de Catalunya, MArch, 2000

PRACTICE
Diego Villasenor Arquitecto y Asociados, 1996–98; Rozana Montiel | Estudio de Arquitectura, 2009–

NOTABLE HONORS
Emerging Voices Award, Architectural League of New York, 2016; Miami Archmarathon Award, 1st Place, 2017; Moira Gemmill Award for Emerging Architecture, *Architectural Review*, 2017; Emerging Architecture Prize, MCHAP, 2018; Venice Architecture Biennale, 2018; National System of Art Creators Grant, FONCA, 2019; Sustainable Global Award for Architecture, Cité de l'Architecture et du Patrimoine of Paris, 2019; Venice Architecture Biennale, 2020

Rozana Montiel's *Void Temple* (2011) established the architect as a unique voice, with a focus suspended between building and landscape, inside and out. One of eight designs along a seventy-three-mile-long pilgrimage route in Jalisco, Mexico, Montiel's tall, white concrete band measures 131 feet in diameter, creating a giant halo. Its site in a pine forest features a significant slope, and a portion of the giant halo rests on the ground in some places and invites you to duck beneath it in others. A space there has been transformed into a place.

The architect describes her firm's placemaking mission as "changing barriers into boundaries, resignifying materials, [and] holding beauty as a basic right." She adds, "More than an aesthetic decision, beautiful design is an ethical stance impacting people's lives."[9] One of Montiel's favorite projects is a book her firm created called *HU: Common Spaces in Housing Units*, which she presented at the 2018 Venice Architecture Biennale. It is a series of pink Post-it notes with observations and hand-drawn diagrams showing actionable research findings from three of her firm's public-space projects in Mexico. Playful, the book's format is engaging not only for its ability to be immediately understood but also because it demonstrates one of Montiel's key design values: "Play is the most serious creative exercise we can think of to produce architectural design. We focus on the social aspects of architecture by staying sensitive to habitability as a principle of human space."

Receiving commissions for public projects was the biggest leap in Montiel's career, especially when she realized the responsibility architects have when designing collective living spaces. "For me, architecture is a text that, in its different expressions, generates patterns, rhythms, and narratives, just like the typography, pagination, and stories of a book."

For Montiel, experimentation is a natural part of the practice—her corrugated concrete module that houses solid-waste incinerators at airports and national ports is in development—as is learning from others. "In my studio we always work with an interdisciplinary team," says the architect. "We have participated in several strategic collaborations with advisors on landscape architecture, permaculture, industrial design, social anthropology, history, photography, art, literature, and filmmaking, depending on the nature of the project. We believe in the horizontality of teamwork, in 'author-shift' more than in 'author-ship.'"

In 2017, Montiel won the Moira Gemmill Award for Emerging Architecture from *Architectural Review* in London, a prize for women architects. She indicates it was an important turning point for her, "not only because the prize validated my studio's approach to architecture but also because it has funded my research. I think this kind of recognition encourages women to keep dreaming big in the architectural field." —*JSE*

Right
Post-its series, Rozana Montiel,
2018. Courtesy Estudio de
Arquitectura

Below
Rural Housing, Ocuilan,
Mexico, Rozana Montiel, 2019.
Photo Jaime Navarro

AMALE ANDRAOS

BORN
Beirut, Lebanon, 1973

EDUCATION
McGill University, BArch, 1996;
Harvard GSD, MArch, 1999

PRACTICE
Atelier Big City, 1996; Saucier
+ Perrotte, 1997–98; Rem
Koolhaas/OMA, 1999–2003;
WORKac, 2003–

TEACHING
Princeton University, adjunct
professor, 2004–11; Columbia
GSAAP, assistant professor,
2011–14, dean, 2014–

NOTABLE HONORS
First female dean, Columbia
GSAPP, 2014; Best of Year
Award, *Interior Design*, 2014;
Firm of the Year, AIA New
York, 2015; Merit Award for
Architecture, AIA New York,
2018; Honor Award, AIA Miami,
2018; Interior Top 50 Award,
Architect's Newspaper, 2019

As dean of Columbia GSAPP and cofounder of the New York City–based studio Work Architecture Company (WORKac), Amale Andraos challenges the field's status quo and reinvents the way we build and inhabit space. Born in Beirut, Lebanon, and raised in Dhahran, Saudi Arabia, Andraos vowed early on that she did not intend to follow in her father's footsteps and become an architect. By the age of seventeen, however, she did an about-face. After a primary education in Paris, Andraos studied architecture at McGill University in Montreal, working as a junior architect for Atelier Big City and Saucier + Perrotte. Andraos later pursued her master's degree from Harvard GSD, studying under Toshiko Mori and Michelle Addington. After graduating, she joined Rem Koolhaas at the Office for Metropolitan Architecture (OMA) in Rotterdam. There, she met her future husband and collaborator, Dan Wood.

In 2002, Andraos and Wood opened the Manhattan office of OMA before starting their own architectural firm together the following year. At first taking on local interior commissions, WORKac has since developed a diverse and international portfolio of projects projects, from a conference center (2014) in Libreville, Gabon and an assembly hall for the summit of the African union, to a master plan for the 2019 Beijing Horticultural Expo. WORKac has received innumerable accolades and international acclaim and in 2015 was awarded the New York State Firm of the Year by the AIA for its exploration of sustainable design, innovative planning, and engagement with social context.

The firm began exploring its signature approach to ecological urbanism starting in 2008, with its winning entry for the MoMA PS1 Young Architects Program.[10] Public Farm One (PF1) was an urban farming project made of a raised garden structure made from inexpensive and recyclable cardboard tubes that doubled as a shaded communal area in the museum's courtyard.

The synthesis between architecture, landscape, and ecology became the premise of WORKac's design of Edible Schoolyard at P.S. 216 (2014) in Gravesend, Brooklyn, and at P.S. 7 (2016) in East Harlem. Working in collaboration with Alice Waters's Chez Panisse Foundation, Andraos and Wood designed a kitchen classroom, greenhouse, and outdoor garden aiming to create a rich learning environment and transform the eating habits of kids. "A structure can make you feel connected to the world, rather than sheltered from it," says Andraos, referring to the ways in which the Edible Schoolyard's interlinked systems of rainwater collection, solar-panel heating, and compost processing communicate to students "how architecture and the environment can work together."[11]

Andraos and Wood have also played a significant role in shaping cultural and educational landscapes through their numerous designs for museums, libraries, and cultural centers, most notably the Blaffer Museum (2012) in Houston, the "Collage Garage" Parking Facade (2018) in Miami, Kew Gardens Hills Library (2017) in Queens, New York, and, most recently, the Student Center at RISD (2019). Some of their current major projects include a public library in Brooklyn and in Boulder, Colorado, and an art museum in Beirut. While each project responds to the specificities of geography and programming,

Collage Garage, Miami Design
District, Miami, FL, WORKac,
2018. Photo Miguel de Guzman

Above
Nature City, Keizer, OR, for MoMA exhibition *Foreclosed: Rehousing the American Dream*, WORKac, 2012. Photo James Ewing

Opposite top
Kew Gardens Hills Library, Queens, NY, WORKac, 2017. Photo Bruce Damonte

Opposite bottom
RISD Student Center, Providence, RI, WORKac, 2019. Photo Bruce Damonte

WORKac consistently pushes the aesthetic envelope through experimental forms and bold uses of color—a style they describe as "polemical optimism."

In addition to their built works, the firm is known for its exhibitions and publications exploring the radical possibilities for urban planning. In 2009, Andraos and Wood combined several years of research into a traveling exhibition and publication entitled *49 Cities*, featuring centuries' worth of unrealized visionary urbanisms in an effort to reflect back to explore the current reality of our own built environments. In a natural extension of this work, WORKac later collaborated with the 1970s architecture collective Ant Farm to design a utopian floating city exhibited at the inaugural Chicago Architecture Biennial. More inspiring yet was the Nature City project for MoMA's 2012 exhibition *Foreclosed: Rehousing the American Dream*, a daring proposal for an Oregon community designed around a compost mountain and high-speed rail network that brought the density, vibrancy, and diversity of an urban center into the suburbs.[12]

In 2014, Andraos joined a growing cadre of female leaders in academia, becoming the first woman to serve as dean of

Columbia GSAPP. Since her appointment, she has oriented the school's curricula around issues pertaining to globalization and the climate crisis, working to cultivate new forms of engagement across architecture, urbanism, infrastructure, and landscape. Her recent research and teachings have focused on the Arab City and the role that architecture plays in the production of cultural narratives. Her book *The Arab City: Architecture and Representation* (2016), coedited with Nora Akawi, investigates inherited conceptions of Islamic architecture, advancing the argument that environmental concerns have an urgency that cut across identity. "Most cities' needs aren't any different from our own," she says. "They need creative solutions to problems involving density, water distribution, energy efficiency, and sustainability, just as all cities do."[13] —*LFR*

HARRIET HARRISS

BORN
Hampshire, England, 1973

EDUCATION
Manchester University,
BArch, 2001; Royal College
of Art, MA Architecture
and Interiors, 2005; AA
School of Architecture,
Graduate Diploma in Building
Conservation, 2006;
Kingston University, Practice
Management & Law, 2007;
Oxford Brookes University,
PhD, Architecture, 2014

PRACTICE
Design Heroine Architecture,
2003–7

TEACHING
Royal College of Art,
Architecture Research
Program, 2014–15; Oxford
Brookes University, MArch,
2009–15; Pratt Institute, dean,
School of Architecture, 2019–

NOTABLE HONORS
Landscape Architecture
Scholar, British School
Rome, 2007–8; Clore Fellow,
2016; European Association
of Architectural Education
Council, 2017; Principal
Fellowship of the UK Higher
Education Academy, 2018;
Aurora Women in Academic
Leadership, 2019; Freeman of
the City of London, Worshipful
Company of Educators,
2019; champion for women
in architecture and design,
Dezeen, 2020

Harriet Harriss is concerned that the profession of architecture is operating like the *Titanic*: heading for impact with an iceberg but doing little to avoid it. As dean of the School of Architecture at Pratt Institute, Harriss's responsibilities require that she navigate the unknown depths of the profession's future. "Will the skills we're teaching endure?" she wonders. "Predictions suggest architects will be doing different things." With technologies like AI, she explains, robotics will bring tremendous changes and new typologies of design production. "What are we architecting?" will finally be the question.[14]

A concern she holds is that students are currently being prepared for careers in architecture *as it is* whereas they will, instead, need to become "propagators for the future." She's already correcting course. And while she doesn't advocate abandoning the traditional curriculum altogether, Harriss encourages engaging students in experimentation. "It's important we teach behaviors, not just skills."

Harriss's pedigree as an agitator was formalized in 2003, when, as a graduate student, she cofounded Design Heroine Architecture in London with Suzi Winstanley, a "conspicuously all-female practice." The partners emphasized storyboarding in their public work, inviting in the community. They coached local residents to become stakeholders for their environments. "We were playful, provocative, and generally committed to proving Ayn Rand wrong," Harriss says. "There's been a blight on the profession since *The Fountainhead* was produced."

Harriss's well-regarded books demonstrate her thinking. She is coeditor of *Radical Pedagogies* (2015); *A Gendered Profession* (2016); *Architects After Architecture* (2020); *Greta Magnuson-Grossman* (2020); and a *Routledge Compendium of Architectural Pedagogies of the Global South* (2012). Before being appointed dean of the school of architecture at Pratt, she led postgraduate research in architecture and interior design at the Royal College of Art in London. She is one of the founding members of Part W, a women-in-architecture activist group committed to calling out gender bias.

"Architecture is the lovechild of conflicted parents, a crucible of contested ideas," says Harriss. "Architecture is a collective endeavor and should not be boiled down to more buildings, to bricks and mortar…Those who trained but don't practice architecture are marginalized and undervalued despite their epistemologically diverse training." She notes that the president of Pratt, Frances Bronet, who is an architect, cites politicians, actors, and filmmakers among the individuals who trained in architecture school yet pursued other professional avenues. "We're responsible for all forms of creative endeavor across a diverse array of sectors, so why not claim these innovators as our own?"

Harriss believes another big omission in current architectural education is the lack of space for entrepreneurship. Her plan is to support students' growth in multifarious applications and eventually get the accrediting boards to sign on. At Pratt, a more robust architectural canon is underway, valuing civil rights and also women like Anne Tyng and Sybil Moholy-Nagy, former instructors at the institute. In Harriss, her students have another fine advocate and mentor. —*JSE*

Top
Radical Pedagogies (2015),
A Gendered Profession (2016),
and *Architecture Live Projects*
(2014). Courtesy Harriet Harriss

Right
Wearable Shelter for Syrian
Refugees, Royal College of Art,
London. RCA students led by
Harriet Harriss and Graeme
Booker, 2016. Photo Joshua Tarn

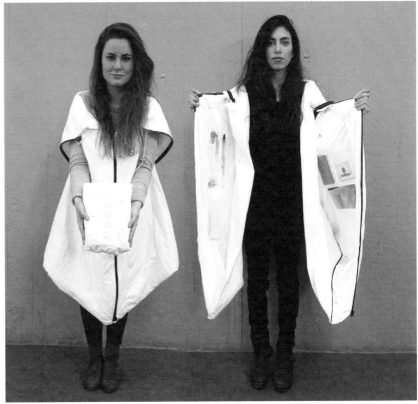

NICOLE DOSSO

BORN
Bronxville, NY, 1974

EDUCATION
Syracuse University,
BArch, 1996

PRACTICE
Perkins Eastman, 1996–98;
SOM, 1998–2019; Vornado
Realty Trust, 2019–

NOTABLE HONORS
Contributions to World Trade
Center site, Presidential
Citation, AIA, 2012; 40
Under 40, *Building Design +
Construction*, 2012; 40 Under
40, *Crain's New York*, 2012;
Fellow, AIA, 2016

Nicole Dosso grew up among construction sites, shadowing her father in his work on water and subway tunnels throughout New York City. It wasn't until she studied Latin in an all-girls Catholic secondary school, however, that she discovered her love for the built environment. "We studied Roman architecture, and it was there that I started becoming interested in history, and architecture in general," she says. In her first year in architecture school at Syracuse University, she initially struggled due to the gender imbalance and her lack of experience with sketching and drafting. "It was a testament of staying the course, which has been a theme throughout my career," she says. After making it through the first year of architecture school, she knew she had made the right choice.

Dosso always knew that she wanted to work in New York. She interned for architect Arpad Baksa, a small business owner she found in the phone book. He offered her a job, and because the firm employed only a handful of people, Dosso gained invaluable experience working within all elements of the firm. "It wasn't enough for me to just be part of the early phase [of design]—I wanted to understand [the whole process]," she says. She describes becoming familiar with codes, gaining hands-on experience at construction sites, and making multiple trips to New York's Department of Buildings.

After leaving Baksa, Dosso spent a year and a half at Perkins Eastman before moving to SOM in 1998. One of her first big projects was the Metropolitan Transportation Authority headquarters (2014) at 2 Broadway. The experience was comparable to being "thrown into the fire," yet it was a pivotal opportunity to build her career.

When 9/11 occurred in 2001, Dosso had been at SOM for three years. The firm's work in commercial office buildings and transportation dissolved for a period of time, forcing SOM to diversify. Within weeks, Dosso was pulled into a redesign of 7 World Trade Center, the last building to collapse that day. The project was able to move forward quickly, partially due to its important role as a piece of infrastructure for New York's Consolidated Edison power company.

Completed in 2006, she calls the project her "legacy" due to the rebirth it symbolized after the trauma of the 9/11 attacks. "Seeing work happening in the midst of chaos at Ground Zero gave people an ability to move forward," she says. Soon afterward, Dosso began work as the senior technical designer on One World Trade Center. When she was brought on to the project, she says, much of the form of the building had been established. Its close proximity to the 9/11 Memorial and the subway made the below-grade elements particularly challenging. Getting to grade, she says, was a major milestone. "Being involved in every aspect of that project was definitely a highlight in my career," she says.

In 2019, Dosso accepted a position as vice president of design and construction at Vornado Realty Trust, marking a new professional chapter. —*KF*

CAROLINE O'DONNELL

BORN
Athlone, Ireland, 1974

EDUCATION
Manchester University, BArch,
2000; Princeton University,
MArch, 2006

PRACTICE
Nettleton Willoughby Williams,
1997–98; KCAP, 2000–2004;
Eisenman Architects,
2006–8; Caroline O'Donnell
Architecture (CODA), 2008–;
O'Donnell Miller Group
(OMG), 2017–

TEACHING
Cornell AAP, Edgar A. Tafel
Professor and director of
MArch program, 2018

NOTABLE HONORS
Susan K. Underwood Prize,
Princeton University, 2006;
First Prize, European 11
Competition, 2012; MoMA PS1
Young Architects Program
Prize, 2013; Top 30 Female
Architects, *Azure*, 2017

Caroline O'Donnell's energetic designs represent a deeper way of thinking about sustainability, one intended to motivate people to act. Her latest book, *Werewolf: The Architecture of Lunacy, Shape-shifting, and Material Metamorphosis*, coedited with José Ibarra, is about change. "I think about designs not as one fixed thing but as existing in different states, varying with context, climate, program," she says.[15] In O'Donnell's hands, simple conditions like weathering, material recycling, and rehabilitation are manifested to come apart and employ the "architectural intelligence" of doing less whenever possible. These are staples in the tool kit of Caroline O'Donnell Architecture (CODA), based in Ithaca, New York.

Party Wall, the 2013 winning design for the MoMA PS1 Young Architects Program competition in Long Island City, New York (built 2014), demonstrates O'Donnell's perspective on multifarious ways a structure is used, viewed, and reused. "Culture is demanding now that temporary architecture (like the pavilions we've been focused on in recent years) not be wasteful," she says. "But when we consider that all architecture is temporary, we realize we need to raise the bar." Party Wall employed leftover cutout pieces from plywood skateboard patterns, temporarily diverting that waste. When the sun hits the forty-foot-high construction at the right time, the letters *W-A-L-L* provide shade for partygoers beneath the structure. "One of my favorite things about this project is that it's about its context—the ground and the sun—that you 'get it' as a concept," says O'Donnell.

Primitive Hut (2017), at Art Omi in Ghent, New York, displays change by integrating the growth and decay of trees into its design. "Every time you see it, it's different," she says. Evitim, a nearby tower that's an outgrowth of Primitive Hut, happened after the design team saw how much waste they were producing at Art Omi. "In most projects today, there is at least as much discarded as used." The structures were conceived and built with Martin Miller, creating the collaborative practice of O'Donnell Miller Group (OMG).

In 2016, she constructed Urchin on the campus, a pavilion for the Cornell Council for the Arts Biennial. Its design employed 360 delicately connected plastic chairs. "In their new configuration in Urchin, the chairs are no longer 'sit-able,' so the viewer is provoked to think about its other aspects," she says. Inspired by James J. Gibson's theory of affordances from his *Ecological Approach to Visual Perception*, O'Donnell opted for form, rather than use, as a design prompt, willing the chairs to lose their typical relationship with the body and the ground.

O'Donnell is the Edgar A. Tafel Professor of Architecture and director of the MArch program at Cornell AAP. Her writing, which she began during the early years of her practice to enable her to explore the practice's typically rushed competition work, helped her to formulate some rules for practice. Writing also helped make sense of her focus on bioclimatics in her undergraduate studies and, later, the type of formalism examined by Peter Eisenman at Princeton, with whom she worked after graduation. While Eisenman sees architecture as communicative, legible, and largely about itself, O'Donnell's experimental work instead explores the legibility of architecture and its relation to its broader context and its role as a small part within that greater whole. —*JSE*

Above
Evitim Hut and Primitive
Hut, Ghent, NY, CODA,
2017. Courtesy CODA

Right
Urchin, CCA Biennial
Pavilion, CODA, 2016.
Photo Joe Wilensky

UPALI NANDA

BORN
New Delhi, India, 1975

EDUCATION
School of Planning and
Architecture, India, BArch,
1999; National University of
Singapore, MArch, 2001; Texas
A&M University, PhD, 2005

PRACTICE
American Art Resources,
2006–12; HKS Architects,
2013–

TEACHING
University of Michigan:
Taubman College of
Architecture and Urban
Planning, 2017–; School of
Public Health, 2017–

NOTABLE HONORS
Certificate of Research
Excellence, Environmental
Design Research Association,
2015, 2016; European
Healthcare Design Research
Award, 2016; Women
in Architecture Awards
Trailblazers, *Architectural
Record*, 2018

Upali Nanda's love of architecture came from an early fascination with people and their environments. "Since childhood, I was always very fond of storytelling, very fond of stage-setting," she says. "[I was interested in] trying to create a theater for human performance, which in many ways, to me, is an analogy of what we do in architecture. We set the stage on which life happens."[16]

Attending India's School of Planning and Architecture in New Delhi, Nanda focused her undergraduate dissertation on exploring the question of what architecture would be if people could not see. She wanted to explore how architecture would be different if it wasn't seen as a field of graphic representation. "My interest in architecture came because I was very interested in human experience," she says.

Nanda went on to pursue a master's degree in architecture at the National University of Singapore and a PhD at Texas A&M University. From 2006 to 2012, she served as the vice president and director of research at American Art Resources, a healthcare fine art firm, where she created the research department. She has been at HKS Architects since 2013, where she established the HKS Lab and the Research Academy programs. Additionally, she currently serves as the executive director of the HKS nonprofit Center for Advanced Design Research and Evaluation.

"In my role as a researcher and then in practice, I'm really invested in making sure that all our decisions are based on something other than pure passion and opinion," Nanda says. Her research focus ultimately carried her into a role as an associate professor of practice at the University of Michigan's Taubman College of Architecture and Urban Planning, where she has been teaching since 2017, and an adjunct role in the School of Public Health. She was drawn to teaching because of what she perceives as the "giant divide" between academia and practice. "In a field that is as applied as architecture, the great divide seems unconscionable," she says. "For me, the balance is really about being a bridge to practice for students and the faculty here."

Nanda's research emphasizes design and health, including healthcare architecture and workplace well-being. One research topic that has gained particular traction is Point of Decision Design (PODD), which uses a framework developed by the Centers for Disease Control and Prevention to build on the premise that if you want people to make healthier decisions, you have to make their environment conducive to those decisions. "When we design environments, if we make the healthy choice the easy choice, we have made a huge leap," she says. She has applied these guidelines to a study on designing healthier college campuses, as well as solutions for childhood obesity.

She is currently working on a design for the Torrey Pines Living and Learning Neighborhood (2021) at the University of California, San Diego, which incorporates PODD in residential, academic, and administrative space. "I was always someone who wanted to transform lives," she says. "I'm really interested in crafting experiences, and architecture [has] allowed me to do that." —*KF*

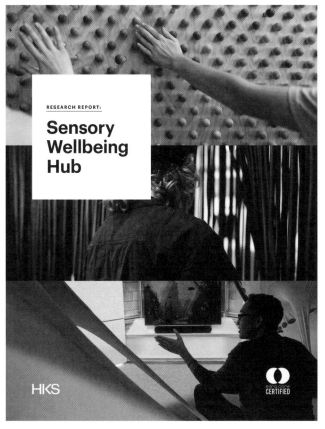

Above
Healthy Choices = Healthy Campuses: Point of Decision Design, Ideation Session, with Upali Nanda, center, 2016. Photo Hannah Jaggers

Left
Sensory Well-Being for Adolescents with Developmental Disabilities, Upali Nanda and HKS Research, 2019. Photo Hannah Jaggers

NERI OXMAN

BORN
Haifa, Israel, 1976

EDUCATION
Technion Israel Institute
of Technology, BArch; AA
School of Architecture,
MArch, 2004; MIT, PhD,
Design Computation, 2010

PRACTICE
MIT Media Lab, 2006–

TEACHING
MIT Media Lab, Sony
Corporation Career
Development Professor and
assistant professor of media
arts and sciences, 2006–;
Mediated Matter Group,
founder, 2010–

NOTABLE HONORS
Future Crucial Design,
International Earth Award,
2008; Graham Foundation
Manny Carter Award, 2008;
Next Generation, *Metropolis*,
2009; 20 Most Influential
Architects to Shape Our
Future, *ICON*, 2009; 40
Under 40, *Building Design +
Construction*, 2012; Senior
Fellow, Design Futures
Council, 2013; Women in
Design Award, Boston Society
of Architects, 2014; Vilcek
Prize, 2014; Emerging Voices
Award, Architectural League
of New York, 2015; 100 Global
Minds: The Most Daring
Cross-Disciplinary Thinkers
in the World, ROADS, 2015;
Innovation by Design, *Fast
Company*, 2015; Collier Medal,
MIT, 2016; Design Innovation
Medal, London Design Festival,
2018; Contemporary Vision
Award, SFMOMA, 2019

MoMA's *Material Ecology* exhibition in spring 2020 displayed the radical thinking and designs of Neri Oxman, an Israeli American professor at MIT. Oxman's interdisciplinary research project of the same name began in MIT's Media Lab in 2006. The intervening years of experimentation resulted in breathtaking innovations (plus multiple awards and a cult following) for her Mediated Matter team, all conceived to unite two distinct worldviews: "Machine or organism, assembly or growth, Henry Ford or Charles Darwin," she says of her interpretation of life's principal dichotomies.

Oxman's mission is to move the architecture and design process away from assembly (an approach stemming from the Industrial Revolution) and closer to growth using synthetic biology. Consider Oxman's Gemini chair (2014), an acoustical chaise lounge with a milled wooden shell and a 3D-printed surface that varies its material properties to receive the body comfortably rather than offering functions like recline or swivel. "I like to think of synthetic biology as a liquid alchemy, only instead of transmuting precious metals you're synthesizing new biological functionalities," she says. In 2015, the San Francisco Museum of Modern Art (SFMOMA) acquired Gemini for its collection.

The joining of science with art seems to come naturally to Oxman. She studied medicine for two years in Israel before attending the AA School of Architecture (both her parents are architects). She also served in the Israeli Air Force from 1996 to 1999.

"Why are we still designing with plastics?" Oxman asks in her 2015 TED Talk, *Design at the Intersection of Technology and Biology*. She quotes *Frankenstein* author

Mary Shelley and "Bucky" Fuller (she's earned the right to the nickname), apt muses for Oxman's somewhat monstrous and awe-inspiring efforts, which include 3D-printed masks for singer Björk that recall the movie *Alien* and the Wanders project, "life-sustaining clothing for interplanetary voyages."

As the TED viewers and SFMOMA visitors witnessed, Oxman's sustainable future relies on nature. At the museum, she recreated the Silk Pavilion, an earlier experiment from 2013. She marvels at the sophistication of silkworm cocoons, which are designed with both tension and compression, "the two forces of life manifested in a single material." Onto a pavilion of robotically spun silk, spotlighted with optimized heat and light, her team attached 6,500 silkworms, lending the structure's tension, or integrity. In two to three weeks, the worms spun 6,500 kilometers (4,040 miles) of silk, "in a curious symmetry, also the length of the Silk Road," notes Oxman. Silkworms are often boiled in their cocoons to access their silk but none of these creatures were harmed.

Keynoting the 2016 AIA conference, Oxman made an important distinction between "nature-inspired design" and "design-inspired nature." Her work falls into the latter camp. "Here's to a new age of creation," she says by way of ending her enthusiastic TED Talk. "One that demands of us for the first time that we 'mother' nature." Oxman is the Sony Corporation Career Development Professor and associate professor of media arts and sciences at the MIT Media Lab. —*JSE*

Above
The Silk Pavilion, *Material Ecology* exhibition, MoMA, New York, NY, Neri Oxman and MIT Media Lab students, 2020. Courtesy Mediated Matter Group

Right
Material Ecology exhibition, MoMA, New York, NY, Neri Oxman and MIT Mediated Matter Group, 2020.
© Denis Doorly

ANNA HERINGER

BORN
Rosenheim, Germany, 1977

EDUCATION
University of Arts and
Industrial Design Linz,
MArch, 2004

PRACTICE
Anna Heringer Architecture,
2005–

TEACHING
UNESCO Earthen
Architecture, Building
Cultures, and Sustainable
Development, chair and
honorary professor; Clay
Storming seminars (with
Martin Rauch) at Harvard
GSD, ETH Zurich, Technical
University of Munich,
Polytechnic University
of Madrid

NOTABLE HONORS
Emerging Architecture,
Architectural Review,
2006; Aga Khan Award for
Architecture, 2007;
UNESCO Chair of Earthen
Architecture, Building
Cultures, and Sustainable
Development, 2010; Global
Award for Sustainable
Architecture, 2010

Anna Heringer promotes building as a tool of self-actualization: "Birds build nests, animals caves. It's in our DNA that we want to build." Mud is Heringer's material of choice. "As every farmer will tell you, [mud is] warm in winter and cool in summer. When you build with earth, there's a psychological aspect that goes deeper than with other materials. It's hard to invent something like this that's already beauti-ful…Mud can return to the earth it came from when the building ages…The more closed and natural the cycle is, the more sustainable. There's no loss of quality."[17] She appreciates that mud is different every-where and that it's vulnerable to climate, which means she can create an architectural language and aesthetic for each place she builds.

Heringer first visited Rudrapur, India, northeast of Delhi, when she was nineteen. She volunteered with a sustainable devel-opment NGO, Dipshikha, which introduced her to the notion of relying on already exist-ing, readily available resources and making the best of them instead of depending on external systems. Those lessons formed the cornerstone of Heringer's practice. "I initially thought that I had to practice in a normal way and it depressed me. I wasn't following my heart. Simplifying my life was a way of getting there."

Heringer has built a Training Center for Sustainability (2011) outside Marrakesh, Morocco, celebrating indigenous building methods, and with Harvard GSD students, a rammed-earth pavilion in Austria, titled MudWorks: A Different Shade of Green (2012).

Heringer describes the difference in building with earth in various places: "When I'm building normally (in Bangladesh), we take responsibility for everything, innova-tion happens and there's trust. In Germany, we delegate the responsibility to insurers, whose concern is liability, and it costs more. It makes me really angry that we cannot afford the most logical way of building in the West. Our economic system around local labor does not support the cheapest, most logical ways. It's all about liability and control in industrial countries."

Heringer and her partner, Martin Rauch, communicate their Clay Storming method to students worldwide, from Harvard GSD to ETH Zurich, using modeling instead of discussion. The workshops include three to five people working with their hands on one object to achieve a result or solution. Often, the participants do not speak the same languages.

Making her own clothes led Heringer, in 2012, to create Dipdii Textiles in the Anandaloy village of Bangladesh, producing unique pieces out of local textile traditions with no electricity. Designed for decentral-ized production, the work enables women to make a living from home rather than leave their families to work in cities. "My team is at the moment 100 percent female. Our focus is on people and harmony." —*JSE*

Top
Modern Education and Training
Institute, Dinajpur, Bangladesh,
Anna Heringer Architecture,
2007. Photo Benjamin Staehli

Bottom
Anandaloy Building, Rudrapur,
Bangladesh, Anna Heringer
Architecture, 2019. Embroided
image by Dipdii Textiles,
Anandaloy village, Bangladesh.
© Günter König

EVA FRANCH I GILABERT

BORN
Deltebre, Catalonia,
Spain, 1978

EDUCATION
Escola Tècnica Superior
d'Arquitectura de Barcelona,
MArch I, 2013; Princeton
University, MArch II, 2014

PRACTICE
Claus en Kaan, 2014; Storefront
for Art and Architecture, 2010–
18; AA School of Architecture,
2019–20

TEACHING
Cooper Union; Columbia
GSAPP; IUAV University of
Venice; Rice University; SUNY
Buffalo; Shanghai Academy of
Fine Art; Princeton University
School of Architecture, visiting
lecturer, 2020–

NOTABLE HONORS
US Pavilion Curator, Venice
Architecture Biennale, 2014;
US State Department, 2016

Eva Franch i Gilabert has been intrigued by math since childhood. A professor of mathematics encouraged her to apply to architecture school. Although unfamiliar with architecture as an area of study, she saw common threads between the ways in which she was solving mathematical problems and the ways that she could solve problems in architecture. After completing a master's degree at Escola Tècnica Superior d'Arquitectura de Barcelona, Gilabert interned at the Claus en Kaan firm in Rotterdam before accepting a full-time position running competitions at the firm, a job she held for almost a year.

Moving to the United States to pursue postgraduate studies at Princeton University, she completed a second master's degree. As Gilabert was considering her next step, Sarah Whiting, her former professor at Princeton, encouraged her to apply for a position at the nonprofit Storefront for Art and Architecture in New York. Gilabert started as director of Storefront in 2010. Among other projects, Gilabert spearheaded the New York Architecture Book Fair, an initiative that brought together authors, publishers, designers, critics, and readers to consider what might constitute a fundamental collection of publications in art and design. Through her work at the Storefront, Gilabert attempted to democratize art and architecture and the ways people interact with it. These ideals culminated in the online initiative Worldwide Storefront.

"Instead of us thinking that culture is something that one produces in museums, or in centers of cultural consumption, culture is something that can happen next door," she says. "My role, or my vision, at the time was to make sure everyone around the world could actually take leadership or take ownership of their own ways of producing culture, and of producing alternative ways of engaging with society and with architecture, and with space at large."[18]

In 2019, Gilabert became director of the AA School of Architecture in London, the renowned center of progressive thought that has educated architects from Rem Koolhaas to Zaha Hadid. She is the first woman to hold the position, and her focus at the association has mirrored the political and cultural movements taking place around the world. "We have an entire new generation who is asking the 'grown-ups' to really understand the social, political, and environmental implications of our actions," she says. "As architects, we always build on behalf of a certain idea of 'other,' and yet what I think makes architecture and architects very powerful is when we are able to speak on behalf of those who are not necessarily embedded within the decision-making process," she says.

In a controversial move within the international architecture community, Gilabert was fired from her role as director of the AA in July 2020 for "specific failures of performance," according to the AA board. Her dismissal prompted an open letter in support of Gilabert's leadership, signed by more than two hundred academics and architects, including Mónica Ponce de León and Tatiana Bilbao. She is a visiting lecturer at Princeton School of Architecture. —*KF*

Top
Sharing Models Manhattanisms,
Storefront for Art and
Architecture, New York, NY,
2016. Photo Naho Kubota

Bottom
US Pavilion, Venice Architecture
Biennale, Architect, 2014.
Commissioned by Storefront for
Art and Architecture, New York.
Photo David Sundberg. Courtesy
Storefront for Art and Architecture

CATIE NEWELL

BORN
Canton, OH, 1979

EDUCATION
Georgia Institute of
Technology, BArch, 2003;
Rice University, MArch, 2006

PRACTICE
Office dA, 2006–9; Alibi
Studio, 2010–

TEACHING
University of Michigan,
Taubman College of
Architecture, associate
professor, 2011–; University
of Michigan, MS in Digital
and Material Technologies,
director, 2019–

NOTABLE HONORS
Oberdick Fellow, University
of Michigan Taubman College
of Architecture and Urban
Planning, 2009–10; Venice
Architecture Biennale,
2012; Rome Prize, American
Academy in Rome, 2013–14;
Kresge Artist Fellow, 2017;
ACADIA Innovative Academic
Program Award of Excellence,
2019; WOJR Civitella Ranieri
Architecture Prize, 2020

The term "site-specific" assumes a novel level of commitment in the architecture of Catie Newell. Her Detroit-based practice, Alibi Studio, opened in 2010, forged with a deep connection to place. Newell grew up nearby, and both her father and brother worked at the local automotive plants. Through her various roles as an innovator and "worker" on her own architecture, she feels an affinity with the industrial craftspeople of Detroit, catalyzed by a need to act when confronted by the city's numerous feral buildings suffering abandonment, arson, or other violence in the wake of economic hardship. "This work seeks out the unforeseen, the troubled, and the shameful," she writes in her essay "This Time: The Vanishing Work of Alibi Studio" in *Waste Matters: Adaptive Reuse for Productive Landscapes* (2020).

In her project Salvaged Landscape (2010), Newell addressed the widespread tragedy of arson in Detroit. The owners of a two-story house that had burned beyond repair desired to replace it with a sculpture garden, yet when she visited the site, "curating the demolition" itself held the most appeal. She and a team of fearless volunteers deconstructed the structure slowly, by hand, until it revealed a sectional cut. By selectively taking apart the building, she witnessed its volumes changing.

Assisted by her father, who worked patiently over two years with Newell on an unsafe building to demolish the structure, Newell then began anew. She cantilevered long, salvaged boards back into the structure to create a new room. Alibi Studio's text about the project talks about "not only registering change but also temporarily suspending it" and the need to both mourn and honor such places of violence.[19]

Photography is Newell's version of drawing. She uses it as a tool to sketch and record, to learn about spaces, and to ensure an afterlife for her fleeting interventions. "We make ghosts" is the way she puts it. As a fellow at the American Academy in Rome, Newell spent a year "chasing darkness" with her camera in European cities. Back home in Detroit, her project Nightly documented how a safety-inspired relighting scheme abruptly changed the city's appearance in spaces that had experienced decades of darkness.

In Secret Sky (2019), Newell challenged herself to take a building and turn it into architecture. "I was commissioned to make something new out of an ailing barn in rural Michigan. With an interest in preserving the barn's iconic shape while also making a project that could work with the wide open sky and its turns between day and night, I created a new space in the barn, one that could be viewed as a subtraction and an addition. The slice cuts across the barn, connecting to its original openings. In a way, I saved two barns by creating an architectural maneuver that became a gift to the sky." Newell describes her conceptual process in Secret Sky as "tending to the space as it existed and listening to it tell me what to do."

Gordon Matta-Clark, Rachel Whiteread, and DoHo Suh's spatial conversations offer inspiration to Alibi Studio. Newell has exhibited her work widely, including at the 2012 Venice Architecture Biennale and at the University of Michigan, where she is director of the master of science in digital and material technologies and associate professor of architecture in the Taubman College. —*JSE*

Above
Secret Sky, Hume, MI,
Alibi Studio, 2019. Courtesy
Catie Newell

Right
Salvaged Landscape, Detroit,
MI. Courtesy Catie Newell

FRIDA ESCOBEDO

BORN
Mexico City, Mexico, 1979

EDUCATION
Universidad Iberoamericana,
BArch, 2003; Harvard GSD,
MArch, 2012

PRACTICE
Frida Escobedo, 2006–

TEACHING
University of California,
Berkeley, College of
Environmental Design, 2007;
AA School of Architecture;
Columbia GSAPP, 2015; Rice
University, 2018; Harvard GSD,
2019–20

NOTABLE HONORS
Young Creators' Scholarship,
Fondo Nacional para la Cultura
y las Artes, Mexico, 2004;
Young Architects Forum
Award, Architectural League
of New York, 2009; Marcelo
Zambrano Scholarship,
2010; Ibero-American
Biennale of Architecture
and Urbanism Prize, 2014;
Emerging Architecture Award,
Architectural Review, 2016;
Emerging Voices Award,
Architectural League of New
York, 2017; Serpentine Pavilion,
London, 2018; International
Fellow of Royal Institute of
British Architect, 2019

Mexican architect Frida Escobedo set up her own practice in 2006, never having worked for anyone else. She creates contemplative spaces, both permanent and temporary, with a complexity that doesn't need to be understood to enjoy them. In 2018, she was the youngest person to create the annual Serpentine Pavilion in London. Her pavilion played with the power of compression and expansion to affect one's experience of space. It also reflected Escobedo's Mexican roots. The building material was a common, concrete roof tile produced industrially in Mexico City and "used in buildings made by people, not architects," she says. "The idea was to use simple material in a more sophisticated way. The lattice creates varying degrees of transparency depending on the position of the sun. In Mexico, we often use a juxtaposition of layers as a way of understanding time and space."[20] The nearby location of the Greenwich Meridian encouraged Escobedo to explore the idea of scientific time versus abstract and social time.

In 2013, Escobedo created the temporary Civic Stage in Lisbon, Portugal. "It tilts when people gather," the concept being that the voice of the speaker is only as loud as the audience. "The visual power of the audience is central here. It's an inversion of the typical orientation." Escobedo transfers ideas from her installations to permanent buildings: "The distilled program offers opportunity to test ideas and materials," she says.

Continuing her personal investigation in her 2019 publication *Domestic Orbits*, she recently taught a studio at Harvard GSD about domestic workers in Mexico being recognized as part of the formal economy.

The brief reads: "How can architectural interventions help recognize, reduce, and redistribute the problems faced by domestic workers? What solutions can be devised to organize access to healthcare, labor rights, decent working conditions, and leisure?" Escobedo has also taught at Columbia University, the AA School of Architecture, UC Berkeley, and Rice University.

Escobedo designed the Mar Tirreno town houses (2018) for developers who allowed her freedom with the program. She provided private corridors for each town house stacked in an atypical configuration, introducing communal patios to economize on cinder blocks. The result reflects the same sophistication exhibited in her Serpentine Pavilion.

"A building is never complete," says Escobedo. "A very liberating way to think about it is to understand it as an open thing that can change instead of something needed to be perfected. Handing it off. I don't have kids, so this may be my way of seeing the projects growing into their own person." —*JSE*

Mar Tirreno, Mexico City,
Mexico, Frida Escobedo, 2018.
© Rafael Gamo

Acknowledgments

Every book involves the dedication of several individuals who contribute their time, talent, and expertise to the work.

For *The Women Who Changed Architecture*, first and foremost are the pioneering architects featured in these pages. All the living architects contributed their valuable time to in-depth interviews with Julie Sinclair Eakin, Katherine Flynn, and Laurel Frances Rogers, and also helped the publisher to curate the artwork that illustrates their brilliant careers. Thank you.

My heartfelt thanks go to Robert and Arlene Kogod of Washington, DC, whose financial support made this book a reality. Bob and Arlene are extraordinary art and architecture patrons on a global scale. They are also lifelong champions of advancing the educational and professional opportunities of girls and women. I am grateful for their faith and confidence in *The Women Who Changed Architecture*.

The Beverly Willis Architecture Foundation, the book's copublisher, founded in 2002 to advance women in the architectural profession, has been a trustworthy partner in this endeavor. Special thanks go to Beverly Willis, Julia Murphy, and Cynthia Phifer Kracauer.

I extend profound thanks to Amale Andraos for the Introduction; to Beverly Willis for the Foreword; to Sarah Allaback for the historical introduction to the "Groundbreakers" generation and for the biographies of nine early pioneers; to Mary McLeod and Victoria Rosner for their penetrating introduction to the "Paving New Paths" generation; to Doris Cole, FAIA, for her insightful introduction to the "Advancing the Agenda" generation; to Margaret "Meg" Birney Vickery for her powerful essay introducing the "Rocking the World" generation; to Julia Gamolina for her spirited introduction to the "Raising the Roof" generation; to Lori Brown for her provocative introduction to the "Innovating for a Better World" generation; to Julie Sinclair Eakin for the forty compelling interviews and biographies, elevating this book to a higher plane; to Katherine Flynn for the thirty-seven unflinching interviews and biographies, ensuring professionalism in each word; to Laurel Frances Rogers for her thirty-three biographies, promising superb research and irresistible histories; and to John Lobell and Andrea J. Merrett for their singular biographies of one very special architect.

I have been honored to work with outstanding colleagues at Princeton Architectural Press. Foremost is associate editor Stephanie Holstein, whose partnership in this mammoth project has been truly magnificent. Jennifer Thompson, executive editor, was an early champion, for which I am grateful. The meticulous expertise of production editor Kristen Hewitt, editor Michelle Meier, office manager Joe Weston, art director Paul Wagner, graphic designer Natalie Snodgrass, and publisher Lynn Grady are noteworthy. Linda Lee, the scrupulous copyeditor, scoured the manuscript to perfection.

Finally, to George Hartman, my husband, I extend loving thanks.

Jan Hartman
Brooksville, Maine

Contributors' Biographies

SARAH ALLABACK ("Groundbreakers") is the senior manuscript editor of the Library of American Landscape History (LALH). She was formerly a historian and editor for the Historic American Buildings Survey and the Historic American Engineering Record and a consultant to the National Park Service. Allaback is the author of *Marjorie Sewell Cautley, Landscape Architect for the Motor Age* (2021) and *The First American Women Architects* (2008); she is a coeditor of *Warren H. Manning, Landscape Architect and Environmental Planner* (2017). Allaback has a BA in architectural history from Princeton University and a PhD from MIT.

AMALE ANDRAOS ("Introduction") is dean of Columbia University Graduate School of Architecture, Planning and Preservation (GSAPP) and cofounder of WORKac, with Dan Wood, her husband, in New York City. Born in Beirut, Lebanon, Andraos holds a BArch from McGill University and an MArch from Harvard University Graduate School of Design. She has taught at Princeton University, Harvard University, and the American University in Beirut. She is the first woman to hold the deanship at Columbia GSAPP. Andraos is the author of *We'll Get There When We Cross That Bridge* (2017) and *The Arab City: Architecture and Representation* (2016).

LORI BROWN ("Innovating for a Better World") is a professor in the School of Architecture and the director of diversity, equity, and inclusion at Syracuse University. She is the author of *Contested Spaces: Abortion Clinics, Women's Shelters and Hospitals* (2013). In 2008, she was awarded the AIA's Diversity Best Practices Honorable Mention, and in 2012, she cofounded, with Nina Freedman, ArchiteXX, a women and architecture group. Brown holds a BS in architecture from Georgia Institute of Technology and an MArch from Princeton University.

DORIS COLE, FAIA ("Advancing the Agenda") is an American architect and author. She was a founding principal of Cole and Goyette (1981–2009) and the founding principal of Doris Cole, FAIA, in 2012. Cole wrote the first book on women in architecture in the United States, *From Tipi to Skyscraper: A History of Women in Architecture* (1973). Other books include *Eleanor Raymond, Architect* (1981) and *The Lady Architects: Lois Lilley Howe, Eleanor Manning and Mary Almy, 1893–1937* (1990). In 2006, the Boston Society for Architecture honored Cole with the Women in Design Award of Excellence.

JULIE SINCLAIR EAKIN, who wrote forty biographies in this book, is an editor and writer with graduate degrees in architecture and the history of architecture from SCI-Arc and the University of California, Berkeley, respectively. She was senior editor at *Architecture* magazine and the editor of *Cite: The Architecture + Design Review of Houston*.

KATHERINE FLYNN, who wrote thirty-seven biographies in this book, is an editor at the AIA and a former senior staff writer at *Consequence of Sound*. Flynn's work has appeared in the *Washington Post*, *CityLab*, the *Huffington Post*, and elsewhere. A graduate of Beloit College and American University, Flynn is a cofounder of *Audia*, a blog that amplifies the voices of women in the music industry.

JULIA GAMOLINA ("Raising the Roof") is the director of strategy for Trahan Architects. The founder and editor of *MadameArchitect.org*, Gamolina has published more than one hundred interviews with architects, designers, publicists, journalists, business developers, and lawyers. Her writing has appeared in the *Architect's Newspaper*, *Architizer*, and *Metropolis* magazine. In 2019, she was named one of Professional Women in Construction's Top 20 Under 40. Gamolina received her BArch from Cornell University.

JAN CIGLIANO HARTMAN is an editor, historian, and book producer. Formerly a senior acquisitions editor at Princeton Architectural Press, Hartman is the principal of Jan Hartman Books and the author or editor of eight books, including *Private Washington: Residences in the Nation's Capital* (1998), *Grand American Avenue, 1850–1920* (1994), and *Showplace of America: Cleveland's Euclid Avenue* (1990). She holds a BA with highest honors in history from Oberlin College and a master's degree in urban planning from George Washington University.

MARY MCLEOD ("Paving New Paths") is a professor of architecture at Columbia University Graduate School of Architecture, Planning and Preservation. McLeod is coeditor of *Architecture, Criticism, Ideology and Architecture Reproduction* (1997) and is editor of and contributor to *Charlotte Perriand: An Art of Living* (2003). Her articles have appeared in *Assemblage, Oppositions, Art Journal, AA Files, Journal of the Society of Architectural Historians, Casabella, Art Journal, Harvard Design Magazine,* and *Lotus.*

LAUREL FRANCES ROGERS, who wrote twenty-three biographies in this book, received her master's degree from Columbia University Graduate School of Architecture, Planning and Preservation and her BFA in photography and BA in art history from San Francisco Art Institute. Rogers has served as editor in chief of *Vacuum* at Columbia and director of Still Lights Gallery in San Francisco.

VICTORIA ROSNER ("Paving New Paths") is dean of academic affairs and adjunct associate professor of English and comparative literature at Columbia University. She is the author of *Modernism and the Architecture of Private Life* (2005) and the editor of *The Cambridge Companion to the Bloomsbury Group* (2014) and *The Global and the Intimate: Feminism in Our Time* (2012, with Geraldine Pratt). Rosner holds a BA from Columbia College and a PhD from Columbia University.

MARGARET "MEG" BIRNEY VICKERY ("Rocking the World") is a lecturer in art history at the University of Massachusetts, Amherst. Vickery is the author of *Landscape and Infrastructure: Reimagining the Pastoral Paradigm for the Twenty-First Century* (2019), *Smith College: The Campus Guide* (2007), and *Buildings for Bluestockings: The Architecture and Social History of Women's Colleges in Late Victorian England* (2000). She earned her BA from Oberlin College and her PhD from Stanford University.

BEVERLY WILLIS, FAIA, is best known for the San Francisco Ballet building and her innovative efforts to develop an early computer software program known as CARLA (Computerized Approach to Residential Land Analysis). She is a cofounder of the National Building Museum in Washington, DC, and founder of the Beverly Willis Architecture Foundation. A graduate of the University of Hawaii, Willis's architecture is rooted in a humanistic approach that is reflected in the functional plans of her buildings.

Credits

Notes

Introduction

1. See, for example, recent profiles such as Amy Waldman, "Jeanne Gang in the Wild," *New Yorker*, May 19, 2014, https://www.newyorker.com/magazine/2014/05/19/the-urban-wild; Justin Davidson, "What Would a World Designed by Women Look Like?" *The Cut*, March 20, 2018, https://www.thecut.com/2018/03/what-would-a-world-designed-by-women-look-like.html; and, more recently, Elisabeth Malkin, "Matching Architecture to People's Needs, by Listening to Them First," *New York Times*, May 7, 2018, https://www.nytimes.com/2018/03/07/arts/design/tatiana-bilbao-architect.html. On the profession, see, for example, Reed Kroloff, "Architecture Is No Longer Just a 'Gentleman's Profession,'" *New York Times*, September 14, 2018, https://www.nytimes.com/2018/09/14/arts/design/women-in-architecture.html; and Allison Arieff, "Where Are All the Female Architects?," *New York Times*, December 15, 2018, https://www.nytimes.com/2018/12/15/opinion/sunday/women-architects.html. After Zaha Hahid died, the *New York Times* launched an informal online questionnaire aimed at getting women to talk candidly about their experience in the profession: https://www.nytimes.com/2016/04/13/arts/design/female-architects-speak-out-on-sexism-unequal-pay-and-more.html.
2. To name but a few: Mónica Ponce de León, dean of Princeton School of Architecture; Deborah Berke, dean of Yale School of Architecture; J. Meejin Yoon, dean of Cornell AAP; Sarah Whiting, dean of Harvard GSD; Lesley Lokko, dean of CUNY's Barnard and Anne Spitzer School of Architecture; Harriet Harriss, dean of Pratt Institute's School of Architecture; Odile Decq, cofounder of the Confluence Institute for Innovation and Creative Strategies in Architecture; Mona Harb, associate dean of the faculty of architecture and engineering at the American University of Beirut and chairperson of the department of architecture and design; and Mona Tabassum, director of the academic program at Bengal Institute for Architecture, Landscapes and Settlements, among others.
3. See, for example, organizations such as the New York City–based group ArchiteXX, which has developed an intergenerational mentoring program to help female graduates make the transition to practice; the Beverly Willis Architecture Foundation, which works to promote women's leadership in the building industry; and Archiparlour, an Australian research initiative, which provides an online discussion forum for issues of gender equity. This sustained work has been joined by more on-the-ground activism, such as the 2013 petition for the Pritzker Prize to recognize Denise Scott Brown; the Voices of Women (VOW) manifesto and demonstration at the 2018 Venice Architecture Biennale; and the Architecture Lobby's efforts to counter sexual harassment in the workplace through its #MeToo Solidarity Bloc (https://architecture-lobby.org/project/metoo-solidarity-bloc/), to name a few.
4. See Laura Mark, "Results of the AJ Women in Architecture Survey Revealed," *Architects' Journal*, January 10, 2014, https://www.architectsjournal.co.uk/events/wia/results-of-the-aj-women-in-architecture-survey-revealed/8657344.article; and the recently published AIA Guides for Equitable Practice or AIASF Equity by Design. See Wanda Lu, "AIASF Equity by Design Releases 2018 Equity in Architecture Survey Findings," *Architect Magazine*, November 6, 2018, https://www.architectmagazine.com/practice/aiasf-equity-by-design-releases-2018-equity-in-architecture-survey-findings_o.
5. Arieff, "Where Are All the Female Architects?"

Chapter 1

1. "Women in Architecture: One Who Has Been Successful in It Talks to Other Women," *Buffalo Morning Express*, March 7, 1881, 6; "Woman Architects: No Demand for Them Unless They Are Willing to Do Men's Work," *Buffalo Courier*, March 7, 1881, 6.
2. Quoted in Sarah Allaback, "Better Than Silver and Gold: Design Schools for Women in America, 1848–1960," *Journal of Women's History* 10 (Spring 1998): 88.
3. Bertha H. Palmer, *Addresses and Reports of Mrs. Potter Palmer: President of the Board of Lady Managers, World's Columbian Commission* (Chicago: Rand McNally, 1894), 15.
4. *The Inland Architect and News Record*, March 1981, 20–21.
5. "The First Lady Architect," *New York Times*, November 12, 1901. Reprinted from the *Pall Mall Gazette* [Paris], October 28, 1901.
6. Sarah Allaback, *The First American Women Architects* (Champaign-Urbana: University of Illinois, 2008), 34.
7. Louise Blanchard Bethune, "Women and Architecture," *Inland Architect and News Record* 17 (March 1891): 20–21.
8. Francis E. Willard and Mary A. Livermore, eds., *A Woman of the Century* (Buffalo, NY: Charles Wells Moulton, 1893), 80–81.
9. Adriana Barbasch, "Louise Blanchard Bethune: The AIA Accepts Its First Woman Member," in *Architecture: A Place for Women*, ed. Ellen Perry Berkeley (Washington, DC: Smithsonian Institution Press), 15–25.
10. Renja Suominen-Kokkonen, *The Fringe of a Profession: Women as Architects in Finland from the 1890's to the 1950's* (Helsinki: Journal of the Association of Ancient Monuments, 1992), 31, 29.
11. Suominen-Kokkonen, *The Fringe of a Profession*, 9, 31; and Riitta Jallinoja, "Women's Path into the Academic World," in *Profiles: Pioneering Women Architects from Finland* (Helsinki: Museum of Finnish Architecture, 1983), 17, 18.
12. Riitta Nikula, ed., *Heroism and the Everyday: Building Finland in the 1950s* (Helsinki: Museum of Finnish Architecture, 1994), 18; Edward Marc Treib, "Lars Sonck: From the Roots," *Journal of the Society of Architectural Historians* 30, no. 3 (October 1971): 228–37.
13. Riitta Nikula, *Profiles: Pioneering Women Architects from Finland*, 18.
14. Allaback, *The First American Women Architects*, 104–17.
15. Andrea Jeanne Merrett, "Lois Lilley Howe," *Pioneering Women of American Architecture*, https://pioneeringwomen.bwaf.org/lois-lilley-howe.
16. Doris Cole and Karen Cord Taylor, *The Lady Architects: Lois Lilley Howe, Eleanor Manning and Mary Almy, 1893–1937* (New York: Midmarch Press, 1990).
17. James F. O'Gorman, "Hill-Stead and Its Architect," in *Hill-Stead, the Country Place of Theodate Pope Riddle* (New York: Princeton Architectural Press, 2009), 54.
18. Allaback, *The First American Women Architects*, 177–82.
19. "Residence of J. P. Chamberlain, Esq.," *Architectural Record*, November 1919, 408.
20. "Interview with Mrs. William Sheffield Cowles [older sister of Theodore Roosevelt] and Mrs. Douglas Robinson—Hotel Belmont," March 19, 1920, Women's Roosevelt Memorial Association Records.
21. Arnold Berke, *Mary Colter: Architect of the Southwest* (New York: Princeton Architectural Press, 2002), 23–24, 28.
22. Berke, *Mary Colter*, 30–31, 34–36.
23. Karen Bartlett, *Mary Jane Colter: House Made of Dawn* (Phoenix, AZ: Nemesis Productions, 1997).
24. "Mary Colter's Hopi House," National Park Service, https://www.nps.gov/grca/learn/photosmultimedia/colter_hopih_photos.htm.
25. Although Colter had the utmost respect and admiration for Native American cultures, she was not exempt from the dominant prejudices of the time. Many have argued that Colter's use of Native American motifs in her designs was exploitative, inevitably having contributed to the development of Native land. See Marta Weigle, "Exposition and Mediation: Mary Colter, Erna Fergusson, and the Santa Fe/Harvey Popularization of the Native Southwest, 1902–1940," *Frontiers: A Journal of Women Studies* 12, no. 3 (1992): 116–50.
26. Berke, *Mary Colter*, 189–90, 201–5.
27. "Profile in Landscape Architecture: Mary Colter," NPS Park Cultural Landscapes Program, https://npsparkclp.tumblr.com/post/141506386922/profile-in-landscape-architecture-mary-colter.
28. Frederick Gutheim, "Griffin, Mary Lucy Mahony," in *Notable American Women, The Modern Period*, v. 4: 292.
29. David Van Zanten, "The Early Work of Marion Mahony Griffin," *Prairie School Review* 3, no. 2 (1966): 6.

30. Allaback, *The First American Women Architects*, 87–88.

31. Elizabeth Birmingham, "Marion Mahony Griffin," Pioneering Women of American Architecture, https://pioneeringwomen.bwaf.org/marion-mahony-griffin/.

32. Sara Holmes Boutelle, *Julia Morgan, Architect* (New York: Abbeville Press, 1995), 16.

33. Boutelle, *Julia Morgan*, 27–31.

34. "The First Lady Architect."

35. Boutelle, *Julia Morgan*, 78–79.

36. Allaback, *The First American Women Architects*, 140–52.

37. "Julia Morgan's Asilomar," brochure, Asilomar State Beach and Conference Grounds, California State Parks, 2018.

38. Duncan Aikman, "A Renaissance Palace in Our West," *New York Times*, July 21, 1929.

39. Boutelle, *Julia Morgan*, 217–33.

40. Quoted in Boutelle, *Julia Morgan,* 44.

41. Mike Boehm, "Hearst Castle's Julia Morgan Is First Woman to Win AIA's Gold Medal," *Los Angeles Times*, December 23, 2013; Christopher Hawthorne, "Gold Medal: Julia Morgan," *Architect*, June 23, 2014, https://www.architectmagazine.com/awards/aia-honor-awards/gold-medal-julia-morgan_o.

42. Rachel Forester, "Early Women Architects of Kansas City, The Mary Rockwell Hook Papers," *Missouri Historical Review* 113, no. 3 (April 2019): 206–9.

43. Mary Rockwell Hook, "This and That" (self-pub., 1970), 25.

44. Page Putnam Miller, National Register Nomination form, US Department of the Interior, National Park Service, 1991.

45. Sherry Piland and Elaine Ryder, "Residential Structures by Mary Rockwell Hook," National Register Nomination, US Department of the Interior, National Park Service, 1983.

46. Lorrie Muldowney, "Siesta Key Architecture a Natural," Sarasota History Alive, http://www.sarasotahistoryalive.com/history/articles/siesta-key-architecture-a-natural/; Hook, "This and That," 61–62.

47. Allaback, *The First American Women Architects*, 101–4.

48. "Visionary Gray Shines Strong," Independent.ie, March 17, 2013, https://www.independent.ie/lifestyle/visionary-gray-shines-strong-29135137.html.

49. Caroline Constant, *Eileen Gray* (London: Phaidon, 2000), 23, 33.

50. J. Stewart Johnson, *Eileen Gray, Designer* (New York: Museum of Modern Art, 1979), 16.

51. Peter Adam, *Eileen Gray: Architect/Designer* (London: Thames and Hudson, 1987), 95–102.

52. Quoted in Adam, *Eileen Gray*, 71–121, 193, 216.

53. Johnson, *Eileen Gray, Designer*.

54. Adam, *Eileen Gray*, 275.

55. Constant, *Eileen Gray*, 175.

56. Constant, *Eileen Gray*, 176.

57. Finding aid for the Eileen Gray architectural drawings, 1930–1947, http://www.oac.cdlib.org/findaid/ark:/13030/c828090m/entire_text/.

58. Adam, *Eileen Gray*, 369–70.

59. "Lilly Reich," Bauhaus Kooperation, https://www.bauhaus100.com/the-bauhaus/people/masters-and-teachers/lilly-reich/.

60. Magdalena Droste, "Lilly Reich: Her Career as an Artist," in Matilda McQuaid, *Lilly Reich: Designer and Architect* (New York: Museum of Modern Art, 1996), 47.

61. Droste, "Lilly Reich," 50.

62. See Despina Stratigakos, "Women and the Werkbund: Gender Politics and German Design Reform, 1907–14," *Journal of the Society of Architectural Historians* 62, no. 4 (December 2003): 490–511; and Esther da Costa Meyer, "Cruel Metonymies: Lilly Reich's Designs for the 1937 World's Fair," *New German Critique* 76, special issue on Weimar Visual Culture (Winter 1999): 161–89.

63. Stratigakos, "Women and the Werkbund," 500.

64. Droste, "Lilly Reich," 50.

65. McQuaid, *Lilly Reich*, 21.

66. McQuaid, *Lilly Reich*, 22.

67. McQuaid, *Lilly Reich*, 22.

68. For more on the impact of fashion and the textile industry on the history of modern architecture, see Mark Wigley, *White Walls, Designer Dresses: The Fashioning of Modern Architecture* (Cambridge, MA: MIT Press, 1996), 128–53.

69. McQuaid, Lilly Reich, 25; Beatriz Colomina, "Collaborations: The Private Life of Modern Architecture," *Journal of the Society of Architectural Historians* 58, no. 3 (September 1999): 462.

70. McQuaid, *Lilly Reich*, 26.

71. McQuaid, *Lilly Reich*, 29.

72. McQuaid, *Lilly Reich*, 35–40. For more on Lilly Reich's silence and complicity in the Werkbund's activities under Nazi leadership, see Da Costa Meyer, "Cruel Metonymies," 172–84.

73. "Lilly Reich," Bauhaus Kooperation; Droste, 57.

74. Droste, "Lilly Reich," 57.

75. Doris Cole, "Eleanor Raymond," Pioneering Women of American Architecture, https://pioneeringwomen.bwaf.org/eleanor-raymond/.

76. Rose Greely, "A Small House of Distinction," *House Beautiful*, November 1922, 423; "House for James H. Cleaves, Winchester, Massachusetts," *Architectural Record*, November 1929, 442–43; "House of James H. Cleaves, Esq., Winchester, Massachusetts," *Architectural Forum*, January 1927, 95–96.

77. Nancy Gruskin, "Frost & Raymond, Suburbia and the Single-Family House of the 1920s," *Windsor Historical Society* 6 (2005): 6; Henry Russell Hitchcock Jr., "Four Harvard Architects," *Hound & Horn* (September 1928): 45.

78. Allaback, *The First American Women Architects*, 183–88.

79. *Eleanor Raymond Architectural Projects, 1919–1973*, curated by Doris Cole, Institute of Contemporary Art, Boston, September 15–November 1, 1981.

80. Allaback, *The First American Women Architects*, 223–24.

81. Diane Y. Welch, "Lilian J. Rice," Pioneering Women of American Architecture, https://pioneeringwomen.bwaf.org/lilian-j-rice.

82. Susanna Timmons, "Overlooked No More: Lilian Rice, Architect Who Lifted a Style in California," *New York Times*, November 21, 2018.

83. Kimberly Merkel Chen & Associates, National Register, nomination, Church Hill North Historic District (Boundary Increase), 2000, section 8, 34.

84. Dreck Spurlock Wilson, ed., *African American Architects: A Biographical Dictionary* (New York: Routledge, 1865), 195.

85. "Records of Pioneering Architect Donated to Library of Virginia," Library of Virginia newsletter, issue 162, March/April 2004.

86. Allaback, *The First American Women Architects*, 80–83.

87. National Register, Church Hill North Historic District, 2000; Harry Kollatz Jr., "What Ethel Built," *Richmond Magazine*, June 2018.

88. "A Guide to the Ethel Bailey Furman Papers and Architectural Drawings, 1928–2003," Library of Virginia, accessed September 14, 2019, http://ead.lib.virginia.edu/vivaxtf/view?docId=lva/vi01215.xml;query=;.

89. Arne Heporauta, "On Aino Marsio-Aalto," in *Aino Aalto*, ed. Ulla Kinnunen (Jyväskylä, Finland: Alvar Aalto Museum, 2004), 21.

90. Riitta Nikula, "Aino Marsio-Aalto," in *Profiles*, 56.

91. Mia Hipeli, "List of Works," in Kinnunen, *Aino Aalto*, 68.

92. Kaarina Mikonranta, "Aino Marsio-Aalto: Interior and Furniture Designer," in Kinnunen, 148.

93. "About Artek,' Artek, https://www.artek.fi/en/company/about.

94. "Artek and the Aaltos: Creating a Modern World," Bard Graduate Center, https://www.bgc.bard.edu/files/16S_Artek_Press.pdf.

95. Mary Harding Sadler, "Amaza Lee Meredith," in Wilson, *African American Architects*, 280.

96. "Amaza Lee Meredith: Teacher, Artist, and Architect," Lynchburg Museum System, http://www.lynchburgmuseum.org/blog/2018/8/24/amaza-lee-meredith-teacher-artist-and-architect.

97. "A Guide to the Amaza Lee Meredith Papers, 1912, 1930–1938," Special Collections and Archives, Johnson Memorial Library, Virginia State University, Petersburg, VA, https://ead.lib.virginia.edu/vivaxtf/view?docId=vsu/vipets00005.xml.

98. Virginia State University, a historically Black college, has gone through a series of name changes since its establishment in 1882. When Meredith began teaching there in 1930, the school was called Virginia State College for Negroes.

99. "A Guide to the Amaza Lee Meredith Papers"; Michael Buettner, "Azurest South Is Milestone for African-American Women," Progress-Index, February 23, 2017, https://www.progress-index.com/news/20170223/azurest-south-is-milestone-for-african-american-women.

100. National Register of Historic Places Registration Form, US Department of the Interior National Park Service, https://www.dhr.virginia.gov/VLR_to_transfer/PDF-Noms/020-5583_Azurest_South_1993_Final_NRHP_nomination.pdf.

101. "Azurest South," Virginia State University Alumni Association, https://www.vsuaaonline.com/azurest-south.

102. "The Visionary Women of Sag Harbor's Historic Azurest Community," Preservation Long Island, https://preservationlongisland.org/the-visionary-women-of-sag-harbors-historic-azurest-community/.

103. David Gebhard, Lutah Maria Riggs: A Woman in Architecture, 1921–1980 (Santa Barbara, CA: Capra Press and Santa Barbara Museum of Art, 1992), 5.

104. The exhibition Picturing Tradition: Lutah Maria Riggs Encounters Mexican Architecture, curated by Kurt G. F. Helfrich, was held at the University Art Museum, September 29, 2004, to January 30, 2005.

105. Finding Aid for the Lutah Maria Riggs Papers, University of California, Santa Barbara Archives, https://oac.cdlib.org/findaid/ark:/13030/kt709nf413/entire_text/.

106. Allaback, The First American Women Architects, 193–204.

107. Finding aid, Riggs Papers.

108. "A Guide to the Margarete Schütte-Lihotzky Biographical Materials, 1993–2000," Special Collections M2001-035, Virginia Polytechnic Institute and State University, Blacksburg, VA, https://lib.virginia.edu/vivaxtf/view?docId=vt/viblbv00646.xml.

109. Susan Henderson, "Margarete Schütte-Lihotzky (1897–2000)," Architectural Review, June 27, 2015, https://www.architectural-review.com/essays/reputations-pen-portraits-/margarete-schtte-lihotzky-1897-2000/8685131.article?search=https%3a%2f%2fwww.architectural-review.com%2fsearcharticles%3fkeywords%3dlihotzky; Juliet Kinchin, "Introduction to Margarete Schütte-Lihotzky," in Margarete Schütte-Lihotzky and Juliet Kinchin, West 86th: A Journal of Decorative Arts, Design History and Material Culture 18, no. 1 (Spring–Summer 2011): 87.

110. Susan R. Henderson, Building Culture: Ernst May and the New Frankfurt Initiative, 1926–1931 (New York: Peter Lang Publishing, 2013), 152–53.

111. Carmen Espegel, Women Architects in the Modern Movement (New York: Routledge, 2018), 194.

112. Natallia Barykina, "Socialist Constructions: Modern Urban Housing and Social Practice," PhD diss., Graduate Department of Geography, University of Toronto, 2015.

Chapter 2

1. Virginia Woolf, A Room of One's Own (1929; repr., San Diego: Harcourt Brace Jovanovich, 1957), 116.

2. Virginia Woolf, "Professions for Women," The Death of the Moth and Other Essays (1942; repr., San Diego: Harvest, 1970), 241.

3. Quoted in Mary McLeod, "Charlotte Perriand's Art de Vivre," in Charlotte Perriand: An Art of Living, ed. Mary McLeod (New York: Harry N. Abrams, in association with the Architectural League of New York, 2003), 10.

4. Mary McLeod, "New Designs for Living: Domestic Equipment of Charlotte Perriand, Le Corbusier, and Pierre Jeanneret, 1928–29," in Charlotte Perriand, 36, https://www.nytimes.com/1999/11/07/nyregion/charlotte-perriand-designer-is-dead-at-96.html.

5. Danilo Udovicki-Selb, "'C'était dans l'air du temps': Charlotte Perriand and the Popular Front," in McLeod, 68–89.

6. Charlotte Benton, "From Tubular Steel to Bamboo: Charlotte Perriand, the Migrating Chaise-longue and Japan," Journal of Design History 11, no. 1 (1998): 34–35.

7. "Greta Magnusson Grossman: A Biography," R & Company, https://www.r-and-company.com/designers/greta-magnusson-grossman/.

8. Caroline Roux, "Interiors from the Archive: Swedish-born Designer Greta Grossman's Work Is Undergoing a Revival," Independent, February 4, 2011; David A. Keeps, "Greta Magnusson Grossman Retrospective to Open in Pasadena," Los Angeles Times, October 24, 2012.

9. Iain Jackson and Jessica Holland, The Architecture of Edwin Maxwell Fry and Jane Drew: Twentieth Century Architecture, Pioneer Modernism and the Tropics (New York: Routledge, 2016), 105.

10. Jackson and Holland, The Architecture of Edwin Maxwell Fry and Jane Drew, 107–8; Susha Guppy, "Obituary: Dame Jane Drew," Independent, August 1, 1996, https://www.independent.co.uk/news/people/obituary-dame-jane-drew-1307641.html.

11. Becky Ayre, "An Architect for Modern Times," Raconteur, February 6, 2014, https://www.raconteur.net/culture/an-architect-for-modern-times.

12. Rhodri Windsor Liscombe, "Modernism in Late Imperial British West Africa: The Work of Maxwell Fry and Jane Drew, 1946–56," Journal of the Society of Architectural Historians 65, no. 2 (June 2006): 190–93.

13. Bryan Marquard, "Sally Harkness, 98; Cofounder of The Architects Collaborative," Boston Globe, July 6, 2013, https://www2.bostonglobe.com/metro/2013/07/06/sally-harkness-cofounder-the-architects-collaborative-was-inspirational-figure-profession/GR8bVdJFc68U5Nhv5TnZvJ/story.html.

14. Guide to the Louisa Vaughan Conrad Collection, https://hollisarchives.lib.harvard.edu/repositories/7/resources/735.

15. Marquard, "Sally Harkness, 98."

16. Michael Kubo, "The Concept of Architectural Corporation," in OfficeUS Agenda (Zurich: Lars Müller Publishers, 2014), 42.

17. Sarah Harkness, interview by Perry King Neubauer, Kate Super, and Doug Cooper, in Still Standing: Conversations with Three Founding Partners of The Architects Collaborative (Cambridge, MA: Perry King Neubauer, 2007). Quoted in Marquard, "Sally Harkness, 98."

18. Benjamin Flowers, "The Architects' Collaborative (TAC)," Encyclopedia of Twentieth Century Architecture, ed. R. Stephen Sennott, (New York: Routledge, 2004), 1324–25.

19. Amanda Kolson Hurley, Radical Suburbs: Experimental Living on the Fringes of the American City (Cleveland, OH: Belt Publishing, 2019), 94–99.

20. Amanda Kolson Hurley, "The Rise of the Radical Suburbs," Architect, April 9, 2019, https://www.architectmagazine.com/design/the-rise-of-the-radical-suburbs_o?utm_source=newsletter&utm_content=Article&utm_medium=email&utm_campaign=AN_050319.

21. "A Guide to the Sarah Pillsbury Harkness Architectural Collection, 1985–1997, 2013," Virginia Polytechnic Institute and State University, Blacksburg, VA, http://ead.lib.virginia.edu/vivaxtf/view?docId=vt/viblbv00526.xml.

22. "Lina Bo Bardi, 1914–1992," O Estado de São Paulo, March 21, 1992, quoted in Zeuler R. M. de A. Lima, Lina Bo Bardi (New Haven, CT: Yale University Press, 2013), 6.

23. Esther da Costa Meyer, "After the Flood," Harvard Design Magazine 16 (Winter/Spring 2002), http://www.harvarddesignmagazine.org/issues/16/after-the-flood.

24. Marcelo Ferraz, "The Making of SESC Pompéia," Lina Bo Bardi: Together, http://linabobarditogether.com/2012/08/03/the-making-of-sesc-pompeia-by-marcelo-ferraz/.

25. Lina Bo Bardi, "Arquitetura como movimento" ("Architecture as movement"), lecture notes, Dance School, Salvador, August 1958, ILBPMB, quoted in Zeuler R. M. De A. Lima, "Lina Bo Bardi and the Architecture of Everyday Culture," Places Journal, November 2013, https://placesjournal.org/article/lina-bo-bardi-and-the-architecture-of-everyday-culture/.

26. Anooradha Iyer Siddiqi, "Crafting the Archive: Minnette De Silva, Architecture, and History," Journal of Architecture 22, no. 8 (December 2017): 1307.

27. Amy Sherlock, "Born 100 Years Ago, Remembering the 'Tropical Modernist' Architect Minnette de Silva," Frieze, September 11, 2018, https://frieze.com/article/born-100-years-ago-remembering-tropical-modernist-architect-minnette-de-silva.

28. Minnette De Silva, Ashley De Vos, and Susil Sirivardana, *The Life and Work of an Asian Woman Architect* (Colombo, Sri Lanka: Smart Media Productions, 1998), 65.

29. Ellen Dissanayake, "Minnette De Silva: Pioneer of Modern Architecture in Sri Lanka," *Orientations* 13, no. 8 (August 1982), http://www.suravi.fr/minnette-de-silva_ellen.html.

30. David Dobson, "Andrew Boyd and Minnette de Silva," *Matter*, https://thinkmatter.in/2015/03/04/andrew-boyd-and-minnette-de-silva-two-pioneers-of-modernism-in-ceylon/#_ftnref14.

31. Piotr Marciniak, "Famous or Forgotten: Women Architects in Communist Poland," June 2014, 855, https://www.researchgate.net/publication/263621129_Famous_or_Forgotten_Women_Architects_in_Communist_Poland.

32. Michał Duda, *Patchwork: the Architecture of Jadwiga Grabowska-Hawrylak* (Wrocław, Poland: Museum of Architecture in Wrocław, 2016), 11.

33. "Anne Griswold Tyng Collection," Weitzman School of Design, University of Pennsylvania, https://www.design.upenn.edu/anne-grisold-tyng-collection-074.

34. Ingrid Schaffner and William Whitaker, "A Life Chronology," in *Anne Tyng: Inhabiting Geometry*, ed. Ingrid Schaffner (Philadelphia: Institute of Contemporary Arts, University of Pennsylvania; Chicago: Graham Foundation for Advanced Studied in the Fine Arts, 2011), 99.

35. Anne Tyng, *Louis Kahn to Anne Tyng: The Rome Letters 1953–1954* (New York: Rizzoli International Publications, 1997), 27–28.

36. Robin Pogrebin, "Anne Tyng, Theorist of Architecture, Dies at 91," *New York Times*, January 7, 2012, https://www.nytimes.com/2012/01/07/arts/design/anne-tyng-architect-and-partner-of-louis-kahn-dies-at-91.html; "Anne Griswold Tyng Collection."

37. Quoted in Detlef Mertins, "Cracking the Glass Ceiling: Look Back at the Career of Trailblazing Architect Natalie de Blois," *SOM Journal* 4 (2006), https://som.medium.com/cracking-the-glass-ceiling-a-look-back-at-the-career-of-trailblazing-architect-natalie-de-blois-b7ef02b28c2b.

38. Mertins, "Cracking the Glass Ceiling."

39. "I am a social animator," *Sztuka Architecktury*, October 5, 2011, http://sztuka-architektury.pl/article/4542/jestem-animatorem-spolecznym.

40. Zbigniew Ihnatowicz, "A lot is won when architectural creativity is not treated as a job but as a hobby," *SARP Warsaw*, 2011, https://sarp.warszawa.pl/architekci/hall-of-fame/halina-skibniewska/; Tadeusz Piotrowski, *Poland's Holocaust: Ethnic Strife, Collaboration with Occupying Forces and Genocide in the Second Republic, 1918–1947* (Jefferson, NC: McFarland, 1998), 118.

41. Adrian Mourby, "Where Are the World's Most War-damaged Cities?" *Guardian*, December 17, 2015, https://www.theguardian.com/cities/2015/dec/17/where-world-most-war-damaged-city.

42. Piotr Marciniak, "Women Architects in the Polish People's Republic," in Mary Pepchinski and Mariann Simon, *Ideological Equals: Women Architects in Socialist Europe 1945–1989* (London: Routledge, 2016), 68.

43. Iwona Szustakiewicz, "Halina Skibniewska's Good Flat," *IOP Conference Series: Materials Science and Engineering*, https://iopscience.iop.org/article/10.1088/1757-899X/603/4/042001/pdf.

44. Marciniak, "Women Architects in the Polish People's Republic," 73.

45. Blanche Lemco van Ginkel, "Slowly and Surely (And Somewhat Painfully): More or Less the History of Women in Architecture in Canada," in *Society for the Study of Architecture in Canada Bulletin* 17, no. 1 (March 1991).

46. "Zofia Hansen, May 13, 1924–January 24, 2013," *Culture.pl*, 2013; English translation, 2017, https://culture.pl/en/artist/zofia-hansen.

47. Marciniak, "Women Architects in the Polish People's Republic," 73.

48. Felicity D. Scott, "Space Educates," in *Oskar Hansen Opening Modernism: On Open Form Architecture, Art and Didactics*, ed. Aleksandra Kedziorek and Lukasz Ronduda (Warsaw: Museum of Modern Art in Warsaw, 2014), 137–60.

49. Agnieszka Sural, "House in Szumin: Oskar and Zofia Hansen," *Culture.pi*, August 12, 2014; English translation, August 26, 2014, https://culture.pl/en/work/house-in-szumin-oskar-and-zofia-hansen.

50. Lukasz Stanek, "Team 10 East: The Socialist State as an Architectural Project," in *Oskar Hansen Opening Modernism: On Open Form Architecture, Art and Didactics* (Chicago: University of Chicago Press, 2014), 61–88.

51. Patricia Morton, "Norma Merrick Sklarek," *Pioneering Woman of American Architecture*, https://pioneeringwomen.bwaf.org/norma-merrick-sklarek/.

52. Natalia Torija Nieto, "Remembering Norma Merrick Sklarek, An Architect of Many Firsts," *Pin-Up*, https://pinupmagazine.org/articles/article-norma-merrick-sklarek-first-liscensed-black-woman-architect-new-york-california-natalia-torija.

53. Elaine Woo, "Pioneering African American Architect," *Los Angeles Times*, February 10, 2012, https://www.latimes.com/archives/la-xpm-2012-feb-10-la-me-norma-sklarek-20120210-story.html.

54. "Norma Sklarek: National Visionary," National Visionary Leadership Project, videos: "NVLP: African American History."

55. Anna M. Lewis, *Women of Steel and Stone: 22 Inspirational Architects, Engineers, and Landscape Designers* (Chicago: Chicago Review Press, 2014), 55.

56. James Murdock, "AIA Lauds Meier, Sklarek, and McKittrick," *Architectural Record* 196, no. 2 (February 2008): 32; "Groundbreaker, Architect, Mentor Norma Merrick Sklarek, FAIA to be Posthumously Awarded the 2019 AIA|LA Gold Medal," July 18, 2019, https://www.aialosangeles.org/news/press-releases/norma-sklarek-aiala-gold-medal-winner-2019/.

57. Blair Kamin, "Gertrude Kerbis, Groundbreaking Architect, Dies at 89," *Chicago Tribune*, June 15, 2016, https://www.chicagotribune.com/news/obituaries/ct-gertrude-kerbis-obituary-kamin-met-0616-20160615-story.html.

58. "Gertrude Lempp Kerbis: 2008 Lifetime Achievement Award," video, produced and directed by Karen Carter Lynch, https://vimeo.com/3268630.

59. "2019 Chicago 7 Most Endangered: Seven Continents/Rotunda Building: Chicago O'Hare International Airport," *Preservation Chicago*, https://preservationchicago.org/chicago07/seven-continents-rotunda-building/.

60. "In Memory: Gertrude Lempp Kerbis, Former SOM Architect," SOM, June 17, 2019, https://www.som.com/news/in_memory_gertrude_lempp_kerbis_former_som_architect; Susan F. King, "Gertrude Lempp Kerbis," *Dynamic National Archive*, https://dna.bwaf.org/architect/kerbis-gertrude-lempp.

61. In Memory: "Gertrude Lempp Kerbis" SOM. June 17, 2019.

62. Kamin, "Gertrude Kerbis."

63. "History of CWA," *Chicago Women in Architecture*, https://cwarch.org/history-of-cwa/.

64. "Remembering Gert Lempp Kerbis," *AIA Chicago*, June 17, 2016, https://www.aiachicago.org/news/entry/remembering-gert-lempp-kerbis/#.XmpqCpNKh0t.

Chapter 3

1. Phyllis Lambert, interview by Julie Sinclair Eakin, September 23, 2019.

2. Gae Aulenti, quoted in Carol Vogel, "The Aulenti Uproar," *New York Times*, November 22, 1987, https://www.nytimes.com/1987/11/22/magazine/the-aulenti-uproar.html.

3. "Gae Aulenti," *Dynamic National Archive*, https://dna.bwaf.org/architect/aulenti-gae.

4. Quoted in Oliver Wainwright, "Gae Aulenti Obituary," *Guardian*, November 5, 2012, https://www.theguardian.com/artanddesign/2012/nov/05/gae-aulenti.

5. "Italy: The New Domestic Landscape," Museum of Modern Art, Release no. 35, 1972, https://www.moma.org/momaorg/shared/pdfs/docs/press_archives/4812/releases/MOMA_1972_0041_35.pdf.

6. Paul Goldberger, "Architecture: The New Musee D'Orsay in Paris," *New York Times*, April 2, 1987, https://www.nytimes.com/1987/04/02/arts/architecture-the-new-musee-d-orsay-in-paris.html.

7. Elaine Woo, "Gae Aulenti, Italian Architect, Dies at 84," *Washington Post*, November 5, 2012, https://www.washingtonpost.com/local/obituaries/gae-aulenti-italian-architect-dies-at-84/2012/11/05/750e5c28-277e-11e2-b2a0-ae18d6159439_story.html.

8. "Gae Aulenti and Olivetti," *Domus*, November 10, 2012, https://www.domusweb.it/en/from-the-archive/2012/11/10/gae-aulenti-and-olivetti.html.

9. "Piazza Gae Aulenti / AECOM," *ArchDaily*, May 31, 2013, https://www.archdaily.com/379624/piazza-gae-aulenti-aecom.

10. Beverly Willis, interview by Julie Sinclair Eakin, July 10 and 26, 2019.

11. Pelin Tan and Ute Meta Bauer, "The Flux of Human Life," *Domus*, March 2013, 105–13; Liane Lefaivre, "Living Outside the Box: Marty Otis Stevens and Thomas McNulty's Lincoln House," *Harvard Design Magazine* 24 (Spring/Summer 2006); Susanna Torre, "Building Utopia: Mary Otis Stevens and the Lincoln, Massachusetts, House," *Impossible to Hold: Women and Culture in the 1960s*, ed. Avital H. Bloch and Lauri Umansky (New York: New York University Press, 2005), 29–42.

12. Mary Otis Stevens, interview by Joan Arnold, *Design Spirit*, 1990.

13. "Alison and Peter Smithson, a Biography" in *Alison and Peter Smithson: From the House of the Future to a House of Today*, ed. Dirk van den Heuvel and Max Risselada (Rotterdam: 010 Publishers, 2004), 233.

14. Steve Parnell, "Alison Smithson (1928–1993) and Peter Smithson (1923–2003)," *Architectural Review*, January 30, 2012, https://www.architectural-review.com/essays/reputations-pen-portraits/alison-smithson-1928-1993-and-peter-smithson-1923-2003/8625631.article.

15. Philip Johnson, "School at Hunstanton, Norfolk, by Alison and Peter Smithson," *Architectural Review*, August 19, 1954, https://www.architectural-review.com/buildings/school-at-hunstanton-norfolk-by-alison-and-peter-smithson/8625095.article.

16. Alison Smithson and Peter Smithson, "House in Soho, London," *Architectural Design*, December 1953, 342–45.

17. Parnell, "Alison Smithson (1928–1993)."

18. Reyner Banham, "Parallel of Life and Art," *Architectural Review* 114 (October 1953): 259–61, featured in *October* 136 (Spring 2011): 8–10.

19. Beatriz Colomina, "Unbreathed Air," *Grey Room* 15 (Spring 2004): 28–59, https://www.mitpressjournals.org/doi/abs/10.1162/1526381041165458?journalCode=grey.

20. Parnell.

21. Dale Allen Gyure, *Minoru Yamasaki: Humanist Architecture for a Modernist World* (New Haven, CT: Yale University Press, 2017), 118.

22. "Obituary for Astra Zarina," *Civita Institute*, https://www.civitainstitute.org/348/obituary-for-astra-zarina.html.

23. "History," Rome Program, Department of Architecture, College of Building Environment, University of Washington, http://rome.be.uw.edu/home/history/.

24. "Our History," UW Rome Center, https://www.washington.edu/rome/about/.

25. "Civita Di Bagnoregio," *World Monuments Fund*, https://www.wmf.org/project/civita-di-bagnoregio.

26. "A New Exhibit in Italy: Astra Zarina in Civita," *Civita Institute*, https://www.civitainstitute.org/3104/astra-zarina-in-civita.html.

27. Julia Gamolina, "A Story No Longer Untold: Astra Zarina's Influence on Modern Architecture," *Metropolis*, July 26, 2019, https://www.metropolismag.com/architecture/rome-teacher-astra-zarina-exhibition/.

28. Maida Goodwin, Finding Aid, Noel Phyllis Birkby Papers, Sophia Smith Collection, Smith College, Northampton, MA, https://findingaids.smith.edu/repositories/2/resources/686.

29. Andrea J. Merrett, "The Alliance of Women in Architecture," *Now What?! Advocacy, Activism and Alliances in American Architecture since 1968*, May 24, 2018, https://www.nowwhat-architexx.org/articles/2018/5/24/the-alliance-of-women-in-architecture.

30. Phyllis Birkby, notes for an article on women and the built environment, quoted in Stephanie Schroeder, "Noel Phyllis Birkby," *Now What?! Advocacy, Activism and Alliances in American Architecture Since 1968*, March 20, 2018, https://www.nowwhat-architexx.org/articles/2018/3/18/noel-phyllis-birkby.

31. Mimi Zeiger, "Building Sisterhood: How Feminists Sought to Make Architecture a Truly Collective Endeavor," *Metropolis*, August 8, 2019, https://www.metropolismag.com/architecture/women-feminism-american-architecture/.

32. Elizabeth Cahn, "The Women's School of Planning and Architecture," *Now What?! Advocacy, Activism and Alliances in American Architecture since 1968*, May 25, 2018, https://www.nowwhat-architexx.org/articles/2018/5/25/the-womens-school-of-planning-and-architecture.

33. Finding Aid, Birkby Papers.

34. Quoted in Patrick Sisson, "Judith Chafee: Dean of Desert Architecture," *Curbed*, August 10, 2017, https://archive.curbed.com/2017/8/10/16120726/judith-chafee-midcentury-architect-tucson.

35. Finding Aid, Joan Forrester Sprague Papers, 1935-1998, 88-M103—98-M166, Schlesinger Library, Radcliffe Institute for Advanced Study, Harvard University, Cambridge, MA, https://hollisarchives.lib.harvard.edu/repositories/8/resources/4843.

36. Jane Thompson and Alexandra Lange, *Design Research: The Store That Brought Modern Living to American Homes* (San Francisco: Chronicle Books, 2010), 130.

37. Finding Aid, Sprague Papers.

38. WALAP, "The Case for Flexible Work Schedules," *Architectural Forum* 137, no. 2 (1972): 53, 66–67, cited in Andrea J. Merrett, "Open Design Office," *Now What?! Advocacy, Activism and Alliances in American Architecture since 1968*, May 24, 2018, https://www.nowwhat-architexx.org/articles/2018/5/24/open-design-office.

39. Quoted in Rita Reif, "Architecture: Feminist Ferment," *New York Times*, August 9, 1975, https://timesmachine.nytimes.com/timesmachine/1975/08/09/76381774.html?pageNumber=33.

40. Merrett, "Open Design Office."

41. The other founding members of WSPA were Katrin Adam, Noel Phyllis Birkby, Ellen Perry Berkeley, Bobbie Sue Hood, Marie I. Kennedy, and Leslie Kanes Weisman. For more on the WSPA, see "The Women's School of Planning and Architecture," *Now What?! Advocacy, Activism and Alliances in American Architecture since 1968*, May 25, 2018, https://www.nowwhat-architexx.org/articles/2018/5/25/the-womens-school-of-planning-and-architecture.

42. Records of the Women's School of Planning and Architecture, Sophia Smith Collection, Smith College, Northampton, MA, https://findingaids.smith.edu/repositories/2/resources/1018.

43. Merrett.

44. Katrin Adam, Susan E. Aitcheson, and Joan Forrester Sprague, "Women's Development Corporation," *Heresies* 3, no. 3 (1981): 19–20, https://archive.org/details/heresies_11/page/n19.

45. A. Ipek Türeli, "Women's Development Corporation," *Now What?! Advocacy, Activism and Alliances in American Architecture since 1968*, May 25, 2018, https://www.nowwhat-architexx.org/articles/2018/5/25/womens-development-corporation.

46. Ada Karmi-Melamede, interview by Julie Sinclair Eakin, December 9, 2019. All direct quotes by Karmi-Melamede published here derive from this interview, unless otherwise stated.

47. Eva Jiřičná, interview by Katherine Flynn, August 23, 2019. All direct quotes by Jiřičná and published here derive from this interview, unless otherwise noted.

48. Sharon Sutton, interview by Julie Sinclair Eakin, August 16, 2019. All direct quotes by Sutton and published here derive from this interview, unless otherwise stated.

49. Yasmeen Lari, interview by Julie Sinclair Eakin, September 2, 2019. All direct quotes by Lari and published here derive from this interview, unless otherwise stated.

50. Merrill Elam, interview by Julie Sinclair Eakin, August 2, 2019. All direct quotes by Elam and published here derive from this interview, unless otherwise stated.

51. Susanna Torre, interview by Katherine Flynn, 2019.

52. Adele Chatfield-Taylor, interview by Julie Sinclair Eakin, August 8, 2019. All direct quotes of Chatfield-Taylor and published here derive from this interview, unless otherwise noted.
53. Julie Snow, interview by Katherine Flynn, October 9, 2019. All direct quotes by Snow and published here derive from this interview, unless otherwise stated.
54. Carol Ross Barney, interview by Katherine Flynn, September 25, 2019. All direct quotes by Ross Barney and published here derive from this interview, unless otherwise stated.

Chapter 4
1. Anna Lebovic, "Refashioning Feminism: American *Vogue*, the Second Wave, and the Transition to Postfeminism," *Journal of Women's History* 31, no. 1 (Spring 2019).
2. Rochelle Martin, "Out of Marginality: Toward a New Kind of Profession," in *Architecture: A Place for Women*, ed. Ellen Perry Berkeley (Washington, DC: Smithsonian Institution Press, 1989), 233.
3. Quoted in Laura Mark, "Francine Houben Named Woman Architect of the Year," *Architect's Journal* 239, no. 6 (February 2014): 8.
4. Zaha Hadid, "Zaha Hadid," *Perspecta* 37 (2005): 130–35, 134.
5. Despina Statigakos, "Why Architects Need Feminism," *Places Journal* (September 2012): 1–7, 5.
6. Peggy Deamer, "The 'Starchitect' Image," *New York Times*, August 10, 2014.
7. Billie Tsien, interview by Julie Sinclair Eakin, September 24, 2019. All direct quotes by Tsien and published here derive from this interview, unless otherwise noted.
8. Tsien, interview by Eakin, 2019.
9. Zaha Hadid, interview, *Design Boom*, https://www.designboom.com/architecture/zaha-hadid-interview-quotes-dies-aged-65-03-31-2016/.
10. Zaha Hadid, interview by Huma Pureshi, *Guardian*, November 14, 2012.
11. Zaha Hadid, interview by Jonathan Glancey, *Guardian*, October 9, 2006.
12. Amale Andraos, interview by Michael Kimmelman, *New York Times*, March 31, 2016.
13. Patricia Patkau, interview by Julie Sinclair Eakin. All direct quotes from Patkau and published here derive from this interview, unless otherwise noted.
14. Peggy Deamer, interview by Katherine Flynn, 2019. All direct quotes of Deamer and published here derive from this interview, unless otherwise noted.
15. Elizabeth Plater-Zyberk, interview by Katherine Flynn, 2019. All direct quotes of Plater-Zyberk and published here derive from this interview, unless otherwise noted.

16. Laurinda Spear, interview by Katherine Flynn, November 22, 2019. All direct quotes of Spear and published here derive from this interview, unless otherwise noted.
17. Toshiko Mori, interview by Julie Sinclair Eakin, September 10, 2019. All direct quotes of Mori and published here derive from this interview, unless otherwise noted.
18. Robin Pogrebin, "Pritzker Architecture Prize Goes to Two Women for the First Time," *New York Times*, March 3, 2020.
19. Shirley Blumberg, interview by Katherine Flynn, October 18, 2019.
20. Quoted in Laura Barnett, "Kathryn Findlay, Architect—Portrait of the Artist," *Guardian*, April 2, 2013, https://www.theguardian.com/artanddesign/2013/apr/02/kathryn-findlay-architect-portrait-artist.
21. Oliver Wainwright, "Kathryn Findlay Obituary," *Guardian*, January 15, 2014, https://www.theguardian.com/artanddesign/2014/jan/15/kathryn-findlay.
22. Findlay, "Kathryn Findlay, Architect."
23. "Kathryn Findlay Obituary," *Telegraph*, February 9, 2014, https://www.telegraph.co.uk/news/obituaries/10627362/Kathryn-Findlay-obituary.html.
24. Jerome Taylor, "'Starfish House' Plans are Left Dead in the Water," *Independent*, August 9, 2008, https://www.independent.co.uk/arts-entertainment/art/news/starfish-house-plans-are-left-dead-in-the-water-889273.html.
25. "Ushida Findlay: A Starfish in Cheshire," *Domus*, February 15, 2002, https://www.domusweb.it/en/architecture/2002/02/15/ushida-findlay-a-starfish-in-cheshire.html.
26. Taylor, "'Starfish House' Plans."
27. "Innovative Scots Architectural Company Goes into Liquidation: Ushida Findlay Closure Casts Cloud over Maggie's Centres," *Herald*, August 5, 2004, https://www.heraldscotland.com/news/12499853.innovative-scots-architectural-company-goes-into-liquidation-ushida-findlay-closure-casts-cloud-over-maggies-centres/.
28. "Poolhouse 2 by Ushida Findlay Architects," *Architect's Journal*, February 19, 2009, https://www.architectsjournal.co.uk/poolhouse-2-by-ushida-findlay-architects/1990546.article.
29. Kieran Long, "The ArcelorMittal Orbit Tower," *Architect*, December 2, 2011, https://www.architectmagazine.com/design/the-arcelormittal-orbit-tower_o.
30. Christine Murray, "Kathryn Findlay Named Winner of the 2014 Jane Drew Prize," *Architect's Journal*, January 10, 2014, https://www.architectsjournal.co.uk/news/daily-news/kathryn-findlay-named-winner-of-the-2014-jane-drew-prize/8657489.article.
31. Jill N. Lerner, interview by Katherine Flynn, September 4, 2019. All direct quotes by Lerner and published here are derived from this interview, unless otherwise stated.
32. Sylvia Smith, interview by Katherine Flynn, September 12, 2019. All direct quotes by Smith and published here are derived from this interview, unless otherwise stated.

33. Deborah Berke, interview by Julie Sinclair Eakin, September 17, 2019. All direct quotes by Berke and published here are derived from this interview, unless otherwise stated.
34. The Museum of Modern Art, *MoMA Highlights since 1980* (New York: Museum of Modern Art, 2007), 79, https://www.moma.org/collection/works/201.
35. Elizabeth Diller, interview by Katherine Flynn, January 23, 2020. All direct quotes by Diller and published here are derived from this interview, unless otherwise stated.
36. Carme Pinós, interview by Julie Sinclair Eakin, December 2, 2019. All direct quotes by Pinós and published here are derived from this interview, unless otherwise stated.
37. Julie Eizenberg, interview by Julie Sinclair Eakin, January 13, 2020. All direct quotes by Eizenberg and published here are derived from this interview, unless otherwise stated.
38. "2020 National Architecture Awards: The Arroyo Affordable Housing by Koning Eizenberg Architecture," *ArchitectureAU*, November 5, 2020, https://architectureau.com/articles/2020-national-architecture-awards-the-jorn-utzon-award-for-international-architecture/.
39. Francine Houben, interview by Amy Frearson, *Dezeen*, August 29, 2013.
40. Doriana Fuksas, interview by Katherine Flynn, January 28, 2020.
41. Odile Decq, interview by Katherine Flynn, October 28, 2019. All direct quotes by Decq and published here are derived from this interview, unless otherwise stated.
42. Quoted in Bodil Blain, "Out of Office: Coffee and Creative Small Talk with Amanda Levete," *Wallpaper*, https://www.wallpaper.com/architecture/architect-amanda-levete-interview.
43. Quoted in Karen Cliento, "12th International Architecture Exhibition Vencie," archdaily.com, August 16, 2010, https://www.archdaily.com/73301/12th-international-architecture-exhibition-venice.
44. Architecture Talk 32: "Intuiting and Uncertainty," https://www.architecturetalk.org/home/32.
45. Marion Weiss, interview by Katherine Flynn, September 19, 2019. All direct quotes by Weiss and published here are derived from this interview, unless otherwise stated.

Chapter 5
1. Quoted in "A Critical Mind Is an Open Mind," *Critical Survival Journals*, August 9, 2020, https://issuu.com/ayvazserdar/docs/journals_all_a4_220720.
2. Karen Bausman, interview by Katherine Flynn, October 9, 2019. All direct quotes by Bausman and published here are derived from this interview, unless otherwise stated.
3. Brigitte Shim, interview by Julie Sinclair Eakin, September 26, 2019. All direct quotes by Shim and published here are derived from this interview, unless otherwise stated.

4. Mary-Ann Ray, interview by Julie Sinclair Eakin, February 2, 2020. All direct quotes by Ray and published here are derived from this interview, unless otherwise stated.

5. *What Is Missing* memorial website, https://whatismissing.net.

6. Karen Fairbanks, interview by Julie Sinclair Eakins, October 25, 2019.

7. Annabelle Selldorf, interview by Julie Sinclair Eakin, November 13, 2019. All direct quotes by Selldorf and published here are derived from this interview, unless otherwise stated.

8. Susan T. Rodriguez, interview by Katherine Flynn, October 9, 2019. All direct quotes by Rodriguez and published here are derived from this interview, unless otherwise stated.

9. Claire Weisz, interview by Julie Sinclair Eakin, October 30, 2019.

10. Dorte Mandrup, interview by Julie Sinclair Eakin, October 8, 2019. All direct quotes by Mandrup and published here are derived from this interview, unless otherwise stated.

11. Alison Brooks, interview by Julie Sinclair Eakin, November 29, 2019. All direct quotes by Brooks and published here are derived from this interview, unless otherwise stated.

12. Carme Pigem, interview by Julie Sinclair Eakin, December 4, 2019. All direct quotes by Pigem and published here are derived from this interview, unless otherwise stated.

13. Yolande Daniels, interview by Katherine Flynn, October 30, 2019. All direct quotes by Daniels and published here are derived from this interview, unless otherwise stated.

14. Mabel O. Wilson, interview by Katherine Flynn, October 17, 2019. All direct quotes by Wilson and published here are derived from this interview, unless otherwise stated.

15. Benedetta Tagliabue, interview by Katherine Flynn, December 5, 2019. All direct quotes by Tagliabue and published here are derived from this interview, unless otherwise stated.

16. Robert Beatty, "Woman at the Head of Architect Firms Breaking New Ground," *South Florida Times*, December 23, 2010, http://www.sfltimes.com/uncategorized/woman-at-the-head-of-architect-firm-breaking-new-ground.

17. IDEA, "African American Cultural Center: Project Details," https://interactivedesignarchitects.com/portfolio-post/university-of-chicago-madd-2/.

18. "Congratulations to the 10 AIA Chicago Members to Receive the 2018 FAIA Distinction," AIA Chicago, February 26, 2018, https://www.aiachicago.org/news/entry/congratulations-to-the-10-aia-chicago-members-to-receive-the-2018-faia-dist/#.YEpzr5NKhMY.

19. Lisa Iwamoto, interview by Katherine Flynn, September 24, 2019. All direct quotes by Iwamoto and published here are derived from this interview, unless otherwise stated.

20. Jeanne Gang, interview by Julie Sinclair Eakin, November 4, 2019. All direct quotes by Gang and published here are derived from this interview, unless otherwise stated.

21. Mónica Ponce de León, interview by Katherine Flynn, October 23, 2019. All direct quotes by Ponce de León and published here are derived from this interview, unless otherwise stated.

22. "On Taking Risks in Architecture with Katie Faulkner," interview by Juliet Chun and Zhanina Boyadzhieva, *Girl Interrupted*, October 16, 2017, https://www.girluninterruptedproject.com/conversations/2017/10/15/on-taking-risks-in-architecture-with-katie-faulkner.

23. Jenna McKnight, "NADAAA Fuses Old and New to Create Daniels Building on Circular Toronto Site," *Dezeen*, May 17, 2019, https://www.dezeen.com/2019/05/17/daniels-building-one-spadina-crescent-nadaaa/.

24. Sharon Johnston, interview by Julie Sinclair Eakin, December 23, 2019. All direct quotes by Johnston and published here are derived from this interview unless otherwise stated.

25. Nathalie de Vries, interview by Julie Sinclair Eakin, October 9, 2019. All direct quotes by de Vries and published here are derived from this interview, unless otherwise stated.

26. Sandra Barclay, interview by Julie Sinclair Eakin, January 7, 2020. All direct quotes by Barclay and published here are derived from this interview, unless otherwise stated.

Chapter 6

1. Sadie Morgan, interview by Julie Sinclair Eakin, November 22, 2019. All direct quotes by Morgan and published here derive from this interview, unless otherwise stated.

2. Lori Brown, interview by Laurel Frances Rogers, October 2019.

3. Zachary Edelson, "New Exhibit Gives Visitors a Tour of Post-1968 Activism in Architecture," *Metropolis*, May 25, 2018, https://www.metropolismag.com/architecture/now-what-advocacy-architecture-exhibition/pic/41486/.

4. Interboro, "Holding Pattern," http://www.interboropartners.com/projects/holding-pattern.

5. William Richards, "Catalyzing Force," *Architect*, August 21, 2014, https://www.architectmagazine.com/aia-architect/aiavoices/catalyzing-force_o.

6. Meg Graham, interview by Laurel Frances Rogers, 2019.

7. Alexandra Caufin, "Superkül Is Our 2020 Designer of the Year," *Design Lines Magazine*, https://www.designlinesmagazine.com/superkul-is-our-2020-designer-of-the-year/.

8. J. Meejin Yoon, interview by Katherine Flynn, October 25, 2019. All direct quotes by Yoon and published here derive from this interview, unless otherwise stated.

9. Rozana Montiel, interview by Julie Sinclair Eakin, March 4, 2020. All direct quotes by Montiel and published here derive from this interview, unless otherwise stated.

10. David Huber, "For WORKac, Building, Research, and Teaching Go Hand in Hand," *Metropolis* January 11, 2017, https://www.metropolismag.com/architecture/game-changers-2017-workac/.

11. Amale Andraos, quoted in "Amale Andraos Appointed Dean of GSAPP," *Columbia Magazine*, Fall 2014, 48.

12. James F. Lima, "Foreclosed: Rehousing the American Dream at MoMA," *Architectural Review*, April 24, 2012, https://www.moma.org/explore/inside_out/2012/07/23/foreclosed-an-urbanist-reflects-on-nature-city/.

13. Andraos, quoted in "Amale Andraos Appointed Dean of GSAPP," 49.

14. Harriet Harriss, interview by Julie Sinclair Eakin, January 21, 2020. All direct quotes by Harriss and published here derive from this interview, unless otherwise stated.

15. Caroline O'Donnell, interview by Julie Sinclair Eakin, November 20, 2019. All direct quotes by O'Donnell and published here derive from this interview, unless otherwise stated.

16. Upali Nanda, interview by Katherine Flynn, November 7, 2019. All direct quotes by Nanda and published here derive from this interview, unless otherwise stated.

17. Anna Heringer, interview by Julie Sinclair Eakin, November 27, 2019. All direct quotes by Heringer and published here derive from this interview, unless otherwise noted.

18. Eva Franch i Gilabert, interview by Katherine Flynn, October 14, 2019. All direct quotes by Franch i Gilabert and published here derive from this interview, unless otherwise stated.

19. Catie Newell, interview by Julie Sinclair Eakin, November 6, 2019. All direct quotes by Newell and published here derive from this interview, unless otherwise stated.

20. Frida Escobedo, interview by Julie Sinclair Eakin, November 11, 2019. All direct quotes by Escobedo and published here derive from this interview, unless otherwise stated.

Index